Pinter's World

Pinter's World

Relationships, Obsessions, and Artistic Endeavors

William Baker

FAIRLEIGH DICKINSON UNIVERSITY PRESS
Vancouver • Madison • Teaneck • Wroxton

Published by Fairleigh Dickinson University Press
Copublished by The Rowman & Littlefield Publishing Group, Inc.
4501 Forbes Boulevard, Suite 200, Lanham, Maryland 20706
www.rowman.com

Unit A, Whitacre Mews, 26-34 Stannary Street, London SE11 4AB

Fairleigh Dickinson University Press gratefully acknowledges the support received for
scholarly publishing from the Friends of FDU Press.

British Library Cataloguing in Publication Information Available

Library of Congress Cataloging-in-Publication Data Available

ISBN 978-1-61147-931-7 (cloth : alk. paper)
ISBN 978-1-61147-932-4 (electronic)

♾️™ The paper used in this publication meets the minimum requirements of American
National Standard for Information Sciences Permanence of Paper for Printed Library
Materials, ANSI/NISO Z39.48-1992.

Printed in the United States of America

For
Harry Keyishian
Doyen of American University Press Publishers

Contents

Introduction and Acknowledgements   ix

Abbreviations   xv

1   The Theatre and Film: Joe Brearley, Repertory (Rep.), Creativity, Peter Hall, and Others   1

2   Passions: Cricket and Other Activities Including Bridge, Tennis, Squash, and Music   45

3   Restaurants and Friendships   77

4   Women   111

5   Politics and Religion   145

6   Literary Influences and Favorites   185

Conclusion   225

Bibliography   227

Index of Works by Pinter   243

Index of People   247

Index of Places and Miscellaneous   257

About the Author   265

Introduction and Acknowledgements

Biographically, the subject of this book has not been neglected. An official biography, Michael Billington's *The Life and Work of Harold Pinter*, written with Pinter's approval, was initially published in 1996. A revised paperback edition appeared in 2007 under the title *Harold Pinter*. It included as an appendix Pinter's Nobel Prize lecture, "Art, Truth & Politics," delivered on December 7, 2005. Malcolm Page's *File on Pinter* (1993) contains much factual detail primarily concerning performances and productions of Pinter's work. A year earlier, Mel Gussow's *Conversations with Pinter* provided a useful guide to its subject's aesthetic and other perspectives.

The present work is a complement to these. It departs from them by drawing upon published and unpublished materials until recently largely unavailable. Prominent amongst recently published work is my *A Harold Pinter Chronology* (2013), which attempts to record almost on a daily basis the *facts* of its subject's life and uses, for the first time, Pinter's annual "Appointment Diaries," now in the Harold Pinter Archive at the British Library. The *Chronology* also mines for factual documentation Billington's biography, Page's compilation, and the memories and perceptions of those close to Pinter, especially his friends. Notable amongst these are those of his widow, Antonia Fraser, in her *Must You Go? My Life with Harold Pinter* (2010); the book covers their initial meeting on January 8, 1975 at a dinner party up through Pinter's death on Christmas Eve 2008.

The present work, *Pinter's World: Relationship, Obsessions, and Artistic Endeavors*, uses these materials, some of which were not available until after Pinter's death, and also sources underutilized by Billington, such as Peter Hall's *Diaries: The Story of a Dramatic Battle*, edited by John Goodwin (1983). This contains a record of Hall's activities during the tumultuous 1972–1980 years that witnessed the creation of the National Theatre; it sheds considerable light upon Pinter and his relationship with Hall and others.

Pinter's World: Relationship, Obsessions, and Artistic Endeavors also taps works written by Simon Gray, whose plays Pinter directed. A close friend of Pinter, Gray dined with Pinter on a weekly basis for over two decades. Gray wrote biographical memoirs including *An Unnatural Pursuit and Other Pieces* (1985), *Enter a Fox* (2001), *The Smoking Diaries* (2004), *The Year of the Jouncer* (2006), and *The Last Cigarette* and *Coda* (both 2008). These works provide a plethora of information concerning Pinter and his habits from the perspective of a shrewd reader of character and one who worked closely and corresponded with Pinter for years.

In her *The Centre of the Bed* (2003), Joan Bakewell illuminates her relationship with Pinter during a period in which each was married to someone else. Their relationship provided the creative stimulus for one of Pinter's most notable dramas, *Betrayal* (1978).

Less well known is the reminiscence of Henry Woolf, Pinter's lifelong friend from school days. Woolf privately produced and published a limited-circulation ring-bound booklet called *Barcelona is in Trouble* (2013), subsequently published by the Greville Press in 2017.

Pinter's World: Relationship, Obsessions, and Artistic Endeavors utilizes these works and unpublished sources, including discussions with those who knew Pinter, such as Anthony Astbury, the founder of the Greville Press, a press that Pinter underwrote. Astbury is the author of two limited-circulation ring-bound booklet tributes to Pinter: *Memories of Harold Pinter* and *Letters to Harold Pinter 1974-2008*, both produced in 2015.

Others who shared their knowledge of Pinter include former members of the Gaieties cricket club with whom Pinter played, such as Dr. Christopher Brookes; those who used to act under Pinter's direction, such as Harry Burton and Doulas McFerran; and the critic and bibliographer Susan Hollis Merritt.

The British Library Harold Pinter Archive contains much material and is continually augmented. Of particular importance is Pinter's correspondence with his friends from childhood, members of what Henry Woolf refers to as Harold's Hackney "gang." The gang includes Woolf himself, Mick Goldstein, and Morris Wernick. Pinter maintained close relationships with these three in particular until the end of his life. Other materials that recently have become available for consultation include letters to and from Joseph Brearley, Pinter's schoolmaster and a formative influence upon him.

Using these materials adds considerably to previous biographical accounts. In the current work, material is arranged around themes, key concerns, the activities of its subject, and, in some instances, a chronology of Pinter's life. It is also careful to document wherever possible Pinter's meetings and endeavors; for instance, with whom he met and when, when he wrote what and when, and his perspective at the time. This work explores Pinter's writing: drama, poetry, prose, journalism, and letters, which are here regarded as part of his aesthetic achievement. Pinter was a wonderful letter writer, especially in his use of language.

Pinter's World: Relationship, Obsessions, and Artistic Endeavors is not a full-scale biography or an exposé but a series of illuminating chapters about Pinter's life, character, and thought, employing new information found in his "Appointment Diaries," recent biographical sources such as Simon Gray's memoirs, and Henry Woolf's reminiscences in addition to personal discussions with several in Pinter's world. This book is a fresh illumination of Pinter's life and art, friendships, obsessions, and concerns.

The first chapter, "The Theatre and Film," encompasses Pinter's school days, his time in—or, in his case, absence from—drama school, his lifelong obsession with the theatre as reflected through the lens of his relationship with schoolmaster Joseph Brearley, and Pinter's work with Peter Hall and others at the National Theatre. This chapter uses the viewpoints of those with whom Pinter worked as a repertory actor in provincial theatres on the British mainland, Northern Ireland, the Irish Republic, and beyond to illuminate his life as an actor and director. This chapter also gives attention to Pinter's autobiographical novel, *The Dwarfs*, his early poetry, work in film, and other creative endeavors. The chapter's structure reveals that as Pinter's career continued and developed, so did his writing.

The second chapter moves from Pinter's fascination with the theatre and film to "Passions" focusing on Pinter's non-theatrical obsessions. It pays special attention to his passion for cricket and other activities, such as the card game bridge. The chapter concludes with a consideration of his love of music, including a discussion of the operas he attended and the composers he preferred, and reflects on their significance to Pinter.

The third chapter, "Restaurants and Friendships," contradicts a perception that Pinter was antisocial, in common with characters in his plays such as *The Caretaker* and *The Birthday Party*. On the contrary, Pinter regarded friendships and loyalty of prime importance and dined out on a regular basis. Analysis of his regular eating out at restaurants reveals that Pinter was a social person who used restaurants to conduct business and for creative and clandestine meetings. He ate out to celebrate milestones such as wedding anniversaries and birthdays. The chapter discusses his favorite restaurants, their ambience, and the choice of food. It reveals that Pinter largely inhabited a seven-mile or so radius of his London W8 postal district home. This contrasts to his early upbringing in the East End of London. His restaurant activities illuminate his collaborative social nature and his capacity for friendship over lengthy periods of time, and forms the foundation for creative transformation in, for instance, his last dramatic work, *Celebration* (2000).

The fourth chapter highlights the women in Pinter's life and attempts to assess their importance to Pinter. The chapter features Pinter's mother, his two wives, two former lovers, three actresses, a translator and producer, a theatrical designer, his agent, and a close friend of both Pinter and his second wife, Lady Antonia Fraser. All played a crucial role in Pinter's professional and private lives.

The fifth chapter looks at "Politics and Religion." It considers Pinter's youthful conscientious objection, drawing upon correspondence with Henry Woolf and Morris Wernick, both of whom were subject to harsh treatment during their National Service. The chapter also considers Pinter's relationship with his father. The political dimensions of Pinter's drama, film, poetry, and prose writing are examined in some detail. Again, previously ignored or unavailable materials are used to reveal Pinter's attitude to religion and to religious issues, which may be regarded as another facet of his "political" perceptions.

The final chapter, "Literary Influences and Favorites," is structured chronologically in its discussion of authors who affected Pinter, from Shakespeare and the Jacobean John Webster to late twentieth-century writers whom Pinter personally knew. The chapter moves from Pinter's early reading and its impact upon him to later literary influences and friendships. As in previous chapters, this chapter uses letters by and to Pinter to reflect on his creative imagination. This chapter supplies information on his reading and his opinions on his reading, and discusses his personal relationship with and influence of authors such as Samuel Beckett, W. S. Graham, and Philip Larkin. Chronologically structured, the chapter places Shakespeare before Beckett, Larkin, and W. S. Graham, but that doesn't necessarily reflect a hierarchy of literary importance for Pinter. It includes writers using languages other than English, such as Proust, Rimbaud, Tolstoy, Turgenev, and Goncharov, before turning briefly to the impact of Aldous Huxley and, at greater length, Henry Miller. Attention then shifts to Pinter's relationship with three contemporaries: Samuel Beckett, W. S. Graham, and Philip Larkin. In one way or another, and in some cases more than others, each of these writers influenced Pinter. As with other chapters in this study, this chapter provides a kaleidoscope of approaches that illuminates the life, personality, and work of the great late twentieth-century writer, Harold Pinter.

How does one sum up another person's life—especially that of a Nobel Prize winner, an accolade that puts the seal on a lifetime's creative achievement? *Pinter's World: Relationship, Obsessions, and Artistic Endeavors* doesn't offer a reassessment of the writer's work but presents a pointillist portrait of him through examining central concerns in his life. These encompass an obsession with the theater and games; his delight in restaurants, demonstrating that Pinter was far removed from the socially awkward, isolated figures who populate his early work; and the women in Pinter's world. Other areas examined include Pinter's political engagement, from his adolescence to his last years, and literary and other creative influences upon him. This work draws upon his papers at the British Library, including letters to others, especially close friends with whom he kept close contact for over half a century. These letters should be regarded on par with his other creative accomplishments. Pinter was a fascinating letter writer, whose letters reveal thoughts at the time of writing often in abrupt and most colorful idiomatic language. His "Appointment Diaries" cannot reveal what actually occurred during his meetings, but they do provide a guide to what he did on a daily basis and whom he met. Memories from his friends, professional colleagues, cricket players, and his second wife, Antonia Fraser, illuminate Pinter's personality and actions. Pinter's first literary love was poetry, and, unlike most other Pinter studies, this one gives attention to his neglected poetic output, which often reveals the real Pinter and the enigma that is at the heart of every great artist.

In addition to those previously mentioned, others from whom much has been learnt include Steve Gale, Francis Gillen, and Alastair Macaulay. Thanks are also due to Judy Daish Associates. Special thanks must go to Ronald Barshinger at the Document Delivery Services Division at Northern Illinois University Libraries and to John Aplin, biographer of William Makepeace Thackeray and editor of the letters of Philip Webb. Also at the British Library Manuscripts Department and the Pinter Archive, Greg Buzwell and the chirpy, knowledgeable Jeff Kattenhorn must be thanked, as must Melissa Birks for her judicious observations on the various drafts of this text, and the anonymous publisher's reader's helpful suggestions and responses. Portions of this work were presented at Shanghai Normal University, Shanghai Jiaotong University, Shanghai, Central Normal University Wuhan, and the School of International Studies, Zhejiang University, Hangzhou, People's Republic of China. Special thanks must go to the deans of faculty and individual faculty members at these universities for inviting me and to the audiences who displayed such an interest in the work of Harold Pinter and provided insights for which I am truly appreciative. This work is dedicated to Harry Keyishian, the distinguished doyen of American academic press publishers who retired in June 2017 after many years of dedicated service at Fairleigh Dickinson University Press. Harry encouraged me to write this and several other books; his advice is always judicious and his encouragement infectious. My debts are so many that if I have inadvertently omitted the person or institution, then my apologies. Any errors are mine and I take responsibility for them. Personal indebtedness includes my daughters Sharon and Karen, their husbands Joel and Marc, and my grandchildren for being such splendid hosts during London visits. Of course my thanks to my wife, Rivka, are beyond words.

William Baker
DeKalb, Illinois
July 2017

Abbreviations

BBC1, BBC2, BBC4: British Broadcasting Corporation television channels

Billington: Michael Billington, *Harold Pinter* (London: Faber and Faber, 2007)

BLADDMSS: British Library Additional Manuscripts: referred to by the Pinter Archive reference numbers assigned by the British Library.

BR: William Baker and John C. Ross, *Harold Pinter: A Bibliographical History* (London: The British Library and New Castle, DE: Oak Knoll Press, 2005)

Chronology: William Baker, *A Harold Pinter Chronology* (Houndmills, Basingstoke, Hants: Palgrave Macmillan, 2013)

Diaries: Peter Hall, *Peter Hall's Diaries: The Story of a Dramatic Battle*, edited by John Goodwin (New York: Harper Row, 1984)

Must: Antonia Fraser, *Must You Go? My Life with Harold Pinter* (London: Weidenfeld & Nicholson, 2010)

Sharp Cut: Steven H. Gale, *Sharp Cut: Harold Pinter's Screenplays and the Artistic Process* (Lexington: University Press of Kentucky, 2003)

TLS: *Times Literary Supplement*

Various Voices (VV): Harold Pinter, *Various Voices: Prose, Poetry, Politics 1948–2005.* (London: Faber and Faber, 2005)

References to Pinter's texts are to his first editions unless otherwise stated. See also under *References*.

ONE

The Theatre and Film

Joe Brearley, Repertory (Rep.), Creativity, Peter Hall, and Others

INTRODUCTION

This opening chapter examines Pinter's obsession with theatre and film and his work as an actor and director. It does so through the prism of his relationship with his schoolmaster Joe Brearley, who profoundly influenced him and with whom Pinter maintained a lifelong friendship. It also draws upon previously unavailable documents. These illuminate Pinter's youthful activities, his theatrical apprenticeship in repertory theatre and struggle to make ends meet, his early creative endeavors, his acting, and his adaptation of a stage name. The chapter discusses Pinter's film work, focusing on his work with another close friend, Simon Gray (see also chapter 3). It includes reactions from actors whom he directed. His relationship with the great theatrical director Peter Hall illuminates Pinter's professional and private life mainly during the 1970s and early 1980s. Chronologically, the chapter follows Pinter through his school days to the early twenty-first century.

JOE BREARLEY (1909–1977)

In his brief introduction to a volume of reminiscences by Joe Brearley's former pupils and friends, Pinter called his teacher an inspirational force.[1] From a Methodist Yorkshire middle-class family, Brearley was educated at Batley Grammar School. Gaining a place at St. John's College, Cambridge, to read English, he came under the influence of I. A. Richards

1

and F. R. Leavis, his supervisor whom he saw twice a week. Before World War II, Brearley also spent time in Germany. A lover of music, especially Bach and Wagner, Brearley possessed a fine voice and, toward the end of his life, frequently sang in church choirs. He began his teaching career at Collyer's School, Horsham, where he taught from 1932 to 1939. He subsequently moved to Hackney Downs Grammar School. He returned to Hackney Downs after serving in the war, becoming its deputy head in 1953. Retiring in 1971, he moved to Germany. There, he met Mara, a much younger painter and sculptor; he spent the rest of his life with her. Following Brearley's death in 1977, Pinter remained in communication with Mara until at least 2002 and his final illnesses.

Brearley's pupils at Hackney Downs included Pinter, Henry Woolf, Moishe (Morris) Wernick, Ron Percival, and others. Brearley regarded the section of London youth whom he taught at Hackney Downs as intellectual elite whom he was privileged to serve. Brearley cast Pinter in leading roles in his productions of *Macbeth* in 1947 and then in *Romeo and Juliet* the following summer. The critic in *Hackney Downs School Magazine* (Summer 1947, no. 162), notes that Pinter as Macbeth wore the costume of a khaki uniform that would have been worn by a post–Second World War British soldier who was serving in the tropics or in Palestine. He writes that "word-perfect, full-voiced, Pinter took the tragic hero through all stages of temptation, hesitation, concentration, damnation. He gave us both Macbeth's conflicts, inner and outer, mental and military, with vigour, insight and remarkable acting resource" (12). The reviewer, however, had reservations concerning Pinter's performance as Romeo. Pinter "flung himself on the floor of the Friar's cell in passionate histrionic abandon" yet seemed to lack the vocal abilities "needed to bring out all the subtle cadences of the poetry" (Summer 1947, no. 165: 18).

During his time at Hackney Downs, from September 1942 until July 1948, Pinter and Brearley went on a series of long walks in North London; this tradition continued for years. Initially, their lives were influenced by Shakespeare; however, as Pinter observes in *Fortunes Fool*, Brearley also introduced him to John Webster and other Jacobean dramatists. Brearley supported Pinter's decision to register as a conscientious objector, meeting with and reassuring Pinter's concerned parents. When Pinter started to write plays, he would send them to Brearley, whose reactions were helpful and encouraging. In 1964 Brearley visited Pinter in Worthing and praised *The Homecoming*. Writing to Brearley in October 1964, Pinter tells Brearley that Brearley and his friends were the true "meaning" of his school days.[2]

Brearley encouraged Pinter's lifelong love of and obsession with the theatre. It was at the Hackney Empire that, in 1947, Brearley took Pinter and his classmates to what was perhaps Pinter's first theatrical experience—and probably theirs—Donald Wolfit as King Lear. Pinter was "staggered" by the performance and saw it six times at various theatres before joining Wolfit's company in 1953. Looking back on these years with his old friend Ronald Harwood, in an interview published early in 2003, Pinter tells Harwood that he went with his parents to see *Death of a Salesman*, which he recalled as a most powerful experience. He saw various performers, including the comedian Max Miller, at the Hackney Empire; at the Palladium, he saw the great comic artist Jack Benny.[3]

On November 20, 1977, Pinter writes to his close childhood friend Mick Goldstein that he heard that Brearley had died.[4] The funeral took place on Wednesday November 23, 1977 at the Crematorium in Nürnberg, Germany, where Brearley had settled. Pinter didn't go; he lunched instead with his son Daniel (*Chronology*: 77). However, Pinter sent a brief tribute that was read at the memorial service; in the tribute, Pinter called Brearley a man of true character, brilliant, and possessed by the theatre.[5]

Shortly after Brearley's death, Pinter wrote one of his finest poems, "Joseph Brearley 1909–1977 . . . (Teacher of English)." It was first published in the little magazine *Soho Square*. In the poem, Pinter doesn't recall his teacher's inspirational school productions and reading of Shakespeare, Webster, Tourneur, and others but rather their walks together through the North London landscape. The poem is replete with specific topographical references, such as Clapton Pond, Stamford Hill, Manor House, and Finsbury Park (*VV*: 163), as if the poet is trying to provide permanence in names to the ephemeral and temporal: The places will remain, those who walked in them do not.

Pinter and Brearley corresponded with each other until the schoolmaster's death: The letters throw light upon their writer's opinions, moods, and events, and illuminate Pinter's work and relationships. In a lengthy typed letter from the Alexandra Theatre Birmingham, where he is acting, on October 27, 1957, Pinter tells Brearley that his wife is expecting a baby in the New Year and that his job at the Alexandra Theatre is the best job he's had from several perspectives. The money is good. The bright spot in the choice of plays is Arthur Miller's *All My Sons* (1947). Pinter played the role of Chris, the idealistic son, and Pinter and Miller subsequently became friendly.

Pinter played at the Alexandra from July 19 to September 30, 1957. His roles included the lead as a vicar in R. C. Sherriff's *The Telescope* (1957). Pinter considered the play to be poorly constructed, verbose, and dull. His two other roles were a minor part in Noel Coward's *Hay Fever* (1925), in which Pinter's then-wife, Vivien Merchant, also appeared, and an inspector in Agatha Christie's *Spider's Web* (1954).

Pinter's minor parts in Coward's dramas such as *Hay Fever* and *South Sea Bubble*—at the Pavilion Torquay following his short honeymoon—provide the opportunity to reflect on Pinter's relationship with Vivien and Pinter's theatrical indebtedness. At the time of his marriage, Pinter was playing minor roles while Vivien had major ones; when he eventually received the limelight and Vivien's glitter faded, the effects on her were devastating and her drinking problem worsened. Many of Coward's themes echoed real-life relationships. In *Hay Fever*, characters are egocentric and play games among each other, withholding information. Conversations are punctuated with silences. The main characters include a father, a writer; a son, an artist; a mother, a retired actress; and a daughter. They invite for the weekend guests whom, in Michael Billington's words, "they ignore, abuse or pass around like erotic parcels." Billington writes that "this is not just proof of their egocentric self-absorption." In fact, receiving guests "is a way of keeping a fractured relationship alive." Charles Spencer, an acute theatrical critic, observes that in the play "we discover the seeds of Pinter's spare, edgy dialogue."[6]

Pinter tells Brearley of his enthusiasm for Beckett, asking Brearley whether he saw *Waiting for Godot*. Peter Hall's production at the Arts Theatre had opened in August 1955.[7] He informs Brearley that his playwriting is going well, although to date nothing has been produced, and that in 1957 he wrote three plays: two one-act plays and a three-act play. He writes that he is in the grip of the playwriting business and enjoys it. A year or so previously, he completed a novel, *The Dwarfs*, but couldn't afford to have it typed and didn't have the time to do it himself. He also gives Brearley an update on two of Brearley's former pupils: Henry Woolf, touring Ireland with McMaster's company, and Jimmy Law, in Naples to try to find pupils for English language lessons. Finally, he tells Brearley of two important informative personal family events: that his mother has been ill and that he's been married to Vivien for more than a year and is happy.[8]

In a letter dated July 22, 1960, following a performance of *The Birthday Party*, Pinter tells Brearley that he was enormously affected by the performance. Pinter objects to the label "Pinterian" that had been placed upon his work. He's also disturbed by his personal relationship to each of the characters in his play—he can't detach himself from them. For instance, at the point when the character of Stanley comes down the stairs in the last act, the character of Petey faces the character of Goldberg and says, "He'll be right here, with us." Pinter observes that his problem is that he's Petey, Goldberg, *and* Stanley. He calls *The Birthday Party* his most significant play to date, comparing it with Martin Luther's thesis nailed to the door.

In a lengthy typed letter dated February 6, 1964, written from 14 Ambrose Place, Worthing, Pinter updates Brearley on his activities and future plans. Pinter is about to begin a film adaptation of L. P. Hartley's "wonderful" novel *The Go-Between*. He is also going to act and will play the lead part of Garcia in Jean-Paul Sartre's *Huis Clos*, directed by Philip Saville. This was transmitted on BBC TV 2 on November 15, 1965. Pinter acknowledges the challenge to see if he can still act—which, after all, Brearley himself first made him do at school. Pinter then will go on to direct *The Birthday Party* at the Aldywch.[9] In fact, he directed this for the Royal Shakespeare Company's production; it opened on June 18, 1964.

Pinter's direction was well received. Writing in *The Observer* on June 21, 1964, Bamber Gascoigne observes: "Apart from the direction of the actors, the main difference in this production [to Peter Wood's premiere in 1958] is that Pinter has tried to make every detail as ordinary as possible—the seaside boarding-house, its inhabitants and the two dark-suited thugs who come to take Stanley away. I see his point—the more familiar the context, the more real the menace which develops—and certainly this theory sometimes works [...] Pinter's production probably reveals the play's meaning more clearly than Peter Wood's."[10]

In his February 6, 1964 letter, Pinter also asks Brearley if he has seen *The Servant*. Pinter wrote the script for the film, which opened in London on November 14, 1963, as well as the script for the film *The Caretaker*, generally released in 1964 (*Chronology*: 16–17). Frequently, Pinter and his former teacher share mutual responses to theatrical productions. In the same February 6, 1964 letter, Pinter tells Brearley that he agrees with him concerning the National Theatre's *Hamlet*, directed by Laurence Olivier. Peter O'Toole played Hamlet; Michael Redgrave, Claudius; and Robert Stephens, Horatio. Brearley found it over-acted. Pinter responds that the performance "has certainly an all-star cast" and then asks, "But where have they all gone? Where have all the flowers gone?" In spite of such a distinguished cast, Pinter tells his former schoolmaster in alliterative language, without elaborating further, that he and his wife left after the first act "like shots from a shovel."

In a later letter dated March 20, 1964, Pinter responds to Brearley's letter dated five days earlier in which Brearley expresses satisfaction with the film of *The Caretaker*, especially in its real presentation of snow and Hackney and Stoke Newington. Brearley is astonished that it "can be so much better than stage performance" and that so much could be done "in such a small place." Pinter found Brearley's critique so refreshing that he shared it with Clive Donner, who directed the film.[11]

Pinter invited his old schoolmaster to the opening night and party of the revival of *The Birthday Party* at the Royal Shakespeare Company at the Aldwych on June 18, 1964. Two days later, Brearley writes Pinter a six-page handwritten reply, expressing his excitement at meeting Margaret Rawlings, whose 1947 performance in Webster's *The White Devil* had so impressed him and others,[12] and also meeting Pinter's close friend Donald Pleasence, who performed the role of David in the initial 1960 production of *The Caretaker*.

In a letter to Pinter on March 15, [1964], Brearley reacts to the film *The Servant*. Pinter's screenplay was so good that he didn't notice it was a script, although Brearley did refer to biographical "bits about fathers having died; mothers having used a particular chair" that reminded him of visits to the home where Pinter grew up. On reflection, he thinks that the film was "a bit too 'theatrical'" and asks questions such as why the girlfriend didn't take action earlier to prevent losing her lover to his manservant. He also notes stylistic features such as the "caricatures of the couple in the country house." He didn't have the right vocabulary to describe the woman in the house at the end of the film. Brearley is annoyed by the close-up of a dripping tap, which he regards as a well-worn gag—he noticed the tap and the paint, so the close-up is unnecessary.

Pinter writes to Brearley on February 6, 1965 that he is in the middle of TV rehearsals and *The Homecoming*. The BBC TV broadcast of *The Tea Party*, directed by Charles Jarrott, took place on March 25, 1965. On the same Thursday evening, *The Homecoming* began its pre-London run, opening in Cardiff. Pinter is also working on the screenplay of Elleston Trevor's ("Adam Hall's") *The Quiller Memorandum* (released November 10, 1966).

Two years later, Pinter's reaction to a New York visit for the production of *The Homecoming* is interesting. Lionized and frequently interviewed, lunching with personalities such as Norman Mailer (February 4, 1967) and attending an evening dinner party hosted by Jacqueline Kennedy (April 20, 1967), he still finds time to spend a day with his old childhood friend Moishe Wernick, then living in Montreal (February 18, 1967). Pinter takes his son Daniel to the Natural History Museum on Saturday February 25, 1967 and confesses to Brearley in a letter written on the same day that it's freezing cold in New York, with bitter weather that makes it difficult to like the city. Regrettably, apart from mentioning the names of Mailer and Jacqueline Kennedy, Pinter doesn't say anything more about them.

The Pinter-Brearley correspondence provides insight into both. Of considerable interest is a lengthy confessional eight-page handwritten letter dated June 1, 1972 from Germany addressed to Pinter. Pinter's old schoolmaster reveals that he has fallen under the spell of a German sculptress named Mara. Brearley draws upon Pinter's knowledge of films to describe her as "a female version of the chap in Pasolini's film *Teorema*," adding that such an occurrence is odd at his age.[13] Brearley was sixtythree at the time. Terence Stamp played the lead role in Pasolini's film in which a guest has sexual relations with each member of the family he is visiting.[14] Brearley adds that he is singing in a Bach choir. He confesses that Bach is the one German pattern that keeps the dark Teutonic gods in their places.[15] The comment is clearly a reference to Brearley's flirtation with German Nationalist ideology, partly stimulated by an obsession with Wagner in the late 1930s, although during the war he was called up for the RAF and torpedoed at sea.

Following Brearley's departure for Germany in 1971, his letters to his former pupil become longer, full of personal information and confidences. Pinter's become shorter. This brevity reflects Pinter's hectic schedule—his writing, theatrical engagements and cinematic commitments, and entangled personal life—rather than a diminution of his indebtedness and friendship with his former teacher. In an example of the schoolmaster becoming dependent upon his former pupil, Brearley sends Pinter an eight-page handwritten letter dated October 3, 1974, almost three years after he left London for Germany. In the letter, he relates the difficulties he is having with renting out his Southgate house in North London. Aware of Pinter's engagement with Proust, Brearley says that he has read the third volume of *À la recherche du temps perdu*. He is never bored with Proust but has his doubts as to whether Pinter will be able to come to terms with Proust's lengthy sentences and similes.

Pinter sent Brearley an advance copy of his latest play, *No Man's Land*, and mentions casting concerns. In his December 3, 1974 letter, Brearley views the play "not in isolation but against an English background which for me is distorted almost beyond hope." In this letter, Brearley asks Pinter about whether there are any legal problems in using real cricketers' names in the play. Regarding casting, for Brearley, John Gielgud possesses a golden voice—full, rich, somewhat degenerate and banal—to play Spooner; the part suits him perfectly. However, the casting for Hirst is complicated. Pinter suggests Michael Redgrave, but Brearley is unsure about his suitability even if Redgrave is available (Pinter has told him he's ill). Redgrave is too clean "and schoolmasterish." For Brearley, the character of Foster in *No Man's Land* is distantly related to Alan Bates's Mick in the first theatrical production and film of *The Caretaker*. "But [Bates] would be fatal in the part—too many memories. And too slight." The part of Hirst would be played by Ralph Richardson and Foster by Michael Feast.

The best summation of the Pinter-Brearley relationship is found in Brearley's July 15, 1977 observation about Pinter's birthday message when Brearley turned sixty-eight. Brearley writes: "'Don't let the fuckers get you down' came as a welcome shot in the arm!"

PINTER'S REPERTORY APPRENTICESHIP

Other perspectives on Pinter's career and personality are found in letters he sent to Brearley's pupils such as Henry Woolf and Moishe Wernick; another contemporary from his youth, Mick Goldstein; and others. After leaving Hackney Downs School, Pinter spent most of the decade, from 1949 to 1959, as a repertory company performer going from production to production in England, Wales, and Ireland—wherever he could find a job and learn his theatrical craft. While on tour with Anew McMaster's touring company in Ireland from September 1951 to the autumn of 1953, he developed an intense relationship with a fellow member of the touring company, Pauline Flanagan (a relationship that will be subsequently explored[16]). She played Portia to his Bassanio, Mrs. Erlynne to his Lord Windermere, and Gwendolen to his Jack Worthing. He also played alongside Anew McMaster, as Iago to the great actor's Othello. Other roles included Sir Robert Chiltern in Wilde's *An Ideal Husband* and Creon in Sophocles's *Oedipus*. In a letter written during the summer of 1952, he tells Moishe Wernick that he had a splendid first night as Iago. He observes that acting is a matter of timing, of a "coincidence" between "internal impulse and an external execution."[17]

On November 8, 1953, toward the end of his second and final tour with McMaster's touring company, Pinter tells Henry Woolf about his stimulating experience in a production of *Rope*. Patrick Hamilton's psychological thriller concerns two Oxford University undergraduates who murder a fellow student to demonstrate their bravado, vanity, and intellectual superiority. They hide the body in a chest and then proceed to host a party for the murdered student's friends and family with the corpse inside the chest, used as a buffet. Pinter plays the role of the bullying Brandon. Patrick Magee, who would subsequently play important Samuel Beckett roles,[18] plays Pinter's nervy cohort, Granillo. Alfred Hitchcock made a 1948 film version with the setting relocated to New York City. Pinter also wrote to Woolf in November 1953 after learning that Woolf too was performing in *Rope*. Pinter muses that he can't see how amateurs could pull off the play because the production is technically quite difficult, adding that his work as Brandon is probably his best work on stage.[19]

An important component of Pinter's work is memory and remembrance. Interestingly, an expression he uses in a letter to Woolf, probably in 1952, remained somewhere in the recesses of his memory to reemerge just over twenty years later as a title for one of his plays, *No Man's Land*. He tells Woolf when discussing a possible meeting location to remember that they don't have to meet in no-man's land.[20]

During the break in McMaster's Irish season, Pinter joined Donald Wolfit's company at the King's Theatre Hammersmith, from February until April 1953. In McMaster's company, he had some major roles; with Wolfit, he was reduced to performing in minor roles. In addition to various small Shakespearian parts, Pinter played the Elder and a Countryman in E. F. Watling's translations of Sophocles's *Oedipus Rex* and *Oedipus at Colonus*. Other roles included the Duke of Normandy and Counsellor in the four-part *The Wandering Jew* by the Anglo-Irish poet and dramatist Ernest Temple Thurston. Pinter's friend Ronald Harwood, who was close to Wolfit, retained a close relationship until Pinter's death.[21] Harwood remembers an ironic piece of casting from those years. According to Harwood, at the initial rehearsal of Thurston's play, Wolfit "glanced at the company of assembled actors and said, 'I want someone to carry the Cross past a window in the first scene.' His gaze rested on one young man; with his voice at its most sonorous, Wolfit called out, 'Pinter.'"[22]

In his "The Knight Has Been Unruly: Memories of Sir Donald Wolfit,"[23] Pinter remembered Wolfit milking a theatrical moment for all it was worth with the help of a stage prop. He specifically recalled Wolfit as Oedipus, standing high on the rostrum, the lights shining on him, with his back to the audience and wrapped in a cloak. When the character downstage had finished what he was saying, the audience anticipated that Oedipus, Wolfit's character, would turn and speak. But Wolfit held the moment, and when he finally turned around, he did so with a swish of the robe, an extraordinary moment of power and savagery. As a dramatist, Pinter effectively used theatrical props and moments; for instance, in Ruth's manipulation of a glass to emasculate Lenny in *The Homecoming* and Mick's smashing of the Buddha in *The Caretaker*.

An illustration of Pinter's practical situation at this time is exemplified in the positive tone of a letter to Woolf dated July 7, 1954. He tells Woolf that he has a six-week tour that, he hopes, would come to the West End after that. He has a small part, but it pays £11. Apart from the money, he believes that a good theatrical run will have positive outcomes, although he's not optimistic, observing that he'll probably be back home in September. Pinter hasn't given up on his other ambition—that is, writing. He is working on the seventh chapter of what would become *The Dwarfs*.

Pinter is excited that he has a role for the summer of 1954 as a leading man at the Whitby Spa Repertory. In June he performed two roles: as the Sophisticated Artist in Agatha Christie's whodunit *Murder at the Vicarage* and in P. King and A. Armstrong's farce *Here We Come Gathering*. He liked Whitby but resigned on a point of principle and in solidarity with the company's assistant stage manager. They had a brief affair, and she was fired. Her landlady reported her to the theatre manager, the local butcher, for staying out late in the evening. Pinter requested unsuccessfully that she be reinstated. Returning home from Whitby to London, Pinter was met by the police at King's Cross for travelling without paying his train fare. The butcher—in in his role as theatre manager—threatened to blacklist him, and Pinter was frightened that he'd never work again in the theatre. The episode reveals two facets of Pinter's character: his firmness of principle in the face of what he considers an injustice and his attractiveness to the opposite sex.

Writing was important to Pinter. In a letter to Henry Woolf written during a visit to London in July, Pinter reveals that his book is on the move and consumes him; he even has a title, although it would not be used: *One Final Summer*.[24] It is during this period that Pinter uses the name "David Baron" as his stage name, possibly out of fear that the Whitby manager had blackballed him. As a writer, he uses his given name or, on three occasions, "Harold Pinta" (Baker and Ross: C5, 7 and 8).

In the summer of 1954, he wrote enthusiastically to Woolf about the minor role as Tops, the actor/cum assistant stage manager in Lawrence du Garde Peach's comedy *A Horse! A Horse!* In the words of Michael Billington, this "was not much of a job: he had to manipulate the ears of a dummy-horse to make it look real and at one performance narrowly avoided dismissal for failing to make the horse 'speak.'"

Yet, in addition to gaining theatrical experience of all sorts, Pinter acquired material that he subsequently put to excellent use in his first full-length stage play, *The Birthday Party.* His rep touring company began its 1954 season at Eastbourne on the Sussex coast and then, during August, toured to Dublin, Cardiff, and other venues. At Eastbourne, Pinter had grotesque, quasi-Dickensian lodging, but he used the experience subsequently for *The Birthday Party.* According to Pinter, he met a former London pianist and heard of a woman who wouldn't leave the pianist alone. Pinter asked the pianist why he stayed in the depressing boarding-house. The response was that there was "nowhere else to go." Three years later, when he came to draft *The Birthday Party,* the image was still there (Billington: 49, 76).

Following a period without work, Pinter's theatrical apprenticeship continued for six weeks or so with the Huddersfield Repertory Company, as he gained further acting experience in diverse roles, appearing in Lois Verneuil's (the pen name of Louis Colin du Bocage) comedy *Affairs of State* as the American diplomat Byron Winkler. The play opened in Huddersfield on November 15, 1954. It was followed on November 22 by Pinter playing the young lover/ amanuensis in Rosemary Casey's comedy *Late Love.* The next week saw Pinter in a leading role in another well-crafted Agatha Christie whodunit, *Ten Little Niggers.*

Inevitably for a rep company actor, another fallow period followed in 1955. From June until the end of September, Pinter acted in Port Stewart, County Londonderry, Ireland. He performed with the Colchester Repertory Company and again became romantically involved with an actress in the company, this time Jill Johnson,[25] with whom he remained in contact until his death. Pinter's diverse parts included the lead role of Orpheus in Jean Anouilh's romance *Point of Departure* (1941), which opened on February 28, 1955: He had taken Dilys Hamlett,[26] a former flame, to see this play during its run at the Lyric Hammersmith in 1950. In a letter dated March 15, 1955, Pinter tells Woolf that he is rehearsing an adaptation of John Steinbeck's 1937 novella *Of Mice and Men,* in which he plays Curley, the bully son of the ranch boss.[27]

At Colchester Repertory Theatre, from October 31, 1955, Pinter played the part of the husband in Denis Cannan's comedy *You and Your Wife,* described in Cannan's *Guardian* obituary as "a neat marital comedy."[28] According to Cannan's *Telegraph* obituary, Cannan "wrote elegant, exhilarating and somewhat fantastical comedies about the absurdities of love and war."[29] Pinter also prepared for a minor role in Phillip King's[30] melodrama *Serious Charge,* which opened at Colchester Rep on November 7.

With time performing in Northern Ireland, Pinter had seventeen roles during 1955 with the Colchester Repertory Company. They included Mayhew, the defending counsel in Agatha Christie's *Witness for the Prosecution* (from November 14). According to David T. Thompson, the play concludes "with twist and counter-twist to the plot" with the central character's "charm and his faithful wife's maniacal vindictiveness" revealed as "fabrications" and a "sensational tableau" on stage. These elements are absent from Pinter's own work, "but he often uses his own kind of dramatic image to end a play . . . with a surprised murder—an ironic final 'twist' to the plot—about to be committed,"[31] such as in the case of *The Dumb Waiter*. During this period, Pinter clearly learned a good deal about stagecraft, including "a fantastic amount about the rhythm and structure of drama and the techniques of theatrical effect." Pinter "absorbed the disciplines of rep drama and [subsequently] applied them to his own peculiar landscape" (Billington: 55).

Pinter continued to write, even while in rep. In a November 10, 1955 letter written from Colchester where he is in rep, Pinter tells Mick Goldstein that he is waiting for "my *Compartment*," probably from the publisher or the BBC. This became his TV drama *The Basement*, shown on BBC TV in February 1967. In another letter to Goldstein written shortly afterwards, Pinter confesses that "*The Compartment*" was a failure. Indeed, it remained in cold storage for more than a decade (BR: W27).

In the same letter to Goldstein, Pinter discusses "The Examination," a short story adapted as a sketch written in 1955. It was performed as a dramatic sketch by the Ambience Lunch-Hour Theatre Club at the Almost Free Theatre on March 12, 1978.[32] The story is concerned with its narrator's failed interrogation of a character named Kullus, who appeared in his prose-poem "Kullus," from 1949. On November 8, 1956, writing from Torquay, Pinter tells Woolf that he is pleased he likes "The Examination." In the same letter, he rambles on about the genesis of "Kullus," who is an old friend of Pinter's whom he met in a Stoke Newington, East End Billiard Hall.[33] In an earlier letter to Goldstein in 1955, Pinter mentions another work from this period, the five-verse poem "The Error of Alarm." He sends a copy to Goldstein and receives a positive response. The poem's female voice discusses her lover and expresses imitations of death, using the conditional "if" six times in the second, third, and fourth verse with a concluding definitive final line: "And he is my bier." The poem appears in *Various Voices*, where it is dated "1956" although seems to have been written a year earlier.[34]

In one of the few observations on his own style, Pinter tells Goldstein in a 1955 letter that what Goldstein wants from Pinter's writing is self-confession. But he's not going to get it. Opening the doors wide is not his purpose. For Pinter, his words are primarily a symbol of an idea; His "aim is stringency, shading, and accuracy." He describes himself as fastidious, especially when striving for an objectivity that his work de-mands. For Pinter, sometimes in his poems, he is not entirely aware of his activity, and the work seems to move on by its own discipline. He, rather, serves as a kind of "go-between."

At the Palace Court Theatre Bournemouth, between his first opening night on March 5, 1956 and his last on September 10, 1956, Pinter performed using his stage name of David Baron. He had twenty-four differing roles ranging from leads to minor parts. Pinter opened as the TV producer in Alan Melville's romantic comedy *Simon and Laura*. In addition to playing the role of a lover, Pinter also developed a reputation for playing detectives or a member of MI5. For instance, a local reviewer of Norman King's thriller *Shadow of Doubt* (from May 7, 1956) observes that "MI5 is at the door in the person of David Baron, black from homburg to toe-cap, a forbidding figure warning the doctors of science of the wrath to come." [35]

BOURNEMOUTH: MARRIAGE,
REPERTORY ACTING, WRITING

A crucial event took place during his time with the Barry O'Brien Company at the Palace Court Theatre in Bournemouth. A liaison with an actress took a different turn. Pinter initially performed with Ada Thomson (Vivien Merchant) during his time in Donald Wolfit's company at the King's Theatre Hammersmith from February to April 1953. They re-met in Bournemouth, began an affair, and married on Friday September 14, 1956 at the local Registry Office. [36]

In letters from Bournemouth, in spite of his heavy repertory commitments and marriage, Pinter discusses his own creative work. Writing to Goldstein on March 1, 1956, Pinter admits that he still has much to learn and that, as he gets older, it becomes harder to compartmentalize. [37] Pinter writes that he is working on a three-act play that would become *The Birthday Party* and provides Goldstein with a synopsis of the plot. The character of Stanley is staying with Meg. Two characters named Goldberg and McCann come along and take them away. [38] Interestingly, at this stage of the project, Goldberg and McCann come after both Stanley and Meg—not just Stanley, as in the final version of the play.

Following a brief honeymoon in Mevagissey, Cornwall, Pinter and Vivien performed for Philip Barrett's New Malvern Company at the Pavilion Theatre Torquay. From his opening role as an author in John Van Druten's *Bell, Book and Candle* (from October 1, 1956) to his final role as the lead in Agatha Christie's *Peril at End House* (from March 6, 1957), Pinter performed in similar repertory fare to that in Bournemouth. From October to December 10, 1956, he appeared in eight plays with lead roles in four: Christie's *Spider's Web* (from October 8); Patrick Cargill and Jack Beale's smutty comedy *Ring for Catty* (from October 22), which formed the basis for the subsequent *Carry on Nurse* films; Terence Rattigan's *Separate Tables* (from October 29); and Paul Osborn's *Mornings at Seven* (from November 5), with a plot anticipating Pinter's *The Homecoming*, in which a fiancé/spouse are introduced into a seemingly close-knit family. Also in 1956, Pinter was cast as a maniacal killer in Christie's *Love from a Stranger* (from November 12), a role he performed in Bournemouth; as a newlywed in Max Rietman's *Love on the Never-Never* (from November 19); and as a rebellious bank manager in J. B. Priestley's comic drama *Mr. Kettle and Mrs. Moon* (from December 10). A local theatrical critic singled out for especial praise Pinter's performance in *Love from a Stranger*: "David Baron [was] suitably sinister. . . . The play culminates in a climax of almost explosive intensity with David Baron attacking his macabre part with the ferocity which would've done justice to the Grand Guignol."[39]

In a 1956 letter, Pinter indicates to Goldstein that he is writing prolifically. He informs Goldstein that chapter 25 of his novel *The Dwarfs* has been typed. The revised version, dated "1952–1956 Revised 1989," has thirty-one chapters. In an undated letter written in late 1956 to Goldstein, Pinter relates that he completed the draft of the book, which he started two and a half years previously. In the same letter, Pinter confesses to writing two poems[40] and is interested in hearing Goldstein's observations on them. One poem consists of six short lines. Titled "Daylight" and dated "1956," this poem appeared in the second edition of Pinter's *Poems* published by the Enitharmon Press in 1971 (see BR: I3b). Its first verse of four lines and second of two lines has a sad lyrical quality, with its opening line, "I have thrown a handful of petals on your breasts," and its closing verse, "Now I bring you from dark into daytime, Laying petal on petal." The second poem, which appears to be unpublished, has five verses of four lines with the opening verse being alliterative.

Late in 1956, Pinter probably wrote an early incarnation of what became the one-act *The Room*, first performed at the Hampstead Theatre Club on January 21, 1960. He sent a copy to Goldstein, who clearly had reservations that Pinter attempted to dispel, writing that the subject of an old woman may not seem interesting to Goldstein, but Pinter believes is a subject that is worthy of treatment. Pinter explains that he is concerned with transformation—of the day, of the place, of furnishings, of the time, of the being. The transformation may be shocking, or unknown by the involved participants, or inevitable; striking a fatalistic note, Pinter adds that what had to happen was bound to happen.[41]

During the early part of 1957, Pinter remained in rep at the Pavilion Torquay for a five-week round of performances. Before leaving Torquay, he told Henry Woolf, who was pressuring him for a play, that he is not a fast worker. He won't let go of work until he is completely satisfied with it.[42]

Pinter wrote a single-sheet typed letter postmarked "February 21, 1957" to Woolf. In the letter, he tells Woolf that he will make several copies of *The Room* for him and that he disagrees with Woolf's observations about the play but agrees to trim down two long bits. He asks if Woolf can recommend an actress who can play the part. If not, Pinter writes, it's not worth taking a chance on producing the play. The observation reveals that finding the right performer for a part is of huge significance to Pinter.

The role of Rose was acted by Susan Engel, who was instrumental in introducing Pinter to his subsequent agent, Jimmy Wax, when Pinter stayed with her in Bristol in July 1957. Engel was friendly with the dramatist John Hall, who at the time had a play running at the Bristol Old Vic. Hall came to visit Engel, bringing Wax with him. "In the kitchen was Jimmy Wax. He told me he had heard about *The Room* and suggested that Susan and I read a scene from the play. So, at midnight in Susan's kitchen, in I think July of 1957, I, as it were, auditioned for Jimmy. He laughed a good deal during the reading and asked me to send him the play." Pinter then "went back to bed" (cited Billington: 73). The following week, he received a letter from Wax offering to be his literary agent; the relationship lasted until Wax's death in 1983.

Shortly afterwards, in another single-sheet typed letter written from Torquay early in 1957, Pinter tells Woolf that he is pleased to hear about Engel and other actors chosen for the parts. Pinter reveals that he is working on another play that became *The Birthday Party* and which is very different from *The Room*. Perhaps revealingly, Pinter adds that, if there is an opportunity to make money from writing, he must take it, especially now that he's married. Pinter always wanted free time to write, but time is limited while acting in repertory theatre. During this period, his letters to friends such as Henry Woolf and Mick Goldstein make little reference to his wife except to say that he is happy.

Following Torquay, during the spring and summer 1957, Pinter and Vivien toured provincial theatres at Leicester, Cheltenham, and elsewhere with Ted Willis and R. Gordon's popular smutty farce *Doctor in the House*. Pinter writes to Woolf from the Palace Theatre Leicester prior to the Bristol May 15–16, 1957 production of *The Room*. He expresses total disillusionment with the theatrical profession, telling Woolf that he is tired of the acting racket. Most of the plays, he complains, are bad. The managements are bad and the audiences are the worst of all. But, for the moment, there's no way out. The next week he and Vivien are going to Bournemouth to perform. In a typed letter written on Saturday June 8, 1957, he springs something of a surprise on Henry Woolf. Pinter tells his close friend that it appears that Vivien is pregnant; their son Daniel would be born on January 29, 1958. Such an important soon-to-be event in his life Pinter conveys almost as an afterthought, as reportage. [43]

THE BIRTHDAY PARTY: 1957–1958

Pinter comments on *The Birthday Party* in a letter written from the Playhouse Theatre Oxford on a Tuesday during the spring or early summer of 1957, when he is on tour with *Doctor in the House*. He tells Goldstein he has completed the play and sent it to Wax. He then writes at some length that there is a difference between the reading and the seeing. The play possesses its own stage rhythm and is on a larger scale than *The Room*. Pinter gives Goldstein a synopsis of the plot: Stanley is staying at the seaside boardinghouse of an aging couple named Meg and Petey. A pair of characters named Goldberg and McGann arrive. According to the old woman in the play, it is Stanley's birthday, so they all have a party. Goldberg's enemy McGann can only be played by one actor, Pinter says: Patrick Magee, with whom Pinter acted in Ireland although he wasn't in the original cast when it was performed. Pinter adds that he is concerned with preserving speech that is accurate to the quality of real spoken speech. He observes that speech "is not dead" and, in fact, it has its own strategy.[44]

On July 19, 1957, Harold and Vivien are acting at the Alexandra Theatre in Birmingham. Pinter has a minor role in Noel Coward's comedy *Hay Fever*, followed on August 2 by his reappearance as the inspector in Agatha Christie's *Spider's Web*. A month later, Pinter plays, according to the *Birmingham Weekly Post*, a "human and convincing" Chris, a young man in Arthur Miller's *All My Sons*.[45] Then on September 30, 1957 he as the lead role, the Parson, "played finely and believably" in R. C. Sherriff's drama *The Telescope*.[46]

Using both sides of a sheet of paper, Pinter manages to type a lot in a letter to Woolf dated Friday September 27, 1957. Pinter has heard that Woolf will join Anew McMaster's company, which begins its tour in Dundalk, County Louth, near the Northern Ireland border. This clearly brings back memories. Pinter tells Woolf that he will find Mac not at his best. Five years previously, when Pinter was with him, Mac was just going "over the peak," although there were some strong performances.

In this letter, Pinter mentions domestic worries. He is concerned about where he and his family will live. He tells Woolf that he heard from the Royal Court Theatre in London that it may be possible to put *The Room* on during a Sunday evening as one half of a double bill. He also learns that the resident producer at the Arts Theatre, Peter Wood, likes *The Birthday Party* and wishes to perform it not at the Arts Theatre but at the Royal Court. In the spring of 1958, Wood directed *The Birthday Party*, first at the Arts Theatre Cambridge and then at the Lyric Hammersmith; it closed after a week. A few days prior to typing his letter, Pinter completed another one-act play provisionally called *The Shaft*, with just two male characters in it. This would become *The Dumb Waiter* and was first presented at the Hampstead Theatre Club on January 21, 1960.

Pinter was with Fred Tripps Company at the Intimate Theatre, Palmers Green, North London, until early April 1958. He played the young schoolmaster with an "underlying seriousness of purpose" in R. F. Delderfield's popular comedy *A Worm's Eye View*, opening on December 26, 1957. His performance as the plainclothes detective in Ian Main's thriller *Subway in the Sky* garnered even more praise from local reviewers: "[T]he outstanding success in the play is David Baron's plain-clothes 'dick.' With his half-ingratiating, half-cynical smile, his lazy, or sudden swift, cat-like movement, he is beautifully in character every moment and suggests all the possibilities of a coiled spring" (see Thompson: 34–33). Pinter's other two roles at the Intimate Theatre included a Detective Constable in Jack Popplewell's whodunit *The Vanity Case* (from March 17, 1958) and Cliff in John Osborne's groundbreaking drama *Look Back in Anger*, first performed at the Royal Court on May 8, 1956 and directed by Tony Richardson. There is only one meeting between Pinter and the highly influential director recorded in Pinter's "Appointment Diaries": at 10 p.m. on Sunday November 10, 1985 (*Chronology*: 145). Writing about *Look Back in Anger*, the local theatre reviewer comments that "David Baron gave a real gem of a performance as Cliff. Unlettered, uncouth, understanding by instinct, friendly by nature, his Cliff Lewis is created so naturally as to add enormously to our acceptance of the thing as a whole."[47]

During a formative time in Pinter's career as a dramatist, April 1958, as a new father he earned his living as an understudy at the Royal Court Theatre in London for two N. F. Simpson plays, *A Resounding Tinkle* and *The Hole*, from April 2 to 12. A month earlier, at the Royal Court from March 10 to 29, Pinter was also an understudy for Osborne and Anthony Creighton's *Epitaph for George Dillon*.

Harold Hobson's Review of The Birthday Party

It isn't an exaggeration to write that Pinter's career was transformed by Harold Hobson's *Sunday Times* May 25, 1958 review of *The Birthday Party*, which opened at the Cambridge Arts Theatre on Monday April 28, 1958. Hobson, a highly influential and respected reviewer, was "willing to risk whatever reputation [he has] as a judge of plays by saying . . . that Mr. Pinter, on the evidence of this work, possesses the most original, disturbing, and arresting talent in theatrical London." For Hobson, *The Birthday Party* "is absorbing. It is witty. Its characters . . . are fascinating." Hobson writes: "[T]he plot, which consists with all kinds of verbal arabesques and echoing explorations of memory and fancy, of the springing of the trap, is first-rate." He then observes that "the whole play has the same atmosphere of delicious, impalpable and hair-raising terror which makes *The Turn of the Screw* one of the best stories in the world." Hobson adds in two subsequently frequently quoted sentences that "Pinter has got hold of a primary fact of existence. We live on the verge of disaster"

(11). Responding the same day as the review appeared, Pinter sends a postcard to Woolf wishing that Hobson may live long and happy.[48]

ADVERSE DOMESTIC CIRCUMSTANCES

In spite of this publicity, Pinter continued acting in rep. Initially *The Birthday Party* was far from a commercial success. Vivien's very painful labor was exceedingly difficult. The couple needed money desperately. They lived at the time rent-free in a depressing Notting Hill Gate West London flat/apartment described by Pinter as a virtual slum. Eventually they found a decent two-room, first-floor flat at 373 Chiswick High Road, where they lived until moving to 14 Ambrose Place Worthing in 1963. But they didn't have the money for a deposit. Vivien happened to tell an admirer, producer Rita Buchan, of their plight. Buchan sent a gift of the money. Pinter writes that this generous act saved them (cited Billington: 75). Further, the theatrical director and impresario Michael Codron, who encountered Pinter after Jimmy Wax alerted him to Harold Hobson's *Sunday Times* review, gave Pinter a £50 option on *The Birthday Party*. In addition, Codron supported Pinter by commissioning him to contribute to theatrical review sketches such as *Pieces of Eight* in 1959 (see BR: W11). Codron also agreed to put on *The Caretaker* at the Arts Theatre in April 1960.

PATRONAGE: ROGER STEVENS

The Hothouse was written in the winter of 1958 when Pinter and his family lived at 373 Chiswick High Road, London W4. Pinter also worked on several radio scripts for BBC radio. Reviews such as Hobson's, as well as hostile ones, bought Pinter public attention at home and overseas. On September 24, 1958, Pinter wrote to Roger Stevens, an American theatrical producer, arts administrator, and real-estate executive, thanking him for financial support that gave him the opportunity to devote additional time to his writing. Jimmy Wax had approached Roger Stevens to support Pinter following *The Birthday Party* debacle and its early closure. Pinter and Wax became close, and Pinter wrote a moving tribute to him in *Jimmy* (1984), a book of commemorative essays, anecdotes, and memoirs (BR: E22). Stevens's patronage in retrospect proved to be something of a cleft stick, as he held the rights to Pinter's subsequent three dramas in exchange for the £1000. The sum, in 1958, was not to be sniffed at for an out-of-work actor and budding dramatist with a wife and young son. Over the years, Pinter tried to claw back the rights to those three plays: *The Caretaker*, and what became *The Homecoming* and *Old Times*.

Pinter continued in rep in 1958 and until late August 1959, when he could afford to devote himself to full-time writing. At the Richmond

Theatre in South London, he was the managing director, a step up from acting, for the production of G. Ross and C. Singer's drama *Any Other Business* that opened on September 29, 1958. Almost a month later, he held the same position with the same play at the Connaught Theatre Worthing (opened October 20, 1958). There, a week later, Pinter had a minor role in Thornton Wilder's comedy *The Matchmaker*. Guy Vaesen, with whom Pinter subsequently worked and who was a lifetime friend of both Pinter and Vivien (see *Chronology*: 322), offered Pinter the Worthing opportunity. Following the opening night of *Any Other Business*, its lead actor became ill. Pinter, still using the name "David Baron," took over the role at short notice. As compensation "for saving the show Pinter was rewarded by the management—he vividly remembers—with a £1 note pressed gratefully into his hands."[49] Pinter then returned to Richmond to be nearer to Vivien and their young son; he would perform one role for the remainder of the year and five in 1959.

NO LONGER "DAVID BARON": SUCCESS

Feeling confident enough to use his given name, Pinter last used the stage name "David Baron" on September 19, 1960 at Cheltenham when he performed the role of Goldberg in *The Birthday Party*. Pinter subsequently devoted his time to writing, screen adaptation, directing, television, radio, and the theatre with infrequent acting appearances. In a letter dated October 29, 1963, Pinter updated Goldstein on his activities including putting on a stage version of *The Dwarfs* at the Arts Theatre Club, jointly directed with Guy Vaesen in September in a double bill with *The Lover*.

Pinter tells Goldstein that a film version of *The Caretaker* has been made under the title *The Guest*; adapted by Clive Donner, it won the Silver Bear at the Berlin Film Festival on June 27, 1963. Other activities at the time included finishing a short screenplay as part of a triple feature. The other two parts—each independent from each other—were written by Eugene Ionesco and Samuel Beckett.[50] This was *Project 1* promoted by the Grove Press, New York, with Beckett's *Film* and Ionesco's *The Hard-Boiled Egg*. Of the three, only Beckett's saw the light of day.[51] Subsequently, Pinter substantially rewrote his piece, called *The Compartment*, for television. He renamed it *The Basement* (cf. BR: B1).

MONOLOGUE

Something of a hiatus occurs in the Pinter-Goldstein correspondence, as both were wrapped up with their own lives. To move forward almost a decade, in 1972 Pinter sent Goldstein a new work that he wanted Henry Woolf to play in. This was *monologue*, presented on BBC television on April 13, 1973. Dedicated to his son and published in a limited edition by the Covent Garden Press (BR: A35), it features a man sitting alone in a chair. He refers to another chair, which is empty (p. [7]) and recalls past events, especially from his youth. There are references to games of Ping-Pong that take on highly suggestive sexual connotations and references to surrealistic painters that are juxtaposed with those of writers, modern and dead. The lines must have struck a deep personal chord in Goldstein, who objects to the play. His reactions upset Pinter, who, in a September 1972 letter tells Goldstein that he is perhaps taking images supplied in the play and using them to make a statement that he's always wanted to make. Pinter does not defend or explain his play apart from saying that it was not addressed to Goldstein or, in fact, to anybody. Baffled and hurt, Pinter won't forgive Goldstein. He accuses Goldstein of misquoting from the text. Two months later, on November 12, 1972, Pinter writes to Goldstein in apologetic tones, explaining that he no longer feels as emotional. He has re-read a letter Goldstein sent him two years previously and has considered their long friendship and all they shared together. He doesn't want to throw that away and wants to keep in touch. They should meet when Goldstein is next in England, he writes.

In a January 7, 1973 letter to Goldstein, Pinter tells his friend that he recorded *monologue* for television and that Woolf played the only role in the play. Pinter calls Woolf remarkable and describes being pleased with the whole production. Currently he is involved with filming *The Homecoming* with four members of the original cast, including his wife, Vivien, as Ruth; Ian Holm as Lenny; Terence Rigby as Joey; and Paul Rogers as Max. In the Aldwych Theatre June 3, 1965 production, Sam was played by John Normington. Cyril Cusack took over the role for the film version. Peter Hall directed both. A week later the shooting was completed, and on February 13, 1973, Pinter looked forward to seeing the initial film cut.

By this time Pinter was successful and sought after. Yet at times he was highly critical and dismissive of production of his work. For instance, on January 18, 1961, *A Slight Ache* opened at the Arts Theatre Club as part of a triple bill called *Three*, before being transferred to the Criterion Theatre. Directed by Donald McWhinnie, who previously directed *The Caretaker* at the Duchess Theatre, *Three* opened May 30, 1960 and enjoyed a long run. *Three* also included John Mortimer's *The Lunch Hour* and N. F. Simpson's *The Form*. Pinter told Goldstein that the production of *The Slight Ache* was terrible.[52]

MARITAL BREAKDOWN, CREATIVE ENDEAVOR, RESPONSES TO PERSONAL SCRIPT COPIES

In the meantime, Pinter's marriage to Vivien had disintegrated. Pinter went to live with Antonia Fraser, who subsequently became his second wife. His first play after moving in with Fraser was *Betrayal*. Hall directed it when it opened at the National Theatre in November 1978. Writing in his *Diaries*, Hall recalls he found it a "bleak and disturbing piece about infidelities" based upon Pinter's own behavior during his marriage to Vivien. "There are plenty of laughs and impeccable style, but my God the prospect is chilling. . . . It weaves a very cunning web" (p. 334). Hall also notes that immediately prior to the opening night, Pinter was "very depressed, tense and moody. He said to me tonight [November 3, 1978] that [*Betrayal*] is the best piece of work he and I had ever done together and it was about to be ruined" (338). A fortnight after its opening night, Pinter observes in a letter to Mick Goldstein that the reviews were generally negative, although there were some exceptions such as Benedict Nightingale in the *New Statesman* (November 24, 1978).

In a November 27, 1978 letter to Goldstein, Pinter reveals that he is about to start writing the screen adaptation of *The French Lieutenant's Woman*, based on John Fowles's novel. Pinter's "Appointment Diaries" reveal that he completed the fifth draft of *The French Lieutenant's Woman* on October 18, 1979, and on November 3 he was on its sixth draft (*Chronology*: 93). Shooting wouldn't begin until May 1980, with release in 1981.

Writing on October 27, 1979, Pinter tells Goldstein that he recently discovered a play that he wrote in 1958 called *The Hothouse*. He had put it in a drawer without showing it to anyone. Pinter re-read it, laughed, and would direct it the following April at the Hampstead Theatre Club.[53] *The Hothouse* opened on April 24, 1980, running until June 14 before being transferred to the Ambassadors Theatre in the West End, opening on June 25. In 1981 it was performed on BBC television. Originally written in 1958 and conceived as a radio play, *The Hothouse* drew upon Pinter's experience as a voluntary subject as a guinea pig for psychological research experiments that took place at the Maudsley Hospital in London years previously. At the time, he needed the small fee being paid. Ronald Harwood, also a Maudsley guinea pig, writes that "nearly all the characters represent some aspect of Harold's personality. The authoritarian director who runs the place embodies his more demonic side." Pinter is "also there in Lamb who is all innocence: Harold still has that same quality of innocence in that something quite ordinary can fill him with wonder." Harwood adds that "even his sensuality is there in the female character" (Billington: 367).

On a regular basis, Pinter sent his friends pre-publication printout copies of his work. In an November 18, 1982 letter, he sends Woolf a copy of the triple bill *Other Places*, which contained *A Kind of Alaska*, *Victoria Station*, and *Family Voices*. It had press night at the Cottesloe, National Theatre, on Thursday October 14. Pinter tells Woolf that the triple bill went over well, with Judi Dench giving a superb performance in *A Kind of Alaska*.

In another letter to Woolf written on September 17, 1983, Pinter confesses that he has had an unsettled year. His own direction of Jean Giradoux's *The Trojan War Will Not Take Place*, with which he was involved from early March until September at the National, was not well received. He resigned from the National Theatre after a row with Peter Hall. He lost his agent and friend Jimmy Wax, who died on April 23, 1983. Pinter attended his funeral on April 25.[54] And he suffered from writer's block, which may well have something to do too with his separation from Vivien and her rapidly deteriorating health.[55]

Nearly nine years later, in a letter of April 6, 1991, Goldstein thanks Pinter for a copy of *Party Time*, which wouldn't be published until early November of the same year (BR: A49). Goldstein says he was gripped by it and thinks it is "of immense importance." On May 1, 1991, Pinter responds by telling Goldstein that he is going to direct it with his *Mountain Language* in October. Both opened at the Almeida in a double bill on October 31, 1991. Pinter tells Goldstein in his May 1, 1991 letter that he is directing *The Caretaker* with Donald Pleasence, who played Davis in the May 1960 original production. The production went on a provincial run to Birmingham, Bradford, Guildford, and Bath before opening at the Comedy Theatre in London in June 1991 with Colin Firth as Aston and Peter Howitt as Mick. Pinter must have also sent Goldstein a copy of his *The Trial* script, because he thanks him in a June 1992 letter for expressing positive remarks about it. The film was not released until a year later, although shooting finished on May 17, 1992. Pinter recalls, too, that in 1965, in *The Homecoming* script he couldn't use the word "fuck" owing to the interference of the Lord Chamberlain's Office, which was abolished in 1968.[56]

Other responses to receiving Pinter scripts came from the dramatist and diarist Simon Gray, one of Pinter's closest friends.[57] On holiday in 1972, Gray writes to Pinter, thanking him for sending him *monologue*: "less stiff and literary as it advances into—I take it—tricky territory." Gray adds that there "is a certain increase of feeling and so a sudden flow." The only character in the play "seems to be speaking from a dreadful privacy, as in a bath in the lonely hours, the tone on the surface marvelously right in its naturalness, but conveying the pain with great economy (and comedy)." Gray's reservation is that the script "gives the initial impression of a forced literary exercise."[58]

One of Pinter's most powerful plays, *Ashes to Ashes*, received a private performance on May 28, 1996 and opened at the Royal Court on September 12 of the same year. Earlier, Pinter sent a script to Goldstein, who responded on February 15, 1996 asking whether Pinter knew "about the echo and light effect when [he had] started it." Goldstein found the play to possess "a strange dignity and reserve," so much so that the occasional "laugh even guffaw, will have shyness as a necessary companion." Pinter responded two days later, saying that despite the grim undertones, the play is inspiring.[59] Woolf directed the North American premiere during the Saskatchewan Summer Festival at Saskatoon. On September 13, 1998,

Pinter wrote to him, saying that he was "chuffed" at the reception and especially by the reviews in the Canadian papers.[60]

Summary

So far this chapter has focused on the impact of Pinter's schoolmaster Joseph Brearley, who encouraged his star pupil during and fostered Pinter's love for the theatre. Brearley also reacted to Pinter's writing, an endeavor he worked on at the same time as his acting activities. Further, the chapter draws upon correspondence with close friends from youth and school such as Mick Goldstein and Henry Woolf and subsequent friendships to throw light upon Pinter's theatrical activities and, at times, his personal life.

PINTER AND FILMS

Another writing skill, and a profitable one, emerged in the mid-1960s. Screenwriting combined Pinter's ability to write dialogue, dramatic situations, and silences with his fascination with the cinema. Pinter's engagement with film went back to his school days. His correspondence with Joe Brearley contains discussion of films they have seen. At school Pinter was active in the debating society. In the final school debate, Pinter seconded the motion that "[i]n view of its progress in the last decades, the Film is more promising in its future as an art form than the Theatre" (*Hackney Down School Magazine*164 Spring 1948: 12). Pinter evidently took such a proposition seriously. A few months earlier, during the autumn of 1947, he addressed fellow pupils on the subject of "Realism and Post-Realism in the French Cinema" (173: 13). His focus was Marcel Carné's film *Les Enfants du Paradis* from 1945, a cinematic exploration of the relationship between life and art, fantasy and reality, which encapsulates what was to become Pinter's poetry of dreams on the edge of chaos and destruction. Carné's wartime film evokes hope and betrayal in Nazi-occupied France. Somewhat ironically, a French wartime writer who also interested Pinter and his friends at school and in the period after leaving school was the Fascist Louis Ferdinand Céline, as is evident from the text of Pinter's autobiographical *The Dwarfs* and short one-act *monologue*. In both works, Pinter draws heavily upon his adolescent experiences and friendships.

At the age of fourteen, Pinter ran his own Hackney film society. In a 2004 interview, he recalled that the film that left the most lasting impression on his imagination was the 1929 silent surrealist film *Un Chien Andalou*, directed by the Spanish Luis Buñuel and the painter Salvador Dalí. The opening sequence of the film haunted Pinter. It contains a juxtaposition of a man sharpening a razor and then slicing a woman's eyeball down the middle with, as a cinematic background, a moon crossing the horizon. He still remembered the Parisian apartment setting, a window three stories up, traffic moving along the street and an assault on a woman by her lover. Other images from the film that he vividly remembered were a surrealistic one of a grand piano, donkeys, and escape by walking out along a beach and the sea. He told his interviewer, Peter Florence, that in his adolescence the cinema was a stronger, more powerful influence upon him than the theatre.[61]

Accident *Adaptation: Nicholas Mosley Correspondence*

It should not come as a surprise that Pinter should take to film adaptation. He worked on his adaptation of Nicolas Mosley's novel *Accident* (1965) between 1965 and 1966. Directed by Joseph Losey, who became a close friend (see *Chronology*: 317), the film starred Dirk Bogarde as Stephen, Stanley Baker as Charley, Michael York as William, and Vivien Merchant as Rosalind. Pinter played the role of Bell and Nicolas Mosley, Hedges. Pinter's friend Terence Rigby played a plainclothes policeman, and Jacqueline Sassard played Anna, an Austrian princess. Among various awards and nominations, the film gained the Cannes Film Festival Special Jury Prize for 1976. Dilys Powell, an eminent film critic reviewing the film in the *Sunday Times*, pointed to important features of Pinter's writing style: "Amazing how little is said and how much is told. Harold Pinter's dialogue—the long pauses, the interchanges which glance along the surface of a scene—is a kind of shorthand of talk; yet its elisions and abbreviations give you the character, the emotion, the situation. Sometimes it is used with ironic effect (there are wickedly funny passages reflecting on the preoccupations of a Senior Common Room)."[62]

Pinter and Mosley met and corresponded during the development of *Accident*. According to Pinter's "Appointment Diaries," they lunched on May 6, 1966 and met again in the late afternoon of June 30, 1966 (*Chronology*: 352). During Pinter's involvement with writing the screenplay, they exchanged lengthy letters. They discussed fundamental concerns of the story, such as whether Anna was a victim or a bitch; they agreed that she was both. In a lengthy typed letter dated April 5, 1966, Mosley reacts to Pinter's script, objecting to what he perceives as extensive changes from his novel. These Mosley identifies as firstly relating to the isolation of Charley, the university teacher who seduces Anna. Mosley questions whether or not Stephen offers Charley and Anna his house for the weekend, as he is resentful and jealous. Mosley is aware that Pinter is being subtle, as the house offer may be perceived as demonstrating Stephen's cynicism and masochism.

Secondly, Mosley is concerned about Anna and Stephen sleeping together, as he regards it as extremely difficult for someone like Stephen to have sex with a twenty-year-old for the first time in any circumstances—

let alone when she is drunk, or suffering from a hangover, semi-con-
cussed, at 5 a.m., and when he has a lot of other issues to consider. It
could be justified as "long as what is shown is the dissociation and slight
madness of sex at 5 a.m. after death in an accident." Mosley adds that
"the danger at this point is that the audience might cynically think—oh
this is what it has all been leading up to, the old usual" Mosley expects
that Pinter "wants to say something about the complexity of human behavior—that there are circumstances in which" someone would put at
risk their professional position as "an urge to self-destruction." Thirdly,
Mosley's view of the latter stages of his novel differs from Pinter's. The
author finds this "inevitable" and has no objection. Mosley emphasizes
the friendship between Stephen and Charley and the positive vibes between the two that emerge following the accident. Pinter's maintaining
their solitariness at the conclusion is valid, and Mosley is full of praise for
Pinter's use of the minor scenes of his novel. The author instances the
tennis match and especially its "dialogue . . . like squibs; very quick; very
undulated." For Mosley, Pinter has captured "the essence" of his novel.

When Pinter sent his screenplay to Mosley, he also sent a letter that he
asked Mosley to read after he had gone through his adaptation. Pinter
says he worked hard to follow Mosley's ending and completed a draft
that followed that course. But he was dissatisfied, complaining that the
long debate in the novel between Stephen and Charley didn't convince
and sustain itself in dramatic terms. The novel differs from screenwriting
and adaptation, with the dramatic structure having its own unique de-
mands. In Pinter's view, Stephen must be alone in his final complicity
with Anna. In dramatic terms the cinematic adaptation narrowed the
focus to achieve a greater intensity. Pinter and Mosley are different people and authors. Pinter tells Mosely that he has avoided distorting anything, as he admires Mosley's book. But he believes that the two writers
have different interpretations of the book. Mosley has an optimistic view
of the ending whereas Pinter, while not saying he has a pessimistic view,
does not feel that the ending is optimistic. Something has taken place and
will always live, on all levels, Pinter adds.[63] Steven H. Gale acutely observes that "with the script for [*Accident*], several things become clear."
For instance, "Pinter continually reworks his materials, trying to produce
the most effective screenplay possible and always endeavoring to remain
true to the essence of his source. He is also becoming increasingly more
adept at working with cinematic elements in his adaptations." In addition, "this is a pattern that has continued throughout his career" (*Sharp
Cut*: 181).

The Go-Between: *L. P. Hartley*

Pinter began working on the screenplay of L. P. Hartley's *The Go-
Between* (1953) for Joseph Losey in 1964. Due to legal issues, he restruc-

tured it and completed the adaptation five years later, in 1969. Pinter praised Hartley's book as superb but then added that he was unable to write a script because of its perfection (Billington: 206). Starring Alan Bates, Julie Christie, and Dominic Guard as the young Leo, the film was released in 1971 and gained several awards, including the Cannes Film Festival Palme d'Or and the British Film Academy Award for the Best Screenplay of 1971. Alexander Walker, the *Evening Standard* film critic, wrote that "Losey is perfectly served by his screenplay writer Harold Pinter, who has adapted L. P. Hartley's novel with scrupulous fidelity, yet adds to it his own uncanny skill at depicting people who use words to conceal themselves rather than reveal their meanings. In this guilty setting of privilege and deceit, Pinter is in his element."[64] On February 1, 1969 Jimmy Wax writes to Pinter to say that the adaptation is "bloody marvellous." Wax is unable to recall anything in Hartley's novel that is excluded from the script, and "the compression and distillation of the essence is little short of fantastic." Wax especially singles out the flash forward, Pinter's treatment of Leo when as an old man he returns to the traumatic scenes of his youth.[65]

Pinter's adaptation also gained L. P. Hartley's approbation. In a lengthy letter dated February 4, 1969, written shortly after Hartley and Pinter met on January 10, 1969, Hartley commends Pinter for his fidelity "to the letter and spirit of" his novel. Hartley particularly praises Pinter's dialogue, presentation of the action, and condensation of the original text. The action led to Hartley crying "at the scene where Leo questions Ted about 'spooning,'" a scene that Hartley regarded as better than his original. There are some caveats. For instance, at the start of Pinter's adaptation, Leo tells Marian that his father "was a pacifist" (*Five Screenplays*: 295). Hartley is skeptical that the word "pacifist" was then in use.[66] The opening direction of Pinter's published script reads: "The action of this film takes place during a span of 3 weeks in August in the summer of 1900 except for certain scenes, which take place in the present" (287). For Hartley, Leo would say that his father was "a 'pro-Boer,' as [his] own father was, and Marian could have replied 'a pro-Boer?'" to which Hartley suggests Leo's answer might have been 'No, a pro-B.O.E.R.,'" instead of Pinter's script in which Marian responds "Ah" and Leo "Mmm" (295). In spite of this caveat, Hartley tells Pinter that he is "quite overwhelmed by the beauty of [Pinter's] script," also by "the ingenuity and convincingness with which you interweave the young Leo and the young Marian with the old Leo and the old Marian."[67]

The French Lieutenant's Woman: *Simon Gray's Response*

Pinter worked on what Gale regards as Pinter's "best screenplay" (*Sharp Cut*: 237), *The French Lieutenant's Woman*, from June 28 to July 6, 1978 through to "June 28, 1979," the date on the title page of the final draft (BR: W42). Directed by Karel Reisz, the film opened in London on October 15, 1981. Pinter sent his friend Simon Gray an advance copy of his script. Gray's extensive, typed, undated letter to Pinter in response, comparing Pinter's script with the film, reveals much about Gray's critical acuity and the frank nature of their friendship, and highlights Pinter's strengths as a scriptwriter and cinematic adapter. Gray admires the "economy," the "deftness" and the "oblique ironies" of Pinter's script, which he regards as better than the actual film itself. The script, for example, conveys tenderness between a man and woman beginning to discover each other, while in the film, they are kept apart from one another. On the other hand, Gray admires director Reisz's "lack of embarrassment over the sheer romanticism of the romance" that exists in Pinter's script. This illustrates some of the "valuable things" omitted from the actual film itself. The film, Gray writes, "doesn't respect the mystery of the characters." This may be seen in the character and portrayal of Dr. Grogan. According to Gray, the final scene in the script in which Grogan appears is "brutally truncated." Gray also fails to "understand why Sam's [the servant of the main protagonist Charles Smithson] revenge and its consequences couldn't have been done" as in Pinter's script.

Jeremy Irons in the role of Charles Smithson/Mike is as always watchable, yet he is "narcissistic—his passion was strongly conveyed as passion, but seems never to be in full contact with its object, i.e., the woman," performed by Meryl Streep. Gray finds this particularly so after they have made love, when Irons "seems more aware of himself and his future in the abstract than his present, which is Sarah, and his future which he intends to make, from whatever complication of feeling, with Sarah." Irons "was at his best . . . when he wasn't playing with Meryl Streep" and especially when he was with the other men in the film. On the other hand, Gray praises Streep's performance, which he regards as "profoundly moving, in all her gestures, her expressions, her eyes-her lower lip swollen with lust, quite extraordinary." There is a caveat, however, as Gray finds "the diction—her rhythms straight-jacketed in the one English cadence that she'd mastered." An English actress would've made more of the speeches; there would've been greater variety, yet Gray would not have wanted anyone else but Meryl Streep to play the role of Sarah Woodruff/Anna. Elements that Gray singles out for particular praise in Reisz's direction includes "self-confidence," the film's "lack of concession to modern equivocation, and its effective transitions between the two worlds of the story."[68]

PINTER AS DIRECTOR

Another facet of Pinter's theatrical versatility is as a director. Ian Smith, with whom Pinter played cricket for the Gaieties side,[69] edited a collection of interviews, reviews, and essays, *Pinter in the Theatre*.[70] The collection features a "Preface" by Pinter, and a concluding section contains impressions of working with Pinter by actors and directors including Sam Mendes; another member of the Gaieties cricket team, Roger Lloyd-Pack; and Peter Hall. For Pinter, actors and directors have been a constant factor in his life. Several are dead, although the ones in the book are quite alive and it was, he writes, a pleasure to work with all of them. While he wouldn't describe them as shy, he has never heard them speak as openly as they do in the pages of the book. He says he learned much from their accounts.[71]

An aspect of Pinter's personality is reflected in his comment on the demise of a number of directors with whom he worked. The observation by association evokes the memory of Alan Schneider, the Russian-born, American theater director responsible for the New York premiere productions of *Birthday Party* (at the Booth Theatre, New York, October 3, 1967), *The Dumb Waiter*, *Collection* (as a double bill at the Cherry Lane Theater, November 26, 1962), and *Other Places* (Manhattan Theater Club, April 3, 1984). Schneider is also noted for his association with Beckett.[72] At the time of his death in London in a road accident in 1984, he was taking a rest from directing *Other Places*. Schneider was close to Pinter (see *Chronology*: 321, 356), who felt that he had betrayed Schneider by not letting him direct the 1981 New York production of *The Hothouse*. Subsequently, Pinter sent Schneider a lengthy letter of apology, dated March 26, 1981. Pinter writes that he behaved hastily and regrets it. Not normally in the habit of apologizing, Pinter concedes that he insulted someone of the utmost integrity and, in turn, discovered a flaw in his own integrity. In June 1984, in a eulogy read at Schneider's memorial service, Pinter confesses to being stunned by Schneider's death and finds it difficult to come to terms with the loss. Pinter is unable to encapsulate in a few words a man of such spirit, character, warmth, and vitality.[73]

Much of Pinter's creative engagement was spent as a director not only of his own work but of others' works, too. The listing under the heading "Directing" compiled on Pinter's website by Mark Taylor-Batty is extensive and extends over much of Pinter's career from 1962 through 2004. It reveals that Pinter directed thirty-seven plays in all, fifteen of those of his own work in the United Kingdom, plus seven for the cinema or television.[74] Chronologically, it begins with *The Collection*, co-directed with Peter Hall for the Royal Shakespeare Company at the Aldwych Theatre. This production opened on Monday June 18, 1962 in a double bill with Strindberg's *Playing with Fire* and was more or less at the beginning of Hall's and Pinter's lengthy and often fractious personal and professional relationship (see *Chronology*: 315–16 and Hall's *Diaries*). Some of the reviews of the initial stage production of Pinter's play drew attention to its "tangles of doubt, jealousy, and domination [that] provide some excellent moments for actors." Martin Shuttleworth, in a far from positive review, observes that the play "is played all the time for ambiguities: ambiguities of time and place and for phrasing and repartee which, in the end, defeated themselves and muffled the central ambiguity of the theme." For Peter Hall, "Pinter productions which remove the ambiguous, contradictory, the enigmatic, actually become very simplistic and boring. The image lacks complexity, and is then *unlike* memory because it is uncontradictory."[75]

Pinter's second production was also of one of his own works and as sole director, although he had an assistant director, Guy Vaesen, for performances of the double bill *The Lover* (1962) and *The Dwarfs* (as a play 1960) at the New Arts Theatre, London, that opened on September 18, 1963. John Russell Taylor, one of Pinter's most acute critics, writes in *Plays and Players* that "as it happens, Pinter's own production [of *The Dwarfs*], though it does not altogether hide the untheatrical nature of the material, does manage to hit on just the right tone. . . . The result is that one does not finally care about whether the play is or is not in theory 'theatrical'; it is a riveting experience in the theatre."[76]

The Birthday Party was the first of his own full-length plays that Pinter directed. This opened on Thursday June 18, 1964 at the Aldwych Theatre for the Royal Shakespeare Company. Acknowledging that Pinter had a fine cast to work with, R. B. Marriott, writing in *The Stage*, is cautious about Pinter's direction: "On the whole [he] has directed with considerable effect, though I consider the production would benefit from a quicker pace throughout."

As will be discussed in the final chapter, an important formative influence upon Pinter was James Joyce.[77] Pinter's attention to detail is singled out in the positive reviews of his direction of Joyce's *Exiles* at the Mermaid Theatre November/December 1970. The removal of a pair of gloves—an apparently meaningless gesture—took on significance in Pinter's direction of Joyce's work. Pinter emphasizes the themes of friendship and betrayal, the wounds from the past that cannot be healed. Martin Esslin in *Plays and Players* (January 1971) writes that "the scene in which, having allowed herself to be kissed by her 'seducer,' Bertha then meticulously reports all that happened to her husband is of astonishing boldness: there is much here of Albee, much also of Ruth's nonchalance about sex in Pinter's own [*The Homecoming*]. On one level this is uncompromisingly honest Edwardian free thinking, on another it is sexual fantasy right out of Pinter's *The Lover*." Another astute reviewer, Ronald Bryden, wrote in *The Observer* on November 29, 1970: "Hushed, deliberate, limpid as crystal, his production forces attention to every murmur of the characters, and in the silences between them you hear the murmur of their hearts."[78]

*Pinter's Direction of Simon Gray's Dramas and Gray's Observations on
Pinter's Plays*

Pinter worked in close collaboration with the dramatist Simon Gray,
and their friendship and working relationship is described elsewhere in
this book[79] and in detail in Gray's various published recollections.[80] Pinter directed ten of Gray's plays, the first being *Butley* (1971); Pinter directed its cinematic version two years later. The last was Gray's *The Old
Masters* in 2004. Following a short run at the Oxford Playhouse in July
1971, Pinter's production of *Butley* transferred to the Criterion Theatre in
London with its first night on July 14, 1971. The designer was Eileen
Diss.[81] Gray observed: "I sat in on [Pinter's] rehearsals which were conducted with clarity, precision and ease. I think what I learned from him is
that directing is simply a matter of the application of common sense.
Anybody should be able to do it who is capable of thinking practically
and specifically about the meaning of this or that line" (Billington: 222).
The American Film Theatre/Cinebill in January 1974 quotes Pinter as saying
of the cinematic version of the play that he wanted to do *Butley* because it
had such energy and mastery of language. He also describes the central
character as a remarkable man and, overall, finds the play witty but also
sad. In his *The Year of the Jouncer*, Gray describes Pinter's "powers of
concentration . . . and the clarity of his intelligence, his quick sympathy
with the actors as well as the command of his presence." Pinter "says he's
exhausted the moment he leaves, and quite tired in the morning when he
gets up, but the moment he's there, in the rehearsal room, he feels galva-
nized, enjoys every minute—'every bloody minute'—scarcely notices the
time passing" (141).

Gray's *The Rear Column*, directed by Pinter in 1978, received hostile
reviews and experienced a short run. One of the few favorable reviews
was from Benedict Nightingale in *The New Statesman*: "Besides Gray's
writing, Harold Pinter's unemphatic directing and a remarkably consistent company supply a super-abundance of that unfashionable theatrical
commodity, individual character" (February 23, 1978). The direction of
Gray's next play, with its appropriate cricket metaphor for a title, *Close of
Play*, occupied a good deal of Pinter's time during 1979. It opened at the
Lyttelton, National Theatre, on May 24, 1979 and ran until August in
spite of Pinter asking Peter Hall to reconsider his decision to close it on
Monday August 13, 1979. It then opened at the Olympia Theatre in Dublin on Monday October 8 with some cast changes. Peter Hall's *Diaries*
note that he attended the initial rehearsal, "a read-through, of Simon
Gray's *Close of Play*. It's mordant, grotesque, and dreadfully funny." Hall
adds that "Harold was in total black, smoking black cigarettes" (416). For
Robert Gordon, "by stressing the predominance of linguistic over gestu-
ral and histrionic effects, Pinter's direction demonstrated Gray's technique of employing conversational prose as a powerful mode of dramatic

action, a technique which Pinter has developed to perfection in his own plays."[82] For Milton Schulman in *The Evening Standard*, "Pinter's sensitive direction, even if it only occasionally hits off the hidden symbolism, beautifully synchronises the petty domesticity with the deep hurt that tears these characters apart even while they are munching their muffins."[83]

Pinter also directed Gray's *The Late Middle Classes*. Set in the 1950s, it concerns a family adapting to post–Second World War life. The winner of the Best New Play in the Barclays Theatre Awards for 1999, the production didn't reach the West End. The failure to do so and the dramatist's attempt to find a suitable West End theater for it are the subject of Gray's *Enter a Fox*, his 2001 diary. The play opened at the Palace Theatre Watford on March 19, 1999 and then moved to Brighton, Plymouth, Bath, and Woking before closing at Richmond on May 22, 1999. For Billington, in *The Guardian*: "Harold Pinter, directing his eighth Gray play, also gets the details exactly right: not just the obvious things like a father's shyness about discussing masturbation with his son but, even more importantly, the sense of guilt that pervades fifties life."[84] Georgina Brown in *The Mail on Sunday* also highlights Pinter's directing, writing that his "atmospheric, absorbing production elicits superb performances from Gray's cast of shell-shocked characters." Paul Taylor in *The Independent* was struck by the "pitch-perfect production, beautifully acted . . . emphasises not only the Rattiganesque stagecraft but a Dickensian range of sympathies."[85]

Gray had his preferences among Pinter's plays. *The Birthday Party* was not one of Gray's favorites. In a letter, Gray responds to its BBC 2 Theatre Night June 21, 1987 production directed by Kevin Ives in which Pinter performs the role of Goldberg. Gray observes to the critic Geordie Greig that *The Birthday Party* "seems to be a series of impulses rather than evolve from a single impulse. In the structure I almost feel a combination of manipulation and arbitrariness." Gray also writes to Greig that Pinter differs from other contemporaries who can be identified by special characteristics such as "the deftness of their plotting, eloquence or otherwise of their dialogue, their political stances." On the other hand, Pinter's plays can be "identified in the course of a short passage by the *atmosphere* of the dialogue." Pinter's speeches, "however different in tone and content, still possess a single voice." This is the reason "perhaps why he is the only living playwright whose name is used as an adjective."

The spring 2005 revival of *The Birthday Party* directed by Lindsay Posner, following a provincial tour, opened at the Duchess Theatre in the West End in the third week of May. Gray, in what appears to be a change in attitude toward the play, told Pinter that he had "been thinking a lot about [*The Birthday Party*] and the whirligig of time—how wonderful for you and for us that this extraordinary play is now nearly fifty years old—Can that be right?—And here it is, in a powerful and frightening new production, as frightening and powerful as if it'd just come into being."[86]

Writing to Pinter at the end of April 2005, Gray tells his terminally ill friend that he keeps "returning to *No Man's Land*—the lightness and the weight of it." It is the Pinter play that Gray most wishes he'd written. Referring to recent revivals of *No Man's Land* and *The Homecoming*, Gray distinguishes between "the play which has its own age and life" and "its reputation which ought to cease to assist the moment one goes into rehearsal." He adds that a recent production of *No Man's Land*, probably referring to the revival at the Royal National Theatre in December 2001 directed by Pinter, "is so new that I felt I've never seen or heard the play performed." Gray contrasts it with *The Homecoming*, a play that resembles "a lying-in-state, a ceremonial unfolding of the doomed creature, a 'classic'—you see, you have to stick around, to do your own productions from time to time."[87] When he learned of Gray's death on August 7, 2008, Pinter put his head in his hands and wept, feeling bereft at the death of his favorite playwright and friend. For Antonia Fraser, Gray's death made Pinter contemplate his own mortality in a way he had not done previously. (*Must*: 322, 273, 322–23).

Other Reactions to Pinter's Directing

Pinter's actors, critics, and other dramatists with whom he worked also praised his directing ability. For instance, Donald Pleasence proclaimed Pinter as "the most truly honest and indeed best director" he ever worked with in the theatre (*Sharp Cut*: 379). Pinter directed Ronald Harwood's *Taking Sides* from April 1995 until August 1995 (*Chronology*: 219–21). For Jeremy Kingston, "Pinter's direction helps to create the sense of danger and the importance of asking what people can best do in such predicaments" (*Times*, May 24, 1995). For a doyen of the London theatrical scene, the critic John Peter, "Pinter's direction has the tidal power of clarity and restraint. He and his actors have set their faces against rhetoric and the temptations of emotional overcharge. Pinter understands and respects Harwood's decision to let the characters make their own case without the luxury of seeing themselves as tragic figures on a world stage. The tragedy is for us to sense" (*Sunday Times*, May 28, 1995). In a public interview on June 17, 2000, Harwood said that Pinter is "a wonderful director . . . because he lets nothing go by. Also, he's a minimalist as a director. When actors get up and start to move, Harold says, 'Why are you moving there?' And they say, 'Well, I just thought . . . I've been sitting here for so long.' 'No. There's no need to move.' And the actors go back and sit. And, what you get from the Pinter production is such a concentration on the text" (Gale: *Sharp Cut*, 379).

Michael Pennington on Pinter as Director

Distinguished actor Michael Pennington played the role of Major Arnold, the American interrogating officer, in Harwood's *Taking Sides*. In his "Harold Pinter as Director," Pennington gives a vivid detailed account of working with Pinter in Harwood's play. At the start of rehearsals, Pinter explained his practical approach: "We would read, stage, practice, find out as we went. The play was sufficient to itself, accurate enough to its period; he trusted his designer, and we were not to be distracted by any minutiae of history that obscured its strong impulse." The company worked continuously over a four- or five-hour period "in the middle of the day," although rehearsals were shortened if the goals for the day were achieved, allowing actors to learn their lines during the evening. Pinter was mutually respectful toward the dramatist and the actors; he was only "sharp to an actor" if an actor were lazy. "Pinter's gentle authority possessed everybody concerned." Furthermore, "there was no theorising, and rehearsals were conducted with an unoppressive punctuality, an uninhibiting sense of discipline."

In his "Harold Pinter as Director," Pennington observes that Pinter disliked "intrusive noise." He objected even "to a fly buzzing in a rehearsal room" and attempted to get noisy traffic stopped. When directing Gray's *Rear Column*, he took a great deal of time when the play started "in establishing the precise dimensions of the fully grown male turtle in order to deduce the necessary size of the crate in which two of them were to arrive." In the case of the production of *Taking Sides*, the sound upsetting Pinter "was that of a great crash which turned out to be his own parked car being reversed into outside the building." An assistant stage manager was told to shut the conversation up in the yard outside where they rehearse. Only small changes in Harwood's script were made during rehearsal, and as the opening approached, Pinter "became highly selective—less of a pause there, more of an emphasis there, a warmer tone perhaps, even a counterpoint between the lines said in the manner of its saying." Even "the pouring of water, the giving of a cup of coffee— should never be rushed, but take the time it takes." Prior to *Taking Sides* opening at the Minerva Theatre, Chichester, on May 18, 1995, Pinter "fought and won an exceptional victory in having the sale of Smarties banned from the theatre confectionery, since the rattling of their tubes during the action was seriously distracting."

Pinter was selective in what he directed. With the exception of Giraudoux's *The Trojan War Will Not Take Place*, he had not "directed a classic"—for instance, John Webster or even Shakespeare. Pennington speculates that "perhaps he distrusts the inevitable flamboyance and expressionism involved in the putting on of," for instance, *The Duchess of Malfi* or *The White Devil*. Essentially, Pennington believes that "there is no special flourish to Pinter the director, no particular methodology, no exotic rehearsal practices. . . . His obligation to nothing but the work in hand can make him seem almost invisible: instead of tiresome panache, there is only a healthy practicality and a hatred of sentimentality."[88]

Pinter's Other Directing Activities

Pinter's directing extended into other areas, too. For instance, on Friday April 10, 1981, he directed excerpts from *The Jail Diary of Albie Sachs* (1966) at the Duke of York's Theatre. Extracts from the diary of the South African antiapartheid activist were read by two eminent actors, Anthony Sher and Donald Pleasence. At the same venue, Pinter also directed and participated with many other luminaries of the London stage including Daniel Massey, Alan Bates, Edward Fox, Eileen Atkins, Judi Dench, Penelope Wilton, Joanna Lumley, and Anna Massey. Held on Sunday October 4, 1981, the production was on behalf of imprisoned writers and included extracts from Fugard, Dostoevsky, Celan, Camus, Anna Akhmatova's *Requiem* (1935–1940), and others (*Chronology*: 110).

To sum up, Pinter's perception of his role as a director is found in an observation Pinter made to Trevor Nunn when Nunn asked him if he'd be interested in directing a Shakespeare play at the Royal Shakespeare Company. Pinter replied: *Othello*. Nunn then asked about Pinter's perception of the tragedy. Pinter replied that he had no perception; he just wanted to realize the text (Billington: 239).

PINTER AS ACTOR

During the Pinter festival at the Gate Theatre Dublin from April 7 to 27, 1997, Pinter performed the role of Harry in *The Collection*. On June 29, 1998, Pinter told Mick Goldstein that he had just concluded playing Harry in the play at the Donmar Warehouse. With eight performances for eight weeks, Pinter found the experience stimulating but exhausting. *The Collection* was an early short play, initially presented by Associated Rediffusion Television on May 11, 1961; Pinter subsequently transformed it into a theatrical one. It opened in the West End at the Aldwych Theatre. Pinter directed it for the Royal Shakespeare Company in one of his earliest collaborations with Peter Hall on June 18, 1962. In it, some of Pinter's perennial concerns are present: triangular desire, sexual ambiguity, and the struggle for dominance, power, and control. Many critics jokingly observed that "Pinter's gesture of stroking the cat, while indulgently sensuous, simultaneously suggested that Harry might just as easily be capable of strangling it, recognizing the aforementioned antinomy of stasis and violence through which the suspense of Pinter's drama is constituted."[89] Alastair Macaulay, reviewing the revival of *The Collection* in *The Financial Times* on May 15, 1998, observes that Pinter in the role of Harry "is full of elegance, danger, aplomb. He takes charge of loaded situations with a partly absurd display of urbanity, he tries to reinforce his authority with petty assertions of power, and often you sense in him the cowardly control-freak secreted behind the polished snarl."

In a September 13, 1998 letter, Pinter tells Henry Woolf that he is acting in Jane Austen's *Mansfield Park*, a 1998 film adaptation by Miramax. Shooting is in Northamptonshire, a beautiful part of England where Pinter has not been before.[90] Pinter has the role of Sir Thomas Bertram in the film, directed by Patricia Rozema. The character, Pinter observes, is civilized and sensible but, in fact, upholding a brutal system from which he derives his money.[91] Reviewing the film in *The Guardian*, November 16, 1999, Peter Bradshaw writes that the film "boasts excellent performances from Frances O'Conner as Fanny Price and especially Harold Pinter as Sir Thomas Bertram, the glowering master of Mansfield Park. Pinter's compelling physical presence and the timbre and control of his voice show him to be a remarkable classical actor."[92]

Other roles include that of John Smith in the TV movie adaptation of Hugh Whitemore's *Breaking the Code*, with Derek Jacobi as a conflicted Alan Turing. Pinter filmed this in November-December 1995. He also played small roles not requiring speech. For instance, in 1960, he makes a non-speaking cameo appearance in his cinematic adaptation of *The Caretaker*. He walks away from a car and then back to it and is accosted in a brief street scene by the tramp Davies. In Joseph Losey's 1964 film of *The Servant*, Pinter has the non-speaking role of a man of society in a very short scene. In *The Accident* (1967), he has a similar role, this time as Mr. Bill, a TV producer. In short, Pinter, over more than forty years, is regarded as a good enough actor to regularly receive acting roles in a highly competitive acting field.

PETER HALL

This chapter concludes by examining the relationship between Pinter and a preeminent figure in the English theatre of the second half of the twentieth century with whom Pinter worked for many years: Peter Hall. Born the same year as Pinter, Hall, the dedicatee of Pinter's *Old Times*, was born in Bury St. Edmunds, Suffolk. After National Service in the RAF, he read English at St. Catherine's College, Cambridge, where he came under the influence of the eminent critic and exponent of close critical reading, F. R. Leavis. On August 3, 1955, Hall directed the English premier of Beckett's *Waiting for Godot* at the Arts Theatre, London. In 1960 he founded the Royal Shakespeare Company (RSC), which he directed for eight years before running the National Theatre from 1973 to 1988. Hall's account of his period at the National is to be found in his *Diaries*, edited by John Goodwin (1983). This provides the source for Hall's version of his often tempestuous creative relationship with Pinter and others.

The first reference to Hall in Pinter's "Appointment Diaries" occurs when, as has been noted, he and Hall co-directed for the RSC *The Collection* at the Aldwych on June 18, 1962. Hall and Pinter met during the intervening years, often on a daily basis, until finally going their separate ways in 1985 and then in 1990 partly reconciling. It was Hall who invited Pinter to join the National Theatre as an associate director, an invitation that Pinter accepted on February 14, 1973. Hall noted that he "never doubted that [Pinter] would direct the odd play, and that he would give me his new plays to direct, as he did at the RSC. But to my pleasure, he is in, heart and soul, though pointing out that he can only do what he can do" (*Diaries*: 33–34).

Hall directed *Old Times* at the RSC, opening at the Aldwych on June 1, 1971. Hall understood the Pinter code, as Ronald Bryden indicates in a revealing review in *The Observer* published June 6, 1971. The review discusses Hall as a Pinter director, Pinter's plays, and the actors' performances, especially, for instance, Vivien Merchant's performance as Anna. Bryden writes that "Peter Hall directs the comedy with a musician's ear for the value of each word and silence which exposes every layer of the text like the perspex levels of a three-dimensional chess board." As an illustration, Bryden cites the line "'Do you drink brandy?'" The question comes from Deeley, the sole male character in the play, who is caught between his wife, Kate, and her friend from the past, Anna. "Vivien Merchant's pause before replying that she would love some is just sufficient to remind you that, on Pinter territory, every question is an attempt to control and every answer a swift evasion."

Hall was also largely responsible for Pinter's emerging reputation as an important dramatist on the European mainland. On Sunday April 16, 1972, he went "to the Vienna to begin directing [*Old Times*] for Vienna's Burgtheater, [his] first play in German." The opening night, June 20, "appeared to be a triumph" (*Diaries*: 7, 11). Relations were so good between Hall and Pinter at this period that Hall stayed up all night on December 17, 1972 reading the film script of *À la recherché du temps perdu*. Hall calls it an "extraordinary achievement," with Pinter managing to condense complex volumes into 221 pages of precise images and dialogue with nothing lost and no simplification.

An interesting diary entry by Hall for Tuesday March 5, 1974 reveals the cordial relations between the two at this time. It is the opening night of *The Tempest*, with John Gielgud as Prospero. Pinter called Hall at 1:15 a.m. on the phone, saying that Pinter and his friend Peggy Ashcroft loved the production. Pinter said that John Bury, the designer, and Hall, the director, should feel proud. Hall thinks that he heard Pinter say that "we should 'dance down Piccadilly with a lily in one hand and a rose in the other'" (*Diaries*: 66, 84).

Hall's *Diaries* well document *No Man's Land* from its gestation to production. On Saturday July 27, 1974, Pinter calls him to report that he is working on a play (*Diaries*: 113). In fact, Pinter started *No Man's Land* slightly earlier—around July 16 (*Chronology*: 55). Hall and Pinter lunch on Wednesday August 7. Pinter is "very excited about his new play," Hall recalls; "for the first time for years he was overwriting, letting it all come out and being less critical of his writing as he worked. He felt freer." On September 11, Pinter telephones Hall to say he has finished *No Man's Land*. Two days later, Hall reads it and is "amazed by it" as the play was "not at all what" he expected. "There is an icy preoccupation with time; and the long sustained speeches have a poetic validity which would have seemed incredible in the days of the brisk, hostile repartee of [*The Birthday Party*]." Hall adds that *No Man's Land* is "extremely funny and also extremely bleak. A play about the nature of the artist: the real artist harassed by the phony artist." Pinter wants *No Man's Land* to be produced immediately and Gielgud in the lead role (*Diaries*: 115, 119–20). Gielgud received a copy of the play from Pinter and told him that it is a "brilliant play"; he would be "really delighted" to play the part of Spooner (*Chronology*: 56).

On November 7 at the Barbican, Hall arranged a dinner party for Pinter and Gielgud to get to know each other. "Harold charmed him and was very specific about [*No Man's Land*]: who was who and what was what. We discussed at length the casting of Hirst. We all want Ralph [Richardson] if we can get him." Hall records that he then had to get a drunk Pinter home in a taxi. Hall spoke to Richardson on November 15 after sending him a copy of the script; he responded enthusiastically (*Diaries*: 129–30). On January 28, at a dinner party in Hall's London apartment, Pinter and Richardson met for the first time: "'I am holding a poet in my hand,' said Ralph as he took Harold's proffered greeting. 'I am holding a great actor in mine,' replied Pinter." On February 9, 1975, Hall records that "the Pinter play all clicked today." He has "a feeling that I really know what it is about—opposites." *No Man's Land* concerns "genius against lack of talent, success against failure, drink against sobriety, elegance against uncouthness, smoothness against roughness, politeness against violence. Now it is inside me I find it a wonderful play." The initial rehearsal, "just a reading," occurred on Monday February 10. The following day, Hall notes that *No Man's Land* "is hard, complex chamber music" (*Diaries*: 141, 145, 147–48).

On Friday March 14, 1975, Hall and Pinter chatted briefly about *No Man's Land*, not then uppermost in Pinter's mind. "He was wildly and happily in love [with Antonia Fraser] . . . he certainly was jubilantly happy, and not terribly interested in his play, which [Hall] found endearing." In early April they deliberated over the use of the word "unscrupulous" in a speech by Spooner. Pinter chose the word "because it shows the ruthlessness of the present, and its ability to lead as it were a life of its own." On Tuesday April 8, Hall and Pinter discussed *No Man's Land* at breakfast. Following "interminable conversation we came up with the line 'the present will not be distorted' instead of 'the present is truly unscrupulous'" (157). A day earlier, Hall rehearsed *No Man's Land* "on the set for the first time, using the stage of the Royalty Theatre. The heating is off. The auditorium is freezing." However, Richardson "was wonderful: absolutely creative and making Hirst (one of the most difficult parts Pinter has ever written) crystal clear." During the afternoon of the same day, there was a costume run-through. Afterwards, Hall and Pinter discussed pauses that Hall found "less potent" than in other Pinter plays. According to Hall, for Pinter *The Homecoming* and *Old Times* "were primarily about sex and the pauses therefore reverberated with half-meanings and suggested meanings. The pauses in [*No Man's Land*] are much more clearly a matter of threat and of tension, as in [*The Caretaker*]." At an afternoon rehearsal on Thursday April 17, Gielgud "asked Harold what the Briggs/Spooner scene was for at the beginning of" the second act. "What did it give the audience? What did it convey? Harold paused, 'I'm afraid I cannot answer questions like that, John. My work is just what it is. I am sorry."

No Man's Land opened on Wednesday April 23 with rumors circulating of a union confrontation with the National Theatre. Pinter asked Hall on the opening night to stay close to him as other rumors were swelling about his relationship with Antonia Fraser. Pinter was afraid that he would lose his temper and hit any reporter who confronted him about the relationship. At the opening night party following the performance, Pinter was the last to leave: "The only thing he was certain of was his relationship with Antonia." Reviews of the play were cautious, and none of the reviewers "actually get to grips with what the play means." Gielgud and Richardson were very pleased, and Hall did "not think any other actor could fill Hirst with such a sense of loneliness and creativity as [Richardson] does" (*Diaries*: 152, 156–60).

On Monday April 28, 1975, Hall spoke with Pinter, who "was at that very moment packed and about to leave home: 'the point is, I am at this moment leaving my home. I'm leaving my house.'" Hall observed that "it is a tough business for him. He told me that whatever happened he thought that he and Vivien were now through."

No Man's Land moved from the Old Vic for a West End run at Wyndham's Theatre in mid-July 1975. On Wednesday October 15, Pinter participated in a fractious National Theatre Associates' meeting at which there was an accusation that many of the associates did not see all of the plays performed. On Thursday January 22, 1976, Gielgud and Richardson threw a dinner at Rules attended by Pinter, Antonia, and Hall and his second wife, Jacky, to celebrate the end of the run of *No Man's Land*.[93] Just over a year later, on February 24, 1977, Hall records in his *Diaries* that *No Man's Land* "back in the Lyttelton repertoire since January, finished tonight after a grand total of 378 performances. Harold benign. The cast presented him with a tiny cricket bat marked 378 not out—for no one believed this was the end of it."

With the backdrop of potential internal unrest at the National, the initial cast reading for Pinter's National Theatre direction of Noël Coward's *Blithe Spirit* took place on Monday May 10, 1976. The cast looked "very good in a biscuit-coloured nineteen-thirties set. How wonderful to have the set there on the first day of reversal. Harold addressed them, saying that the dramatist "calls this play an improbable farce. Well, I just wish to make one thing clear—I do not regard it as improbable and I do not regard it as a farce" (*Diaries*: 161, 190, 207, 284–85, 232). Mel Gussow asked Pinter, "Do you particularly like Noel Coward?" Pinter responded that, while he hadn't read much Coward, he was asked by Hall to do the play. He read it and thought it would be fun—in fact, it was quite difficult. When asked if he has an affinity with Coward, Pinter replied that he admired a great deal about Coward, whom he described as a dramatist of range. Pinter loved the fun and games of *Blithe Spirit*. Still, he could find the exposition somewhat labored. Nothing could be done about it; that was the play.[94]

Hall's final direction of a Pinter play was *Betrayal* at the National and subsequently in New York. Its opening night was on November 15, 1978 at the Lyttelton, National Theatre. Hall's *Diaries* record the early stages of preparing the play for production. On Thursday August 25, 1977, Hall and Pinter spend most of the afternoon together. Pinter alludes to working on another play. Hall observes that Pinter is "writing again: being in no man's land is over. He's moved into Antonia's house" at 52 Campden Hill Square, W8. Pinter did so on Friday August 12 (*Must*: 83) "and he has a little study there where he feels at peace. His books are up, and he can work. Hard graft is required he says, but I [Hall] can expect a play." Hall adds that Pinter "has been obsessed with time ever since he wrote [*Landscape*] and working on Proust confirmed that in him. [*Betrayal*] begins at the end, with a crisis-written heartbreaking scene, and ends seven years earlier, at the beginning of the affair. It weaves a very cunning web, and the metaphorical structure is extraordinary." Hall makes astute observations concerning *Betrayal*, writing that "it is an advance for Harold, this play. The tension builds up at an enormous rate. It's not fanciful to think of Mozart. From my point of view there's the same precision of means, the same beauty, the same lyricism, and the same sudden descents into pain which are quickly over because of a healthy sense of the ridiculous" (*Diaries*: 382).

During the run of *Betrayal*, the National Theatre was beset by industrial action in the form of strikes. On the evening of November 3, 1978, a "very depressed, tense and moody" Pinter tells Hall that he is worried that *Betrayal*—the best work they'd done together—might be ruined if there were sporadic strikes and they couldn't have previews; without previews, the play might not come together and all would be lost. Hall tells Pinter "not to be silly . . . I don't believe we shall open on time, but we shall open, and it will be good." The preview did take place on Tuesday November 14; still, "Harold is walking about like a sad zombie, wondering whether [*Betrayal*] is to open or not." The play had its first night on Wednesday; it "had been born, not at all under the happiest circumstances."

To use Hall's words, "the critics range from the patronising to the bad, and are now taking him [Pinter] to task for being *un*-enigmatic. They find the play small, inconsequential, and about a segment of society, upper middle-class intellectuals . . . who are not worth writing or thinking about." Pinter, however, remained cheerful even though the actors were angry at the reviews. He was proud of their work. On Monday January 8, 1979, Hall notes that *Betrayal* "seems to found its audience and is successful." He tells this to Pinter who, Hall observes, is "hiding in the Grand Hotel, Eastbourne, writing the film script of [*The French Lieutenant's Woman*]." (*Diaries*: 388–91, 406).

Betrayal gained the Society of West End Theatre Managers' best play award. Pinter was surprised at the accolade, given the hostility of the critics and especially of Michael Billington, who wrote "that he wasn't interested in the sex lives of Hampstead intellectuals. He wanted social issues." (Pinter's subsequent reaction to Billington changed and, in the last decade of the twentieth century, Billington became his trusted official biographer and close friend.) *Betrayal* opened in New York on Saturday January 5, 1980. The final reference to Pinter in Hall's *Diaries* occurs on Sunday January 20, 1980: "Harold rang me tonight to tell me *Betrayal* is now a hit, and is expected to do even better" (*Diaries*: 423, 477, 482).

Inevitably, the relationship between the two suffered from a bitter breach. Both were charismatic, vocal, creative characters. Mutually, they benefited from a fruitful artistic partnership. For Pinter, his plays were produced by the most influential theatrical company in the United Kingdom with the best actors, directors, and so on to draw upon. He had the opportunity to direct and work with such a company and its personnel and to witness almost on a daily basis its changing fortunes and difficulties at a microscopic level. Increasingly, the relationship turned sour, especially concerning the National Theatre's production of Giraudoux's *The Trojan War Will Not Take Place*, which Pinter directed in May 1983. The play's subject was Hector and his attempt to prevent war. It proved topical: Britain was recovering from the impact of the Falklands War, attempting to find its place in a fractious world, and there was industrial unrest at the National. The play was difficult to direct, and Hall, who asked Pinter to direct it, went during the production to Bayreuth to direct Wagner's "Ring Cycle."

According to Billington, Pinter told the journalist Stephen Fay that they had both at some point become selfish. Unlike Hall, Pinter wasn't just thinking of himself but of a production at the National Theatre—*The Trojan War Will Not Take Place*—for which he was, finally, responsible. Pinter promptly resigned as a National Theatre associate director. The final straw for Pinter concerned the 1983 publication of Hall's *Diaries*, edited by John Goodwin and published by Hamish Hamilton. Pinter felt that revelations concerning his private life breached his strong code of friendship. For Hall: "What I wrote in the *Diaries* was written out of love and compassion. Certainly nothing I said about him and Antonia had not been said—and much worse—in . . . public." Indeed, Billington's own biography of Pinter that first appeared in 1996, and in a subsequent edition eleven years later, contains far more revelations of a personal nature.

A reconciliation of sorts took place in 1990, with Hall's production at the Comedy Theatre of a revival of *The Homecoming*. In the meantime, after a six-year breach, Pinter wrote to Hall to compliment him upon a production. Subsequently, they met at a dinner party arranged by Edna O'Brien,[95] and, according to Billington, Pinter wrote to Hall asking to make up because life is too short. Billington observes that "though sudden and quick in quarrel, Pinter is also a great believer in reconciliation" (*Diaries*: 290–91, 324).

SUMMARY

In this chapter, we have seen Pinter's trajectory from a repertory theatre actor in small roles to his rise as an acclaimed actor, playwright, and screenwriter. Ambitious, creative, sometimes prickly in his relationships—see the frayed but ultimately almost repaired relationship with Peter Hall—Pinter was constantly working. His formative alliances with Joe Brearley, Hall, Simon Gray, and others formed the foundation for his career. Pinter's loyalty to his friends from his school days is reflected in their correspondence for over fifty years; they shed light upon Pinter's career and obsessions. These correspondences and the reminiscences of others show that Pinter always gave credit to those who helped and influenced him along the way.

NOTES

1. *"Fortune's Fool": The Man Who Taught Harold Pinter: A Life of Joe Brearley*, ed. G. L. Watkins. Aylesbury: Twig Books, 2008: 7–9.

2. BLADDMSS 88880/7/2.

3. http://www.independent.co.uk/arts-entertainment/theatre-dance/features/when-harold-met-ronald-118150.html, accessed October 24, 2016.

4. BLADDMSS: 889208/5/2.

5. BLADDMSS: 88880/7/2.

6. For Pinter and Miller, see *Chronology* 315. Michael Billington: https://www.theguardian.com/stage/2012/feb/26/hay-fever-review, accessed April 10, 2017; http://www.telegraph.co.uk/culture/theatre/theatre-reviews/9108057/Hay-Fever-Noel-

Coward-Theatre-review.html, accessed April 10, 2017. See also Billington, "Familiar Spirits," *Guardian* 7 (July 1976): 8.

7. See chapter 6.

8. BLADDMSS: 88880/7/2.

9. BLADDMSS: 88880/7/2.

10. Cited http://www.haroldpinter.org/directing/directing_bday.shtml: accessed October 9, 2016.

11. Letter to Joe Brearley dated March 20, 1964, responding to Brearley's letter dated five days earlier: BLADDMSS: 88880/7/2.

12. See chapter 6.

13. BLADDMSS: 88880/7/2.

14. https://en.wikipedia.org/wiki/Pasolini_(film): accessed August 22, 2016.

15. For Brearley's love of Wagner and flirtation with German Nationalism, see *"Fortunes Fool"* (cf. n 1 above).

16. See chapter 4.

17. BLADDMSS: 88880/7/2.

18. For Patrick Magee (1922–1973), see *The Letters of Samuel Beckett 1957–1965*: 700.

19. BLADDMSS: 89094/2.

20. BLADDMSS: 89094/2.

21. See chapter 3.

22. *Sir Donald Wolfit: His Life and Work in the Unfashionable Theatre*. London: Amber Lane, 1983: 225.

23. *The Listener* 79 (April 1968): 501. BR: E13.

24. BLADDMSS: 89094/2.

25. See chapter 4.

26. See chapter 4.

27. BLADDMSS: 89094/3.

28. October 17, 2011: www.the guardian.com: accessed August 25, 2016.

29. November 2, 2011: www.telegraph.co.uk : accessed August 25, 2016.

30. See http://www.dig.planet.com: accessed August 25, 2016.

31. David T. Thompson, *Pinter The Player's Playwright*. Houndmills, Basingstoke, 1985: 45–46.

32. BLADDMSS: 88920/5/2; see BR: W4; prose text of *The Examination* in *VV*: 88–93.

33. BLADDMSS: 890941/2.

34. BLADDMSS: 88920/5/2. "The Error of Alarm" was published in Kathleen Nott, C. Day Lewis, and Thomas Blackburn's *New Poems 1957*. London: Michael Joseph, 1957. See BR: C10.

35. Cited Thompson: 33.

36. For Ada Thomson (1929–1982), Vivien Merchant: see chapter 4.

37. BLADDMSS: 88920/5/2.

38. BLADDMSS: 88920/5/2.

39. Cited Thompson: 33–34.

40. BLADDMSS: 88920/5/2.

41. BLADDMSS: 88920/5/2.

42. BLADDMSS: 89094/5.

43. BLADDMSS: 89094/4.

44. BLADDMSS: 88920/5/2.

45. September 6, 1957: 6; cited Thompson: 34.

46. *Enfield Gazette and Observer*, January 3, 1958: 14; ibid., 34.

47. *Enfield Gazette and Observer*, March 26, 1958: 11; cited Thompson: 35.

48. BLADDMSS: 89094/4.

49. Cited Thompson: 30.

50. BLADDMSS 88920/5/2.

51. See *The Letters of Samuel Beckett 1957–1965*: 745.

52. BLADDMSS: 88920/5/2.

53. BLADDMSS: 88920/5/2.

54. BLADDMSS: 89094/5.

55. See chapter 4.

56. BLADDMSS: 88920/5/2.

57. See chapter 3.

58. BLADDMSS: 88880/7/6 f4.

59. BLADDMSS: 88920/5/2.

60. BLADDMSS: 89094/5.

61. "Orange Screen Writers Season at the British Library," Harold Pinter interviewed by Peter Florence at the British Library (February 9, 2004), British Library Sound Archives: cf. Baker 2008: 21.

62. http://www.haroldpinter.org/films/films_accident.shtml%20%20accessed%2011%20June%202016.

63. Cited Mosley, autobiography *Efforts at Truth*: 164–65; see also BLADDMSS: 88880/2/1-2.

64. Cited http://www.haroldpinter.org/films/films_gobetween.shtml, accessed June 10, 2016.

65. BLADDMSS: 88880/2.

66. The word *pacifism* was coined by the French peace campaigner Émile Arnaud (1864–1921) and adopted by other peace activists at the tenth Universal Peace Congress in Glasgow in 1901." https://en.wikipedia.org/wiki/Pacifism, accessed June 11, 2016.

67. BLADDMSS: 88880/2.

68. BLAddMSS: 88880/7/6 f.11–12.

69. See chapter 2 and *Chronology*: 357.

70. Nick Hern Books, 2005.

71. *Pinter in the Theatre*. London: Nick Hern Books, 2005: 7.

72. See *The Letters of Samuel Beckett Volume III: 1957–1965* ed. G. Craig et al. CUP 2014: 763–64.

73. BLADDMSS: 88880/7/0.

74. http://www.haroldpinter.org/directing/index.shtml, accessed November 21, 2016.

75. Bamber Gascoigne, *The Spectator* (June 29, 1962); Martin Shuttleworth, *The Listener* (June 21, 1962); Peter Hall, "Directing Pinter; cited M. Page, *File on Pinter*, 70–71.

76. Cited: http://www.haroldpinter.org/directing/directing_lover.shtml%20accessed%2014%20September%202016.

77. See chapter 6.

78. All the reviews are cited http://www.haroldpinter.org/directing/directing_bday.shtml, accessed November 22, 2016. Mention should be made, too, of the interview with Pinter and Alan Haydock within the "Options" program on BBC Radio 4, broadcast November15, 1970. This was recorded at the Mermaid Theatre and relates to the production of Joyce's *Exiles* (BR: J33).

79. See chapter 3.

80. See for instance Gray's *Enter a Fox: Further Adventures of a Paranoid*, London: Faber, 2001; *The Smoking Diaries*, London: Granta Books, 2004; *The Year of the Jouncer*, London: Granta Books, 2006; *The Last Cigarette: Smoking Diaries Volume 3*. London: Granta Books, 2008.

81. See chapter 4.

82. Robert Gordon in "Experimental Drama and the Well-Made Play" in Katherine Burkman (ed.), *Simon Gray: A Casebook*, London: Garland, 1992: 7–8.

83. May 25, 1979: cited http://www.haroldpinter.org/directing/directing_bday.shtml, accessed September 16, 2016.

84. March 27, 1999: cited http://www.haroldpinter.org/directing/directing_bday.shtml, accessed September 19, 2016.

85. Cited http://www.simongray.org.uk, accessed September 19, 2016.

86. BLADDMSS:88880/7/6: ff.33, 55.

87. BLADDMSS:88880/7/6: ff.22, 33, 50, 55–56.

88. "Harold Pinter as Director," *The Cambridge Companion to Harold Pinter*, second edition: 150, 153, 156–158.

89. "3 by Harold Pinter," *The Pinter Review*, 1997 and 1998: 146–50.

90. http://www.haroldpinter.org/acting/acting_forstage2.shtml; BLADDMSS:8909 4/5.

91. Publicity for *Mansfield Park*, 1998.

92. Cited www.haroldpinter.org/films: accessed September 28, 2016.

93. Pinter ate on at least four occasions at Rules, a restaurant in Covent Garden founded in 1798 (cf. chapter 3 and see *Chronology*: 372).

94. *Conversations with Harold Pinter*. London: Nick Hern, 1994: 61.

95. See chapter 4.

TWO

Passions

*Cricket and Other Activities Including
Bridge, Tennis, Squash, and Music*

Any consideration of Pinter's life, his personality, and his activities must examine his great obsessions: cricket, bridge, tennis, squash, and music. Each represents different facets of his personality: from the physically competitive to the nostalgic, love for England, and need for verification to the cerebral. Cricket was a lifelong love with Pinter; in perhaps his final interview, he took great pains to differentiate cricket from what he referred to as "this obsession with bloody football."[1] For Pinter, cricket represented an ideal world. At a key moment in his life, when he decided to become a conscientious objector in the autumn of 1948, Pinter wrote to his close friend Henry Woolf that he wanted a quiet game of cricket to forget for a while and rest.[2] This attitude never changed. The game frequently appears in one form or another in his work, in his letters, and in his film adaptations.

Pinter's team was the Gaieties Cricket Club. One of many incidents shows his dedication to the team and the sport. In late 1987 the Gaieties' fast bowler, Ossie Gooding, was transferred from the Home Office for which he worked in London to Newcastle. His departure left the team looking for a young, fit, fast bowler who would maintain a good bowling length on a regular basis. At the time, Gaieties was half a century old. In late December 1987, Pinter made a payment to the magazine the *Cricket World* to print the announcement that his team had lost its bowler. Pinter added that the team would welcome refugees from league cricket.[3] According to the Gaieties website, Gooding was a "once-terrifying Caribbean fast-bowling sensation, still favours three gullies." Inigo Thomas, who played for the Gaieties in the 1980s and early 1990s, notes that Good-ing "played into his sixties and was a legend on the club circuit in and around London."[4] His "finest hour: 25 years fast bowling of the highest class" and "not likely to say: 'Come on you slips, you're way too deep.'"

The Gaieties website describes its history: "Gaieties Cricket Club is a wandering side which plays cricket in the Home Counties. It was founded in 1937 by the Hackney-born music hall artist Lupino Lane [1892–1959], whose company was at that time based at the Gaiety Thea-tre, in London. After the death of Lupino Lane, the club was captained by his son Lauri Lupino Lane, who was succeeded in 1972 by Harold Pinter as Chairman. . . . The Gaiety Theatre has now been demolished, but a plaque marks its site in the Strand and the cricket club continues to thrive."[5]

In the autumn of 1973, Pinter sent a series of letters to one of the team's players, Winston Stafford; the letters illustrate Pinter's perspective on the team and the sport. Pinter congratulates Stafford for scoring in a match at Teddington. Apparently, Stafford had felt let down by the rest of his team's fielding and its general standard of play. Pinter acknowl-edges that Stafford's cricket is of a professional standard but adds that it is unrealistic to expect other members of the Gaieties team to be as good as Stafford in all departments. After all, the Gaieties are amateurs and, consequently, must field teams of various strengths on a weekly basis. It is a wandering club that, of course, plays to win and plays with enthu-siasm; however, its performances must inevitably vary a great deal, and Stafford can't expect fielding on a consistently professional level. Pinter believes that Stafford expects far too much and that, on the field, he expresses too much anger and disgust at fielding errors. Stafford's atti-tudes have their origin in his total involvement in the game and are understandable, Pinter writes, but such attitudes are not just and create team tension that does not make the Gaieties improve their perfor-mances. Pinter is not suggesting that it's humanly possible to shrug off an important dropped catch.[6]

In the letter to Stafford, Pinter uses cricket as a metaphor for life. As in life, cricket is full of mishaps, mistakes, dropped catches, missed oppor-tunities, and misjudgments of all kinds. Indeed, Pinter cannot envisage or remember a game when such occurrences didn't take place, and even Stafford himself is not immune from them. Stafford is a gifted player, and this means that he should be more reasonable about the frailties of his fellow players. In a reply dated September 28, 1973, Stafford comments on many of Pinter's observations, which he regards as "harsh" and bor-dering on the "unfair." He also asserts that he has never attacked a player "who has made an effort"—his "anger and disgust" is reserved for what he describes as the team's "prima donnas . . . who never make the effort to improve their game."[7] This must have struck a chord in Pinter. His "Appointment Diaries" reveal that, during the winters over many years,

Pinter regularly participated in indoor nets at Lords to improve his batting—another testament to the fact that he took his cricket very seriously.

Indeed, dropped catches and ones taken became something of an obsession with Pinter and form the foundation for the privately printed
illustrated prose work *The Catch: A Correspondence* with Alan Wilkinson
published in 2003 (BR: H69). The text is concerned with a fine catch that
Pinter took while playing for the Gaieties. It celebrates Pinter's love of
cricket and memorializes a great "catch off Ossie [Gooding] at Stokesley"
many years previously. A fellow member of the club recalled that he had
"never seen a better catch at any level of cricket" ([7]). The text reveals
Pinter's encyclopedic knowledge and memory of cricket and its language, rituals, and customs. Wilkinson heard about the catch over a
drink and, on January 21, 2002, wrote to Pinter asking a number of questions about it. Pinter replied on January 24 and 31, 2002. The main text
consists of Wilkinson's questions and Pinter's responses.

Pinter was not always able to play for the Gaieties during the cricket
season due to work commitments, productions, rehearsals, film shoot-
ings, holidays, and so on. There were also health issues. For instance, the
May 1981 season began with a lot of rain that month. The team won its
first match, but the next two were abandoned due to the weather. Pinter's
"Appointment Diaries" do record that he played in a match on Sunday
May 24, 1981 (*Chronology*: 107). Gaieties is a strong side, Pinter tells a
correspondent in Ontario in a letter dated May 11, 1981; however, he
didn't appear much for them as his "bones creak too much."[8]

Cricket became something of a family celebration for Pinter. For instance, at the end of July 1992, he celebrated a decisive victory for his
team, "Pinter XI," in its annual match against the staff of the *Guardian*.
Pinter's team declared at 168 runs for five wickets down, and the opposition scored 87 for the loss of nine wickets. One of Antonia's sons scored—
to use Pinter's words in a letter dated July 27, 1992—"an absolutely
splendid 50."[9] Pinter went to matches regularly, sometimes with Antonia. For instance, on Saturday June 22, 1991—the day after Pinter attended Peggy Ashcroft's funeral—they both joined Donald Trelford, editor of *The Observer* from 1975 to 1993, in his box at the Mound Stand
Lord's to see England and the West Indies (*Chronology*:189).

The Gaieties skipper (or captain) at the time was Christopher Brookes,
with whom Pinter shared a deep love of cricket. Brookes worked in a
freelance capacity for the government. Like Pinter, he was preoccupied
with other matters but managed to turn out on a regular basis for the
club. Brookes authored *English Cricket: The Game and Its Players through the
Ages* (1978), a revision of his University of Leicester doctoral thesis, and
His Own Man: The Life of Neville Cardus (1985). He initially met Pinter late
in 1972 at the Middlesex County Cricket Club indoor school in North
London. According to Brookes, it was "a wet, cold Saturday morning and
I was feeling terrible. Harold—who had just taken over the captaincy of

the Gaieties cricket club—assessed my potential for some time before concluding that I might become a member of his team." Apart from their love of cricket, they had in common "an often decidedly irreverent view of many aspects of formal conversation. In 1976, I succeeded him as captain" following a "slight disagreement during the match, an event that—despite what others might have assumed—did nothing to undermine a close friendship that lasted until his death." Brookes adds that "in addition to cricket, we also played tennis and bridge together on many, many occasions, and lunched together frequently" often at the Royal Society of Arts (RSA) club along from Waterloo station.

Other venues included Le Caprice, where they lunched on June 10, 1994 and again on June 15, 2004 (*Chronology*: 212, 286 and see also 338). Brookes writes that "through [Pinter he] came to enjoy and appreciate worlds and people that otherwise I could never have expected to experience. For that, as for his friendship, I will always be greatly in his debt."[10] Brookes has in his possession a copy of an unpublished three verses of five lines each Pinter poem titled "Old Man at a Cricket Match." In the first verse, the only recourse a team has to save its situation is for it to rain, with rain pouring down on the scorer's shed. The team is seven wickets down for 45 runs, the fielders are appealing constantly to the umpire, and "the swifts [are] squealing" overhead. The batsman, like an old man, awaits what his fate will be, in spite of the elements and the opposition: "Life and the weather mending worse| Or worsening better." Again, there is the constant theme for Pinter that cricket is a metaphor for life and the journey through life. It is noteworthy, too, that Pinter in his correspondence is fascinated with the minutiae of the game, with its details, of who scored what when, who bowled, what the weather was, and so on.

The love of cricket and the associations of the game are evident from Pinter's earliest days. Every time he was evacuated from London during the war, he "took his cricket bat with" him (*New Yorker*, February 25, 1967: 36). At Hackney Downs Grammar School, his cricket achievements were mentioned in its magazine. He was awarded his cricket colors in the summer of 1948, and the cricket notes refer to him as school vice-captain and for the best individual batting performance (27).

Pinter's memories of Lord's from the 1940s are enshrined in his "Memories of Cricket" published in the *Daily Telegraph Magazine* on May 16, 1969, subsequently reprinted under the title "Hutton and the Past" (BR: E15). Staccato sentences convey memories of the post-war era and the heroes of the past. These included two Nottinghamshire and England players, Joe Hardstaff and Reg Simpson. For the cricket correspondent Colin Bateman, "Hardstaff was one of the most artistic batsmen ever to set foot on a cricket field."[11] With distinctive curly hair, Simpson was "a fearless and effective player of fast bowling, but had a habit of getting out to spin bowlers, who he regarded with contempt."[12] In "Memories of

Cricket," Pinter's schoolboy heroes are starkly contrasted. Hardstaff is described as golden haired and Simpson as dark. Pinter conjures up images of them at Lords when Nottinghamshire played Middlesex in 1946 or 1947. Pinter notes their physical features as batsman. They both had upright stances. As the runs accumulated, they didn't need to run between the wickets, and they placed their shots precisely. They scored 70 quickly: "Hardstaff hooked, immaculate, no sound. They crossed, and back. Deep square leg in the heat after it." Middlesex then put on their leg break bowler Jim Sims at the pavilion end. Pinter's memory of such detail from his childhood yesteryear is phenomenal, and the accumulation of the detail conveys the atmosphere of the occasion from his youth.

The connection between cricket and halcyon days is recalled with memories from the winter of 1946–1947 in damp, cold, and bleak Hackney. Pinter would get up early in the morning to listen to the fight for the Ashes[13] between Australia and the MCC, as the visiting English cricket team was called, from Australia. He listened every morning of the 1946–1947 series while he was in his final year at school. This included listening to the exploits of Len Hutton, who in 1952 became the first professional cricketer of the modern era to captain England in Test Matches. In 1953, under his leadership, England defeated Australia to regain the Ashes.

Pinter greatly admired Hutton and frequently mentioned him in his correspondence to his closest friends. Pinter lunched with his childhood hero—by then Sir Leonard Hutton (Hutton was knighted in 1956)—during the opening day of the England versus New Zealand, Lord's Test Match on July 24, 1969 (*Chronology*: 32). Also at the lunch was the poet Alan Ross, literary editor of the *London Magazine* and cricket correspondent for *The Observer* from 1953 onwards.[14] Pinter remembered that at the Sydney Test Match during the MCC 1946–1947 tour of Australia, he heard on the radio early in the morning in Hackney that Hutton had hit "37 in 24 minutes and was out last ball before lunch when his bat slipped in hitting a further four, when England had nothing to play for but a hopeless draw." Pinter adds in his "Memories of Cricket" that Hutton never explained why he did that. Pinter's desire for verification shows when he notes that he wasn't there to see and regret it, but he wasn't surprised to hear about it because every stroke Hutton made surprised him. The commentator he heard on the radio was Alan McGilvray, a legendary radio commentator and voice of Australian cricket in the post–World War II years.

Hutton was forever associated in Pinter's mind with England's regaining of the Ashes against Australia at the Oval in 1953. Immediately after recall of Hutton in 1946–1947 from Sydney, Pinter writes that he heard Edrich and Compton in 1953 clinch the Ashes for England (*Daily Telegraph Magazine*, May 16, 1969: 25, 26). "Edrich" is a reference to Bill Edrich, who played for Middlesex alongside his more well-known batting partner, Dennis Compton. Compton has named after him a stand at Lord's and a cricket ground called the "Dennis Compton Oval" at Shenley Cricket Center in Hertfordshire, where the Gaieties regularly played.

It was seeing Compton at the Oval in 1948 when he was thirteen that transformed Pinter's close friend Simon Gray into a lifetime love for cricket (see *Jouncer*: 206). In June 1991, Antonia's father, Lord Longford, arranged a lunch at the House of Lords for Pinter and Compton (*Chronology*: 181). Pinter writes that he knew Hutton and Compton to be the two greatest English batsmen.[15] Yet it is not Compton but Hutton whom Pinter memorializes in one of his shortest pieces of verse entitled "Poem" (1986), consisting of three run-on lines with each line separated by a space. The poem enshrines using rhyme and repetition a vanished world and time: "I saw Len Hutton in his prime | Another time" with its last line repeating the previous second line.

Pinter's letter to Henry Woolf from the summer of 1948 illustrates its writer's fascination with the particularities of cricket and its players. Pinter compares Hutton and Compton. Pinter describes Compton as a feminine player who doesn't hit the ball but rather caresses and woos and then wins it from the bowler's hand. Compton, according to Pinter, seduces the fielders with the charm of his strokes. For Pinter, Compton reminds him of the great English "anarchist," Romantic poet Percy Bysshe Shelley. He then contrasts Compton with Hutton, saying that Compton may be a prince but Hutton is a king who garners immediate attention. As soon as Hutton enters the field, anyone can see that he is a great batsman. His perched cap is regarded as one of the best things in cricket. He is majestic, surveying the field as from a lofty throne. His strokes curb handsomely in amazing spirals over the ground, and Hutton paints their path in the air. As with Compton, there is something feminine, too, in Hutton: He moves with grace and ease. He is at his best when the sky is black with dark clouds. Pinter describes Hutton as almost superhuman with a whimsical, delightful leg-glide and majestic drives that render the opposition helpless. Pinter asks Woolf a rhetorical question: "But what do you think of cricket meaning so much to me?" Certainly, writing about Hutton, Pinter heaps a prose paean of praise upon him.[16]

It is curious why Pinter didn't revisit his words on Hutton and print them. They contain his fullest affirmation of a cricketer; perhaps he regarded them as too emotive. In Pinter's library there is a copy of Sir Leonard Hutton's *Cricket is My Life*, a reprint in the original dust jacket of a work initially published by Hutchinson in 1950. It is inscribed on the front end paper: "Presented to Harold Pinter by his friends, Gaieties Cricket Club, Summer 2000" and signed by Hutton on the half title.[17] In 1990, Pinter sent Woolf a cassette copy of a conversation he had with Brian Johnston, the legendary cricket commentator (see BR: J45). This was one of a series of conversations held during Test Match lunch breaks; this conversation took place at the Oval on August 25, 1990, during the England versus India Text Match (*Chronology*: 182). The conversation included, among other cricket memories, some of Pinter's recollections of Hutton, who died shortly after the discussion, on September 6, 1990. It exemplifies Pinter's abiding love of the game, his veneration for Lord's cricket ground, and his patriotism and anti-Americanism that emerged in his political stances later on in his life. Pinter told Johnston that a four-teen-year-old schoolboy heard a report that the Americans were going to play baseball at Lord's. This resulted in Pinter telephoning Lord's and requesting to speak to the chief administrative officer there, called the MCC secretary. Pinter told the secretary that he was a schoolboy who felt that it would be disgraceful if Americans played baseball at Lord's. According to Pinter, the MCC secretary responded, "Don't worry, my dear fellow, I don't think you should take these reports too seriously. I don't think we're actually going to allow it to happen."[18]

Cricket has positive associations for Pinter. On Monday September 6, 1948, after empathizing with Woolf's account of the brutality, cruelty, and savagery he is experiencing during his service with the RAF, Pinter says that his life is divided into phases: escape with his then-girlfriend Jennifer and cricket. In 1948, Pinter left school. In the autumn of that year, encouraged by his teacher Joe Brearley, he began at the Royal Academy of Dramatic Art. He was unhappy and attended irregularly. He remembers a morning in 1949 when he feigned illness and walked down into Gower Street. There, he boarded a bus and ran into Lord's at the Nursery end "to see through the terraces Washbrook late cutting for four, the ball skidding towards me."[19] Cyril Washbrook, renowned for his refusal to sign autographs, played for Lancashire and frequently opened the batting for England with Len Hutton. Michael Billington in the *Guardian* piece, "Harold Pinter and the Hackney Gang," observes that a friend maintains that Pinter's sentence that follows his recollection of Washbrook—"That beautiful evening Compton made seventy"—constitutes "one of the most evocative" sentences "even written about cricket."

On taking an initial glimpse at Pinter's letters at the British Library, Billington writes that "if discovery of" the works of Samuel Beckett "binds the Pinter letters, so too does Pinter's love of cricket." In July 1955, for instance, while Pinter "was excited about the imminent premiere of *Waiting for Godot*, he was no less stirred by the news that a young York-shire man called Doug Padgett, who for a time was thought to be in the mold of Pinter's beloved Len Hutton, had scored a century against War-wickshire."[20] Pinter informs in a letter to Mick Goldstein that he is waiting for *Waiting for Godot* to be performed in August 1955 at the Arts Theatre. He then confesses that he "was bowled for a duck fifth ball by a man called Percival"—shades of Pinter's schoolboy nemesis are hard to resist and resurface from the shadows.[21]

There was an unsettled period after Pinter left school, went to and then left drama school, and lived at home until 1951. He spent his days at

Lord's, where time seemed suspended in sun, according to his 1951 memoir "The Queen of all the Fairies."[22] From January to July 1951, Pinter was a student at the Central School of Speech and Drama. From September 1951 to the autumn of 1952, he joined Anew McMaster's repertory company touring Ireland. In his letters, Pinter remembers Hutton's successes and failures. For instance, Pinter recalls England playing against New Zealand in 1949 at Lord's. Hutton opened the batting "quietly, within himself, setting his day in order." After the first hour of play, England had scored 40 for none; Hutton looked set to score. Through variations in short sentence lengths, Pinter conveys the expectations of the crowd while Hutton is at the wicket. The New Zealand "slow left hand" bowler, Tom Burtt, "took the ball at the nursery end, tossed it up." Hutton to this first ball made "a superb square drive to Wallace at deep point. Wallace stopped it." The repetitive pattern continues in Pinter's description of the combat between batsman, bowler, and fielders, then the variation: "Burtt in, bowled. Hutton half way up the pitch immediately driving straight. Missed it. Clean bowled. On his heel back to the Pavilion." The detail, the precision, comes from the memory of being a witness, a participant, even as a spectator. The construction of a two-word sentence, the liberties with formal grammatical construction, owes much to his early reading of James Joyce and Samuel Beckett.

Pinter remembered Hutton's triumphs, too. In 1950 the West Indians visited. Pinter recalls that G. H. G. Doggart, fielding in the slips for England, "missed" the great West Indian batsman Clyde Walcott and that Walcott went on to score an unbeaten 168. This was in the second innings of the Second Test at Lord's and helped the West Indies to their first Test victory over England, assisted by the spin bowling of Sonny Ramadhin (and Alf Valentine). Pinter adds, "Hutton scored 202 not out against them and against Goddard bowling breakbacks on a bad" Oval wicket.[23]

Pinter's close friendships also evoke sporting memories, especially cricketing ones. In his correspondence with Goldstein, there is much banter and reminiscence over cricket and legendary past players; cricket memories represent a chord between them. The attention to detail seems an attempt to prevent the passing of time, to recapture the experience and moment. In a 1956 letter, Pinter comments on the Australian all-round Keith Miller, who was a fighter pilot during the Second World War, which had a profound impact on his attitude toward life. Associated with Miller and memories of 1948 is the great cricket writer Neville Cardus. Pinter wrote to Woolf in the autumn of 1948 of the "marvellous" Neville Cardus.[24]

In his "Memories of Cricket," Pinter wrote of the Lord's MCC match against the Australians on a Monday in 1948. On the Saturday, "the Australians had plastered the MCC bowling." "On Monday morning Miller hit Laker[25] for five sixties into the tavern."[26] Keith Miller[27] is the subject of observations in letters from Pinter to Woolf. In the summer of 1948, the summer Pinter left Hackney Downs Grammar School, the Australians, captained by Don Bradman (subsequently Sir Donald Bradman and dubbed "The Don") were running riot against England.

Pinter confesses to Woolf that he is intrigued and fascinated by cricket. He attends part of the Second Test Match at Lord's, which the Australians won by 409 runs. In their first innings, the Australian left-hander Arthur Morris scored 105 runs. Pinter tells Woolf that Morris is like a well-oiled machine, a powerful batsman whom one can never get out.[28] In fact, Morris, who made a very "slow start, made 105 runs out of a total of 166 scored while he was at the wicket, including 14 fours and one six. His innings included 14 fours and one six, and was noted for powerful, well-placed cover drives."[29] The diminutive Lindsay Hassett, who captained Australia during the 1953 tour of England, helped rebuild the innings after Miller was quickly dismissed. Pinter records that Hassett— small and compact—had stylized stokes that were a pleasure to watch. For Pinter, Miller, who objected to Bradman's ruthless tactics employed against England in the immediate post-war 1948 tests, "is indeed the uncontrolled genius. He is not aware"—a word usage more expressive in its context than "unaware," revealing Pinter's own genius for transforming the language—"of the limits to his own greatness. He does everything with careless panache! He is from the village green . . . his face disappears beneath the waterfall of hair."[30]

LETTERS TO AND FROM MICK GOLDSTEIN

Subsequently, Pinter returned to the subject of Miller and memories of yesteryear. On February 18, 1993, Pinter was engaged in drafting *Moonlight*, a drama obsessed with memory—its unreliability and the impossibility of returning to the past. After thanking Mick Goldstein for his kind words about the play, Pinter launches into cricket subjects and memory. He recalls meeting Keith Miller, who told him that Bradman was definitely caught by Ikin in Brisbane in 1946 for 28. However, Miller was given not out and went on to amass a large total. Pinter is referring to Jack Ikin, who played for Lancashire and England, a left-handed all-rounder. During the first test against the Australians in the 1946–1947 Ashes series played at Brisbane, Ikin fielded at second slip-not on the boundary and—as Pinter remembered—caught the great Bradman when he had scored 28. The umpire said it was not out, and Bradman indeed went on to make 187 runs.[31] Returning to the subject of his play, memories, and the unreliability of recall, Pinter tells Goldstein that *Moonlight* would be performed in September.[32] On February 24, 1993, Goldstein responds, "Of course we all thought Ikin made the catch." He also tells Pinter that he is "just in the middle of a book by Keith Miller and R. S. Whittington called *The Catch*. On page 224 is a picture of Len Hutton making a drive of Neil Harvey's bowling. It is one of the best pictures of Hutton I have ever seen." According to its subtitle, the book is "an account of two cricket tours." Pinter didn't have a copy of it.[33]

In his 1956 correspondence with Goldstein, Pinter laments what he considers to be the demise of cricketing characters such as Miller and fiery Yorkshire and England fast bowler Fred Trueman. For Pinter, the game sadly isn't what it used to be. Hutton retired from first-class cricket at the conclusion of the 1955 season, and the game has all but gone. A sense of Pinter's somewhat diminished enthusiasm is conveyed in 1957 when, watching the final day of a Test Match against the visiting West Indians on television, Pinter observes to Goldstein that Trueman has become the most formidable fast bowler. Pinter is subsequently annoyed when Trueman is omitted from the 1956–1957 MCC touring party to tour South Africa, in which England relied on other pace bowlers. Pinter describes Tom Graveney as an immaculate gentleman; his *Daily Telegraph* obituary describes him as "the greatest, as well as the most elegant and graceful, professional batsman to emerge in Britain in the years after the Second World War" and as "a throwback to cricket's golden age" with his attacking power and technique.[34] The West Indian opening bowler Roy Gilchrist, Pinter tells Goldstein, is fast and a pleasure to watch.[35]

Pinter's cricketing recollections were not entirely of the past. Occasionally he mentioned contemporary cricket matches. For instance, in an October 1963 letter, Pinter tells Goldstein that he went to the June 12, 1963 Sussex and Yorkshire one-day match at Hove on the Sussex coast. Sussex player Jim Parks "hit a fumbulating ninety including two sixes over cover point." The other top scorer in the match was Geoffrey Boycott, then at the start of what was to be a great career; he made 71 for the losing side Yorkshire, who lost the match by the relatively narrow margin of 22 runs. Pinter describes Boycott as a "colt and a doughty boy." When he ran himself out, Brian Close, the Yorkshire captain, "stormed with a filthy and terrible curse out of the balcony to meet Boycott on the stairs."

Goldstein must have had some cricketing ability, as Pinter in a May 14, 1971 letter informs him that he is getting up a team to play the Guardian newspaper staff on Saturday June 12 at their home ground in Gunnersbury Park. He asks whether Goldstein will be available. At the time, Goldstein was living in Sutton Coldfield in the West Midlands. By June 1972, he had moved to Victoria in Australia. On July 5, 1972, Pinter tells Goldstein that a few weeks previously, his team, Harold Pinter's XI, played against the uardian, and the match was drawn.

What troubles Pinter was his missed opportunity, his mistake. In fact, as Pinter's correspondence with Alan Wilkinson in the early years of the twenty-first century enshrined in *The Catch* demonstrates, he was obsessed with catches. They become a metaphor for life, for opportunities missed, roads not taken. In July 1972, Pinter describes missing a vital catch that came down from a colossal height. By January 1973, Goldstein had moved to Melbourne. On January 3, 1973, Pinter wrote to Goldstein that he was still every Saturday morning going to net practice at Lord's; he was improving but paradoxically getting worse as an actual player. He also reminded Goldstein of an experience the previous summer. He attended the Lord's Test Match against Australia (June 22–26, 1972). Dennis Lillie, the Australian fast bowler, "bowled Boycott middle stump" in the England second innings. This "was a sight and a half."

Another batsman to impress Pinter was David Gower, the fair-haired, left-handed batsman who played for Leicestershire and captained England in the 1980s. Pinter senses his potential, writing to Goldstein at the end of October 1979 that Gower was wonderful and that he hadn't seen anyone quite like him. He drew upon his encyclopedic knowledge of the history of cricket: Pinter had a fine run of Wisden's, replete with cricketing facts from the past and regarded by many as the cricketer's bible, that lined his study at 52 Campden Hill Square. He observed that the only other player perhaps better might have been Frank Woolley, but he never saw him play.[36] Frank Woolley, a left-handed batsman and bowler who played as a professional for Kent and England, was described as "one of the finest all-rounders" to play cricket. Playing sixty-four tests for England between 1909 and 1934, "there was all summer in a stroke by Woolley, and he batted as it is sometimes shown in dreams," the cricket writer R. C. Robertson-Glasgow wrote.[37] Incidentally, on the back of the envelope of his letter to Goldstein, Pinter adds, "But you've seen Gower-of course!"

In the same letter, written on Saturday October 27, 1979, before the annual Gaieties dinner, Pinter assessed their cricketing achievements for 1979. They had a pretty good season and finished triumphantly, beating Sidcup, whom they'd never beaten before, on Sunday September 23. There are echoes in the name "Sidcup" of Pinter's early dramatic success *The Caretaker*, where Davies the tramp wishes to go to pick up mysterious papers that will affirm his identity.[38] To return to Pinter's and the Gaieties cricketing achievements, his personal highlights included taking a blinder at mid-off "to get rid of their best batsman, a left-handed Indian called Modi" and "hitting a straight six which nearly knocked off the umpire's hand and hit the sight screen like a bullet." Pinter adds with a sarcastic and ironic nuance, "Naturally stirred by this, I tried to do it again, missed and was bowled, demonstrating again my great cricketing intelligence." In a subsequent letter to Goldstein, he ushered in the New Year with a cricketing metaphor: "[L]et 1980 enter like a shot off a shovel!" Six years later, cricket is still present in their correspondence, with Pinter writing on Sunday July 27, 1986 to report that his team lost their match played yesterday against the *Guardian*. Pinter doesn't mince his words. He "hit a straight drive for four but fucked up an exquisite leg glide." He looks forward to seeing Goldstein when Goldstein is in London in early September; they'll go to watch cricket.

Pinter's signing off a letter to Goldstein dated January 25, 1994 encapsulates exactly the mood and spirit of his sense of his lengthy friendship with him: "How zat?" he quips and immediately writes, "Not out!" and "Love Harold."[39] Somewhat surprisingly, Goldstein doesn't comment on the copy he received early in 1995 of Pinter's four-verse poem "Cricket at Night" (*VV*: 172). Kerry Packer used floodlights for evening and night cricket during his World Cricket Series initially on November 27, 1977 at the Adelaide Oval between the Australian World Cricket Series team and the West Indian one. The first use of floodlights in England for cricket didn't occur until 1997, when it was used at Edgbaston, Birmingham. Pinter's poem is dated two years earlier. Lacking punctuation, the poem has two verses of three lines each, the third verse has six lines and the final verse a single line. Pinter repeats many words, a technique he uses in many poems. The poem begins and ends with the same line: "They are still playing cricket at night." The pronouns "they" and "they're" occur nine times, always at the start of lines. There are also at the end of lines effective rhymes reflecting the poem's preoccupations with "night," "light," the "dark," "black," and "white."

Two years later, Goldstein tells his friend that he received as a birthday present a biography of Bradman. In the same letter, dated February 15, 1996, he thanks Pinter for a copy of his play *Ashes to Ashes*. Written in January 1996, its title conjures images of the England versus Australia Test Matches played for possession of an urn containing ashes. But the play has nothing to do with cricket and is replete with imagery of brutality and savagery. The idea for the play came from Pinter reading, not a book about cricket, but rather Gitta Sereny's biography of Albert Speer, Hitler's minister for armaments and munitions (*Chronology*: 225).

Among the subjects touched in a lengthy letter to Goldstein dated January 4, 1997 is the progress of the Gaieties the previous year. They won seventeen matches, drawing four and losing two. Pinter played for them twice, on Sunday afternoons on June 23 and September 8 in Hampstead (*Chronology*: 228–29). Pinter tells Goldstein that he "retired hurt: having made six," pulled a muscle "and caught at mid-off," having failed to "get to the pitch of the ball!" In a letter dated January 13, 1998, Goldstein thanks Pinter for sending him a copy of *Runs in the Memory: County Cricket in the 1950s* (1997) by Stephen Chalke with illustrations by Ken Taylor, the former Yorkshire and England batsmen. Goldstein tells his old friend that he is "sure that heaven cannot promise anything better than to partake in a game with some of the cricketers of old."[40]

LETTERS TO HENRY WOOLF

Pinter's early letters to Woolf at times mix cricket with sexual metaphors and personal inside jokes. They also display Pinter's sense of humor. At the Theatre Royal, Huddersfield, during November 1954, Pinter appears with the Huddersfield Repertory Company in two comedies. One is *Affairs of State* by the French-born dramatist Louis Verneuil. Pinter has the lead role of a United States diplomat, Byron Winkler (for the week of November 15, 1954). The following week, he plays the young lover and amanuensis in Rosemary Casey's three-act comedy *Late Love*. Starting November 29, he has the leading part in Agatha Christie's whodunit *Ten Little Niggers*. In spite of such a hectic schedule, he has time to write to Woolf that if Woolf "strikes a length," the Yorkshire and England left-arm spin bowler, or Wardle's rival for a place in the England Test side, who also played for Yorkshire Bob Appleyard, the right-handed off break and fast medium bowler, "can forget about" gaining a place in Hutton's Test team. Continuing in this sarcastic vein, Pinter tells Woolf that his selection is "highly probable," but Pinter adds the caveat that Woolf is "by report, an odd type and changes his jockstrap three times a day." Both Wardle and Appleyard toured Australia with Len Hutton's MCC side in the English autumn/winter of 1954. Pinter then refers to the great Australian batsmen Arthur Morris and Neil Harvey and uses a Yiddish word that will appear again in *The Birthday Party*: "to mention only two" of the Australian batsmen who "have very little *nacchas* for your bowling." The Yiddish word means pride and happiness in someone's achievement(s). In this context, Pinter is using the word to mean satisfaction.

The early correspondence between Pinter and Woolf at times contains obscene language, especially of a sexual nature, that subsequently sometimes reoccurs in Pinter's drama. In an instance from an early letter, Pinter gives Woolf a final word of advice—to "keep off the cunt if he hope[s] to pull [his] weight on the great day." At the letter's conclusion, Pinter jokes at his friend's age, saying that he was seen playing with the deceased English cricketer and captain Archie MacLaren, who was noted for, among other achievements, leading the MCC to four defeats in Ashes series against Australia. Pinter signs his letter "Ivan Karamazov,"[41] an allusion to the major character in Dostoyevsky's classic philosophical novel *The Brothers Karamazov*. Dostoevsky was among the authors Pinter started reading voraciously on his own initiative by the age of twelve (Billington: 10). The reference to Ivan—the novel's poet and rationalist who hates his father and falls in love with his brother's betrothed— reveals much about the relationship between Pinter and Woolf, a relationship dramatically explored through the memories of a single character performed by Woolf in Pinter's *monologue*. The obsession with cricket, with its factual minutiae and names of players from the past who take on at times a legendary status, is juxtaposed in *monologue* with intellectual references and sexual innuendo.

In the middle of a hectic schedule at the Pavilion Theatre Torquay on a Tuesday in October 1956, Pinter writes to Woolf. After asking how he is doing, Pinter continues in a questioning fashion full of playful sexual innuendo: "Which wicket are you playing in and what's it like? I take it you're still piercing the field, playing off your legs as of old."[42] In an earlier letter to Woolf dated Saturday 18 [July 1953] from Dundalk County Louth, Pinter comments on the Lord's Test Match against the Australians that had taken place between June 25 and June 30. The letter demonstrates Pinter's superb knowledge of cricket and his memory of the details from specific matches, details that can be confirmed from *Wisden's*, the cricketing almanac, and other information. Pinter regards England as the better team apart from the great Australian fast bowler Ray Lindwall. Lindwall frequently opened the bowling for Australia with Keith Miller. Pinter notices a loosening and fraying at the edge of the Australian team's concentration. Pinter would never understand why the Australian captain Lindsay Hassett didn't put Lindwall on to bowl following the tea break on the final day at Lord's nor why the left-handed batsmen Willie Watson and Trevor Bailey were dismissed. Pinter is unimpressed with Reg Simpson playing for England and would like to see him replaced by another batsman, Cyril Washbrook. He wonders when Simpson "again will . . . play an innings of the same power and authority as his 156 at Melbourne in 1951, which virtually won us the 5th Test?"

In addition, Len Hutton, the England captain, should "bowl Compton more often." Pinter regards the selection of the Worcestershire batsman Don Kenyon as "stupid" because Kenyon "never *was* Test class." In his praise of Compton's bowling, Pinter is probably thinking of Compton's capturing the wicket of the Australian batsman Arthur Morris in the second innings. Compton bowled three overs, took one wicket, and had 21 runs scored off him. The Second Test was drawn; Kenyon, who opened the innings, was out for three and two; Willie Watson scored four and in the second innings 109, saving the match. Trevor Bailey, the Essex all-rounder, scored two and an invaluable slow 71 in partnership with Watson. Lindwall took in the first innings five wickets for 66 runs and in the second innings two for 26 after not being bowled much. The Third Test played at Old Trafford Manchester from July 9 to July 14, 1953 was also drawn; this time, rain stopped play. Simpson, who wasn't selected for the Second Test, played and scored 31. Kenyon was dropped; Compton wasn't called upon to bowl.[43]

ARTHUR WELLARD

Pinter met the former Somerset and England batsman Arthur Wellard through the Gaieties Cricket Club. Wellard played for them and then became their umpire for four years following his final game for the Gaieties in 1975 at the age of seventy-three; he had played cricket for around half a century. In the year following Wellard's death, Pinter published a powerful prose tribute. Affixed to the half title is a photograph of the Gaieties team taken in 1975 with Wellard seated at the bottom right (BR: E21A). Tom Stoppard, another lover of cricket, received a copy from Pinter, and in his thank you letter dated October 10, 1980, refers to it as "a marvellous piece."[44] In his tribute to Wellard, Pinter exhibits his knowledge and recall of the game of cricket and transforms Wellard into a hero. Pinter recalls his hero in the fading light, last man at the age of seventy-two winning a game in the final over: "the ball had gone miles, in the long-on the area, over the boundary for four."

As an umpire, Wellard was impartial by the highest standards, Pinter writes. Wellard's reminiscences of legendary names from the past—such as the great batsman Wally Hammond, whom "nobody could stop. . . . Never anyone to touch old Wally on the offside, off the back foot," or Harold Larwood—"quickest thing I ever saw"—are succinct and quintessential. Wellard was not afraid to take Pinter down a peg or two. Pinter recalled that "once, on a beautiful wicket at Eastbourne I suddenly played a covered drive for four, probably the best shot I ever played in my life." Shortly after this, Pinter was clean bowled. Arriving at the front of the Pavilion, Wellard met him and chastised Pinter for getting out to a terrible shot. Pinter reminded him of the wonderful drive he had made previously. Wellard dismissed this and told Pinter not to play back to a full-length ball. Pinter apologized to Wellard, and Pinter was not by nature an apologetic person. He concludes his tribute with nostalgia, gratitude, puns, and double entendres, with which his work is replete. In the case of cricket, they are associated with idyllic times and memories. For instance, Wellard "gave me [Pinter] his England cap and the stump he knocked over when he bowled [Jack] Badcock" (*VV*: 46–53), the Australian batsman, second ball in the Lord's Test of 1938 against Australia.[45] Pinter's kindness to Wellard is seen in a short note his hero sent him dated December 18, 1974. Wellard thanks him for a "lovely Xmas present," adding that Pinter has "been so kind to [him], especially during the cricket season. [He] shall never be able to repay" him.[46]

RAMONA KOVAL INTERVIEW

Pinter's obsession with cricket is placed in perspective in his observations in a wide-ranging interview toward the end of his life with Australian writer Ramona Koval. The interview took place at the Edinburgh International Book Festival on August 25, 2002 and subsequently appeared in extract format in the *Guardian*, August 28, 2002. It was broadcast on the Australian Broadcasting Corporation's Radio National program *Books and Writing* on September 15, 2002.[47] In it, Pinter describes cricket as a civilized form of warfare that he finds "aesthetically pleasing." The reasons for his love for cricket are related to its shape and "the general environment of" the game. Additionally, the details of the game fascinate him. Pinter tells Koval that when he played cricket, he "had little concentration, patience, or the most important thing of all: true relaxation; and my judgment was distinctly less than impeccable!" Pinter could hit very hard—but typically, fielders would get in the way and catch the ball. Pinter likes the game's rules, which he says are for the benefit of mankind. It is noticeable that Pinter's great affection for the game is associated with order, with rules, with a perception of Englishness, the English countryside, and—perhaps ironically—the weather, in a climate given to summer rain that frequently prevented play.

SIGNIFICANCE OF CRICKET?

Pinter's obsession with the past and with memory—its unreliability and the need for verification—are related to his obsession with cricket. The psychological hinterland of cricket may be perceived as an attempt to hold on to the past, to memories that live on inside the heart and in the mind. The game is associated with the mood and the aspects of childhood, with long evenings in which in England the light gradually fades; in remembering it, idyllic days of youth may be rediscovered. Through cricket perhaps there is an attempt to find the meaning of life, of fulfillment that has been taken away in the process of growing up and everyday existence. Pinter's continuous involvement with the game, with playing it, remembering it, may be seen as part of this, of a process to arrest maturation. It is not without significance that his cricketing memories are reinforced in letters to his closest friends from childhood including Mick Goldstein, in faraway Australia, and Henry Woolf. The cricketers he largely celebrates, such as Hutton and Compton, are associated with Pinter's immediate post-war world of Hackney and friendships and escape. Interestingly, a friend of later years (see *Chronology*: 179) is the former English captain Mike Brearley, who since retiring from the game became a writer and psychoanalyst. According to Jon Hotten in his *The Meaning of Cricket* (2016), Brearley observed that the game of cricket prepares one for death and heightens awareness of one's own mortality. After all, when the umpire's finger is raised, one is out.[48]

For Antonia Fraser, her husband's love of cricket is associated with his attitude toward his country, his patriotism. In *Must*, she writes that "Harold was captivated by the natural beauty of Dorset since he loved anything that could be construed as 'England.'" She adds, "which was perhaps why cricket appealed to him aesthetically so much, the cricket on the village green, the cricket match of a David Inshaw painting" (234). Pinter and his wife went to the David Inshaw exhibition on October 15, 2004. It featured "a huge new cricket picture which we had been told David was keen for Harold to have. . . . All the same, I think he was a bit relieved when the picture didn't fit the measurements of [Pinter's] Super-Study" (277–78).

CRICKET AS AN ASSOCIATIVE LINK:
BECKETT, GRAY, LARKIN

Cricket is an important associative link for Pinter not only with his close friends from youth such as Woolf and Goldstein, but with others including fellow authors Simon Gray, who became a very close friend, Philip Larkin, and Samuel Beckett.[49] To take the example of Beckett: In a letter to Pinter dated August 1, 1973, Beckett thanks Pinter for sending him a copy of "Hutton and the Past" (BR: E15), which Beckett "much relished." Beckett demonstrates an extensive knowledge of cricket and writes on the assumption that his correspondent Pinter possesses that knowledge, too: "[T]alking of Woolley set me thinking of Gregory since out. F.E.W. was one of the few to stand up to him and MacDonald. Two near centuries in the same Test. Early Twenties must've been." Beckett is referring to "Australian bowlers who challenged [Frank Woolley]: Jack Gregory . . . and Edward A. (Ted) MacDonald." Beckett's memory is not playing tricks, as "in the 1921 Test match between Australia and England at Lord's, Woolley scored 95 in England's 1st innings and 93 in their 2nd innings."[50] In a letter to Barbara Bray written from Tangier and dated June 26, 1975, Beckett writes that he receives the *Sunday Times* on a Tuesday and "saw about Harold's names." This refers to Pinter's confirmation "that he had named the characters in" his *No Man's Land* after "prominent cricketers," according to Joan Bakewell in her "One Women's Week" (*Sunday Times*, June 15, 1975: 28).[51]

CRICKET IN PINTER'S WORK: PINTER'S FINAL DAYS

Cricket is enshrined in Pinter's creative work, and the ways in which Pinter's love for the game manifests itself in some of his films and plays has been critically explored. For instance, Peter Thomson in his "What's in a name? Cricket in *No Man's Land*"[52] contains a survey of the cricketing aspects of the deployment of characters' names and linguistic strategies in *No Man's Land*. Tim Miles[53] discusses the use of cricket as a device in *The Birthday Party*, *The Caretaker* and two Pinter screenplays: *The Servant* and *The Quiller Memorandum*. Given the pervasive obsession Pinter had for cricket during his life, it is perhaps surprising that Antonia doesn't use cricket metaphors to describe her husband's last days, but instead draws upon metaphors from tennis and football. Pinter collapsed at dinner on October 12, 2007 and was taken to the casualty department at St. Mary's hospital. This was followed by eight days of intensive care. He was suffering from "prolonged internal bleeding." On November 10,

2007, Antonia attempted to compose a poem, "Death v. H.P.," encompassing all the devices Pinter had stored up to ward off the inevitable. The poem admitted that Death "only needs one goal," but somewhat over-optimistically she thought that Pinter "on the whole" was winning.[54] Antonia observes that "she read it to Harold, but it was not as good as I thought" (*Must*: 315–17). Cricket is associated with happiness and nostalgia in Pinter, not necessarily with personal mortality. The occurrence in his letters of cricketing names, scores, when such a game was played, who bowled whom, who caught whom, how many runs were made, and so forth represent something concrete and definite to hold onto faced with the vulnerability of memory and recall—a permanent theme in Pinter's work.

BRIDGE

Karel Reisz

Karel Reisz, the Czech-born cinematic director, arrived in England in 1938. Following attendance at Leighton Park School, Reading, and service in the RAF, he went to Emmanuel College, Cambridge. Reisz and Pinter worked together on *The French Lieutenant's Woman* (1981), and they subsequently formed a close friendship lasting until Reisz's death. Their friendship was cemented by their passion for the game of bridge (see *Chronology*: 355). In 1963, Reisz married the American-born actress Betsy Blair. Following her husband's death, she continued to play bridge with Harold Pinter and Antonia and remained a close friend. Antonia recalls that as preparations went ahead for performances of *Betrayal*, and before Pinter and Karel Reisz went to Lyme Regis to check out locations for *The French Lieutenant's Woman* in September 1978, "the Reiszes . . . come to dinner and play bridge." She adds that "this was the beginning of a lifelong friendship between the four of us" (*Must*: 100–1). It was Reisz who encouraged Pinter in 1987 to work on the screenplay of Margaret Atwood's *The Handmaid's Tale*. He directed the restaged *Moonlight* at the May 1994 Pinter Dublin Festival and also on Broadway four years later. In 2001 at the Lincoln Center, Reisz directed *Landscape* and *A Kind of Alaska*.

It is significant that Pinter, in his oration at Karel Reisz's funeral on the first day of December 2002, doesn't begin with Reisz's direction of such notable films as *Saturday Night and Sunday Morning* (1960), *This Sporting Life* (1963), or perhaps his *Morgan: A Suitable Case for Treatment* (1966). Rather, Pinter begins with bridge and remembers that it was one of the things Reisz loved most in the world. As they sat down to play, Reisz would clap his hands together and say, "This is the life."

An accomplished and rational player, Reisz would, Pinter recalls, occasionally allow himself a wild gambit, declaring six of spades, for instance. "On seeing his partner's cards, he would say, with a twinkle in his eye, 'One of two things will have to be right. But more often than not he would actually make 6 spades and he received our congratulation with modesty and grace." He was, Pinter says, a man of grace but also toughness. Pinter mentions that Reisz directed four of his plays with skill and dedication. The longest time they spent together was when they worked on the script of *The French Lieutenant's Woman* between May 1980 and the following April. Pinter recalls an anecdote from that period. Pinter showed Reisz a rewritten scene relating to what was to follow the Victorian love scene between Jeremy Irons and Meryl Streep, which took place in Exeter. Both actors meet at Exeter station, where Streep is waiting to take a train to London. Irons says, "I want you," to which Streep replies, "But you've just had me in Exeter." At the funeral oration, Pinter recalls that Reisz looked at him and said, "Audacious!" Then Reisz winked at Pinter, and Pinter never forget that wink.[55]

Bridge Partners

According to Antonia Fraser, it was her editor at Weidenfeld & Nicolson, Christopher Falkus, who taught her husband to play bridge during a weekend that she, Pinter, and the Falkuses spent together at Sissinghurst in Kent, March 6–7, 1976. She adds, "A great success, confirming my theory of Harold's naturally brilliant brain" (54). Following Falkus's early death, his widow, Gila, continued to play the game on a regular basis with Pinter and Antonia. Bridge became a family game; for instance, during a family holiday in the Algarve in 1980, four of them played and changed partners. Fraser adds that her son Damian, then aged fifteen, was the best player. The teenager played for his school, Ampleforth. The other player was her son Orlando. In 1983, three years later, she records "how bridge is strangely brilliant these days." She adds that she and Pinter "win and win, defeating far better players" such as the economist and journalist Peter Jay and William and Caroline (Burrows) Waldegrave (*Chronology*: 322). Baron William Waldegrave was the Conservative politician and cabinet member (1990–1997) who left politics and became provost of Eton College in 2009. Waldegrave also played tennis with Pinter and Antonia. Antonia penned a poem for her wedding anniversary, dated November 27, 1983, called "For My Partner," which "expresses [her] romantic feelings about [her] union in that respect (as Susanna Gross says much later: bridge, because it's about partnership, is a romantic game)" (*Must*: 119–20, 139).

Bridge is a game revealing friendships, of time spent together in cerebral competition with personalities from differing walks of life and political opinion. In addition to Betsy Reisz, other long-standing friendships formed over bridge included the Israeli-born actress Haya Clayton (Neuberg/Harareet), who was best known for her performance as Esther in *Ben Hur* (1959) and widow of the British film director Jack Clayton. Clayton directed Penelope Mortimer's *The Pumpkin Eater*, for which Pinter wrote the screenplay in 1963. A year after Clayton's February 25, 1995 death, Pinter said in a professional tribute that Jack Clayton had great sensitivity, intelligence, and flair. Pinter remembered him as a gentle man with a wry sense of humor, rigor, and fierce determination.[56] On the final day of 2005, Antonia recalled that Betsy Reisz and Haya Clayton came to play bridge. For her husband, 2005 was his worst year. It was, she added, worse than 2002 when he was only in the hospital for two weeks. "The Nobel Prize hardly seems to count in the field of his emotions" (*Must*: 299).

Simon Gray closes his memoir *The Year of the Jouncer* (2006) with an image of Pinter playing cards. Gray is in a bar in a Barbados hotel. He envisions seeing Harold and Antonia: "At their table are two elderly ladies, whom I can't identify—I think they're playing bridge—yes, Harold made a movement, an emphatic putting-down-a-card—take-that! Kind of movement" (117–18, 282). Other regular bridge players included the eminent pianist Mitsuko Uchida and her partner, the distinguished diplomat Robert Cooper. Uchido's performance of the Mozart Piano Concerto No. 27 at the Barbican on Sunday September 30, 2007 was probably "the last concert Harold ever [went] to (the physical strain of reaching the auditorium was so great)." Antonia observes that the friendship with Uchida and Cooper was "among the solaces of these years" (*Must*: 316). Just over a year later, on December 24, 2008, Pinter died.

SQUASH/TENNIS

Pinter was an obsessive squash and tennis player. He played tennis well into his seventies, as illustrated by Antonia noting on October 12, 2002 that "shortly after his seventy-second birthday, Harold played tennis again" (*Must*: 265). For over half a century, he played fiercely competitive squash and tennis against Ronald Harwood. He enjoyed going to Wimbledon, as he did, for instance, on Saturday June 29, 1991, Thursday June 25, 1992, Monday June 24, 1996, and Wednesday June 30, 1999 (*Chronology*: 189, 197, 228, 252). According to Antonia, in 1985 she and Pinter, then aged fifty-five, joined the Vanderbilt Club, which was "perched on top of a railway hanger" in Shepherd's Bush in West London. Pinter comments that he will concentrate on tennis because he pulls a muscle every time he plays cricket. Antonia adds that "there were those that maintained Harold remained a maniacal squash-player to the end of his days on the tennis court." His service was weak: "[T]he art of serving certainly eluded him: as against that, he had been Pinter the Sprinter at school—as he often reminded us—and could outrun many younger men." In 1948 he equaled the Hackney Downs Grammar School 100 yards record and created a new 220 yards school record. However, following his illness and operations, on the final day of 2002, he had to give the Vanderbilt up: "'Just too exhausting' . . . our beloved Vanderbilt Club came to an end" (*Must*: 196, 268).

Pinter's competitive nature, his need for physical exercise, to keep fit, to keep trim, like the speaker in his *monologue*, is seen in 1970. He plays squash during the morning of April 7, again on the morning of July 20, again on the morning of September 24 and October 2 followed the next day, a Saturday, by morning cricket nets. All the squash matches are against Ronald Harwood. On Sunday June 21, 1970, he plays cricket for the Gaieties and then, in one of the few references to football, in the evening watched the World Cup Final on TV. Incidentally, unlike his friend Samuel Beckett, Pinter showed no interest whatsoever in rugby; the reason may be because Pinter was at a football- rather than rugby-playing school (see *Must*: 145). The next year, 1971, sees him playing squash on the morning of January 28 with the writer and producer Michael Kustow; on the morning of February 25, with Peter Willes, who had become a close friend after Willes assisted with the screening of *The Birthday Party* in 1960; and then again with Ronald Harwood on the morning of August 2 (*Chronology*: 36–39, 40–41, 43). In 1972, after the cricket season finished, on the morning of November 29 he plays squash again with Ronald Harwood. Somewhat surprisingly, there seem to be no more references to either tennis or playing squash in his "Appointment Diaries" until January 16, 1974, when he picks up his routine of playing squash in the morning with Harwood and again on May 31, after which he and Harwood lunch. On the final day of January 1975, the same pattern is followed: morning squash and then lunch with Harwood. On March 18, 1976, he plays squash in the morning with an unnamed player. On the morning of October 28, 1977, squash is played with Christopher Falkus. Four days later, Pinter is back in the morning battling it out on the squash court with Harwood and then they go for lunch. He has an unnamed opponent on the morning of November 17, meets his son Daniel for lunch, and then at 8 pm on the same evening settles down to the more cerebral bridge. The morning of December 2, 1977 sees him again playing squash with an unnamed opponent. The morning of March 7, 1978 records Pinter playing squash with Harwood and then lunching with him, and on March 10, his opponent is the stage, television, and production executive Christopher Morahan. One of the final references to Pinter's playing squash found in the "Appointment Diaries" is on April 19, 1978, when he plays in the morning with Christopher Falkus (*Chronology*: 318, 81).

In Pinter's drama, squash—"a subject Robert and Jerry discuss aggressively in" *Betrayal* (*Must*: 113)—becomes a code word for sexual activity and sexual rivalry. For instance, in *Betrayal*'s scene four, the date is the autumn of 1974 and the setting is Robert and Emma's living room. Robert describes Casey, with whom Emma his wife is now having an affair, as a "brutally honest squash player" and tells Jerry, his literary agent who previously had an affair with Emma, that "we must play. You were rather good." Jerry responds, "Yes, I was quite good. All right. I'll give you a ring." Robert responds, "Why don't you?" Jerry, "We'll make a date." Robert tells Jerry, "The man who wins buys the lunch." Emma wishes to watch: "Why can't I watch and then take you both to lunch?" Robert replies, "Well, to be brutally honest, we wouldn't actually want a woman around, would we, Jerry? I mean a game of squash isn't simply a game of squash, it's rather more than that." He elaborates at some length on the perception of the rituals of squash: "You see, first there's the game. And then there's the pint. And then there's lunch. After all, you've been at it." The word "it" could here refer to sexual intercourse. Robert continues, with the repetitive "don't want her" taking on ironic reverberations: "You've had your battle. What you want is your pint and lunch. You really don't want a woman buying you lunch. You don't actually want a woman within a mile of the place, and of the places, really. You don't want her in the squash court, you don't want her in the shower, or the pub, or the restaurant. You see, at lunch you want to talk about squash, or cricket, or books, or even women, with your friend and be able to warm to your theme without fear of improper interruption. That's what it's all about." He then asks Jerry, "What do you think, Jerry?" Jerry responds abruptly, "I haven't played squash for years" (4: 12–14). There are, of course, associations with male bonding, rivalry, and sexual infidelity.

TABLE TENNIS

Somewhat surprisingly, Pinter's "Appointment Diaries" do not contain references to a once-favorite game of his adolescence: table tennis. Although he and Mick Goldstein didn't go to the same school, they were obsessive table tennis players at Hackney Boys' Club. Jasper Rees, in his "Ping Pong with Pinter," relates that he "once asked Pinter what he recalled of" Woolf's performance in the first production of *The Room*. "He was a bit in and out," Pinter replied. But that didn't stop him writing [*monologue*] for Woolf in 1973. Rees adds "that the short BBC drama makes nostalgic reference to their joint fondness for ping-pong. Woolf says that Pinter's table tennis 'was completely unorthodox, unlike anybody else's.'"[57] The play has a single character called "Man" obsessing about his past rivalry with a "former" friend for dominance over a woman. It opens with the suggestive "I think I'll nip down to the games room. Stretch my legs. Have a game of ping pong." Then, he addresses a chair that is empty, utilizing pronoun repetition, asking, "What about you? Fancy a game? How would you like a categorical thrashing?" He is "willing to accept any challenge, any stakes, any gauntlet you'd care to fling down."[58] Table tennis becomes associated with rivalry, with conflict, with adolescent memories. It is surprising that Pinter doesn't draw more in his work upon the interminable games of table tennis he must have played against Goldstein, Woolf, and Moishe Wernick at the Hackney Boys' Club.

GAMES AND THEIR SIGNIFICANCE

Games as enactment for the conflict between people, for sexual rivalry and competition, are also found in Pinter's film script of *Sleuth*, adapted from Anthony Shaffer's play. Pinter completed the tenth and final draft in May 2005 (*Chronology*: 295). The film stars Michael Caine and Jude Law in the main roles; Pinter appeared as a man on TV. *Sleuth* depicts the struggle between the aging, successful author Andrew Wyke (played by Caine) and the much younger, aspiring actor Milo Tindle (played by Law) over Wyke's wife, Maggie, with whom Milo is having an affair. Wyke invites Milo into his mansion, well equipped with electronic devices, to enact revenge. There he plans to play squash with him and soundly thrash the younger man. Power shifts continually in the script, in the psychological battle of wills triggered by the fight to possess Maggie between the older and younger man. Pinter "explores male insecurity, the addictive gamesmanship, the unreliability of narrative and the politics of dominant power, all classic Pinter themes" (Billington: 419–20).

In the second act of *The Birthday Party*, Goldberg's reminiscences about the East End ascend to a muted lyricism when he remembers "the sun falling behind the dog stadium" (46). In his work, correspondence, and "Appointment Diaries," there are few other references or allusions to greyhound racing, the dog track, horse racing or betting, or even sports that Pinter successfully participated in at school, such as running or football. Although Pinter played Ping-Pong, tennis, and squash (not badminton) and later in life was an adroit bridge player, it is cricket that dominates as metaphor, as direct reference, from his earliest days until the end of his life. In his "Afterword: Harold Pinter and Cricket," John Fowles[59] writes of what he considers "as a kind of secret gate-key to [Pinter's] work. That is his very intense and evident love of cricket." Fowles observes that "whatever it is in Harold's past that first led him to this very English invention [cricket] is undoubtedly what needs to be explored and commented on by those who favour his dramatic work."[60] Simon Gray in *Jouncer* writes that cricket "was at the heart of England, of being English" (204). On July 18, 2006, Pinter's family celebrated the Nobel Prize award "by taking a box at Lords"—a day of "total happiness (of eighteen people)" (*Must*: 304). In an interview published in *The Guardian* on December 27, 2008, three days following Pinter's death on Christmas Eve 2008, Andy Bull cites Pinter as saying: "Cricket, the whole thing, playing, watching, being part of the Gaieties, has been the central feature of my life."[61]

MUSIC

Apart from cricket, Pinter's other great obsession and "love" was music, although he didn't play a musical instrument. Larry Bensky asked Pinter in an interview published in the *Paris Review* (Fall 1966: No 39) whether music had influenced his writing. Pinter answered that he didn't know how music can influence writing, but both jazz and classical music were important to him. He feels a sense of music in writing—which is different than being influenced by it. He names Boulez and Webern as composers he listens to often.[62] Alastair Macaulay, chief ballet critic of the *New York Times*, and one of Pinter's most acute critics, in his reflections on Pinter's achievement and legacy (*New York Times*, January 9, 2009) writes that, in 1996, Pinter told him that he thought "choreographically." He adds that, in the late 1940s, Pinter "was something of a balletomane"—an interest that seems not to have been subsequently sustained.

A ballet from that period had a particular impact upon Pinter. He saw in London "Roland Petit's one-act "Le Jeune Homme et la Mort" (1946), set to a libretto by Jean Cocteau." Macaulay observes that "no Pinter play has a hero committing suicide onstage, as does the Young Man of Mr. Petit's ballet. But 'Le Jeune Homme'"—set to music by Bach, Pinter's favorite composer—"has something of the suspensefulness, the mixture of menace and eroticism, and the aura of the inexplicable that Pinter was to start putting into his plays" more than a decade later. Petit's ballet has not stood the test of time as well as Pinter's work, and Macaulay writes that "[i]t seems unlikely to me that the choreography of Mr. Petit or any other dancemaker exerted any serious influence on Pinter's work." Rather, "the sources of [Pinter's] feeling for movement . . . are more likely to be found in cinema, in the plays he loved, from Shakespeare to Beckett, and, not least, in cricket (which Pinter revered to the point of rating it somewhat higher than sex)." Macaulay adds that, in Pinter's plays, "as in cricket, you often seem to wait and wait while the characters concerned stand still; then something happens fast, and everything has changed irreversibly. The movement, like the words, has an unmistakable rhythm."[63]

Pinter's aunt on his father's side was very musical. Aunt Sophie was an "excellent pianist" whose husband, Isidor, a taxi driver and chess enthusiast, also possessed musical abilities. His paternal grandfather, Nathan, was dominated by his wife, Fanny Baron, Pinter's favorite grandmother. A Polish-born ladies' hairdresser, she "preferred listening to records by the great Beethoven and Mozart pianist Artur Schnabel [1882–1951] to doing housework." His close lifelong friend Goldstein was obsessed by music; he was a fine violinist, and their correspondence is replete with references to Beethoven, Mozart, Haydn, and other composers. In Pinter's autobiographical novel *The Dwarfs*, "Len Weinstein, working as a porter at Euston Station and haunted in his imagination by hallucinatory dwarfs whom he finally banishes, is a variance on the music-loving Michael Goldstein" (Billington: 3, 58). Len, a violinist, loves Bach—as did Pinter—and finds subtle differences between Bach and Beethoven. After a visit to a concert at the Conway Hall and hearing Beethoven's Grosse Fuge Opus 133, a one-movement composition for string quartet, Len somewhat ambiguously observes, "I've never heard anything like it. It's not musical. It's physical. It's physical. It's not music. It's someone's sawing bones in a coffin" (*The Dwarfs*: 69).

During Pinter's last years, Dame Mitsuko Ushida, the eminent Japanese-born pianist and conductor and foremost interpreter of Mozart's piano works, with her partner, the diplomat Sir Robert Cooper, become close friends and frequent visitors at Pinter's home. Indeed, one of the last concerts the Pinters attended, according to his "Appointment Diaries," was to hear Mitsuko Uchida perform Mozart's Piano Concerto No. 27 at the Barbican on Sunday September 30, 2007 (*Chronology*: 302; for Ushido and Cooper's visits see 359, 340). According to Antonia, they "had wonderful seats from where we could see her miraculous hands." She added that "it may be the last concert Harold ever goes to (the physical strain of reaching the auditorium was so great) but what a concert!" (*Must*: 316).

When Antonia was a guest on the BBC radio program *Desert Island Discs*, broadcast on Sunday July 27, 2008, she was asked her personal selections of recordings to take if she were cast away on an imaginary desert island. Her eighth and final choice was the final movement of Mozart's 23rd Piano Concerto performed by Mitsuko Uchida. Antonia has been a castaway twice on the program. On the first occasion on June 2, 1969, her final choice and favorite was different: Beethoven's 9th Symphony. Pinter was a guest only once on the program, on June 14, 1965. His eight choices were eclectic. He chose three Bach works: the fourth Brandenburg Concerto in G major, the sixth Brandenburg in B flat major, and the Orchestral Suite No 3 in D major with Janos Starker as the cello soloist. He chose four jazz pieces: Charlie Parker's "Funky Blues"; the Modern Jazz Quartet playing "Pyramid"; Thelonious Monk and Gerry Mulligan's "Round Midnight"; and Charlie Parker's Reboppers "Flamenco Sketches." Pinter's eighth and final choice, the castaway's favorite, was Beethoven's String Quartet No 15 in A minor, Opus. 132. This work is Antonia's seventh choice for her second castaway session.[64] On July 27, 2008, Pinter and Antonia listened to her *Desert Island Discs* choices, which "delighted" Pinter, who "was immensely touched" with her choice of Beethoven's Opus 132—Pinter's "favourite [sic] piece of music" (*Must:* 316, 322).

Pinter's relationship with Antonia nurtured his love for music and, combined with his creative success, presented him with the additional opportunity to attend with her operatic performances at Covent Garden, Glyndebourne, the London Coliseum, and elsewhere. These reflected his eclectic taste both for contemporary and classical composition. For instance, on the evening of Wednesday May 7, 1969, he attended a performance of Pierre Boulez's "Pli Selon Pli" at the Royal Festival Hall. He was particularly interested in the work of Harrison Birtwistle. Birtwistle, under Peter Hall, became head of music at the National Theatre and wrote the music for Pinter's direction of Giraudoux's *The Trojan War Will Not Take Place*. On May 14, 1976, Pinter and Birtwistle met at 6 p.m. to discuss music for Pinter's upcoming production of William Archibald's *The Innocents*, and on August 30, 1976, they lunched together. On January 21, 1983 at 5:30 p.m., Pinter went to the September 2, 1987 tribute to Birtwistle at the Queen Elizabeth Hall beginning at 7:45 p.m. On June 8, 1991 at Covent Garden, Pinter heard Birtwistle's *Gawain* opera. The final public musical experience that Pinter was well enough to attend was on Saturday March 15, 2008, when he went with Antonia to Birtwistle's two-act opera *The Minotaur* at Covent Garden (*Chronology:* 337).

A twentieth-century British composer who seems to have had a particular fascination for Pinter is Benjamin Britten: both were conscientious objectors. Pinter went outside of London and the Home Counties to hear Britten's work. Britten's dramatic subjects appealed to Pinter to such extent that, in the early months of 1994, he contemplated directing the Glyndebourne production of Britten's rarely heard "pacifist" operatic adaptation of Henry James's short story *Owen Wingrave*. The initial record in Pinter's "Appointment Diaries" of hearing Britten was on Sunday July 5, 1981, when he went to Glyndebourne to see *A Midsummer Night's Dream*, an opera that he experienced again on the evening of 21 21, June 1995 at the London Coliseum. During Pinter's stay in Suffolk with the novelist Angus Wilson and his partner Tony Garrett, Pinter went to Aldeburgh to see Britten's *The Turn of the Screw* on Saturday June 11, 1983. He saw this opera on two further occasions: at the Barbican on the evening of October 4, 1997 and at Glyndebourne on the evening of October 24, 2000. On the evening of March 4, 1988, Pinter (and Antonia?) heard Britten's *Billy Budd* at the Coliseum. They (?) also saw the opera at the same venue on the evening of October 3, 1991 and also in Bristol during the evening of April 7, 1998 in a performance by the Welsh National Opera. Pinter saw *Peter Grimes* five times at evening performances: on June 11, 1988 at Covent Garden; April 20, 1991 at the Coliseum; at Glyndebourne on June 16, 1992; on April 22, 1995 at Covent Garden; and at the Coliseum on March 30, 1999. He saw the rarely performed Britten opera *Death in Ven-*

ice during the evening of March 21, 1992 at Covent Garden. In Leeds on January 13, 1994, Pinter heard another rarely performed Britten opera, *Gloriana*, with its William Plomer libretto based on Lytton Strachey's 1928 biography *Elizabeth and Essex: A Tragic History*. Pinter recorded attending two live performances of Britten's *The War Requiem*: at the Royal Festival Hall on November 15, 1988 and at the Royal Albert Hall on February 21, 1993 (both performances were evening ones: *Chronology*: 338). Antonia writes that toward the end of her husband's life, on November 9, 2008, they listened on Radio 3 to *The War Requiem*. She "found tears pouring down [her] face at" Wilfred Owen's line "I am the enemy you killed, my friend." She adds that "Harold, who did not, I think, notice, wept silently at 'Let us sleep now.'" It may have been at the back of their minds that on August 7, 2004, Pinter was "awarded the Wilfred Owen prize, specifically for *War*, the pamphlet and for his services to the anti-war cause" (*Must*: 325, 276).

One of Pinter's final creative works was a just under half-an-hour collaboration with British composer James Clarke, with whom, in the words of Alice Jones, he shared "similar tastes in music, including admiration for the work of the contemporary French composer Pierre Boulez." Clarke describes Boulez as "precise and economical."[65] *Voices*, broadcast on BBC Radio 3 on October 10, 2005 in honor of Pinter's seventy-fifth birthday, has nine actors, solo musicians, and an orchestra. It features Pinter's text completed in 2000, which, in the words of Harry Derbyshire, expresses Pinter's "political concerns through artistic means" and depicts a universe "of public terror, nightmare and persecution" in a "complexly textured soundscape of brutalisers and brutalised."[66] Writing on *Voices*, Jones relates that the work initiated with a 1996 letter from Clarke to Pinter written after Clarke saw *Ashes to Ashes*. Following a meeting in 1997, Pinter recalls that they decided on collaboration. Pinter told Jones that they both walked together into hell—the hell that they all share here and now. Jones adds that the Pinter "plays from which he has culled his lines share a preoccupation with the power relationship between bully and victim, torturer and tortured, master and slave. Against a backdrop of unspecified totalitarian states, Pinter focuses on interrogators, torturers and guards and their violent mistreatment of innocent prisoners."[67]

The relationship between music, politics, and religion engaged Pinter in his last years. In *Must*, Antonia relates that when she and Pinter were staying at Westbrook House Dorset during August 2008, they heard "an exquisite late-night Prom of Bach Cantatas" and "discussed whether Bach's belief in God validated Him." The answer from Pinter's point of view was in the negative, Antonia's in the positive. Her "point . . . is that Bach's belief in God does mean that Harold (who worships Bach as God) can't dismiss all people who believe in God as hopeless nincompoops." She then adds that she "wouldn't care if Bach voted for Mussolini, this is the most perfect music I have ever heard." For Antonia, "it's the old

Wagner-the-anti-Semite argument: does Wagner's anti-Semitism stop him being personally great? Yes. Does it stop his music being great? No" (*Must*: 315).

Similar issues are explored in Ronald Harwood's *Taking Sides*, which Pinter directed.[68] Pinter's "Appointment Diaries" record him as seeing five Wagner operas. He went with Antonia on August 22, 1987 to *Tristan and Isolde* at the Coliseum and also saw it at the same venue on March 16, 1996. On October 14, 1990, he went to Covent Garden, probably with Antonia, to *Die Walküre*, and also at the Garden on February 19, 1991 to *Götterdämmerung*. Other Wagner operas he heard at Covent Garden include *Die Meistersinger* on November 13, 1993 and on February 17, 1997 *Lohengrin* (*Chronology*: 360).

Pinter's love of music went back to his formative years. In a letter to Woolf postmarked "September 16, 1948," Pinter writes of hearing an "overpowering performance of" Beethoven's Grosse Fugue performed by the BBC (Symphony Orchestra) conducted by Rafael Kubelik. Pinter refers to some of the works of Beethoven's last period as transcending art and adds that the same can be said of Mozart. At the time, he found a recording of the "liebestod" from Wagner's *Tristan and Isolde* overpowering.[69]

Pinter's "Appointment Diaries" record from 1970 to 2008 regular attendance at Covent Garden and the Coliseum. The first attendance at the Royal Opera House was to Michael Tippett's *The Knot Garden*, directed by Peter Hall on December 2, 1970, and the last for an opera by another modern composer, Harrison Birtwistle's *The Minotaur* on March 15, 2008. The first visit to the Coliseum was to an evening ballet, again a modern one, Maurice Béjart's *Ballet of the 20th Century* with the music of Karlheinz Stockhausen. The last recorded visit is to a late twentieth-century opera, *Nixon in China* by John Adams. He saw it with Antonia for a second time in June 2007. Pinter first heard it at Covent Garden on June 17, 2000 (*Chronology*: 359, 336, 53, 335).

Harold and Antonia heard the well-known standard operatic repertory ranging from Beethoven, Bellini, Berlioz, Giordano, Gluck, Gounod, Handel, Mozart, Mussorgsky to Puccini, Rossini, Tchaikovsky, and Verdi. Interestingly, apart from hearing Rostropovitch perform at the Barbican on October 27, 1990 and some other exceptions, apparently Pinter attended few purely orchestral concerts. The exceptions were piano recitals by his friends Alfred Brendel and Mitsuko Uchida. Also somewhat surprisingly, given Pinter's long-standing friendship with the musically obsessed Mick Goldstein with his love for string quartets, Pinter made infrequent visits to London's Wigmore Hall, the leading venue for chamber music. On September 30, 1975, he attended a piano recital, and on December 14 of the same year, a guitar recital by Simon Munting. He heard Mitsuko Uchido in a Mozart piano recital on the evening of June 15, 1982. The first recital recorded that Pinter attended at which she performed was a Sunday afternoon Chopin recital at the Queen Elizabeth Hall on December 9, 1979. On the evening of July 6, 1999, Pinter went to a concert of music by his beloved Bach at the Wigmore Hall, and his final recorded visit there was again to hear Mitsuko perform on February 2, 2000 (*Chronology*: 57, 116, 94, 252, 256). In short, all the evidence points to a deep and abiding passion and love for music, especially opera—a passion and love that almost stands alongside that for cricket.

NOTES

1. https://www.theguardian.com/culture/2008/dec/26/harold-pinter-final-interview%20accessed%2014%20October%202016.
2. BLADDMSS: 89094/3.
3. BLADDMSS: 88880/7/15.
4. "Beware Bouncers," *LRB* (blog), November 27, 2014.
5. http://www.haroldpinter.org/cricket/theteam2.shtml%20Accessed%2026%20May%202016.
6. BLADDMSS: 88880/7/14.
7. BLADDMSS: 88880/7/14.
8. BLADDMSS: 88880/7/14; Pinter to Judy Cachart of Whitby, Ontio.
9. Pinter to Paloma Fraser: BLADDMSS: 88880/7/14.
10. Personal communication, April 17, 2013; cf. *Chronology*: 311.
11. https://en.wikipedia.org/wiki/Joe_Hardstaff,_Jr., accessed May 27, 2016.
12. https://en.wikipedia.org/wiki/Reg_Simpson, accessed May 27, 2017.
13. "The Ashes is a Test cricket series played between England's cricket team and Australia's national cricket team. The Ashes are regarded as being held by the team that most recently won the Test series." See https://en.wikipedia.org/wiki/The_Ashes, accessed May 14, 2017.
14. Alan Ross (1922–2001). See https://en.wikipedia.org/wiki/Alan_Ross, accessed May 14, 2017.
15. *Daily Telegraph Magazine*, May 16, 1969: 25.
16. BLADDMSS: 89094/1.
17. See Baker, "Harold Pinter's Library," 254.
18. "Harold Pinter OM" in Brian Johnston, *A Further Slice of Johnners*. Barry Johnston, ed., London: Virgin Books, 2002: 306.
19. BLADDMSS: 89094/1.
20. *Guardian*, November 29, 2014.
21. BLADDMSS: 88880/5/4.
22. BLADDMSS: 88880/4/17.
23. *Daily Telegraph Magazine*, May 16, 1969: 26.
24. BLADDMSS: 89094/1.
25. 1922–1986; in 1956 he became a legend taking 19 wickets for 90 runs at the Old Trafford Manchester Test Match against the Australians.
26. *Daily Telegraph Magazine*, May 16, 1969: 25–26.
27. https://en.wikipedia.org/wiki/Keith_Miller, accessed May 29, 2016.
28. BLADDMSS: 89094/1.
29. https://en.wikipedia.org/wiki/Arthur_Morris_with_the_Australian_cricket_team_in_England_in_1948, accessed May 15, 2017.
30. BLADDMSS: 89094/1.
31. See https://en.mwikipedia.org/wiki/Jack_Ikin, accessed May 31, 2016.
32. BLADDMSS: 88920/5/2.
33. Neil Harvey, more noted for being an attractive left-handed batsman than his right-arm off spin bowling, played in seventy-nine Test Matches for Australia between

1948 and 1963; see https://en.mwikipedia.org/Neil_Harvey%20Consulted%2031 %20May%202016.

34. "Tom Graveney, cricketer obituary, Daily Telegraph (November 3, 2015), accessed May 30, 2016. For Fred Trueman (1931–2006) see https://en.wikipedia.org/wiki/ Fred_Trueman, accessed May 15, 2017.

35. BLADDMSS: 88920/5/2.

36. BLADDMSS: 88920/5/2.

37. https://en.wikipedia.org/wiki/Frank_Woolley, accessed May 31, 2016. For David Gower (1957–) see https://en.wikipedia.org/wiki/David_Gower, accessed May 15, 2017; and for Jim Parks see https://en.wikipedia.org/wiki/Jim_Parks_(cricketer,_born_ 1931), accessed May 15, 2017.

38. Revealing his "cantankerous nature," Pinter in 1966 told a schoolboy inquirer that "Davies papers were in Sidcup because that's where they are." http://www. telegraph.co.uk/culture/7902767/Harold-Pinter-sent-sarcastic-letter-to-pupils-who-sought-hidden-meaning-in-his-plays.html, accessed April 18, 2017.

39. BLADDMSS: 88920/5/2.

40. BLADDMSS: 88920/5/2.

41. BLADDMSS: 89094/3; see https://en.wikipedia.org/wiki/The_Brothers_Karamaz ov#Major_characters, accessed April 19, 2017. For Archie MacLaren (1871–1944) see https://en.wikipedia.org/wiki/Archie_MacLaren, accessed May 15, 2017.

42. BLADDMSS: 89094/3.

43. BLADDMSS: 89094/2. For Ray Lindwall (1921–1996) see https://en.wikipedia. org/wiki/Ray_Lindwall; Lindsay Hassett (1913–1993) see https://en.wikipedia.org/ wiki/Lindsay_Hassett; Cyril Washbrook (1914–1999) see https://en.wikipedia.org/ wiki/Cyril_Washbrook; Don Kenyon(1924–1996) see https://en.wikipedia.org/wiki/ Don_Kenyon; Trevor Bailey (1923–2011) see https://en.wikipedia.org/wiki/Trevor_ Bailey; accessed May 15, 2017.

44. BLADDMSS: 88880/7/10.

45. For Arthur Wellard (1902–1980), see Arunabha Sengupta, http://www. cricketcountry.com/articles/arthur-wellard-one-of-the-biggest-hitters-in-the-game-who-twice-pummelled-five-sixes-in-an-over-24991, accessed May 27, 2016; and for Wally Hammond (1903–1965) see https://en.wikipedia.org/wiki/Wally_Hammond; Harold Larwood (1904–1995) see https://en.wikipedia.org/wiki/Harold_Larwood; for Jack Badcock (1914–1982) see https://en.wikipedia.org/wiki/Jack_Badcock; all accessed May 15, 2017.

46. BLADDMSS: 88880/7/10.

47. BR: E51, G117; full transcript available on http://www.haroldpinter.org.

48. BBC "TMS [Test Match Special] Podcast, The Meaning of Cricket with Jon Hotten," from a BBC "Test Match Special" lunchtime—"Ed Smith is joined by author Jon Hotten to discuss his latest book"—August 4, 2016. For Mike Brearley (1942–) see https://en.wikipedia.org/wiki/Mike_Brearley, accessed May 15, 2017.

49. See chapter 6.

50. *The Letters of Samuel Beckett: Volume IV, 1966-1989*: 339–40 and n.2. For Frank Woolley (1887–1978) see https://en.wikipedia.org/wiki/Frank_Woolley; for Edward A. MacDonald (1891–1937) see http://adb.anu.edu.au/biography/mcdonald-edgar-arthur-ted-7336; for Jack Gregory (1895–1973) see https://en.wikipedia.org/wiki/Jack_ Gregory_(cricketer); accessed May 15, 2017.

51. See *The Letters of Samuel Beckett: Volume IV, 1966–1989*: 403–4 and note 1. For Hirst (George Hirst, 1871–1954) see https://en.wikipedia.org/wiki/George_Hirst; Spooner (Dick Spooner, 1919–1997) see https://en.wikipedia.org/wiki/Dick_Spooner, and/or Reggie Spooner (1880–1961) see https://en.wikipedia.org/wiki/Reggie_Spooner; Foster (Frank Foster, 1889–1958) see https://en.wikipedia.org/wiki/Frank_Foster_ (cricketer); Briggs (Johnny Briggs, 1862–1902) see https://en.wikipedia.org/wiki/ Johnny_Briggs_(cricketer); accessed May 15, 2017.

52. *Studies in Theatre and Performance*, 2011, Vol. 31, i: 5–15.

53. In his "Playing cricket shots in my mind: Cricket and the drama of Harold Pinter," *Studies in Theatre and Performance*. 2011. Vol. 31, i: 17–31.

54. BLADDMSS: 88920/5/2.

55. BLADDMSS: 88920/1/8.

56. See Neil Sinyard, *Jack Clayton*, Manchester University Press, 2000: 225–28.

57. http://www.telegraph.co.uk/culture/theatre/drama/3666531/Ping-pong-with-Pinter.html, accessed October 16, 2016.

58. My reference is to *Ashes to Ashes and Other Plays*, New York: Dramatists Play Service, 2008: 57.

59. In Peter Raby ed., *The Cambridge Companion to Harold Pinter*, second edition, 2009, 310–11.

60. Ibid., 310–11.

61. https://www.theguardian.com/culture/2008/dec/26/harold-pinter-final-interview, accessed October 14, 2016.

62. http://www.theparisreview.org/interviews/4351/the-art-of-theater-no-3-harold-pinter, accessed November 7, 2016.

63. http://www.nytimes.com/2009/01/10/arts/dance/10pint.html?pagewanted=all&_r=0, accessed November 7, 2016.

64. See http//www.bbc.co.uk/radio4/features/desert-island discs/find-a-castaway, accessed November 7, 2016.

65. Alice Jones, "Voices," *The Independent*, October 7, 2005, http://www.independent.co.uk/voices, accessed November 9, 2015.

66. Derbyshire, "Pinter as Celebrity" in *The Cambridge Companion to Harold Pinter* second edition, Peter Raby, ed., 2009: 268; Mary Luckhurst "Speaking Out: Harold Pinter and Freedom of Expression" in Raby: 116; also citing Billington speaking in a post-broadcast interview to *Voices*, BBC Radio 3, October 10, 2005: 119.

67. Alice Jones, "Voices," *The Independent*, October 7, 2005, http://www.independent.co.uk/voices, accessed November 9, 2015; and cf. chapter 5 of the present work.

68. See chapter 5.

69. BLADDMSS: 89094/1/3.

THREE

Restaurants and Friendships

An important facet of Pinter's personality is his fascination with food, restaurants, and dining out and his capacity for friendship. The two— eating in restaurants and friendships—are intertwined and put to artistic use in his work. This third chapter places Pinter within an approximately seven-mile radius of his home(s), from his early upbringing in the East End to his move to West London and Campden Hill Square, focusing on his choices of where to eat and with whom. Pinter regarded many friendships as sacrosanct, including friendships with his old mates from childhood such as Michael (Mick) Goldstein, as well as dining partners including Simon Gray, Ronald Harwood, John Casey, and Tom Stoppard, among others. Pinter, in fact, was very sociable in spite of appearances to the contrary and the social ineptness of many of his characters, especially in his early dramas. Pinter used restaurants for business, creative, and clandestine meetings. An examination of restaurants and friendships reveals Pinter's progress from pub-crawling in the East End and also in provincial towns where he appeared in repertory theatre to dining at some of the most sophisticated and expensive London restaurants. His final play, *Celebration*, is set in a posh upscale restaurant, a different world from the East End cafés of his youth, and reflects its author's own journey.

In Pinter's work, there is a clear distinction between private and public eating. The former usually occurs in the form of breakfast or, as in the *Homecoming*, in the manner of eating on a daily basis in which those who serve are transformed by the end of the drama into those who are served. In other words, those who are dominant at the start of play—those who are served—become by its end subservient to those who have served. Basic breakfasts in earlier works consist, for instance, of cornflakes or toast and tea. Meals mutate, in later work, into champagne (the drink of the wealthy), caviar, Dover sole, and other expensive delicacies. The frustrations expressed by servers in the early *The Dumb Waiter* are transformed in his last play, *Celebration*, into the poetic meanderings of the waiter expecting an expensive tip.

THE DWARFS

Pinter's only novel, *The Dwarfs*, is dated at its conclusion "1952-1956 Revised 1989" (183). Clearly autobiographical, it reflects themes running throughout Pinter's work: the politics among people and the conscious or unconscious struggle for dominance, power, and position between them. It also includes conversational non sequiturs, interrogative questions, staccato utterances, London topographical references, the naming of various works of art, artists, and cultural icons. These extend from Johann Sebastian Bach to Shakespeare to T. S. Eliot, among others. Cultural and other innuendos and direct references move swiftly from the sublime to the ridiculous, from the mood of Shakespearean tragedy to that of the local musical hall. In the private world or spaces in which the characters live in Pinter's novel, there are teapots, loaves of bread, kettles, and ordinary London tap water. The public world, as in Pinter's life, is not that of the expensive restaurants that he subsequently frequented when successful.

In *The Dwarfs*, there are innumerable references to food and its appurtenances such as cups and saucers. The female figure in the novel is Virginia, or "Ginni." Mark and Pete—based on Ron Percival, Pinter's fierce rival for girls when young—fight for possession over her. Ginni usually collects the cups and saucers and does the washing up. Henry Woolf in his *Barcelona is in Trouble* writes of the "beautiful, devilish Ron who could hypnotise twelve girls at once" (39). Pinter was at odds with Percival, who was one of the main reasons why Pinter had been feeling so awful, as he confesses in an autumn 1948 letter to Woolf. He complains to Woolf of Percival's admiration of Russia.[1] This is ironic in hindsight, given Percival's subsequent racism and alignment with extreme right wing positions, but does reveal a consistency in his advocacy and attraction to extremist positions.

The novel opens with Pete and Len in their flat/apartment: "Pete waited for the kettle to boil, poured water into the teapot and took it into the living room, where he set two cups on the table." Roles are reversed when Len pours the tea; however, Pete brings the milk and is unable to find any sugar. They inhabit a domestic world of cups of tea and loaves of bread. Subsequently, there are suggestions of cocoa and bagels (46). The text refers to various kinds of tea, such as "Black tea. Pure tea" (9) and "lemon tea and a canopy" in Pete's fantasy (62). A glass of tea becomes a sexual prop at Virginia's, a part of her attraction (98). The characters inhabit public spaces including cafés such as "the Swan Café," where Pete and Mark meet Virginia, who "sat back, tapping her spoon on the table" (80–81). At Virginia's flat/apartment, cups of tea are consumed and Virginia chews crumbs (85). In their private world, interestingly, Len uses a food metaphor to describe his reactions to poetry as being "like the old women eating onions and knitting when the guillotine falls." Further, he describes writing, the process of writing a poem, in terms of getting up, squeezing "a lemon, a drop of juice comes out, and that's the poem" (97). At an unspecified public place for a picnic, nobody clears up anything; the remainders are left for the rats, whose "ratsteak" becomes a gruesome metaphor for life (106). The dessert at the picnic along the "east bank of the river" was not lavish, just "cheese and biscuits" (108). In his own private world, the omniscient narrator (Pinter) describes Len and Mark as settling "down for the night with ginger beer and a doughnut" (120). At Sonia's, "Mark skated through eggshells, potatopeel and baconrind to kiss her" (128). It is unclear whether the speaker is Mark or Sonia (probably Mark) when he says, "[G]ive me a pigfoot and a bottle of gin, slay me cause I'm in my sin. Slay me cause I'm full of gin" (129).

PUBS

An obvious public place is the pub (in the opening scene of *Betrayal*, Emma and Jerry meet at a pub). The pub is the setting for an early poem called "New Year in the Midlands," dated "1950" and written during Pinter's time in rep when he frequents a "Whitbread Ale town" and "the yellow pub" where he drinks "ambrosial bitter weed." The noisy pub is filled with miscellaneous people driven by lust including the landlady Freda, a prostitute, "Sailor boys," and "Young men and old" (*VV*: 119). All appear to enjoy the festivities celebrating the arrival of the New Year that no doubt Pinter celebrated on many occasions in similar towns where he managed to pick up acting work for short periods, such as Chesterfield, where he appeared in the Christmas pantomime. In a letter to Henry Woolf from May 1954, Pinter describes a meeting with his friend Barry Foster, with whom he acted in rep, and Jimmy Law from school days. Jimmy was drunk; they got thrown out of two pubs and spent the night "kipping" on a friend's floor.[2]

The Dwarfs depicts, to use Francis Gillen's words, "the passionate, personal discussions of Shakespeare, art, philosophy, friendship and love"[3] that are not only fictionally depicted and also dramatized in the one-act *monologue* but are also a reflection of Pinter's life in his late teens and the immediate years after he left school. This is a world not of fancy restaurants but of working-class pubs, of bed sits, of landladies and their food: of tea, beer, potato peel, bacon rind, doughnuts, and toast. It's a world, too, of betrayal, of close friendship and disillusionment. Jennifer

Mortimer, upon whom Virginia in the novel was based, recalled this period of Pinter's life. She knew Pinter "since he was fourteen when I met him and the others at the Hackney Club. As a group they were terribly tight-knit, very loyal and extremely admired . . . if I was educated, it was by sitting around in cafés in Hackney listening to them all talking. They talked about and quoted Shakespeare all the time." She added that *The Dwarfs* "is absolutely how it was even to the moment when Ron [Percival] flung a book at me for daring to quote from *Hamlet*. . . . The real fight was over the fact that Harold was that much more powerful as a person and Ron was fighting this because he wanted to be king" (Billington: 59).

LOCALS OF THE EARLY YEARS

In "The Queen of all the Fairies," Pinter's unpublished autobiographical memoir of the Hackney of his formative years, Pinter describes Hackney as an East End satellite that was replete with milk bars, Italian cafés, tailors, and barber shops. It was a place where younger people gathered outside the delicatessen and one Jewish saloon. Christians, on the other hand, hung around the pubs and fish-and-chip shops.

The Café Torino

Pinter writes of the Café Torino in Compton Street,[4] located at the corner of Old Compton Street and Dean Street, with a large, ten-foot mannequin perched above the door. Café Torino was a favored café for many of the art sects prevalent in London in the mid-1950s. According to reminiscences: "Officially, it was a restaurant serving pizza, spaghetti and risotto, but you could talk for hours over a small cup of coffee."[5] By the late 1940s, "milk bars had evolved to include not only groceries, but also became places where young people could buy ready-made food, non-alcoholic drinks and could socialise. Milk bars often used to include jukeboxes, pinball machines—later upgraded to video games, with tables and chairs to encourage patrons to linger and spend more money."[6]

Quentin Crisp

Pinter writes, too,[7] of an initial meeting with Quentin Crisp (real name Dennis Charles Pratt), a writer and subsequently gay icon and frequenter of Bohemian Soho. Crisp is associated with food and images of food. They met in the summer of 1955 at the ground-floor flat of an actress friend Veronica Nugent; the flat was part of a house in Fulham in West London. In the words of Paul Bailey, Crisp "lived in a variety of furnished rooms before settling into 129 Beaufort Street, where Chelsea meets Fulham. The room he occupied on the first floor became famous for its squalor, since he had at an early age abandoned the housewifely duties of cleaning and dusting. It inspired Harold Pinter to write his first play, *The Room*."[8] Written two years later, the image at its opening is that of a solitary silent man. Pinter recalls that "a large man, wearing a cap, was sitting at a table reading a comic," and a woman is fussing around him cooking him bacon and eggs. Pinter recalls that also present was Crisp, "a small man who smiled and waved from the stove." Crisp, or as Pinter refers to him, "Q.C. . . . slapped the bacon and eggs onto a plate"; he then took "the plate to the table, placed it, poured tea into a cup, cut a chunk of bread, buttered it, all the while chatting away merrily to us." The other man in the room began "to eat, his comic propped up in front of him. His name was never disclosed and" he "never looked up." Crisp conducts a monologue as he continually cuts and butters more bread and pours more tea, shoveling salt and sauce over what was left of his egg. Pinter clearly didn't forget this scene in the room.[9]

Eating Places and Their Associations

Eating places, including pubs, are associated with friendships, business, meeting actors from Pinter's past, and lovers. In an early poem called "School Life," dated 1948, Pinter refers to "Cold glasses" and meetings in "the Ritz bar"—probably the bar of the local Ritz, as opposed to the very expensive West End hotel. "The Ritz" at that time was a common name for a cinema in British towns. In his last lines in the poem, Pinter mentions wanting his dinner and to "poetasters. | From the Greek?" The question mark adds to the ambiguity of the lines: Is the reference to the ancient Greek, or to a Greek restaurant or café, or to both?

The earliest mentions of the "pub" in Pinter's "Appointment Diaries" occur when he moves from Worthing on the Sussex coast to London. On Tuesday May 10, 1966, he attended a PEN dinner at the Cock Tavern, Fleet Street. Recognition and success and, above all, friendships are reflected in different eating places. A few months previously, on January 18, 1966, he met with one of his oldest friends, Michael (Mick) Goldstein, at Ward's Irish House (*Chronology*: 21, 19). According to Ian Nairn in his *Nairn's London* (1966), the Irish House was "a basement under the angle between Shaftesbury Avenue and Coventry Street. It is not trying to be Irish; it just is. A big, bare room with a central zinc-topped bar; no concession to comfort, but on the other hand some of the best draught Guinness in London. . . . It has surely got the fairies on it, though mentioning fairies in this rough, shabby, real place you might get some strange looks."[10]

Mick Goldstein

Over the years, Pinter didn't specify meeting places—with some exceptions. The exceptions are from Pinter's later years and reflect the longevity and closeness of friendships with, for instance, Mick Goldstein. Twice they met at Cibo's and at Orsino's, on each occasion for lunch at 1 p.m. On November 4, 2003, in what must've been one of their last meetings prior to Pinter's death, the venue was Cibo's. An Italian restaurant near Holland Park, located at 3 Russell Gardens, London W 14, it reveals Pinter's predilection for Italian cuisine and intimate atmospheric restaurants. They also met at Orsino's, a small, contemporary trattoria serving Italian/Neapolitan dishes and a selection of homemade desserts, located in South Kensington at 8A Thurloe Place, London SW7 2RX. Both restaurants appear to have been favorites of Pinter's, especially for meeting close friends, as may be seen from the number of lunches and dinners eaten there recorded in his "Diaries." Both restaurants have excellent Italian wine selections (*Chronology*: 371–72, 237). Unfortunately, Pinter records the location of meetings but not what is discussed over lunch or an evening meal.

Born in 1930, the same year as Pinter, Mick Goldstein was the dedicatee of four of Pinter's works: *Other Places: Three Plays* (1982); *Other Places: Four Plays* (1984); *Poems* (1968); and *Poems, Second Edition with Nine Added Poems* (1971). Their friendship lasted for over half a century and they regularly corresponded. Goldstein and Pinter didn't go to the same school, Hackney Downs; Mick went to the Raine's Foundation School. Both were very keen table-tennis players at the Hackney Boys' Club. As a member of what Woolf called "Harold's Gang," Mick and Pinter were very close. In fact, Len Weinstein, the music-loving porter in *The Dwarfs*, is probably based on Goldstein's personality. In his memoir *Barcelona is in Trouble*, Woolf describes Pinter as "my very own mucker, mate and bosom pal" and describes Goldstein as "the Talmudic violinist whose mystic moments were a perfect cover drive or a double check-mate at chess" (134, 39). Pinter sought Goldstein's advice in the early 1950s during the period when he was close to marrying Pauline Flanagan. During school holidays, he and Pinter would go to Lord's to see the opening game of the cricket season. After having settled in Australia and when returning to London to visit, Goldstein would meet with Pinter. Following Pinter's death, Goldstein became an important source of recollections for Pinter's early years. In the summer of 1990, Pinter sent Goldstein a pre-publication copy of *The Dwarf*—Faber published it in early October 1990 (see BR: D8a). Goldstein was completely engrossed in its reenactment of "those times so long ago, and yet ever present to me." They are "etched" in his "brain." He writes to Pinter: "What a strong pong the book has."

In the early twentieth-first century, Goldstein recalled conversations with Michael Billington. Pinter and his mates encountered, in the immediate post-war period, Fascist thugs on Ridley Road in the East End of London. On one particular occasion, he and Pinter were walking behind their friends Woolf, Moishe (Morris) Wernick, and Jimmy Law. Goldstein and Pinter were just missed by a huge onion that had been hurled at them by at least six thugs. Pinter, according to Goldstein, stood his ground and turned to face them while Goldstein went to seek help from the others who by now were around the corner in Dalston Lane. Some of the Fascists had bicycle chains, while others were carrying jagged-edged broken milk bottles. Jimmy Law bravely stood with Pinter, breaking the ring of the attackers. Fortunately, a trolleybus slowed to round the corner, and Pinter and his friends managed to get on it and away (cf. Billington: 18).

Letters to and from Goldstein extend from July 1953, when Pinter was in rep in Tipperary, until 2003. In a letter dated July 7, 1953, Pinter responded enthusiastically to reading both parts of *Henry IV*. He has enjoyed the reading as much as any Shakespeare and finds the prose extraordinary. On July 29, he told Goldstein that he has penned a prose poem evoked by Mistress Overdone's question ("What's his offense?") to Pompey in *Measure for Measure* in Act One Scene 2:

> POMPEY Yonder man is carried to prison. MISTRESS OVERDONE Well; what has he done? POMPEY A woman. MISTRESS OVERDONE But what's his offense? POMPEY Groping for trouts in a peculiar river.

Unfortunately, Pinter's prose poem has disappeared. The letters to and from Goldstein not only reveal Pinter's literary enthusiasms such as his discovery of Beckett, but they also reveal his seeking Goldstein's advice on literary matters and the progress he is making on his own work (see chapter 6). A single instance will suffice. In *Various Voices*, there is the text of "Latest Reports from the Stock Exchange." This was written in response to an *Evening Standard* headline reading "Gottwald in Coma" — a reference to Klement Gottwald (1896–1953), the Czech Communist leader and prime minister who died on March 14, 953 from a burst artery shortly after attending the funeral of Stalin in Moscow on March 9, 1953. Pinter also wrote the piece in response to his "general mystification at the stock exchange reports in the . . . presses of the national newspapers" (*Various Voices*: 82). In his original version, Pinter referred to the anti-Semitic reference to Jewish people as "kike." Goldstein recalled how at a much later date, and specifically at a Gaieties-against-Hampstead cricket match around 1990, Pinter asked Goldstein's opinion as to whether or not he should change the "kike." Goldstein's advice was not to change anything, advice that Pinter didn't take. The printed text refers twice to the less pejorative "Jews" in the newspaper headline (*VV*: 84). In January 1994, Pinter was in New York for David Jones's production of *No Man's Land* on January 28; he and Antonia flew to Mexico City the next day, then to Oaxaca from February 2 to 4 where they stayed in a hotel that was a converted convent (*Must*: 230). Then they went to Puerto Vallarta for four days before returning to Mexico City and arriving back in London on February 11. In a letter sent before they left London, Pinter asked Goldstein if he has a copy of what Pinter referred to as "Last reports from the Stock Exchange." If Goldstein has a copy and Pinter hasn't seen it for what must be forty years, he'd love to have a copy. In a note written three years later, dated January 21, 1997, Goldstein noted that he has seen the changed text and that the word "Reds" has replaced "kikes" in the lines "Reds scoring against the clock" and "The Reds have cleaned out the sheep pens and are seven up with three to go" (*Various Voices*: 83), which is most appropriate.

In their correspondence, Pinter reveals details concerning his relationships with women. For instance, on November 30, 1955, he mentioned that Jill Johnson, with whom he acted in repertory in Ireland, would not be accompanying him to Colchester, where he was to perform in repertory. Following his marriage to Vivien Merchant on September 14, 1956, he wrote to Goldstein from Bournemouth that he and Vivien have settled together (March 28, 1956). He requested that Goldstein wrap up texts he has ordered on Pinter's behalf, such as Beckett and Proust. Interestingly, in letters to Goldstein, Pinter evokes memories from their cultural past that they have a less than reverential attitude to. He describes the sky as "a cross between Rabbi Ben Ezra and Tintorelli [*sic*]." This is followed by an invitation to Goldstein to visit him in Bournemouth, where Goldstein can smell the rhododendrons. Pinter then reported that Vivian was ill following a dental treatment for two impacted wisdom teeth and that she now drinks Guinness. In another 1956 letter, Pinter played upon multiple meanings of the Yiddish word "shamus," a watch man in the Synagogue. In cockney, it's slang for a "copper" or policeman, or perhaps even the Irish name "Seamus" and the word's associations with the Pope.

In a letter dated December 11, 1960 to Goldstein, Pinter apologized concerning his apparent rudeness and abruptness, a characteristic for which he became noted in his public persona. In fact, in private and to friends such as Goldstein and other members of the Hackney gang, he was unstinting in his time. He wrote to Goldstein concerning the poet and fellow East Ender Emanuel Litvinoff (1915–2011), whom Pinter appeared to have offended. Litvinoff had spent his childhood moving from one grim tenement flat to another in Whitechapel, Bethnal Green, Hackney, and Dalston. Litvinoff's worn-down mother haunts the pages of his powerful autobiography *Journey through a Small Planet* (1972) with its "vivid re-creation of the variety and complexity of Jewish life in the East End during the inter-war years." Somewhat sarcastically, Pinter told Goldstein that he was "contrite to hear about Litvinoff" and asked Goldstein that if he saw Litvinoff, he should assure him that Pinter meant no offense. He wouldn't dream of offending anyone in a million years—least of all, in a reference to Litvinoff, a rabbi (in fact, Litvinoff was not a rabbi). In view of Pinter's subsequent legal and other battles and given that most of his characters are in perpetual conflict with one another for supremacy one over another, his remarks may be viewed as wishful thinking and ironic. As Pauline Flanagan remembered, Pinter during the early 1950s enjoyed giving frequent recitations from T. S. Eliot's *The Waste Land*. Pinter's remarks concerning Litvinoff, coupled with his and Goldstein's sarcasm at the expense of Jewish religious figures, might well have had something to do with Pinter's predilection for Eliot's poetry.

Litvinoff contributed to small poetry magazines such as that of the Anglo-Welsh poet and medical doctor Dannie Abse's *Verse* and *Poetry and Poverty*. In 1949 the initial issue of *Poetry and Poverty* contained Litvinoff's "To T. S. Eliot." This subsequently frequently anthologized poem was written in reaction to Eliot's decision to include some of his anti-Semitic poems in his *Selected Poems* (1948). In January 1951, Herbert Read arranged inaugural poetry readings at the Institute of Contemporary Arts. During the readings, Eliot appeared. Litvinoff read his poem, causing a great commotion. Stephen Spender "rose angrily and shouted that Litvinoff had grossly insulted Tom Eliot," but Eliot was heard to murmur that it was a "very good poem."

Their letters are punctuated by inquiries over family matters and health matters, the arrival of an addition to the Goldstein family, and Pinter suffering from a cold. A hiatus in their correspondence worried Pinter, who was concerned that Goldstein, in Australia, had not responded to a detailed letter he had sent him two months previously in September 1972 concerning *monologue*. From Pinter's letter of September 4, 1972, it seems that Goldstein had personally objected to something in the text of the play, although it is unclear what annoyed Goldstein. In a November 12, 1972 letter, Pinter mentioned a letter that Goldstein had sent him two years previously in which he referred to the title of Martin Esslin's *The Peopled Wound: The Work of Harold Pinter* (1970). Pinter told Goldstein that it moved him and led him to think about all the time they've known each other and all that they have shared. He added that he wants to keep in touch and that they should meet when he's back in England.

On occasions, Pinter's communications to Goldstein juxtapose the mundane, for example their habits of drinking tea, with the philosophical. Such a mixture of moving quickly from the everyday to the almost sublime is characteristic, for instance, of the one-act *monologue*. Writing from 14 Ambrose Place, Worthing, on October 29, 1963, Pinter asked Goldstein the price of a cup of tea and follows his question with the observation: "As Engels said to Kant: who's in front?" There are personal revelations.

In August 1975, Pinter and Antonia Fraser began to live together at a house in Launcester Place Kensington with Pinter's son, Daniel. Pinter was hounded by the press on a daily basis. In a letter written from 33 Launcester Place, London W8, dated "Christmas Day. 1975," Pinter told Goldstein that the year has seen total upheaval. The private pain and public horror has been unimaginable; he won't go into it. Woolf and others, Pinter observed, have been friends to him. He reported that his marriage to Vivien was over and that he and Vivian would have to find "another shape to [their] life and lives." Meanwhile, Vivien was in a bad state over Pinter's relationship with Antonia but was beginning to get her head "above water," Pinter wrote. He confessed to being exhausted but alive. He ended the letter by saying that his son Daniel has won a scholarship—in fact, an Exhibition—to Magdalen College Oxford and that Daniel "is a joy to me." In light of what would later happen, these are sad and ironic words. Pinter's letters to Goldstein more than once evoke associations with Daniel. In an earlier letter dated December 11, 1960, for instance, Pinter remarked that Daniel remembered Goldstein and his then-wife Helen sitting on the armchair when he came in the room. Another letter was written from 14 Ambrose Place, Worthing, on the Sussex coast, dated October 29, 1963, where he moved with Vivien and wrote *The Pumpkin Eater* film script and *The Homecoming*. Pinter described the "Regency" house on a quiet road, a short distance from the sea. He and Vivien were happy there, and Daniel was almost six years old. On October 1, 1965, he tells Goldstein that Vivien and Daniel were fine and Moishe [Wernick] visited last summer with three kids from Canada.

On March 24, 1976, Pinter told Goldstein that Daniel has changed his name to that of "Brand," his maternal grandmother's maiden name. According to Billington, "Pinter, however, does not see this as a symbolic rejection of himself; it was, he claims, a largely pragmatic move on Daniel's part designed to keep the press, who had been relentlessly hounding him also, at bay" (255). However, writing from Antonia's home at 52 Campden Hill Square, London W8, where she and Pinter had moved on August 12, 1977, in a letter dated November 19, 1977, Pinter confessed to Goldstein that his son has experienced a nervous breakdown and that he could not put Goldstein up during an upcoming visit to London because Antonia has six children, all of whom would be visiting over the Christmas period; there was literally no room. A day later he informed Goldstein that his old schoolmaster, Joe Brearley, has died and that he was extremely upset. Owing to work pressures, such as his direction of Simon Gray's *The Rear Column*, he could not go to the funeral. A year later, in a typed letter addressed not only to Goldstein but to Moishe Wernick and Woolf, dated November 27, 1978 from 52 Campden Hill Square, Pinter informed them that the house he lived in with Vivien at 7 Hanover Terrace, Regents Park, from 1964 has been sold. His news about Daniel was not so good. He and Daniel have gone their separate ways, and they do not meet or talk. Pinter received what he described as a vicious letter from his son. Pinter is very sensitive about playing a favorite from his three old friends. His typed letter is addressed in three separate ways with "Mosie," "Mick," and "then "Henry" appearing initially. He added that he loves them all the same, followed by two exclamation marks.

In a letter to Goldstein dated October 27, 1979 from Campden Hill Square, Pinter referred to a brief meeting they had. It lasted for less than an hour, but they seemed to pack the "whole world" into that time. He didn't specify where they met. Pinter responded to the news that Goldstein's marriage is over. Pinter said he can imagine what his friend is going through. Most of the letter concerns cricket; at its conclusion, Pinter said that he and Antonia are well and that she has had tremendous success with her book *King Charles II* (published by Weidenfeld & Nicolson in 1979) that took five years to write. In a fortnight, they would both be off to New York for rehearsals of *Betrayal*.

Vivien died on October 3, 1982. On November 18, 1982, Pinter thanked Goldstein for what he has said about her and added that Antonia has been wonderful. Letters from Goldstein to Pinter reveal that Goldstein was preoccupied especially at this time with marital issues, his relationships with women, and especially triangular relationships of a lesbian nature. He told Pinter that he has been working for the computer firm Honeywell, an American multinational conglomerate company that produces a variety of commercial and consumer products, and that he has a long service leave due in 1986. He would be able to visit London. To move forward a few years, in a April 6, 1991 letter to Pinter, Goldstein revealed that he has left his job, and while he never thought he would miss his computer work, he does. In a letter written a few years earlier, Goldstein told Pinter of his other obsessions that concern "perfecting [his] interpretation of the Haydn string quartets by holding regular chamber music sessions" on Sunday mornings with players from the Waverley Philharmonic Orchestra that he leads. Additionally in his letter of July 3, 1984, Goldstein reports that he read of Joseph Losey's death on June 22, 1984.

Pinter and Goldstein met when Goldstein was in London in early September 1986. On February 5, 1990, Pinter sent Goldstein a lengthy letter containing a vitriolic attack from their old East End combatant Ronald Percival on Salman Rushdie, who was under a fatwa calling for his assassination for his *Satanic Verses* (1988). The Pinters had given Rushdie refuge. On May 4, 1990, Goldstein told Pinter that he has worked for so long for an American company that it was becoming increasingly difficult for him to laugh. Goldstein knew Pinter's parents. In a letter of November 20, 1991, after telling Goldstein that he would be in London at the end of January 1992 and including some reviews of his *Party Time*, Pinter added that his father was almost age ninety and that his mum was almost eighty-eight. On the whole, they were in good health for their respective ages and their minds were as sharp as ever. In a letter dated February 18, 1993, following observations on Goldstein's reactions to *Moonlight* and comments on cricket, Pinter added that he hasn't informed Goldstein about the sudden death of his mother at the age of eighty-eight on October 5 of the previous year. Pinter observed that his father cries but retains a clear head and, at the age of ninety-one, is well looked after. Earlier, in January 1993, Pinter sent Goldstein a check for £5000 as a loan—yet another illustration of Pinter's generosity and kindness. Later in February, Goldstein apologized about its non-repayment and that he was still working in a full-time capacity as a technical writer. In a letter dated May 8, 1993, Pinter told Goldstein that *Moonlight* would be produced in September. It opened on September 7, 1993 at the Almeida, transferring in November to the Comedy Theatre. Judy Daish, Pinter's agent, sent Goldstein an invitation to attend the opening night party.

To repeat, friendships are indissolubly associated with food, drink, and meetings at restaurants. Later letters to Goldstein contain references to their favorite drink: Guinness. In congratulating Pinter on receiving the David Cohen British Literature Award for a lifetime's achievement on March 15, 1995, Goldstein brings up something from the past. He recalls a specific kind of drink, family relationships, money, and poetry. In his "A Speech of Thanks" on receipt of the award, Pinter recalled that only a single member of his family when he was growing up appeared to have money. He referred to his great-uncle Coleman, who was a businessman. Pinter recalled him as always wearing felt carpet slippers and skullcap at home and being a very courteous man. Pinter's father encouraged his son to show his uncle his poem "New Year in the Midlands," which had just appeared in *Poetry London*. In the poem, there is the line, "straddled, exile always in one Whitbread Ale town." Pinter and his parents sat silently while the uncle read the poem. When Uncle Coleman came to that line, he stopped, looked over the magazine at them and said, "Whitbread shares are doing very well at the moment. Take my tip" (*VV*: 61).

In a March 15, 1995 letter, Goldstein told Pinter that he had the impression that he remembers encountering David Cohen when he worked for a short time as a postal clerk at the offices of the British Board of Jewish Deputies in Upper Woburn Place. Pinter's Uncle Coleman's last name must have been "Cohen," for Goldstein comments that Pinter's "Uncle Coleman was blessed with the right name." Goldstein is making an allusion to Jewish ritual, when on Yom Kippur of the Day of Atonement, the "Cohens," or descendants of the High Priests, bless the congregation. They have a privileged role and are singled out from the congregation. In a communication dated January 4, 1997, Pinter told Goldstein that, in the week following, he and Antonia would celebrate the twenty-second anniversary of their first meeting and that she was doing well. She is with Pinter in everything at the same time she is independent. He recommended her latest book, *The Gunpowder Plot: Terror and Faith in 1605*, published by Weidenfeld & Nicolson in 1996.

By January 1997, Pinter and Goldstein have started corresponding not by the letters sent by airmail that took a week or so to reach each other but by using the internet and email. On January 4, 1997, Pinter told Goldstein that he still used an old Olympia portable typewriter and that he never got around to computers, although his personal assistant uses one and he dictates to her. He wrote from 52 Campden Hill Square at the time, and Pinter added that he wrote *The Caretaker* on a portable in Chiswick High Road many years before. In the same email[11] from early 1997, Pinter informed Goldstein that he and Antonia were going to Mexico for a holiday and to see their latest grandchild, their ninth. Antonia's son Damian and his wife Palona lived in Mexico City. The Pinters were in Mexico from January 11 to 25, 1997. In April, he told Goldstein that that there would be a festival of his drama in Dublin. Pinter played Harry in *The Collection*, which ran at the Gate Theatre from April 7 to 27, and he also directed *Ashes to Ashes*, which also ran in Dublin during the festival. Furthermore, a new production of *The Homecoming* opened at the Lyttelton at the National Theatre on January 9, 1997. So we have in these letters to Goldstein Pinter as director, as actor, as dramatist, as family man, and as close friend.

In July 2000, Pinter told Goldstein that he rejected writing the screenplay of *Voss*, by the great Australian writer and Nobel Prize winner Patrick White with Joseph Losey as its director. *Voss* (1957) was White's fifth published novel and revolves around the life of Ludwig Leichhardt, the nineteenth-century Prussian explorer and naturalist who vanished while on an expedition into the Australian outback.[12] The film was never made. Over three years earlier, on January 21, 1997, Goldstein told Pinter that he was correct to regard the film *Shine* as great. This was a 1996 Australian biographical drama film based on the life of pianist David Helfgott, who suffered a mental breakdown and spent years in institutions. Pinter added that at last he and Goldstein have found the right women, or so it seemed. In the same email, Goldstein remembered that Pinter had recalled to him a dream he had had in which a crocodile or alligator had got hold of him around the waist and wouldn't let him go. Pinter's father died on Wednesday September 10, 1997, and Pinter immediately penned one of his finest poems, "Death (Births and Deaths Registration Act 1953)," on the occasion of his having to identify the body at Hove Town Hall. Two days later, Pinter told Goldstein that his father has died and that he has been buried next to his mother.

In October 1999, Pinter sent Goldstein a copy of what would turn out to be his last play, *Celebration*, with its rambling monologues about the past. This led Goldstein to reminisce and to reveal much about his early years. In this instance, he recalled his late younger brother David, who was curator of Hebrew Manuscripts at the British Library. In a most moving tribute published in the *British Library Journal*, his colleague Albertine Gaur wrote that David, three years younger than Pinter, was "the youngest of five children, three sons and two daughters. His parents owned a drapery shop in Hackney. In 1939, when he was six years old, the family home was bombed and David, together with one of his brothers, was evacuated to the country." Back in London, David, like Pinter, attended "the Hackney Downs School where he distinguished himself in French, Latin and Greek but showed as yet no special interest in Hebrew or Hebrew literature." It wasn't until after Oxford, where he read English, that David became interested in studying Hebrew. His other interests included being a member of the MCC! Perhaps his most widely known work is his 1966 translation *Hebrew Poems from Spain*. Revised and expanded, it appeared in 1971 under the title *The Jewish Poets of Spain 900-1250*. Like Pinter, David Goldstein, when he wasn't adopting a public persona, "had no time for hypocrisy or pretension." [13] In his reply to Pinter, Goldstein told him that the copy of *Celebration* brought to Goldstein's mind an anecdote concerning his brother David going to the flat/apartment of a distinguished predecessor to see if there were any of the British Library's (the British Museum as it was called then) Hebrew collections at the flat/apartment. He found copies of the *London Times* going back dozens of years and also a hundred or so ancient Hebrew books and manuscripts that had never been cataloged.

Clearly, *Celebration* evoked a flood of disconnected memories; for instance, in an October 1999 email to Pinter, Goldstein mentioned an old flame, a Norwegian girl whom he should have married. The play's setting is an upscale West End London restaurant. Sitting at two separate tables are Russell and Suki: the former is a shady investment banker; the latter has been a secretary. At a much larger table, a wedding anniversary is being celebrated by a group of former East Enders who enjoy insulting one another. There are confessions of infidelity. For Goldstein, the timing of the entrance of Russell and Suki in the play is exactly right, and the waiter around whom the play revolves is an invention of momentous proportions. In an email of December 8, 1999 to Pinter, Goldstein predicted that the play "will go down as one of your greatest dramatic feats." Some of the reasons are that it contains "a laugh a minute" — an experience echoed by Pinter, who started to write the play, one drawn from accumulated memories and experiences, when he was on holiday in Dorset with his family. Pinter's family asked him to read aloud what he was writing; as he read, the family started collapsing with laughter (Billington: 403–4). Goldstein observed that the "characters seem unaware of any dignity [and] the intrusion of an artificial attempt at such dignity by the owner and his partner is seen for what it is" — a sham. For Goldstein, this "is a brilliant touch."

The play may also have had its genesis in a six-verse poem that Pinter sent to Goldstein and others around this time. Called "Restaurant" and dated "1989," in its final verse the narcissism of the diners is transformed in another setting once they leave the restaurant: "And they shed tears for it ǀ in the back of the taxi home." [14] Restaurants in this poem are associated with food, with friends and laughter, with appearances, and also with sadness.

In June 2000 the death of a close relative who was buried in Waverley cemetery "overlooking the ocean" led Goldstein to reveal to his old friend that he has reserved a plot for himself in the same spot, one where the Australian author Henry Lawson, one of Goldstein's favorite poets, is buried. In the same cemetery are legendary Australian cricketers such as Victor Trumper; A. C. Bannerman, a member of the first Australian team to tour England in 1878; and Jack Fingleton, a cricketer, journalist, and commentator. On July 16, 2000, Pinter told Goldstein that a cataract operation he had two weeks previously was unsuccessful; his eye resisted the invasion and this led to complications. He experienced considerable pain, has a stitch in his eye, and can barely read. Jill Johnson[15] —from his early days in repertory—would record for a BBC Radio 4 production of his early short radio play *A Slight Ache*. Its title is echoed in the drama—the character Edward experiences "a slight ache" in his eyes (12)—he becomes a powerful symbol of powerlessness and impotence.

On October 13, 2000, Pinter reported to Goldstein that his seventieth birthday was on October 10 and that their old sparring partner and rival from school days, Ron Percival, had sent birthday greetings. Pinter and Percival spoke and they might meet in a few weeks. They had met from time to time over the years; for instance, when Pinter was appearing in repertory in the spring of 1956 in Bournemouth, he saw Percival in London. What Pinter omitted in his October 2000 email was that his seventieth birthday was celebrated at the upscale Ivy Restaurant, a favorite of Pinters, located in Covent Garden in the heart of the theatre district. Guy Dimond writes in *Time Out* on its reopening following extensive refurbishment and posted online June 17, 2015: "Once upon a time, if you were a celeb, you went to The Ivy. . . . In the 1990s and 2000s, pretty much all you had to do to be a celeb was to go to The Ivy, and then be pampered as you left. It was exclusive." Favorite dishes, what Dimond calls "comfort food," include "shepherd's pie . . . with its rich browned-meat flavours, along with old-fashioned seafood dishes such as plaice with earthy brown shrimps, doused in a buttery sauce."[16] Andrew Bovell, an Australian dramatist, encountered Pinter and Antonia dining together there in 2007. He commented: "Harold and Antonia are still at their table at The Ivy. Harold is having dessert. Apple pie and cream. He likes a good piece of apple pie."[17] Dining at such an upscale, expensive restaurant obviously demonstrates that Pinter has made a great deal of money and is highly successful. It is somewhere that his friend Goldstein just couldn't afford to go to eat.

In 2001, Goldstein told Pinter that he has just turned seventy-one and that their mutual friend Henry Woolf beat him to that age by a few weeks. He added that "apart from immediate family I have known him longer than anyone else." Goldstein saw *Old Times* at a local theatre near Sydney, an experience that recalled an evening in May 1971 at the Cambridge Arts Theatre when Vivien won a bottle of champagne that Peter Hall awarded to the first actor who got all his or her lines right. He also remembered that Pinter wasn't too pleased that Vivien won the champagne. In a postcard, rather than an email, dated November 4, 2000,

Pinter objected to Goldstein addressing him as "Sir." In fact, he told Goldstein that he turned down a knighthood; he is "just plain Mister." Goldstein, too, had playwriting pretensions. In an email of February 27, 2003 on the outbreak of the American invasion of Iraq, Pinter told Goldstein that, because of the war, he has been unable to concentrate on the play script Goldstein sent him. Following Pinter's rapidly declining health and serious illnesses and Goldstein's increasing personal problems and ill health, their friendship and communication over a more than sixty-year period dwindled away. It had been marked by mutual memories of girls, of shared experiences, of families who had known one another, by their love of cricket, by a shared love of Guinness.[18]

Simon Gray

Someone else who formed a close bond with Pinter over many years was Simon Gray. Their friendship was celebrated in innumerable meals and restaurant visits. Pinter contributed a "Foreword" to Gray's journal of the production of Gray's play *The Common Pursuit*, directed by Pinter at the Lyric Hammersmith in 1984 (BR: H7). Pinter directed, at Gray's request, the stage version of Gray's *Butley* (1971), "his most successful work, both artistically and financially" (*Sharp Cut*: 456, n.30). In his "Introduction to Simon Gray Plays," Pinter wrote that he found *Butley* savage with lacerating wit. Pinter subsequently directed seven more Gray plays, concluding with *The Late Middle Classes* in 2000. Pinter and Gray formed a fast friendship, with Pinter calling his involvement with Gray's work a uniquely rich and vivid part of his professional life.

For Pinter, the extraordinary thing about *Butley* is the character who hurls himself toward destruction while living in the fever of his intellectual hell. According to Pinter, the play is a remarkable creation.[19] The stage premiere was at the Oxford Playhouse on July 7, 1971. One week later, it moved to London's Criterion Theatre, and then at the end of October 1972 started an American tour at New York City's Morosco Theatre. At the premiere, Susan Engel played the part of Anne Butley and Alan Bates played Ben Butley. For Pinter, Bates gave a performance of a lifetime. Pinter also told Goldstein on February 12, 1973 that he was preparing to direct his first film, which would be *Butley*. It was released a year later with Engel and Bates in the main roles.[20]

In May 1997, rehearsals opened for Pinter's production of Gray's *Life Support*. Alan Bates played the main character with Eileen Diss the set designer.[21] The play opened at the Yvonne Arnauld Theatre, Guildford, on June 10, 1997 and received favorable if not ecstatic reviews. Writing in the *Daily Telegraph*, Charles Spencer observed that "Harold Pinter's production is spare, scrupulous and continually involving. It's a rich and affecting evening" (August 7, 1997).[22] In Gray's 1975 *Otherwise Engaged*, directed by Pinter, Bates's role was very different from that of Ben Butley.

According to Pinter, its central character, Simon Hench, is solely obligated to self-protection.[23]

The friendship of Gray and Pinter serves as a further illustration of aspects of Pinter's character: his loyalty and fidelity to his close friends and his quickness to forgive perceived slights. For instance, in the character of Hector Duff in the televised version of *Unnatural Pursuits*, Gray depicted Pinter as "the world's most famous playwright." Gray wished Pinter to play the role of himself; Pinter declined to do so. Gray changed the name, a mistake in casting took place, and the character became "a waspish Scot. In the end, what irked Pinter was that the playwright was mocked for his sense of political engagement, but the momentary coolness between the two writers was soon settled by a cordial lunch" (Billington: 389). Indeed, as Pinter's "Appointment Diaries" reveal, he and Gray met for lunch or dinner on innumerable occasions extending from 1971 until the last day of December 2007. Restaurants they lunched at included Venezia's with its Italian dishes, for instance on September 26, 1974, and they got together for dinner at Odin's with its French cuisine on January 20, 1976. Other venues included Grouchos in Mayfair and Chez Moi. The meetings were not confined to periods during which they were involved with Gray's plays. They sought each other's company, especially during the difficult period following Pinter's separation from his first wife, Vivien Merchant; Gray's separation from his wife, Beryl; and Gray's subsequent divorce and relationship with Victoria Rothschild, who became his second wife. Gray and Victoria then dined frequently with Pinter and Antonia (see *Chronology*: 345).

Gray's letters to Pinter reveal that their restaurant meetings had a creative and other significance for both. For instance, Gray wrote a 2002 letter after Pinter had had his esophagus operation to remove a tumor from his throat on April 25, 2002 and was undergoing a painful period of chemotherapy (see *Chronology*: 272–73 and *Must*: 256–57). Gray recalled his own operations for lung cancer and that he was fortunate post-operatively. Around the time of Gray's operation, Pinter directed one of Gray's plays and this gave him "a strong, direct line of support, being in some way looked after, out in the world, by you." All Gray can do is daily "prayers and thoughts" on Pinter's behalf until Pinter is "sitting in [his] rightful place at the right table at Chez Moi" — one of their favorite restaurants.

Some idea of the nature of the Gray-Pinter friendship may also be glimpsed in the May 24, 2002 letter Gray sent Pinter following the latter's April 25 cancer of the esophagus operation followed by chemotherapy. Pinter was discharged from the Royal Marsden Hospital on Wednesday May 8. Gray and Victoria visited Pinter and Antonia on Tuesday May 21, 2002 at 8 p.m. (*Chronology*: 272–73). Two days later, Gray wrote, "It was good to see you on Tuesday night, not so good to see you so depressed and hear what you've been going through [and] undoubtedly still are."

Gray then spoke from his own experience. He told Pinter that "we're never prepared for the post-operative state." Gray adds "I think the thing is that while our bodies are brutalized our minds are withdrawn from the process—though God knows *what* the nature of that withdrawal is—what the anaesthetised [sic] mind actually lives through with its beloved fleshly self being sliced over, gorged into, stitched up, etc. but I suspect that it takes some time [for it] to get together again." For Gray, both the mind and the body are "in shock, bewildered, suspicious etc. of each other—and to both therefore, the world is a frightening, futile place" and, he adds, "the people in it noisy *and* shadowy, distant and aggressive." Gray reassured Pinter that "it will pass—you can't believe energy will come back, but it will—your body is getting stronger but not telling you it is—and the same is true of the mind, I believe." Gray recommended to Pinter Andrew Marvell's poem "A Dialogue between the Soul and the Body," which he found during his own post-operative condition "immensely helpful."

In an earlier lengthy handwritten letter to Pinter written from the "Grand Hotel dis Castelli" near Genoa, Italy, dated "August 4, [1990]," Gray remembered a lunch that he and Pinter had a few months previously at Grouchos. At the conclusion, "we found ourselves discussing our different understanding of the nature of faith." Gray remembered a subsequent lunch encounter at this venue in which Pinter said suddenly that he'd "love to direct another" of Gray's plays. He then told Pinter that between the two lunches, Gray found himself "embarking on a play about faith, *English* faith" that has "a rural C[hurch] of E[ngland] Vicar etc.; And to my astonishment I finished it very quickly," approximately a week prior to writing his letter to Pinter. He preferred Pinter not to direct it.[24] "The real reason is personal, to do with you and me, and what you have come to mean to me as a friend," Gray explained, adding that their relationship "moved rapidly from professional to a great deal more, and through further professional entanglements and personal trust to the near disaster (I mean *personally*) of The Common Pursuit." He was referring to their intense rows during its production. Gray then added that "each professional encounter tested us by fire-sometimes by ice—sometimes, by God, by both—and strengthened it (for me anyway) until it's become one of the most important elements in my life." For Gray, it is through Pinter that he has "come to know everything that I do know about the theatre." Consequently, Gray is "not yet ready for one more adventure together." Revealingly, Gray wrote that "the extremes to which our respective natures carry us in rehearsal (that have led to fire and ice) the testing times, etc., and *they're* what I'm not yet ready for." In short, Gray needed Pinter "as a friend far more than" he needed him "as a director." He added, and this perhaps essentially sums up the importance for him of their lunches, that "when I get back we can talk about" these matters "more fully over lunch," if Pinter felt inclined to do so. In a postscript, Gray added that family matters left him "feeling fragile . . . the head still liable to burst . . . and actually dependent on stable relationships with the people that I know and love." Pinter replied to him immediately in a brief three sentences dated "August 10." He told Gray that he agreed with every word he wrote and was eager to read Gray's play. Pinter's last sentence informed Gray of the latest cricket score with Australia batting at Old Trafford.[25]

Gray and Pinter met regularly for lunch and for supper at the Groucho Club, 45 Dean Street, London W I., "a private members club open to men and women" that officially opened on May 5, 1985. According to its website, it was "dreamt up by a group of publishers as an alternative to stuffy gentlemen's clubs who wanted somewhere to meet and relax." Both Gray and Pinter enjoyed their drinks and eating together. As Gray wrote to Pinter in an undated letter, not without a touch of sarcasm, it had "dawned on" him "that the world *needs* two such calm and reasonable men to discuss its affairs over lunch." Gray added that he is "free almost any day this week and next. What about you?" A mention of Pinter having dinner at the Club is found in his diary for Thursday March 13, 1986. He then lunched with Gray on Friday April 18, 1986 at the Club and with his poetry publisher, Tony Astbury, and others in a supper party on Friday September 5, 1986 prior to the evening performance of Pinter's direction of Donald Freed's *Circe and Bravo* at the Wyndham's Theatre.

Pinter's "Appointment Diaries" have twenty-eight mentions of going to the Groucho Club. Most of these were to have lunch with Simon Gray. Noticeably, these lunches started around 1:15 p.m. and Pinter records no subsequent events for the same day. They often took place on a Monday or a Friday. An indication that the venue was a favorite watering hole for Pinter and Gray is reflected in the fact that it was the chosen venue to celebrate Gray's sixtieth birthday on Sunday October 27, 1996 at 8 p.m. Pinter also lunched there on more than one occasion was his agent, Judy Daish. He dined with her, for instance, on April 3 and July 1, 1978, both Fridays. Pinter arranged two Gaieties meetings in the private room of the Groucho Club: Friday April 15, 1988 at 8 p.m. and Sunday September 17, 1989 beginning at 1:30 p.m. Among Pinter's final visits to the Groucho Club was Monday April 7, 2004 for what seems to have been a brief meeting with his old sparring partner Peter Hall, accompanied by the actor Edward Fox—probably to keep the peace—at 7 p.m. At nine thirty the same evening, Pinter dined with Louis Marks, the BBC producer, director, and scriptwriter who worked with him on *The Hothouse* and on the 1993 adaptation of Kafka's *The Trial*. This meeting occurred at another of Pinter's favorite restaurants, Odin's. Pinter's last meal at the Groucho Club took place just over a year later, on Monday April 18, 2005, when he lunched at 1:15 p.m. with Michael Colgan, the organizer of the Dublin Pinter Festival, and Judy Daish (*Chronology*: 371).

Gray and Pinter were from different backgrounds, united by a love for the theatre, an obsession with cricket, and a delight in eating out. They watched matches together on an almost weekly basis during the cricket season until Gray's death on August 7, 2008. Both had a predilection for chain-smoking cigarettes and drinking, among other elements in common, including personal chemistry. Dramatist, diarist, novelist, academic, Gray was the dedicatee of Pinter's *Betrayal* (BR: A37), and Gray's eight volumes of diaries are an important resource for information on Pinter, their meetings, and about Pinter as a theatrical director. Gray was not from the East End of London. He was born on Hayling Island, Hampshire, the second son of a Scottish-born medical practitioner. Gray studied English at Dalhousie University, Halifax, Nova Scotia, and then at Trinity College, Cambridge, where he was influenced by the ideas and personality of F. R. Leavis, as were two other Pinter directors, Peter Hall and David Jones.[26] In 1965, Gray was appointed to a lectureship at Queen Mary College London. He resigned from this position in 1985. In 1965, Gray married Beryl Mary Kevern, with whom he had two children; the marriage was dissolved in 1997 following his eight-year affair with Victoria Katherine Rothschild, who also taught at Queen Mary. The couple married in 1997.

Gray, in common with Pinter, was an obsessive smoker; Gray smoked sixty cigarettes a day for at least half a century. Both also drank alcohol often to excess. Diagnosed with cancer in 2007, as Pinter had been at an earlier date, Gray died a year later. So close was the friendship between Simon Gray and Victoria and Harold and Antonia that they spent time together on vacation in Barbados. The Pinters' final visit, as it turned out, was between January 5 and 19, 2005. The Grays subsequently joined them. Antonia records "torrential rain." The visit was "dismal. Harold developed a painful chest and heavy cough" (*Must*: 280). In one of their final communications, at the end of April 2005, Gray sent his old friend a letter from the Coral Reef Club, St James, Barbados, written at "one in the morning." He was "sitting near the table where the four of us had so many lunches and dishes—the waiter taking it in turns to bring your bill every time you raised your glass to your lips."[27]

FOOD AND HEALTH

Pinter's declining health in the early years of the twentieth century is marked by a decrease in his appetite and a decline in his eating out. Antonia Fraser records that her seventy-third birthday on Saturday August 27, 2005 was spent at Bernhurst, her parents' family home. Pinter's health became "really worse, eats nothing . . . [has] lost his voice, coughs and splatters all night long" (*Must*: 288). On the final day of August, he went to the Princess Grace Hospital, returning home on Wednesday September 14 following treatment for pemphigus. On Friday September 16, he saw Dr. Chris Bunker, a dermatologist. On Monday September 26, Pinter was unwell and using a stick to walk; he was taking steroids that made his feet sweat and his voice croaky (*Chronology*: 297). In spite of his frail condition, he still found time to write to Woolf, giving him a detailed account of his condition. Pinter started with the good news that his cancer had not returned. However, the pemphigus was another thing altogether. This is a rare skin disease in which the skin attacks itself; it can be fatal if not controlled. In Pinter's case the condition was located in the mouth and was extremely uncomfortable. At the time, Pinter was on a strong dose of steroids, which had not yet worked. He would later start on a weekly routine of injections of another drug, which doctors hoped would improve his condition. He told Woolf that he had total confidence in his medical advisors. He added that Antonia was wonderful but worried about his loss of weight: He had lost two stone and felt weak. He ate soup and pasta and assured Woolf that he was not ready to die. On June 20, 2005, Pinter somewhat prophetically wrote to Woolf, asking rhetorically, "How can we respond to death?" Pinter answered his own question: "We can't find the appropriate words. There aren't any."

THE ESSENCE OF FRIENDSHIPS

In an earlier undated letter to a depressed Moishe Wernick in Canada, Pinter cited the words of South African–born deaf poet David Wright that his old friends are either dead or on the wagon. As for himself, Pinter added, he's neither. As for Wernick, Pinter believes he will always be the same stubborn, critical, wry old bugger he met when he was sixteen. He then commented in words that summarize the quintessence of his friendship with Woolf and others, saying that they all share something unique. Although they are miles away geographically—Wernick and Woolf in Canada, Goldstein in Australia—their spirit does not die and won't even after they are all dead.[28]

Pinter learned that he had been awarded the Nobel Prize for Literature on October 13, 2005. Over a month later, on November 25, following a bad fall at home, he was readmitted to the Royal Marsden Hospital (*Must*: 295–96). He remained there until December 13, when he returned home to be treated daily by a nurse. On November 29, 2005, Anne Hudson, Pinter's personal assistant at the time, wrote Woolf an account of Pinter's situation. She told him that his old friend was once again in hospital, as he was "suffering from an infection that was causing him great pain in both his legs and making it almost impossible for him to walk." Over-optimistically, she assured Woolf that Pinter was much better; however, owing to doctor's advice, the trip to Stockholm to receive the Nobel Prize had been cancelled. She provided details of his Nobel presentation speech, informing Woolf that his Nobel lecture would be recorded in advance by Channel 4. In Pinter's absence the speech would be screened on video from the Swedish Academy in Stockholm on December 7. Simultaneously in the United Kingdom, it would be broadcast over Channel 4's new digital channel. Pinter recorded his Nobel speech, "Art, Truth and Politics," on Sunday December 4 at 3 p.m. Per Pinter's direction, Anne Hudson assured Woolf that Pinter was on the mend and that he didn't need to worry about him. He sent Woolf his love.[29]

Ronald Harwood

Another friend of long standing was Ronald Harwood, with whom Pinter shared a love of and knowledge of the theatre and with whom he ate out on many occasions. Pinter sent Harwood his Proust adaptation. In a detailed response dated February 21, 1973, Harwood confessed to his "shame" not to have read Proust's novel. For Harwood, reading Pinter's script was "an overwhelming experience from which I have not yet fully recovered." Harwood was "still haunted by the characters and the imagery, and inexplicably involved with them. At one level it was like reading the most superior detective story, so that one was intrigued and fascinated by the flashbacks and flash-forwards as one is by clues in a more conventional tale. All one's perceptions were focused on trying to discover, to guess what each image or recollection would mean to Marcel, and when the revelation occurred the excitement was almost unbearable." Harwood told Pinter that he didn't "know how [he] managed it, but I was not once confused by what, after all, is a complex structure. I knew always where I was in time and place. And this is just from *reading* the script." Harwood has been "given insight into human behaviour that I had never even glimpsed before. . . . There will be those who will be hooked by the sheer suspense of the narrative technique, and others will be savaged by the power and duty of the story." Furthermore, "what on a personal level pleased me as much as anything, was that the whole piece seems to me part of you and your work. I mean a *central* part. And I don't think I can pay Proust a greater compliment than that!"[30]

The dramatist, director, author, and literary administrator born Ronald Horwitz in Cape Town, South Africa, moved to London in 1951 to pursue an acting career. He and Pinter met two years later when they auditioned at London's Waldorf Hotel for Sir Donald Wolfit's theatrical company: Harwood was a member from 1953 to 1958. Subsequently, Harwood wrote a biography of Wolfit.[31] Harwood was waiting for his audition and recalled when Pinter came "bounding down the stairs in a state of high excitement and saying to the beautiful red-headed girl who was waiting for him, 'I've got it. I've got it'" (Billington: 46). A friend of Pinter's for over fifty years, they played fiercely competitive squash and tennis against each other and shared a mutual love of cricket. With his wife, Natasha (Riehle), whom he married in 1959, he frequently visited Pinter and Antonia and also stayed with them. Pinter directed Harwood's *Taking Sides* (1995) with its depiction of the complex situation of the great conductor Wilhelm Furtwängler during the Nazi regime. Harwood won an Oscar for his screenplay *The Pianist* in 2002, and he played an active role in PEN, serving as the English president from 1989 to 1993 and of PEN International from 1993 to 1997. He was also president of the Royal Literary Fund from 2005. He was appointed CBE in 1999 and knighted in 2010 for his services to the theatre.

Harwood and Pinter shared meals together at different London restaurants over a thirty-year period. The different venues also serve to exemplify where Pinter ate, entertained, and conducted business. Pinter's "Appointment Diaries" reveal that they lunched together on Thursday January 21, 1971 and their last recorded lunch is on Thursday November 21, 2002 at Orsino's, following a meeting together at 11:30 a.m., probably to discuss PEN or other professional matters. Of the many recorded restaurants they went to together, six were for supper engagements, usually with their wives, and the remainder for lunch with usually just the two of them. The favorite restaurant was Orsino's with its Italian cuisine, located in the Holland Park area of West London. Pinter and Harwood lunched there on five occasions and dined there in the evening three times (*Chronology*: 40, 277, 209, 237, 253, 259, 262, 267, 277). They went to Cibo's on five occasions—once for dinner (ibid., 182, 186, 206, 209, 213). They lunched twice at Odin's and twice at Da Mario's, on both occasions in the evening. On three occasions, they lunched at Thompson's (ibid., 56, 248, 169, 173, 91, 93, 157). There were other restaurants where they lunched once. These included Giovanni's, the Athenaeum, Garrick Club (113), Hilaire, Kingfisher, Pegasus, and the Ritz (ibid., 77, 116, 113, 150, 161, 218, 120) but not one of Pinter's favorite restaurants: Le Caprice. A somewhat curious lacuna in Pinter's "Appointment Diaries" occurs in late 2002 and early in 2003. There is an absence of the date on which the recorded conversation between Pinter and Harwood took place, when they discussed at Pinter's home celebrity casting, musicals, the critics, and early theatrical visits in London. Their conversation was published in the *Independent* on February 6, 2003.[32] The final recorded meeting between them took place at 11 a.m. on November 21, 2002 at the Pinters, and they then went to lunch at 1 p.m. at Orsino's.

For Harwood, "the thing people don't understand about Harold is that he's always been the same. It's not fame that's made him vibrant, aggressive or anti-authoritarian. That's how he always was" (Billington: 46–47). Harwood also volunteered for the same psychological testing work as Pinter had done at the Maudsley Hospital in the early 1950s. For Harwood, Pinter's play that draws upon his experiences at the Maudsley, *The Hothouse*, is very autobiographical: "Nearly all the characters represent some aspect of Harold's personality. The authoritarian director who runs the place embodies his more demonic side." Pinter is also present in the character of Lamb, "who is all innocence: Harold still has that same quality of innocence in that something quite ordinary can fill him with wonder. Even his sensuality is there in the female character. They're all aspects of Harold in the same way that Ibsen's characters are fragments of the author." Harwood observed that "if I really was in trouble, financially or emotionally, I would turn to Harold because I know he would be rock solid in support (Billington: 367, 393).

John Casey

To turn from a man of the theatre and fellow dramatist to someone else from a different walk of life, a surprising friendship and restaurant companion revealed in Pinter's "Appointment Diaries" is Dr. John Casey, the Conservative thinker, formerly college and university lecturer in English, and lifetime Fellow of Gonville and Caius College, Cambridge. Rumored among his contemporaries to be the Cambridge University talent spotter for British Intelligence recruitment,[33] Casey was educated at the Irish Christian Brothers' School, St Brendan's College Bristol. In 1975 he founded the Conservative Philosophy Group with another right-wing thinker, the philosopher Roger Scruton, with whom there are four meetings with Pinter noted: September 10, 1977 for lunch, March 22, 1979 for dinner, December 12, 1980 mid-morning, and on the evening of February 20, 1980 with Tom Stoppard (*Chronology*: 356). Associated with the right-wing *Salisbury Review*, Casey also wrote for newspapers and journals such as the *Daily Mail*, the *Evening Standard*, *The Spectator*, the *Sunday Times*, and most notably for the *Daily Telegraph* on a wide range of subjects including interviews with Latin American Liberation theologians. His theatrical reviews included "highly flattering" praise of Pinter in the *Daily Telegraph* (see Billington: 369–70). In addition to extensive journalism and academic articles, Casey authored four monographs.[34]

The first mention of Casey in Pinter's "Appointment Diaries" is on May 19, 1977, when Pinter heard Casey give the British Academy Chatterton Lecture on Poetry. The topic was T. S. Eliot—and "Language, Sincerity and the Self." Pinter was not in the habit of attending British Academy lectures, even on subjects and writers that he was interested in, and he may have been encouraged by Antonia Fraser to hear a leading Catholic intellectual speak. Pinter was sufficiently impressed that on December 9, he heard Casey lecture in Cambridge. On March 4, 1978 at 8 p.m., he met with Casey, the distinguished actress Claire Bloom, and her then-partner Philip Roth (both were also dining and lunch companions) (*Chronology*: 337, 356).

Pinter and Casey met for lunch or dinner infrequently over the years. The final appointment seems to be on December 20, 1999, when they lunched at 1 p.m. at Chez Moi, in Holland Park. What may be deduced from these infrequent but regular encounters over more than two decades between Pinter, with his known radical sympathies, and a redoubtable Cambridge academic and journalist known for advocating Conservative positions? Perhaps their mutual sympathy for the cause of the Sandinistas in South America; perhaps their mutual love of T. S. Eliot's poetry; perhaps Casey's friendship with Antonia Fraser (although Antonia was absent from their meetings); perhaps their love of England and objection to its apparent subjection to the United States. Cricket was not a common denominator, as Casey didn't appear interested in the game.

According to Billington, in 2003 Pinter objected to a citation used by Casey in the *Daily Telegraph* relating to *Mountain Language* in which the suggestion was made that the play was "very close to home." Pinter objected to the word "torture," telling Bllington that "there is no torture as such in [*Mountain Language*], there is simply brutality" (369–70). Such a disagreement with something Casey wrote took place after their meetings. Perhaps they had found each other, so different in many ways, intellectually stimulating and useful for mutual advice on literary and political matters. It would be foolhardy to speculate that Pinter and Casey consulted over intelligence matters of mutual concern.

Tom Stoppard

A less surprising restaurant companion was fellow dramatist Tom Stoppard. Pinter and Stoppard met more than twenty-five times over a period of thirty years. Each saw the other's work and criticized and praised it. They played cricket together, Stoppard on occasion as wicket-keeper for the Gaieties. Both were members of PEN, and they worked actively against censorship. Before Stoppard separated from his second wife, Miriam, in 1992, Pinter, Antonia, Tom, and Miriam went to the theatre together and Pinter also invited Stoppard to join him at Lord's. Stoppard attended Pinter's private funeral on December 31, 2008 at Kensal Green Cemetery. On the occasion of Stoppard's fiftieth birthday dinner held at the Garrick Club on June 30, 1987, Pinter observed that Stoppard was his own man. Nobody, Pinter said, pushes Stoppard around. He writes what he likes, not what others want him to write, and has succeeded in writing serious, popular plays. He also added that Stoppard didn't look fifty.[35]

Pinter's responses to Stoppard's work are of interest, too, and especially Pinter's reaction in what must have been one of his last communications to Stoppard. The subject was Stoppard's full-length play *Rock 'n' Roll* (2006), which met with mixed reviews. Pinter wrote to Stoppard on January 19, 2006 on his reaction to receiving an advance copy of the script (*Chronology*: 299). Pinter told his friend that his play is about historical legacies and the obligation to make sense of these legacies. Pinter added that Stoppard's play looks at various human and political aspirations head-on, and he felt in it a profound sense of loss, specifically relating to British cultural life. Pinter acutely told Stoppard that he found nothing abstract in the work because Stoppard created such vivid, concrete characters. He then asked Stoppard two questions. First, he asked of the scene between the characters Esme and Alice, "What is it doing exactly?" Second, of the scene between Max, Eleanor, and Lenki, he asked whether the character "Lenki [is] (perhaps) too clever by half? Or am I stupid?" The response by Stoppard, who was an obsessive reviser, is not known.[36]

Stoppard's reactions to Pinter's plays, poems, direction, and cinematic adaptations are interesting and found usually in cryptic form on the back of the thirty-six or so postcards that he sent Pinter dating from the October 1979 period—when Stoppard and his then-wife, Miriam, moved to Iver Grove, Iver, Buckinghamshire—to the period just before Pinter's final illness. Stoppard wrote to Pinter following receipt of an advanced script of *Ashes to Ashes*, observing that "the sense of an abyss under the conversation is very strong" (March 5, [1996]). On March 2, 1978, he told Pinter that he saw his production of Simon Gray's *The Rear Column* and was "mystified and disturbed by the commercial failure of it." On March 25, 2002, he wrote to Pinter following a reading of Pinter's "Cancer Cells" (BR: C40). "It's an unforgettable poem, it ends but it doesn't stop. . . . The poem is bloody good." In a letter from 2004, Stoppard thanked Pinter for sending him some poems. "To My Wife" dated "June 2004" (BR: C48) "clutches the heart. It's only sayable as a poem, it had to be a poem." Stoppard had more detailed observations on "The 'Special Relationship'" dated "August 2004" (BR: C49). He told Pinter that the poem starts well and that Pinter was "on to a good thing playing with the verb 'go', and then switching prepositions, from 'off' to 'out' goes bang, really good." Stoppard wished "to write your poem but I want to stick with go—plus—preposition, I want 'the war goes on' and something 'goes in'—well bullets go in but I don't want two-syllable words *anywhere*." For Stoppard, line 13—"A man bows down before another man"—"takes the pressure off, off the poet—I expect you have a deliberate effect in mind but the better effect is the one you've already brought off, i.e. saying it all with only four monosyllables per line allowed, like winning the trick with no picture cards." Stoppard then asked, "How did you resist 'A man goes down | And sucks the last?'—You don't need 'another man' because he's there in the title."[37]

The previews of *Celebration* and *The Room* on March 20, 2000 brought back memories to Stoppard of his time in Bristol in 1957. He wrote to Pinter that "it was *The Room* that really got to me" as it recalled "being there in Bristol in 1957 when I was 20 and the sense of all that it led to. . . . It is still a strange wonderful play which your subsequent plays taught us how to meet half way. How I wish I'd seen it then, so that I might now get a sense of the distance between me then and me now."[38]

To give two further examples of Stoppard's reaction to seeing a Pinter play: On January 18, 2002, at a time when Pinter was losing his hair and on "horrendous" diets after receiving chemo (*Must*: 248; *Chronology*: 271), Stoppard sent him "a postscript after having been to" a revival of *No Man's Land*. Stoppard was "struck by how clear" Pinter's plays are in revival. "Their surroundings in the interim have come into harmony with the play, leaving one to wonder 'what was the problem?'" Stoppard recalled "being taken with [*No Man's Land*] for the first time round as a mysteriously absorbing event. Now that seems to have been a sort of blindness (And the long top of act 2 is funnier than [Coward's] *Private Lives*, which I'd seen the previous day)." The revival of *No Man's Land*, directed by Pinter, opened at the Royal National Theatre on December 8, 2001 with Corin Redgrave as Hirst and John Wood, known for his roles in Stoppard's plays, as Spooner. For Stoppard, Redgrave "was spot on for my money: John was overselling it slightly—it's his way of telling an audience they're not good enough as an audience."[39]

Stoppard's reaction to *Moonlight* is interesting, too. The play opened at the Almeida on September 7, 1993 and was transferred to the Comedy Theatre on November 4, 1993. Antonia commented that it was "even better than at the Almeida. Boys speedier, wittier. Half the critics think it is a tragedy of a mother alienated from her sons, the others think it's a father ditto. Why not both?" (*Must*: 212). Stoppard was one of the few to find humor in the play, writing to Pinter on November 12 that he went to see it the previous evening and that the play "seemed to [him] perfectly expressed and moment to moment poetry—what a wonderful play it is—I wanted the two main duets particularly to not stop, I think the boys' passage are as funny as anything you've ever done, I sat like a saucepan-lid kept just on the boil, then came home and read it again."[40]

Occasionally in his postcards to Pinter, Stoppard commented on other matters. On one occasion, he told Pinter that "I am afraid my life is bounded by rehearsal—I see nobody outside it" (September 12, 2002), and on another, "I am not a very enthusiastic grandparent but I have my uses." Stoppard occasionally shared a joke with Pinter. He told him that he read in a review of Ira Nadel's biography of himself[41] "that—apparently—I wrote *Schindler's List*" (screenplay) and that on another occasion S[tephen] Spielberg sent me a checque [*sic*] for one million dollars!" (June 23, 2002).[42]

On other occasions, they exchanged messages on versification and, for instance, the triolet: "a Fr[ench] fixed form with eight lines, two rhymes and two refrain lines, patterned ABaAabAB" that "may be split into two quatrains or employed as a stanza form, although poems of one strophe are typical. Line length and meter are not fixed."[43] In a letter written from Fernleigh near Maidenhead where Stoppard lived between August 1972 and October 1979, he told Pinter that "the repeated opening line is a feature of the triolet" and provides illustrations.[44] Stoppard might have been responding to receiving a copy of Pinter's eight-line "magic poem called 'Paris'" dated 1975 (*Must*: 19; *VV* 159). However, the poem is hardly a triolet, perhaps a variation on the form.

Pinter's written communications with Stoppard are either in the Pinter Archive at the British Library or in some instances among Stoppard's correspondence extending from the late 1950s until 2000 and beyond, now at the University of Texas's Harry Ransom Humanities Research Center. They shared each other's work and attended performances of plays and cinematic adaptations. Their meetings were sometimes with others: Stoppard with his second wife, Miriam, or with Felicity Kendall, Stoppard's partner between 1991 and 1998, and Pinter with Antonia. They met at meetings of PEN and shared other causes relating to freedom of expression and performances of the Belarus Free Theatre. One example occurred on April 13, 2007, when the Belarus Free Theatre company performed *Being Harold Pinter*, which Stoppard introduced. Pinter and Antonia attended Stoppard's annual garden party in London on September 4, 1999 and July 5, 2003 (*Chronology*: 301, 253, 282). Pinter saw Stoppard's *Voyage*, the first part of his *The Coast of Utopia* trilogy at the Olivier Theatre (National Theatre) on the evening of July 23, 2002. On July 12, Pinter had been "officially cleared of the oesophageal cancer" (*Must*: 262). At 10:30 p.m. following the performance, Pinter and Stoppard dined at the Ivy, where Pinter regularly either lunched or took an evening meal for a quarter of a century. The first reference to his eating there in his "Appointments Diaries" is on May 30, 1980 when he lunched with David Aukin, the theatrical and executive producer who from 1975 to 1984 administered the Hampstead Theatre. The last reference to the Ivy in Pinter's "Appointment Diaries" occurs on April 9, 2005 when he lunched there with Ronald Harwood (*Chronology*: 274, 98, 294).

The over forty years of friendship between Pinter and Stoppard consisted of a not uncritical mutual admiration society. On May 24, 1976, Pinter, Antonia, Stoppard, and Miriam dined at Odin's. At this dinner, Stoppard confronted Pinter about the extent of the obscene language used in *No Man's Land*, telling Pinter that "'this must be something in you, Harold, waiting to get out.' Harold: 'But I don't plan my characters' lives.' Then to Tom: 'Don't you find they take over sometimes?' Tom: 'No'" (*Must*: 58).

SPECIFIC RESTAURANTS

The evidence provided in Pinter's "Appointment Diaries" and *Must* reveals that many key moments of Pinter's life are associated with restaurants. The venues, then, reveal his circle of friends. When his divorce from Vivien finally took place on August 1, 1980, although Pinter was suffering from bronchitis, he took Antonia "to the Belvedere restaurant where he originally proposed" to her (*Must*: 119; *Chronology* 100; see also chapter 4). Clearly the Belvedere, a restaurant dating back to the seventeenth century in Holland Park, West London, with private dining facilities and sumptuous surroundings, was a favorite Pinter venue, especially for lunch, although occasionally he went there for dinner, too. His "Appointment Diaries" mention at least fifty visits, the first on Friday June 13, 1975, when he met Antonia. They lunched together there on March 5, 1985. The last reference occurred when his health was fading on March 1, 2005; he met the artist David Inshaw for lunch. On December 15, 2004, he met his agent, Judy Daish, there, for the last time, also for lunch. They lunched there on seven occasions, initially on May 10, 1984, although of course they lunched elsewhere, too. It was also a favorite lunching place—not the only place where they met to eat either—for Pinter and Simon Gray. They had at least eight lunches at the Belvedere, the first on December 22, 1982 and the last on February 19, 1987. The Pinters dined there with Gray and Victoria Rothschild on April 8, 1999; the restaurant clearly must have had a good wine list as Pinter and Gray certainly enjoyed fine wine and spent a good deal of money, gained, in Pinter's case, from his lucrative screenwriting career.

In spite of Joan Bakewell's issues with Pinter's dramatic depiction of their seven-year affair in *Betrayal* in 1978, she and Pinter subsequently met at the Belvedere for at least four lunches, the first recorded on July 19, 1983 and the last on February 18, 1987. The restaurant was a location where Pinter met other former lovers, too. For instance, it was one of the restaurants where he lunched on at least three occasions with Jill Johnson, with whom he had a close relationship in the mid-1950s while in repertory at Colchester. These lunches were not necessarily business ones but probably nostalgic, as they occurred after he and Jill recorded *A Slight Ache* for the radio in July 2000 and she performed in Pinter and Di Travis's November 2000 adaptation of *The Proust Screenplay*.[45] They lunched at the Belvedere on August 7, 2001, September 27, 2002, and September 8, 2003. In the late 1960s and early 1970s, a close relationship developed between Pinter and the much older great actress Peggy Ashcroft (see chapter 4). The initial record of them lunching together at the Belvedere is on January 27, 1982; they also lunched there February 10, 1986, and again on September 1986 (*Chronology*: 370, 336, 348, 335).

Clearly, the Belvedere provided a suitable ambience for private, discreet lunches. Pinter and Antonia's daughter Flora lunched together on May 31, 1999 shortly after she formally introduced her new partner, Peter Soros. They subsequently divorced. On the occasion of her and Pinter's lunch, perhaps she shared her doubts and sought Pinter's opinion as to her relationship with Sorus. Pinter met one of Antonia's sons, Orlando Fraser, a barrister who specialized in commercial law, for dinner on November 23, 1984. He dined with him on several occasions at various restaurants. Over the years, Pinter met with his accountant and financial consultant Harold Goodman, with whom he had been at school. The Belvedere was a chosen lunch venue for September 30, 1983 and June 15, 1988. Pinter dined at the Belvedere with another old school friend, the wealthy Maurice Stoppi, with whom he stayed in the West Indies, on September 21, 1984. He lunched on four occasions with Kenneth Ives, the actor-turned-director who produced for television Pinter's *A Kind of Alaska* (1984), *The Dumb Waiter* and *Other Places* (1985), and *The Birthday Party* (1987). This demonstrates Pinter's delight, especially in the 1980s, in lunching at the Belvedere and his combining pleasure with business. He and Ives lunched there on December 2, 1985, August 20, 1986, May 30, 1989, and February 19, 1992. Pinter lunched, too, at the Belvedere on July 9, 1984 with the actor Edward de Souza and the BBC Radio drama producer, Cherry Cookson (*Chronology*: 370, 343–44, 358, 347, 340, 339). This lunch was probably a prelude for "Players," Pinter's recollection about two great players from the world of theatre and cricket: Andrew McMaster and Arthur Wellard. With Edward de Souza and with Pinter's narration, this was produced by Cherry Cookson and broadcast on BBC Radio 3, on Sunday March 17, 1985 (BR: W20: 3).

Pinter's creativity on occasion was inspired at restaurants. According to Antonia, on May 19, 1983, Pinter began to write what became *One for the Road* at the French cuisine–based Le Caprice. He started to talk about a play "about imprisonment and torture." She responded to him, "Quick, quick, there must be a paper and pencil here. This is a Le Caprice, Jeffrey Archer's favorite restaurant" (*Must*: 142).[46] The first record of Pinter's eating at Le Caprice, situated in St. James's, Piccadilly in Central London, is on July 14, 1982 when he met for lunch the actor Terence Rigby, who played the role of Briggs in Peter Hall's 1975 production of *No Man's Land* (*Chronology*: 117).[47] Pinter's final visit to the restaurant is for a dinner with Antonia's son Damian and his wife, Paloma, on the evening of July 28, 2005 (*Chronology*: 297).

Between the period 1972 and 2005, Pinter frequented Le Caprice upward of at least 139 occasions. He met Antonia there, as noted, on May 19, 1983. They celebrated her birthday there on August 27, 1984, and her birthday dinner took place there the following year. Pinter's fifty-fifth birthday celebration dinner on October 10, 1985 took place there; the Fraser family Christmas dinner, too, on December 22, 1985. Pinter and Antonia dined at Le Caprice on her birthday August 27, 1991. They had lunched that day at the Connaught Hotel in Mayfair, where they had celebrated by throwing a party for their third wedding anniversary on Sunday November 27, 1983. Saturday September 18, 1993 saw them lunching there, and on Wednesday November 27, 1996 after lunch at the Ivy in Covent Garden, they celebrated their wedding anniversary by dining late, at 10 p.m., at Le Caprice. On March 11, 1997, Pinter dined with Antonia's daughter Flora and Peter Soros, at Le Caprice. Pinter and Antonia were joined at Le Caprice by Louis Marks for a 9 p.m. dinner on

Thursday December 2, 1999. Pinter and Marks lunched together at the restaurant on March 31, 2002 and again on September 17, 2003 (*Chronology*: 371).

On February 5, 2002, Pinter had an endoscopy. Another family occasion at the restaurant occurred at 8:30 p.m. a few days later following Pinter's "magnificent performance in" *Press Conference* at the Lyttelton at the National Theatre on February 8, 2002 at 6 p.m. (*Must*: 251): Harold and Antonia, Flora, her sister Rebecca Fraser and her husband, Edward Fitzgerald, all dined together (*Chronology*: 272). However, Antonia records in Must that on the following day her husband was "totally exhausted and the bloody indigestion acute." She adds that "terrible days followed of sickness, the problem of eating and so on" (*Must*: 251). On October 20, 2003, Pinter dined with Orlando Fraser; on November 14, 2002, he lunched with Antonia's brother Sir Michael Pakenham and his wife, Mimi, also at Le Caprice (*Chronology*: 276, 284, 277).

Le Caprice was also one of the restaurant venues for meetings with his agent, Judy Daish. They used it on at least fourteen occasions between June 2, 1983 and January 17, 2003, meeting there for lunch. They met there on August 23, 1983, and then, following auditions held at the Haymarket Theatre for *Old Times*, also for lunch on March 11, 1985. Pinter subsequently traveled to Guildford for a dress rehearsal of the play and used the restaurant again for one of their frequent lunch meetings on May 8, 1987. They lunched there on November 15, 1988; on August 14, 1990, two days after an afternoon meeting; also on November 23, 1990; on July 10, 1991 before Pinter went to demonstrate at the House of Commons; and again for lunch on July 28, 1993 before Pinter dined at an unspecified location with the extremely powerful and well-connected publisher George Weidenfeld. Another lunch between Pinter and Daish at Le Caprice occurred on April 6, 1994, and again on September 26, 1995 after Pinter had participated in the PEN protest condemning the hanging of Ken Saro-Wiwa and eight other Ogoni activists. Following their lunch, Pinter went to a rehearsal of Ronald Harwood's *Taking Sides* that he was directing. He then met Geno Lechner, who was performing the role of Emmi Straube in the drama, and at 8 p.m. on the same evening, he and Antonia joined Carlos Fuentes for a dinner at the Mexican Embassy. On another day replete with engagements, after attending a Guatemala Memorial Ceremony, Pinter met Daish for lunch at Le Caprice on March 21, 1996 and in the evening went to a production of Jeremy Sams's translation of Schiller's *Mary Stuart* at the Cottesloe Theatre, the National Theatre. One other lunch at Le Caprice should be mentioned: He met Daish at noon on November 13, 2001 (*Chronology*: 124, 278, 125, 140, 157, 169, 182, 184, 190, 205, 211, 222, 226, 270). Two days later, he wasn't feeling well. This may have had nothing to do with the restaurant, as Antonia writes that "Harold has not felt well since he returned from Canada, a month ago, absolutely exhausted, no energy. Both of us, in it together, feel a kind of despair which luckily we can discuss" (*Must*: 244). Perhaps in an effort to revive his spirits, Pinter lunched with former flame Jill Johnson at Le Caprice at noon on November 16, before departing on November 17–18, 2001 to Berlin to receive the German PEN Hermann Kesten medal recognizing his outstanding commitment on behalf of the cause of persecuted and imprisoned authors (*Chronology*: 270).

Le Caprice was also one of the restaurants where Pinter ate with friends such as Alan Bates, Barry Foster,[48] Edna O'Brien,[49] and Ronald Harwood.[50] Pinter used its private facilities for group dinners. For instance, on March 17, 1985, it was the setting for the cast dinner for *Old Times* prior to its revival at the Theatre Royal Haymarket directed by David Jones on March 24, 1985. Just over ten years later, on August 11, 1995, the cast dinner for Ronald Harwood's *Taking Sides* began there at 10 p.m., its final Chichester performance having taken place on Saturday June 3, 1995. It had opened at London's Criterion Theatre on July 3, 1995. The previous evening, the cast supper for the revival of *Old Times*, due to open at Wyndham's Theatre on June 30, 1995, had taken place at an unspecified location. On November 4, 1987, Pinter arranged a dinner for the fast bowler Ossie Gooding and other Gaieties members to mark Ossie's departure from the team (*Chronology*: 140–41, 160, 220–21, 191).

CONCLUSION

Specific restaurants appealed to Pinter and provided the settings for meetings with friends and groups of friends and those closest to him. An examination of whom he dined with where and when illuminates his friends but cannot reveal the nature of what took place over the meals. Perhaps in the instance of Pinter's friendship with Simon Gray this is fortunate, as both enjoyed their fine wine and no doubt under its influence made comments that subsequently they might regret. Perhaps their love of wine was a consequence of their chain-smoking over the years and the impact that had upon their throats. An account of what occurred during a restaurant meeting is provided in Sir Nicholas Hytner's reminiscences *Balancing Acts: Behind the Scenes at the National Theatre* (2017). Craig Brown reviewed the book in the *Daily Mail*. According to Brown, "Nicholas Hytner's account of running the National Theatre is a heartfelt, gossipy delight." Hytner writes that "one minute you're having to schmooze a sponsor, the next you're dealing with a revolving stage that refuses to revolve and, just when you think it's all over, you're faced with one of Harold Pinter's volcanic rages." Brown's review continues:

> "You're a f****** liar," Pinter shouted at Hytner in a hushed restaurant. "You're a f****** liar, and you're a f****** s***." Years before, Pinter had tried to offload two very minor plays on Hytner; Hytner had hummed and hawed, which Pinter took to be a thumbs-up.

"I'm really sorry if I gave you that impression, Harold. That wasn't my intention. I'm genuinely sorry."

"Don't f****** apologise to me. I'm not interested in your f****** apology. You're a s*** and a liar, and now I've f****** told you."[51]

Certainly, Pinter was not unaware that restaurants are an escape from reality and places where a lot of wine is consumed. His very late short drama *Celebration* "was simply drawn from accumulated memories and experiences" (Billington: 403–4). Set in an upscale London restaurant, the play concerns two groups of diners insulting each other, then joining together and the chief waiter taking over. For him, the restaurant represents "my womb" (33)—the restaurant as a microcosm of existence. In common with so much of Pinter's other work, this play is preoccupied with possession, power, sexual conflict, linguistic games, memory, and mutability. Pinter himself may well have moved from eating cornflakes in shabby boardinghouses and theatrical digs in Eastbourne to the finest London restaurants. His characters likewise moved from East End thugs such as McCann and Goldberg in *The Birthday Party* to former East-Enders, some of whom have made lots of money, in *Celebration*. The restaurant settings are posher and much more expensive. His achievements gave Pinter wealth and friendship, yet his vision remained the same: the weasel underneath the table.

NOTES

1. BLADDMSS: 89094/1.
2. BLADDMSS: 89094/3.
3. Francis Gillen, "From Chapter Ten of *The Dwarfs* to *Mountain Language*: The Continuity of Harold Pinter," *The Pinter Review*, II, i (1988):1.
4. BLADDMSS: 88880/4/17.
5. http://www.classiccafes.co.uk/torino_special.htm, accessed November 26, 2016.
6. https://en.wikipedia.org/wiki/Milk_bar%20accessed%2026%20November%202016.
7. BLADDMSS: 88880/4/17.
8. http://www.oxforddnb.com/view/article/73162, accessed November 26, 2016.
9. BLADDMSS: 88880/4/17.
10. http://boakandbailey.com/2014/03/ian-nairn-wards-irish-house/, accessed November 27, 2016.
11. A printout is with the Pinter Archive, BLADDMSS: 88920/5/2.
12. See https://en.wikipedia.org/wiki/Voss_%28novel%29, accessed June 10, 2016.
13. http://www.bl.uk/eblj/1989articles/pdf/article1.pdf%20accessed%2027%20November%202016.
14. Pinter, *Collected Poems and Prose*, London: Faber, 1991: 52.
15. See chapter 4.
16. http://www.timeout.com/london/restaurants/the-ivy, posted June 17, 2015, accessed June 26, 2016.
17. https://dailyreview.com.au/xenophobia-and/52522/, accessed November 27, 2016.
18. BLADDMSS: 88920/5/2.

19. BLADDMSS: 88920/18. Pinter's remarks are found in published form in Simon Gray's *Key Plays Introduced by H. Pinter*, published by Faber in 2002.

20. For reactions, see http://www.haroldpinter.org/directing/directing_butley. shtml%20accessed%2027%20November%202016.

21. See chapter 4.

22. http://www.haroldpinter.org/directing/directing_life.shtml.

23. See http://www.haroldpinter.org/directing/directing_engage.shtml.

24. *The Holy Terror: Melon Revisited* is a reworking of Gray's earlier play *Melon* (1987). Gray directed the revised version at the Temple of Arts Theatre, Arizona, February 15, 1991, http://simongray.org.uk/plays/the-holy-terror.

25. BLADDMSS: 88880/7/6: ff.51, 27–30, 51–52.

26. See chapter 1.

27. BLADDMSS: 88880/7/6: f.56.

28. BLADDMSS: 88880/7/2.

29. BLADDMSS: 889094/5.

30. BLADDMSS: 88880/6/26.

31. Ronald Harwood, *Sir Donald Wolfit: His Life and Work in the Unfashionable Theatre*, London: Secker and Warburg, 1971.

32. See Baker and Ross: G120.

33. Information from former students of Dr. Casey.

34. John Casey, *The Language of Criticism*, London: Methuen, 1966, reissued 2011; *Morality and Moral Reasoning*, London: Methuen, 1971; *Pagan Virtue: An Essay in Ethics*, Oxford: Clarendon, 1991; and *After Lives: A Guide to Heaven, Hell and Purgatory*, Oxford: Oxford University Press, 2010.

35. BLADDMSS: 88880/6/15.

36. BLADDMSS: 88920/5/2.

37. BLADDMSS: 88880/7/10.

38. BLADDMSS: 88880/6/20.

39. BLADDMSS: 88880/6/21.

40. BLADDMSS: 88880/7/10.

41. Ira Nadel, *Double Act: A Life of Tom Stoppard*, London: Methuen, 2002.

42. BLADDMSS: 88880/6/15.

43. R.Greene et al., *The Princeton Encyclopedia of Poetry & Poetics*, fourth edition, 2012: 1460.

44. BLADDMSS: 88880/7/10.

45. See chapter 4.

46. When Pinter received the Nobel Prize, Jeffrey Archer (1940–) commented, "I thought nothing could surpass winning the Ashes. I was wrong," cited Billington: 425. No meetings between Pinter and Archer seem to be recorded in Pinter's "Appointment Diaries."

47. Rigby played Joey in Peter Hall's 1965 production of *The Homecoming* and Davies in Lindsey Posner's 2003 Bristol production of *The Caretaker*. The initial mention of him in Pinter's "Appointment Diaries" is on February 9, 1966; in addition to the lunch at Le Caprice, they also met on March 13, 1972 and lunched together on September 7, 2004 (*Chronology*: 19, 46, 290).

48. See also chapters 1 and 6.

49. See chapter 4.

50. See also chapters 1 and 2.

51. See http://www.dailymail.co.uk/home/event/article-4447988/Nicholas-Hytner-Balancing-Acts-review-gossipy-delight.html, accessed May 1, 2017.

FOUR

Women

On December 2, 1979, Antonia Fraser records that at the Society of West End Theatre Managers' Awards—subsequently named the "Oliviers"—Pinter's *Betrayal* gained the award for the "Best New Play." Pinter makes "another speech to anybody that will listen." Antonia quotes him: "I love women. I'm resolutely heterosexual. Listen, a woman's waist is the most beautiful thing in the world." Antonia adds: "He puts his arm around the nearest waist which happens by pure coincidence to be that of a woman, and by a further happy coincidence, mine" (*Must*: 112). The reminiscences of Pinter's closest friends while growing up—Mick Goldstein, Moishe Wernick, and Henry Woolf—are full of their encounters with girls. For instance, during the summer of 1949, Pinter and Wernick hitchhiked around Cornwall. Pinter remembered that they met two Yorkshire girls, but it rained and they parted. They returned to London and the summer finished. Wernick became a soldier in Germany. Ron Percival disappeared. Pinter "loved and was loved."[1]

In his *Barcelona is in Trouble*, Woolf remembers meeting "the beautiful Joan Bakewell who made every thinking man's pulse quicken when she appeared on the nightly television program 'Late Night Line-Up.'" Pinter said to him after arranging a meeting of the three of them at the Whitbread Pub in St. George's Square, near the BBC: "Look, Henry, we're in a bit of a fix, Joan and I. We'd like to see a bit more of each other, if you see what I mean. But we have nowhere to go." "I know a clue when I hear one. Well, my place is a bit grubby but you're welcome to visit any time," Woolf responded. This detail is omitted from Pinter's dramatic rendition of their relationship in *Betrayal*, which focuses on the flat in the house where Pinter and Bakewell conducted their seven-year affair. Woolf added that "I wasn't surprised that Harold's darling was beautiful. He attracted beautiful girls all the time. Look at Judith Foster,[2] still absolutely lovely,[3] and Dilys Hamlet,[4] who dumped him when he was a drama school. I remember him being terribly cut up about that. . . . They weren't just good-looking, though, they were High Quality Goods." For Woolf, "two seconds after meeting them, one forgot whether they were beautiful or not because they were so different from each other and so interesting: sometimes mysterious, like Vivien," then Woolf adds in parenthesis, "(did she know anything about his relationship with Joan?)," and continues, "sometimes buzzing with brains and glamour, like Antonia Fraser. Harold was so proud of her." Correctly Woolf adds that "she kept him happy for over thirty years, and in the end, when he was so ill, she nursed him devotedly for what must've been seven terribly difficult years. 'I'm a lucky man, Henry,' he would say to me towards the end. 'A very lucky man. In Antonia, I mean.'"[5]

There is no doubt that women played an important part in Pinter's life. What follows is an alphabetically arranged account of twelve who may be regarded as among the most important ladies in that life. These include Pinter's mother (Frances Pinter), his two wives (Vivien Merchant and Antonia Fraser), three actresses (Peggy Ashcroft, Pauline Flanagan, and Jill Johnson, at least two of whom were also his lovers), other former lovers (Joan Bakewell, Barbara Stanton), a translator and producer who played an important role in Pinter's early career (Barbara Bray), a theatrical designer (Eileen Diss), his agent (Judy Daish), and Edna O'Brien, a longtime mutual friend of both Pinter and Antonia Fraser.

PEGGY ASHCROFT

In 1975, Peggy Ashcroft was playing one of the lead roles in Peter Hall's production of Ibsen's *John Gabriel Borkman* at the National Theatre. Hall records in his diary for Wednesday January 15, 1975 that Pinter told Ashcroft that "he was coming to the run-through. So Peggy, who adores him, got in an emotional state and said she couldn't possibly act if Harold were there." Hall started to lose his temper, saying that he needed help, too. "She got more emotional." Hall "just managed to control [himself] and cool the whole situation." He didn't "want her in a low creative state. . . . So [he] stopped Harold from coming and got on with it."

An indication of the closeness of the Pinter-Ashcroft relationship during this period is further reflected in an entry in Hall's *Diaries* for Monday March 23, 1975. He records that, on the previous Tuesday, March 18—a meeting not noted in Pinter's "Appointment Diaries"—"Harold went to see Peggy and told her he was in love with Antonia Fraser. He also said he would have to tell Vivien, and that he was anxious above everything else that his marriage should not break up." Hall continues, "Today, Harold phoned Peg to say he'd told Vivien, who had, he said, taken it surprisingly well." Hall observes that he feels "uneasy about [Pinter's] state. And also very uneasy about Vivien. Apparently, the Antonia Fraser romance began some six weeks ago. Since then, it has raged passionately" (143, 154). In *Must*, Antonia notes that on June 11, 1980, Peggy Ashcroft "came to lunch, having indicated that she would like to do so." Antonia adds, "So I am FORGIVEN! (She had feared that my arrival as the first person in Harold's life would disrupt the *amitié amoureuse* both treasured: which of course it didn't)." For Antonia, "of all the people [she knows] Peggy is the only one who treats old age with absolute astonishment and outrage. It's because she really is so young inside that she cannot be reconciled to it" (118); Peggy Ashcroft, born in 1907, was seventy-two at the time!

Edith Margaret Emily Ashcroft, known as "Peggy," was born in Croydon in Surrey; her mother's side of the family were of Jewish origins. Recognized as one of the great British actresses of the twentieth century, when she came on the stage, in the words of John Gielgud, "it was as if all the lights in the theatre had suddenly gone up" (*Chronology*: 306). Very active in her commitment to liberal and left-leaning causes, especially the Campaign for Nuclear Disarmament, she encouraged Pinter to believe that as a dramatist and public figure his espousal of political causes would have considerable influence. She and Pinter were very close from the late 1960s onward. Indicative of this closeness are the nearly fifty references to Peggy Ashcroft in Pinter's "Appointment Diaries" (see *Chronology*: 335). Pinter chose her rather than his then-wife, Vivien Merchant, to play the role of Beth in *Landscape* on the radio in April 1968, directed by Guy Vaesen. Ashcroft subsequently appeared in the role in July 1969 at the Royal Shakespeare Company under Hall's direction. She was the second voice in *Family Voices*, broadcast on BBC Radio 3 in January 1981 and at the National Theatre Platform Performance under Hall's direction a month later.

Awarded the CBE in 1951 and becoming Dame Peggy five years later, she was very important in fostering the development of the Royal Shakespeare Company and encouraging Hall. Michael Billington, her biographer, observed in his *Oxford Dictionary of National Biography* (*ODNB*) entry on her: "She seemed to have an especial affinity with Pinter: as Beth in *Landscape* she sat in a humble kitchen chair with a cardigan draped around her shoulders, remembering the past with erotic ecstasy but entirely estranged from the husband sitting opposite her. It was as if a door had come down between them. 'Not, I feel, an ordinary door,' said Pinter, 'but a great big clanking, iron door that she had pulled down between her and the rest of the world.'"

In addition to their political affinities, she and Pinter shared many characteristics. Both attempted to protect, not always successfully, their personal lives. Billington "was always stimulated by her willingness to discuss theatre, politics, books, cricket, and people, yet also aware of an aura of solitude, as if she lacked the consolation of permanent companionship." An important difference is that in Antonia Fraser, Pinter found such "companionship" and love. Both possessed their own kind of "granite-like integrity"[6]—in Pinter's case also especially with his close friends from childhood.

To repeat, Peggy Ashcroft and Pinter met on many occasions over nearly thirty years until her death in June 1991. These encounters were not confined to rehearsals for her appearances in *Landscape* and *Family Voices*. Frequent meetings from 1979 to 1981 reflect a concern with National Theatre matters and the industrial relations at the company. Both served as associates during a difficult period. She and Pinter met following Pinter's drafting of *One for the Road* in the spring of 1984; Pinter accompanied Ashcroft to a performance of *Mountain Language* on November 3, 1988; both met with the actor Michael Kitchen, who doesn't appear to have performed in a Pinter play or been directed by Pinter, at the La Barca Restaurant on February 13, 1981. If these encounters are considered as evidence, it appears that Ashcroft advised Pinter on casting issues (129, 131, 168, 104).

Some of Ashcroft and Pinter's meetings seem to have been of short duration; for instance, in the early evening, prior to supper often spent with others, again suggesting that they were discussing professional matters. Generally, Pinter doesn't record where he and Ashcroft met for lunch; they rarely, if ever, met for evening dinner. When they lunched, it would be at the Belvedere or Wilton's. The last record of their lunching together is at Ivy's on August 31, 1990, a short time after Pinter and Antonia's marriage was "convalidated" on August 27, 1990 (113, 147, 151, 156, 183). Pinter attended Peggy Ashcroft's funeral on June 21, 1991. Three days later, he went to the Westminster Abbey Deanery at 3:10 p.m. to make arrangements for her memorial at the Abbey, and on June 6, 2005 was present when a plaque in her memory was dedicated at Westminster Abbey (189, 190, 296). According to Michael Billington's *ODNB* entry on Peggy Ashcroft, Pinter and Peter Hall gave addresses at her memorial service held in Westminster Abbey on November 30, 1991. However, Lady Antonia Fraser doesn't recall Pinter giving an address, and, as she observes, "I was there and don't remember an address."[7] All serve to exemplify a major Pinter concern: fallibility, the unreliability of memory, and the need to verify!

JOAN BAKEWELL

Television presenter, newsreader, journalist, and Labour Peer Joan Bakewell (née Rowlands) was dubbed by Frank Muir in the popular press and elsewhere as the original "thinking man's crumpet."[8] Born into a working-class home in Stockport in Cheshire in 1933, Bakewell was educated at the local High School for Girls and gained a scholarship to Newnham

College Cambridge. A powerful account of the early years, experiences in the male-dominated media world, and of her seven-year affair with Pinter from 1962 to 1969, conducted while each was married to other partners, is found in her autobiography *The Centre of the Bed* (2003). Another account of the affair, her forty-five-minute drama *Keeping in Touch*, written in the 1970s as a riposte to Pinter's *Betrayal*, received its premiere on BBC Radio 4 on April 22, 2017. A lifelong Labour Party supporter, Bakewell was awarded a CBE in 1999, became a DBE in 2008, and in 2010 a lifetime peerage.

Her relationship with Pinter formed the foundation for his *Betrayal* (1978), written in late 1977, and they continued to meet on a regular basis until just before his death. In fact, their first meeting recorded in Pinter's "Appointments Diaries" is on April 23, 1966, when he visited Bakewell and her then-husband, Michael, who was a radio and television producer, director, and formally BBC head of plays. They were married from 1955 to 1972 and had two children. She then was married to Jack Emery, the director, writer, and stage producer, from 1975 to 2001. The final meeting between Pinter and Bakewell is recorded on July 11, 2003, when they met for lunch. In other words, Pinter and Bakewell's friendship survived over a tumultuous half century, as they knew each other as early as 1962.

Bakewell's first husband, Michael, was an early BBC advocate of Pinter's work. He unsuccessfully supported the broadcasting of Pinter's thirty-minute radio play *Something in Common* in 1958 (BR: W8) and *The Dwarfs* as a radio play, broadcast in December 1960. Bakewell produced the Third Programme broadcast of *The Examination* in June 1962 and Pinter's *Review Sketches* (nine of them) on BBC Radio in May 1964 (BR: W11). He also produced Pinter's reading of *The Tea Party* as a short story on BBC Radio in April 1964 and was also involved with supporting the TV production of *A Slight Ache* in February 1967. His friendship with Pinter ended with *Betrayal*. However, in 1995 he adapted Pinter's *Proust Screenplay* into a two-hour radio play.[9]

In an over-sensationalized newspaper headline, "Why Is the Thinking Man's Crumpet So Proud of Being A Husband Stealer? As Joan Bakewell Uses Her Harold Pinter Affair to Plug A New Book, How Women Flaunt The Betrayals Which Tear Families Apart," Barbara Davies writes in the *Daily Mail* (October 26, 2016) that at the time that Joan and Pinter started their sexual relationship in 1962, later renting a Kentish town flat where they could meet, they and their spouses went to dinner parties at each other's homes. Harriet, the daughter of Joan and Michael, was a guest at one of Daniel Pinter's birthday parties. The "magical moment" when Pinter in play threw Joan's daughter into the air and caught her is frequently recalled by Bakewell and occurs in *Betrayal*. According to Bakewell, "[T]here was never any talk of leaving their marriages." However, Davies writes that Pinter's "letters reveal that Pinter was privately thinking of doing exactly that." In a letter concerning "Vivien at the height of his affair with Bakewell in February 1967, he wrote 'it appears quite possible that we will separate (how?). . . . We certainly can't go on like this. I now feel that I'm more at fault than she is and have been. But one can't talk about fault.'" As Davies indicates, "[I]n the end, as Bakewell's own TV presenting career took off, it became increasingly difficult for the pair to meet and they ended their affair by mutual consent in 1969." Davies adds that "'there was no harshness, no recrimination,' Bakewell wrote in her autobiography, behind the scenes, however, Pinter's marriage to Vivien was already coming apart at the seams."[10]

For Michael Billington, Bakewell's *Keeping in Touch* "is lighter in texture and brisker in tone than Pinter's [*Betrayal*] and" according to Bakewell, "her version is closer to the facts of the matter. It deftly tells the story from her perspective and raises fascinating questions about the frustrations of bourgeois marriage." It places the actual events at a little distance. Her heroine, named Rachel, is a professional translator who after spending three years at university remains at home with small children. Her life changes through meeting an eminent architect named Tom who, with her husband, is working on a TV documentary and "ardently pursuing her. They meet in pubs and parks and Rachel palpably enjoys the sense of engaging in a flirtatious relationship that seems to be leading in one inevitable direction." The play "is, very clearly, about an intelligent woman trapped in a domestic life that denies her fulfilment. She also has a crucial speech in which she talks about the way marriage cuts you off from attractive and beguiling people and becomes 'a limit on life.'" Billington adds that "Pinter's play is also not simply a re-creation of an old affair but a study of the multiple betrayals, not least of our youthful aspirations, that we all experience."[11]

Antonia writes that, on November 27, 1977, "Harold has begun to write a new play." This became *Betrayal*, although it was referred to as *Unsolicited Manuscript* and then *Torcello*. It "began with the image of Harold finding out from Michael Bakewell that he, Michael, had long known of Harold's affair with his wife Joan—from Joan herself." Antonia continues, "[B]ut Bakewell had not let on to Harold when he met him in the role of radio producer. Harold began by saying: 'I hope Joan won't mind.'" Antonia had not read the play then and "thought that [Joan] would be flattered." Joan and Antonia "got on well" and occasionally met for lunch. Joan helped her with some of Antonia's own work. Her relationship with Pinter, as she described it to Antonia when they initially met, "was very much an on-off affair with prolonged gaps; it was also complicated by the fact that without Joan's knowledge (or Vivien's for that matter) Harold became obsessed with a woman in America [Barbara Stanton] whom he described as looking like Cleopatra, so there were many levels of deception." Antonia also observes that Michael Billington's Pinter biography created a press "tizzy about the revelation of Harold's affair with Joan Bakewell in the sixties" and some close to Bakewell consider that she "has made rather a meal of the whole thing in the book" (*Must*: 85–86, 223).

For Bakewell, reflecting on her affair with Pinter and scenes in *Betrayal* such as the throwing of her daughter in the air reveal an important element in Pinter's work: its autobiographical nature. She told Michael Billington that Pinter "mines exhaustively what is happening to him. It's very difficult to talk about this without talking about [*Betrayal*] which is about my relationship with Harold; and which is all true. It's accurate in its chronology and its events." She added that the play resembles "a diary and so I was upset when I first read it. Harold kept saying, '[I]t's a play—it's a play.' I was upset, however, because it was called *Betrayal*. It's such a judgemental [*sic*] word. But we go on betraying, don't we? . . . The irony is that the process never ends." For Pinter, on the other hand, the play gave them pause *after* he'd written it. At the time, the compulsion to write overrode everything else. Pinter knew that he was getting into something related to his past, but not literally his own past. "The experience was transmuted into something else." He and Michael Bakewell were not at all close; they had simply worked together and got along well. But, Pinter said, the play "just happened." And Pinter tells Billington that the kind of questions he is asking "only start to arise when you send the play to the person involved"—that is, Joan Bakewell (Billington: 265–66).

David Jones, Joan's contemporary at Cambridge, worked with Pinter on many productions and also writes about her and Pinter's reactions to *Betrayal*. In his "Staging Pauses and Silences," Jones recalls dining with Joan before *Betrayal* was produced; she told Jones about her affair with Pinter and the fact that Pinter had written a play about it. She "didn't know how to stop him doing this play. It can't happen." Jones responded that there were two pertinent questions to consider: "'Number one is it a good play?' She said, 'Dam it, yes.'" Jones then asked her, "'So, do you think people will recognize you?' And she said, 'I don't know.'" Jones responded that she will have to take the risk and observed that "she didn't blow up the production." Jones was subsequently offered the film of *Betrayal* to direct. Early in 1982, a week prior to filming, Pinter invited him home for a drink and told Jones, "Well I've got to tell you quite frankly, this movie is about myself. What happens in the movie, it happened to me." He then tells Jones about his affair with Bakewell. Jones responded that he'd known about it for four years. "How do you know that?" Pinter asked. Jones responded that Bakewell had told him and that Pinter didn't "have to tell him now." Jones added that this "was a marvellous copy of what happens between the two men in the play." He added that "strangely [*Betrayal*] was the play about which [Pinter] was the least possessive. It has hardly any camera instructions" and Pinter didn't "ever talk to [Jones] about how he thought [Jones] should shoot it."[12]

Billington cites Bakewell as saying that "Harold and I are very fond of each other . . . and have terrific lunches" (265). There are over one hundred meetings between them and sometimes with others recorded in Pinter's "Appointment Diaries" between 1966 and 2003. Many of the venues are not noted by Pinter; others are. Over the years, their favorite lunch venue seems to be Cibo's—Pinter went there frequently—an Italian restaurant in Holland Park West London. Other haunts included the Belvedere, Le Caprice, Odette's, Little Acropolis, Clarke's, and Orsino's. Other restaurants where they ate at least once included the upmarket Waldorf, the Café Royal, Odin's, La Barca, and Sheekey's. Pinter was present at Bakewell's fiftieth birthday party on April 17, 1983 and her sixtieth birthday party on May 2, 1993 (*Chronology*: 123, 203). In the record of his friendships it is difficult, with the exception of his three schoolmates, Woolf, Goldberg, and Wernick, and Pinter's agent Judy Daish, to find such a consistent pattern of meetings and relationships, which even survived a lengthy affair and dramatic enactment, as that between Joan Bakewell and Harold Pinter.

In 2016, she observed, "To be with Harold Pinter was to enjoy yourself. He was very witty, he was a great raconteur and he knew a great deal of poetry off by heart and would recite it. We remained friends throughout his life and he would occasionally say, 'We did have fun, didn't we Joan?' And yes we did."[13]

BARBARA BRAY

Barbara Bray (née Jacobs) was a translator, critic, producer, and close friend of Samuel Beckett, with whom she enjoyed a triangular relationship following his marriage. An identical twin, she was born in Maida Vale, West London, on November 24, 1924. Her father was a clerical officer at the Ministry of Health. After attending Preston Manor County Grammar School, Brent, in North West London, she gained a state scholarship in 1942 to Girton College Cambridge, where she read English and also studied French and Italian, gaining a first class degree in English. Following graduation, she married John Bray, an Australian-born fellow student who'd been a RAF prisoner of war and who was five years older than her. They then spent three years teaching English in Cairo and Alexandria prior to returning to London. In 1953, Bray obtained a position as script editor in the drama department of the freshly inaugurated BBC Third Programme, where she commissioned and translated avant-garde writing including Beckett and others. "Although life was not always kind to her,"[14] according to Dan Gunn, "when Bray's husband died in an accident in Cyprus in early 1958, leaving Bray in sole charge of her two young daughters, Francesca and Julia, Beckett wrote her a condolence letter that indicated how close he believed their two (strictly irreligious) attitudes were, towards life and towards death."[15]

At the BBC, she greatly encouraged Pinter's early work, and he was grateful to her throughout his life for her crucial early support. She commissioned for BBC Radio *A Slight Ache*, *A Night Out*, and *The Dwarfs*, which she directed as a radio play broadcast on the Third Programme on December 2, 1960. She was the script editor in May 1957 for *The Room*, subsequently rejected by the BBC. In November 1958, Pinter sent her a detailed synopsis of *The Hothouse* (see Billington: 101), and she fought hard for opportunities to gain radio hearings for his work, for instance, assisting him after the failure of *The Birthday Party*.

From 1961 onward, she lived in Paris as a freelance translator, known for translating Flaubert, Marguerite Duras, Julia Kristeva, Jean Genet, and others. In 1980 she was awarded the PEN translation prize, and on four occasions she received the prestigious Scott Moncrieff translation prize. She worked with Joseph Losey and Pinter for many years on their Proust translation. Finalized in 1973, the screenplay remained un-filmed, but she assisted with the 1995 radio production. Pinter dedicated its 1977 publication to Bray and to Losey (see BR: B3). Later on in her career, she co-founded a Paris-based theatre company where she directed lesser-known works by Pinter and Beckett, among others.

Pinter and Bray communicated frequently in the early years of his career, and they worked on the Proust translation. His "Appointment Diaries" record their meetings from 1960, although they began earlier, until 2003. At the end of July 1970, Pinter met her and Beckett in Paris. In November of the same year, he met her to discuss his directing of Joyce's *Exiles*, then running at the Mermaid Theatre. In October of the next year, Pinter again met her during his visit to Paris to see the French production of his *Old Times* at the Théâtre Montparnasse. In December 1971, they worked together adapting Proust, a project that preoccupied them and Losey throughout the following year and after. For instance, on February 14, 1972, he and Bray lunched together, and at 5 p.m. that afternoon, Losey joined them to discuss the Proust adaptation. They worked together on the project the following day. A month later, Pinter was again in Paris discussing Proust with her, and he then returned to London following a visit with Beckett. During the morning of July 19, 1972, Pinter, Bray, and Losey went to the BBC TV Centre to view a Proust film and then lunch together. There was further collaborative work in September and October 1972. On October 5, 1972, Pinter and Bray lunched together at Odin's, with its French cuisine, located near Madame Tussaud's and Regents Park (*Chronology*: 371). They may have been celebrating the completion of a version of the Proust adaptation, as a copy of the film script with the date "Oct. 25, 1972" is located "in the Gregory Peck Collection, Margaret Herrick Library, Academy of Motion Pictures Arts and Sciences,

Beverley Hills, Calif [that] suggests that [Gregory] Peck was considered for one of the roles in the film" (*Sharp Cut*: 440).

Bray's name doesn't occur in Pinter's "Appointment Diaries" for almost another five years until April 21, 1977 when they lunched together. Nearly a month later, they met in Paris before Pinter returned to London and industrial unrest at the National Theatre. They met again on June 27, 1977 and lunched after Christmas of the same year when Pinter's *Betrayal* was gestating. On the same date, December 28 a year later, this time while Pinter was at work on the film script of *The French Lieutenant's Woman*, they lunched together again (*Chronology*: 338).

On May 14, 1979, Pinter and Antonia spent an evening with Beckett and Bray. Pinter at the time was directing Simon Gray's *Close of Play*. According to Antonia, Beckett's eyes shone wide at Pinter's depiction of the play. She added that Bray behaved well until at the end, when she started claiming that everything in art is political. At the time, Bray was rehearsing for her appearance on *The Critics* program on the radio, and Antonia suspected Gray's play would not fare well. Responding to Bray, Pinter surprisingly said that nothing he has written is political. Beckett added that the absence of politics is a political statement in itself. Bray couldn't leave it at that, according to Antonia, and finally, Beckett lit one of his little black cheroots and asked why she talks so much. Everyone in the group got along better after that, with Bray no longer "lecturing" Pinter on his own work (*Must*: 104–5).

Bray's behavior didn't prevent her and Pinter meeting for lunch on May 16, 1980 at Little Acropolis, a Greek restaurant situated in Gunnersbury Lane, Acton, in West London (see *Chronology*: 371). There is no record of their meeting for almost another seven years, until they lunched together in London on April 14, 1987. More than three years later, they again lunched at Little Acropolis, on August 7, 1991. Nearly five years later, on February 8, 1996, Pinter records that Bray and Tom Stoppard, among others, were corresponding about his recently opened play, *Ashes to Ashes*. He and Bray met twice for lunch in 1998. They corresponded in September 1999 regarding *Celebration*. Their final two meetings after nearly half a century of engagement are both for lunch: on April 21, 2003 and March 28, 2005. On this final occasion, they met at 12:30 p.m. prior to Pinter being interviewed at 5 p.m. that afternoon on French television followed by an 8 p.m. dinner with the distinguished Parisian-based publishers Gallimard. Two days later, *The Caretaker* opened in Paris, directed by the eminent French director Roger Planchon (*Chronology*: 338).

JUDY DAISH

Judy Daish is Antonia Fraser's "dramatic agent as well as Harold's agent and our close friend" (*Must*: 281). She also managed Simon Gray's theatrical works. Gray's *The Year of the Jouncer* begins in the Barbados when he is on holiday with his wife, Victoria Rothschild, in the winter and New Year of 2003–2004. Gray observes that Pinter's "capacity for explosive anger is currently diminished because of his recent poor health" (54). Gray illustrates Daish's long reach. She rang Gray in Barbados to tell him that she had just heard that "the artistic director of the Birmingham rep" would like to stage *The Old Masters* (60)—Pinter went on to direct it. Following the first London performance of Gray's *The Holy Terror* at the Duke of York's Theatre in 2004, he and Victoria were accompanied by William and Caroline Waldegrave and Daish and "her new chap Gordon . . . the first chap I can remember with husband status" at dinner. Gray writes that she has been his "agent for twenty-five years or so, a great beauty with many sympathetic features—a kind, generous, thoughtful and I would say caring, if I could bear the word" (116–17).

Among her duties were to convey the tenor of reviews to the dramatists, assuming that they hadn't already read them. In the case of Simon Gray, for instance, he seems to have avoided reading reviews, whereas Pinter and Antonia read them.[16] She also reported on the phone or in person on advance ticket requests and interest, whether "we look set for a decent run, there's been foreign interest," matters including cinematic and television rights and interest, requests for media interviews, and so on (*Jouncer*: 173). These were all handled by Daish as were all "official" correspondence, such as requests from all over the world to translate Pinter's work, to reprint it, to cite from it, to clarify whether or not there was and still is a copyright issue involved. Correspondence might well relate to requests to perform Pinter or to request that he contribute to something, or there might be letters from the office of a prime minister offering an honour [*sic*]. Gray in *Jouncer* gives an account of Daish sending by messenger a letter that "had just arrived at her office . . . from the Office of the Prime Minister" offering Gray an honour in the "New Year's list" (256). Other Daish functions included handling requests to speak, to become associated with this or that cause, to give money, and so on; in other words, the myriad activities that a writer's agent performs as well as skillfully acting on the author's behalf in terms of negotiating contracts, film rights, and so on.

Jimmy Wax, a leading literary agent, founded Theatrical and Cinematic Limited (ACTAC) in 1946 after serving as a judge in the British Army of Occupation in post-war Europe. He took a first in law at New College, Oxford. In July 1957, Wax wrote to Pinter proposing that he represent him, which he did until Wax's death on April 23, 1983. Pinter and many others indebted to Wax contributed to a volume of commemorative essays and memoirs, *Jimmy* (Pendragon Press, 1984; BR: E22). He was succeeded by Daish, whom he had trained for five years. Ever protective of Pinter, who dedicated *The Dwarfs* to her (BR: D8), she represented his estate as well as Antonia Fraser's dramatic rights. With

notable exceptions such as Antonia Fraser, Daish met Pinter more frequently than others following Wax's death until 2006. The final meeting
between them was recorded by Pinter on December 21, 2006 at 1 p.m.,
following Pinter's discharge from the Royal Marsden Hospital on December 13, 2006 (*Chronology*: 299).

There is a pattern in their meetings, which took place usually on a
twice-monthly basis when they met for lunch or dinner or both from May
12, 1983 until their 2006 lunch meeting at L'Epicure. They would meet
following Pinter's overseas visits soon after he returned to catch up as,
for instance, their lunch on October 9, 1984, a day after Pinter returned
from New York. At 6:30 p.m. on the same day, she again met him with
the director David Jones, probably to discuss plans for an upcoming production. Sometimes, they ate with others. For instance, on January 11,
1984, Gray joined them. If something urgent appears to have cropped up,
they met as, for instance, at 11 a.m. five days later on January 16, 1984;
although in this instance as in others the "Appointment Diaries" do not
reveal what the frequent meetings specifically were about. In March 1984,
they met on March 7 at 6 p.m., then a week later on March 14 at 6:30 p.m.
On March 20, they met at 11 a.m. and then again at 6 p.m. at a party for
the publication of *Jimmy* and then on March 26 at 1 p.m. for lunch where
they were joined by Alan Bates. This was followed by lunch at 1 p.m. at
the Belvedere on May 10, 1984 following a May 3 1 p.m. lunch (*Chronology*: 299, 135, 129, 131–32).

The choice of restaurants where business was conducted followed a
pattern and frequently included Pinter's favorite ones: Figuring prominently were Orsino (*ibid.*, 228, 229, 235), Le Caprice (124, 157), L'Epicure
(129, 144), Thompson's (156, 159), Chez Moi (161, 164) and the Belvedere
(see, for instance, 132). Two meetings pre-date Jimmy Wax's death. The
first recorded is on October 28, 1975 at 6 p.m. with no location given (63)
and June 21, 1978 for lunch in the company of Wax and Gray (82). Unre-
corded is Daish's presence at other occasions, such as, for instance, the
Europa Theatre Prize at Turino, Italy, from March 8 to 12, 2006 when
Pinter, accompanied by Antonia Fraser, received the European Theatre
Award. Judy Daish was a discreet presence, protecting her client's rights.

Clearly, Pinter and Daish found other means over the years to communicate, such as on the phone as opposed to meals. The frequency of
their meetings suggests that they enjoyed each other's company and that
Pinter preferred to conduct his business affairs face-to-face. He also was
not afraid to show who the boss was. There were occasions when his
agent refused permission on Pinter matters. Once she heard that Pinter
had allowed something, she quickly backed down.[17] During Pinter's final
illness, Antonia records that Pinter fell at night. Daish and her husband
came instantly when summoned at 3 a.m. (*Must*: 296).

EILEEN DISS

Eminent cinematic and film production designer, Eileen Diss was educated at the Central School of Arts and Crafts at St. Martin's. Diss began working for the BBC in the early 1950s, focusing on children's television. She became, in Michael Codron's words, Pinter's "most regular designer, with a special gift for giving a fairly conventional setting a crucial dislocation or nudge from naturalism."[18] She and Pinter initially met when they worked together on the television production of *The Tea Party* in 1964. They later worked on *The Basement* and Joyce's *Exiles*. In his interview with Diss in *The Stage* (May 21, 2015), Nick Smurthwaite noted that "in the 1970s, she began designing for the theatre as well, prompted by an invitation from Harold Pinter to work on a revival of James Joyce's *Exiles* he was directing at the Mermaid Theatre. 'I'd done a couple of TV plays with Harold, so we got on quite well together. We were both a bit nervous about doing a stage play. He was very meticulous. If he didn't like something, he'd tell you.'"[19]

Diss worked with Pinter on his final play, *Celebration*, at the Almeida in 2000, and they worked together on his production of Simon Gray's *The Old Masters* in the spring of 2014. She also collaborated with many other dramatists, including Simon Gray, with whom she worked extensively (including his *Butley, Otherwise Engaged, Quartermaine's Terms, The Rear Column, Cell Mates, Life Support,* and *The Old Masters*), Ronald Harwood (*Taking Sides*), and David Mamet (*Oleanna*). Diss was the production designer for the cinematic adaptation of *Betrayal*, nominated for the 1983 Academy of Motion Picture Arts and Sciences Awards; it won the awards for Best Picture Writing and the "Best Screenplay Based on Material from Another Medium" (*Sharp Cut*: 256). In fact, during the course of her career she won six BAFTA awards.

In one of the few discussions of the significance of her sets for an appreciation of Pinter's work, Marc Silverstein draws attention to ironic juxtapositions in his "'Talking about Some Kind of Atrocity': *Ashes to Ashes* in Barcelona." He comments that her set for *Ashes to Ashes* "creates an aura of bourgeois comfort and security [and] underscores the insularity of a class that 'creates' the reality it chooses to recognize. . . . Diss's set design perfectly captures the 'idyllic' self-enclosure from such 'horror' that the play increasingly erodes through its insistent deconstruction of the opposition between private and public" (*Pinter Review* [1997 and 1998]: 75). There are also characters in *Celebration* who believe that their money and lifestyle will protect them. They adopt a similar stance to characters in Pinter's cinematic adaptation of Fred Ulhman's *Reunion*, set in Stuttgart just before the Nazis seized power, which depicts the illusion of German Jewish families who believed that their wealth and position and war service would protect them from historical reality, the reality of the everyday.

In an interview conducted on March 15, 2005, Diss was asked by Ewan Jeffrey about working with Pinter on *The Tea Party* in 1964. Pinter wrote it as a television play for the BBC TV, European Broadcasting Union; it had been written the previous year as a short story and was televised on March 25, 1965. Charles Jarrott directed, Leo McKern played Disson, and Vivien Merchant played Wendy (see BR: W23). Diss told Jeffrey that this was the first time she met Pinter, and although she had more contact with Jarrott on that production, Pinter "was round quite a bit, but I didn't really have a lot to do with him, but the next one we did was *The Basement*, I think the following year . . . it was 1965. On that occasion, Harold played Stott with Derek Godfrey alongside him" with Kika Markham in the role of Jane. This was broadcast on BBC-2, February 20, 1967. *The Basement* presented technical difficulties. For instance, it features both a fish tank being smashed and a cricket match. Diss recalls that they produced it at the Ealing Studios and the room had to change "from what it was to suddenly becoming Swedish Modern and then becoming Italianate . . . Renaissance and put it on film." They "did some exteriors, too, on the beach"; these "were obviously on film." Further, they "built the set inside the tank, at Ealing. Because the BBC at that time owned Ealing Studios and all their interior filming was done on the stages there." They built the set inside the fish tank and all the water spilt out and they rushed "about with buckets after the shot . . . picking up flapping goldfish . . . putting them back into the water. I don't think we lost one at all."

Jeffrey then asked her about her move to the theatre from television and the difference. "The first time was in fact, *Exiles* for Harold at the Mermaid. It was the Mermaid, and they had very little money. And really the terrific difference then was the lack of back-up, you know, having been used to the BBC where there was a big workshop." Jeffrey then turned to "the double-bill of [*Celebration*] and *The Room* and how [Diss] prepared that." Jeffrey asked her whether she referred to designs used for previous Pinter productions. Diss responded that *The Room* was very early Pinter, set at the beginning of the 1950s. They were thinking about a "room in a house full of bed-sits and small flats, rather crumbling, and I imagined it somewhere around the Tottenham or Shepherd's Bush area." The people who lived in them shared bathrooms. "Life hadn't changed very much since the immediate post-war really, for these people [with] the sink in the room and the gas-fire in the room. They're living in one room." Diss adds that "it is something of both a haven and a prison for Rose—she doesn't go out really, except to the shops perhaps." Consequently, "she's very defensive [about] who comes to the door." In addition, "Harold and I had the same sort of memory, I think—of that sort of life." How Diss conveyed this in her design was initially "to take note of where you are. And we were at the Almeida, which is certainly elliptical." All the action has to be accommodated into a small space: "cooking at the stove, water from the sink, looking out of the window, lighting a gas fire, opening the door onto a landing." The design also has to create "the impression that this is a real room."

The much later *Celebration*, dating from 1999 (BR: W62), features the feeling of security within its restaurant space and opulence that has "a lot to do with the maître d'" who gives the diners "their sense of importance." The design for *Celebration* was in some respects simpler, as "there's 50 years between the two plays, so the difference in those 50 years is startling, really, in every way [for] both the people and the setting. And the play itself, the contrast between the two is extraordinary." Jeffrey adds that "it's extraordinary too, knowing now that, according to Pinter . . . that that will be his last play." [20]

The first meeting between Pinter and Diss recorded in Pinter's "Appointment Diaries" occurs during the morning of August 26, 1970. Diss did not design the sets for James Hammerstein's double-bill productions of *The Tea Party* and *The Room* that opened at the Duchess Theatre on September 17, 1970, so the two subsequent 1970 meetings between Pinter and Diss must have concerned the set designs for the upcoming production of Joyce's *Exiles* that opened at the Mermaid on November 12, 1970. Pinter and Diss met over one hundred times between August 26, 1970, and their final meeting is recorded in Pinter's "Appointment Diaries" on May 3, 2004 when Pinter directed Gray's *The Old Masters*. Diss designed. The great majority of meetings seem to be brief and relate to professional matters: Diss's designs either for Pinter's own work in the theatre or on film. For example, Diss was the production designer for the film *Betrayal*, directed by David Jones and released in 1982. Discussion may also have been on the plays Pinter was directing, such as those by Gray or by Robert East; Pinter directed East's *Incident at Tulse Hill* at the Hampstead Theatre in late 1981. Another example would be David Mamet's *Oleanna*, directed by Pinter in the spring of 1993.

Pinter directed and Diss designed the sets for his own work that also went on provincial runs such as *The Caretaker* in the spring and early summer of 1991. Sometimes they met with others, for instance, in the company of Gray during the production of his plays (see March 23 and May 1, 1981) or on February 4, 2000 at 6 p.m. with Dany Everett, who was the costume designer for *Celebration* and other Pinter works. There are a few occasions on which Diss and Pinter lunched together; they don't appear to have dined together. They met for lunch on October 24, 1979 at L'Epicure, just after Pinter had spent the morning with Václav Havel discussing demonstrations, and on May 30, 1980 at 12:30 p.m. for drinks with the theatrical and executive producer David Aukin at the Ambassadors. Their meetings were arranged at eleven in the morning before Pinter went to a luncheon appointment with someone else (see, for instance, October 18, 1995), or at 6 p.m. prior to Pinter's dining with another (see

July 29, 1996), providing additional testimony to the professional nature of the long-standing Pinter-Diss relationship (*Chronology*: 341).

PAULINE FLANAGAN

Pinter met Pauline Flanagan when they both were members of the same repertory company during the 1951 to 1953 period. Following his first stint in Anew McMaster's touring company, Pinter wrote to Henry Woolf from the King's Theatre Hammersmith where Pinter performed with Donald Wolfit's company. On May 13, 1953, Pinter tells Woolf that he and Flanagan are getting married as soon as possible and that he is leaving for Ireland immediately after the season ends. Following his return to Ireland, Pinter writes in a bawdy manner to Woolf that both men have always appreciated the "female buttock." With echoes from *King Lear*, he adds, "Pauline, of course. . . . She is you know. As flies to wanton boys. Women? Both of us, mates . . . you and me both." Some months later, probably in September, while in Waterford, Pinter has learned that Woolf and his girlfriend have parted. Pinter tells Woolf that love, to some degree, still remains on both sides but the "twoness" of it is no more. For Pinter, love has "spiked deep into my soul, and scalded my being." He says that the moon changes people, and Pinter would never lose faith in such things.

A lengthy handwritten letter from Pinter extending over six sheets of paper from digs in Seatown, Dundalk, County Louth, dated Saturday 18 [July 1953] well expresses Pinter's mood at the time. He tells Woolf that both he and Flanagan are deeply happy. Every morning is a new discovery, and the discovery never ends. With a foreboding note, he observes that whatever the future holds, it cannot take away from the present. The "beat and tick" of his life is now Pauline; he is in love with her. In September from Listowel, County Kerry, Pinter tells Woolf that Flanagan sends her love to him and that they are both well.[21] Similar sentiments are echoed in a letter from Dundalk to Mick Goldstein on July 29, 1953, in which Pinter admits to living in Pauline's world and that life is extraordinarily balanced at the moment. Pinter also speaks of cricket, Lewis Carroll's *Alice in Wonderland*, "a preliminary examination of" Shakespeare's *Measure for Measure*, Franz Kafka's *The Trial*, portions again of Henry Miller's novel *Black Spring*, published in 1936 (see chapter 6) and Pinter's own miscellaneous prose.[22]

Writing to Woolf toward the end of his stay in Ireland, from Carlow, County Carlow on November 8, 1953, Pinter first says that God is enriched by Flanagan's presence. But then, he reveals that they will not marry. At Christmas, Flanagan might go to America. He doesn't know their future. Shortly afterward, in a letter written from Westport, County Mayo, he informs Woolf that Flanagan barely escaped death by fire when a paraffin stove set her dressing room ablaze. She jumped at the last moment. Pinter describes the experience as the most "sickening body blow" that he has ever received. She was not hurt. In closing, he tells Woolf that the two are happy but, again, affirms that they will not marry. In what appears to be his final letter while in Anew McMaster's company, written from Castlebar, County Mayo, Pinter reveals that he can't contain his delight in Flanagan, whom he describes as shy and lovely. They go, he says, from strength to strength.[23] However in a letter postmarked two days later, on Tuesday "November 10, 1953," Pinter writes to Mick Goldstein, saying that Flanagan is going to America and the two will not marry. He adds that he will be home, back in Hackney, in December.[24]

He writes to Woolf, in a letter postmarked "May 4, 1954" using his parent's return address of 19 Thistlewaite Road, London E5, that 1954 is the worst year so far. He knew when he left Flanagan that it would be so. In July 1954, Pinter writes to Woolf from Whitby, where he is appearing with the Whitby Spa Repertory Company, that although he likes the peace and quiet of Whitby, he feels Flanagan's absence more as the days go by. This didn't, however, prevent him from a two-week fling with a girl in the company, whom he describes as a treasure. They had sex on the seafront at night, with the sea roaring. The fling cost him his job, as both of them were fired.[25]

One of the reasons why he and Flanagan parted was due in part to the strong objections of Pinter's mother when he took her home: "Pinter's mother, although hospitable, was deeply concerned about the idea of her son marrying an Irish-Catholic girl. Maybe also she was worried, understandably, about their economic prospects" (Billington: 40). The separation may also well have had something to do with Pinter's own reaction to Catholicism. He wrote to Woolf in a letter dated Saturday September 22, [1951], just after he'd begun in Anew McMaster's touring company and met Flanagan, that one of the girls was in "this Catholic business." In a later letter to Woolf written from Thurles, County Tipperary on a Tuesday in the summer of 1952, Pinter tells Woolf that he and Flanagan have parted even as he is in love with her, and it's been the sweetest, gentlest relationship he's had. Pinter on October 10, 1951 turned twenty-one. He confesses that he is confused, because while he loves Flanagan, he hates Catholicism. His bitterness has turned him cruel and rotten. In another letter to Woolf, probably written in the autumn of 1951 shortly after his relationship with Flanagan had begun, Pinter writes about the all-pervasive influence of Catholicism: Flanagan is under its spell. She, like others, has injected it from birth.[26]

Flanagan went on to have a highly successful acting career. Based in New York, she married George Vogel in 1958 and had two daughters. Born in Sligo, she was from a politically committed Republican family; both her parents served as lord mayor of Sligo.[27] She and Pinter maintained contact over the years. For instance, on June 27, 1976 Pinter flew to New York for the casting of *The Innocents*, which he directed, and cast her in the leading role as Mrs. Grose (*Chronology*: 68).

ANTONIA FRASER

Pinter and Antonia Fraser met on January 8, 1975 at a dinner party at the home of her sister Rachel (who served as the president of English PEN from 1998 to 2000) and her husband, Kevin Billington, the theatre, film, and television director. Pinter gave her a lift home and remained until 6 a.m. Shortly after, Pinter sent her the typescript of *No Man's Land*. Peter Hall records that on Sunday August 17, 1975, Pinter went to Hall's Wallingford home "bringing with him his son Daniel who is to stay with us. . . . Harold was tense but pretending to be happy. Tonight, Antonia joins him in his new rented home. Photographers and reporters are all round it. He has, he says, filled the house with flowers." In the evening, Pinter left to collect Antonia at the airport. Afterward, they moved to 33 Launceston Place, South Kensington (*Diaries*: 180; *Chronology*: 308–9, 57–62; *Must*: 32–33).

On Christmas Day 1975, Pinter wrote from 33 Launceston Place, London W8, to inform Mick Goldstein that 1975 has been a year of total upheaval. The private pain and public horror have been unimaginable. He's living with Antonia in a rented house. His son Daniel lives there, too. His wife, Vivien, meanwhile, is in a bad state but coming out of it. He adds that Woolf and others have been wonderful friends to Vivien. Pinter tells Goldstein that he can't say anymore except that his marriage to Vivien is over. He is in love with Antonia, exhausted but alive.

Antonia's account is more upbeat, although she may have been away on Christmas Day when Pinter wrote his letter to Goldstein. She had gone to Scotland to spend Christmas with her children. She wrote on the occasion of their Christmas party held on December 21 that "Harold could remember nothing the next day except for a warm glow of feeling that everyone had enjoyed themselves." On January 8, 1976, she wrote that neither she nor Pinter regretted their "fatal meeting," adding "then, having celebrated, we could go back to being neurotic for the rest of the year" (*Must*: 45–46).

Pinter finally moved in with Antonia at her family house, 52 Campden Hill Square, W8 on August 12, 1977. With him, he had his desk, chair, and Guy Vaesen's cricket picture from his former Hanover Terrace home (*Must*: 83). Writing to Goldstein from his new address on November 19, 1977, Pinter reported that Antonia and he are there and "happy"—but elsewhere, things were not good. Daniel was going through a nervous breakdown. Antonia has six children, and especially at Christmastime there is literally no room to put Goldstein up.[28] In a letter to Woolf dated

September 17, 1983, Pinter confessed to a writer's block but lightened up when he told his old friend that Antonia is great. A hard worker, she finished a book on seventeenth-century English women. Pinter expressed his pride in her fantastic achievement.[29]

Life between Pinter and Antonia had its ups and downs, which is hardly surprising for two such creative, argumentative people from different backgrounds. Antonia records that in New York on October 20, 1996, Pinter had a dispute with a political commentator at her publishing party for *The Gunpowder Plot*. This displeased Antonia, who reports that she and Pinter then had a row at the end of the evening, "which no doubt marks many of the happiest of marriages. . . . Even Harold's usual mantra, 'We are two strong characters in the same marriage' did not assuage my wrath and the sundown must have been one of the latest ever. We were finely reconciled." On June 13, 1997, she noted in her diary that Pinter was "morose" and they were unable to communicate over lunch. The following day Pinter explained his sorrow at the state of the world, to which she responded that this should not "spill into our relationship." He told her, "You're the one thing . . ." to which she replied that all she could "do is [to] shelter [Pinter] under the wide umbrella of [her] love." Yet she has to accept that this is part of Pinter's character that will never be eliminated (*Must*: 217–18). Antonia's favorite of the poems that Pinter wrote her is "It is Here," dedicated to her and dated "1990." It opens with the questioning single-line verse "What sound was that?" and concludes with two other single-line verses: "It was the breath we took when we first met.| Listen. It is here." (*VV*: 169; *Must*: 124; BR: C27a).

Born Antonia Pakenham in 1932 in Westminster, a distinguished author in her own right, Lady (subsequently Dame) Antonia Fraser was Pinter's partner and closest influence upon him from August 1975 until his death on Christmas Eve in 2008. She was the dedicatee of many of his works. The eldest of eight, she grew up in Oxford. Her father, Frank Pakenham, became seventh Earl of Longford on the death of his elder brother, who died childless in 1961. He taught politics at Christ Church College and was a Labour politician who failed to win a seat at Oxford in the 1945 election swing to Labour, but who subsequently became a peer and a member of the House of Lords. His causes included campaigning for prisoners' rights, conducting an inquiry into pornography, and campaigning for the abolition of the death penalty. Antonia's mother, born Elizabeth Harman, had her own Labour parliamentary hopes. Her husband converted to Catholicism in 1940; she followed six years later. She subsequently wrote biographies of Queen Victoria and the Duke of Wellington. In common with her husband, she suffered from bouts of depression. With the help of nannies she raised her brood of eight children: four sons and four daughters.

As Antonia relates in *My History: A Memoir of Growing Up* (2015), as a youngster she spent four years learning Greek and Latin at the Dragon

School near her Oxford home. She played rugby and was one of twenty girls out of four hundred pupils. The Dragon School was followed by a short unhappy period at a Church of England boarding school in Salisbury, then St. Mary's Convent, Ascot. The Pakenham family had their origins in Ireland as part of the Protestant Ascendancy. Antonia regarded herself as "Anglo-Irish . . . and with my brother Thomas had visited Ireland all through our shared youth, including wartime" (*Must*: 232). Peter Stothard writes in his *TLS* review of *My History*: "[T]hreaded through the text are potent shards of Harold Pinter's life before their marriage in 1980, times not shared but contemporaneous," such as Pinter's "wartime evacuation to Cornwall, hers to an Oxfordshire Manor, his stealing of one library book when she was removing an illustration from another, appearances at the Gate Theatre in Dublin at different times, his fear of flies, her fear of the dark" (July 10, 2015: 21).

Prior to going to Oxford, Antonia worked in various jobs: as a typist and in a hat department at a large store. Following a crammer, in 1950, she went to Lady Margaret Hall, Oxford, to read first PPE before changing to history. Post-Oxford, she worked in publishing for George Weidenfeld who, in 1948, founded the firm of Weidenfeld & Nicolson. He subsequently published her work, and he, Antonia, and Pinter spent many hours socially together (see *Chronology*: 360). On September 25, 1956, she married the fourteen-years-older Hugh Fraser, who came from a prominent Roman Catholic family. Fraser had a distinguished Second World War record and was an MP from 1945 until his death in 1984, holding many prominent government positions. In 1975 he was unsuccessful candidate for the Conservative Party leadership. He and Antonia had three sons: Benjamin, "Benjie," a banker and poet; Damian, the managing director of an investment banking firm in Mexico; and Orlando, a barrister specializing in commercial law. They also had three daughters: Rebecca, wife of the barrister Edward Fitzgerald QC; Flora; and Natasha, wife of Jean-Pierre Cavassoni. All three daughters are authors. There are eighteen grandchildren. Following her relationship with Pinter, her children became close to Pinter, who spent hours lavishing devotion on Antonia's grandchildren (see *Must*, and photographs between 264–65, and *Chronology*: 342–43).

Antonia wrote her first best-selling historical novel, *Mary Queen of Scots*, in 1969—her young baby Flora responding well to the sound of her typewriter. This book was followed by other successful historical biographies and detective novels including the Jemima Shore series, television, and radio drama. A former president of the English PEN (1988–1990) and broadcaster, she was made CBE in 1999 and DBE in 2011 for services to literature. Since 1975, her life, until his December 2008 death, was on a daily basis intimately associated with Pinter's. His "Appointment Diaries" recording their frequent joint receipt of honorary degrees, visits in the UK and overseas, social gatherings, opera outings, [30] and Pinter's celebration on an annual basis of their initial meeting. For instance, on January 8, 1985, the tenth anniversary of when they met, Antonia writes in *Must* that Pinter gave her a giant Georgian ring containing a pale golden stone set in gleaming dark paste diamonds and masses of white flowers. She gave him two silk shirts (176 and *Chronology*: 138). Her birthday on August 27 was celebrated by a lunch or dinner (see, for instance, the celebration of her sixty-third birthday on August 27, 1995 with its "amazing lunch party" (*Must*: 213)). Christmas and the New Year were celebrated with her family. Her friends, social circle, and family became his. On occasion, to write, they escaped London, secluding themselves, for instance, at the Grand Hotel Eastbourne from January 3 to 6, 1989 and November 2 to 7, 1989.

Antonia looked after Pinter during his final illnesses and protected him (see *Chronology*: 170, 176, 342–43). As he wrote in the final verse of "To My Wife" dated "June 2004: "You are my life| And so I live" (*VV*: 179). Since his death, in addition to another historical work, *Perilous Question: The Drama of the Great Reform Bill 1832* (2013), Antonia has written her memoir of her life with Pinter and *My History: A Memoir of Growing Up* also published by Weidenfeld & Nicolson. It contains memories of Pinter prior to their marriage—their parallel lives. On September 22, 2012, she unveiled the Harold Pinter plaque at his childhood home, 19 Thistlewaite Road, Hackney. Additionally in 2017, the travel diary she kept during a trip to Israel with Pinter in May 1978 was published, with accompanying color photographs under the title *Our Israeli Diary, 1978. Of That Time, of That Place*. In it, she describes on an almost daily basis the sights, the shopping, the conversations, and the culture shocks they experienced.[31]

JILL JOHNSON

Pinter and Jill Johnson became lovers when they appeared together in rep at Colchester in 1955. Pinter wrote to Woolf that he was very happy with Johnson. However, memories of Flanagan intruded when he wrote on July 18, 1955 that "the south" of Ireland is far off, "something across a border, remaining, continual, placed in my blood." The repertory company he was with toured the north of Ireland during the summer of 1955. He confessed to boredom with this kind of existence and with his continual movement from place to place. In a letter to Woolf from Colchester dated March 15, 1955, Pinter confided that Johnson was the best girl he's had. She was spirited, with temper and loveliness and a little "savage"; they were very fond of each other. On Sunday November 6, 1955, as part of a ten-page, double-sided letter begun on Tuesday November 1, Pinter confessed to Woolf that "there can be no absolute lock for my key. Too many doors in the corridor. And so I shall never marry, or it is highly doubtful." Pinter added, "Again, I see a formula attached, and aware of it, despise it—for years now—the masochism of women, I am not referring specifically to Jill, who is lovely." Pinter added that he did a summer season in Northern Ireland for three months on the seashore with Johnson. It was fine, but Johnson had at this point returned to London. Things always change, he observed.[32] Johnson remembered that when they were together at Colchester, Pinter "was writing poetry, the prose-pieces that became *The Examination* and *The Black and White* and his novel [*The Dwarfs*]." She added that "one knew he had this amazing talent but it never occurred to me he would be a playwright simply because he wasn't writing plays." She "also wondered if he'd be a bit obscure. He'd produce a poem and I'd say 'Wonderful—but what does it mean?' Even then, you didn't say that to Harold. He'd say 'I don't know—you tell me what it means.'" (Billington: 51).

Pinter and Johnson kept in contact until Pinter's last years. They met on a regular basis, lunching together at various restaurants such as the Grill St. Quentin (GSQ) or on several occasions at Cibo, too. They had lunch other times as well, especially during the 1990s, for instance, at Orsino's and the Belvedere. Frequently, Pinter didn't indicate in his "Appointment Diaries" the restaurants where they met for lunch. Their final lunch encounter seems to be on July 26, 2005 at an unspecified restaurant (see *Chronology*: 348).

Johnson performed in Pinter's work, participating in the June 1987 production of *A Slight Ache* in Vienna in the role of Flora with another fellow actor whom he met at the Central School of Drama, Barry Foster as Edward. Directed by Kevin Billington in collaboration with Pinter, this was seen early in June at Vienna's English Theatre. Pinter wrote to Mick Goldstein on July 16, 2000 that the week after next, he and Johnson would be recording *A Slight Ache* for radio, and she would also be in the Proust at the National[33] that opened at the Cottesloe, Royal National Theatre, on November 23, 2000. Johnson played the role of the Marquis de Villeparisis. She played Flora with Pinter in the role of Edward in the BBC Radio 4 production of *A Slight Ache*, broadcast on October 13, 2000 (*Chronology*: 261). She is a clear illustration of Pinter's continuing relationship with former lovers—in her case, continuing almost fifty years after their physical relationship ceased.

VIVIEN MERCHANT (ADA BRAND THOMSON)

Under the name Vivien (from Vivien Leigh, the actress she admired) and Merchant from her brother who was in the Merchant Navy, Vivien Merchant began on the professional stage in 1942 in repertory. She obtained West End parts, for instance, in Noël Coward's musical *Sigh No More* (1945–1946) and his *Ace of Clubs* (1950). By the early 1950s, she had become a leading repertory company lady. She met Pinter when they both were in rep at Bournemouth. She also was in various films such as *Alfie* (1966), for which she received Academy Award and Golden Globe nominations as the best supporting actress, in addition to winning awards from BAFTA Award and the National Board of Review. She was in *Accident* (1967), Hitchcock's *Frenzy*, and in the same year, 1972, Sidney Lumet's *The Offence*. Following her September 14, 1956 marriage to Pinter, she appeared in the lead roles in many of his works, including the revival in 1960 of *The Room*, *A Slight Ache*, *A Night Out*, *The Collection*, and *The Lover*. For the Associated-Rediffusion TV production of *The Lover*, she played Sarah and won the *Evening Standard* Theatre Award for Best Newcomer and also the BAFTA Best Actress Award. Directed by Joan Kemp-Welch, with Alan Badel as Richard, it was shown on March 28, 1963. In 1965 she appeared as Wendy in *The Tea Party*, and in the same year she played the role of Ruth in Pinter's *The Homecoming*, both in London and in 1967 in New York. She was nominated for a Tony, and she was in the 1973 film version directed by Peter Hall. The final Pinter work that Vivien performed on the stage was in 1971 as Anna in *Old Times*. Among her other notable performances was as Lady Macbeth in Hall's 1967 Royal Shakespeare Company production with Paul Scofield as Macbeth.

In the early years of his marriage, Pinter appeared besotted with Vivien, telling Woolf in a letter dated September 27, 1957 that Vivien was with him as he typed his letter. Sitting by the fire, she was knitting a delicate, delightful baby garment. He described himself as "bonkers" about her.[34] In spite of the birth of their son, Daniel, on January 29, 1958, the marriage began to disintegrate. Pinter's affair with Joan Bakewell lasted off and on from 1962 to 1969. There were other Pinter relationships, too, especially with the wealthy New York socialite Barbara Stanton. His relationship with Antonia Fraser began in 1975; Pinter told Vivien about it in March 1975. At first, she reacted without too much hostility. But according to Guy Vaesen, who remained friendly with both Vivien and Pinter after their increasingly bitter separation, Vivien's mind was gradually poisoned against Antonia following a visit by one of Vivien's female friends (Billington: 253).

Vivien filed for a divorce and gave inflammatory press interviews to the London tabloid press with scathing remarks about Antonia such as, "He didn't need to take a change of shoes. He can always wear hers. She has very big feet, you know."[35] Antonia received a divorce in 1977. Following deliberate stalling on Vivien's part, her divorce went through in 1980. By the end of November 1978, the Pinter home at 7 Hanover Terrace, Regent's Park, had been sold. Vivien did not move out until the second week of January. She then moved into her new home in Blackheath, and financial matters were agreed between her and Pinter.

Vivien Merchant lapsed into a deep depression following the break with Pinter, and on October 3, 1982, aged fifty-three, died from "chronic alcoholism." Billington writes that Pinter "did everything possible to support" his ex-wife until her death. Pinter deeply regretted his subsequent estrangement from their son, Daniel, who became a recluse and, following his parents' separation, adopted as his surname that of his maternal grandmother's maiden name Brand. The immediate impact upon Pinter was a writing block: "[N]ot until he and Antonia moved back into her Holland Park family home in August 1977 was he able even to contemplate a new play: so there was a three-year writing block in the late 1970s and early 1980s. [36]

Vivien was the inspiration for Pinter's early work. As acknowledgement of his indebtedness to her, he dedicated the first Methuen edition of *The Birthday Party*, published as a single play, "To Vivien." She was also the dedicatee of the first edition and early editions of *The Caretaker, The Birthday Party and Other Plays, The Caretaker and The Dumb Waiter, A Slight Ache and Other Plays, The Room and The Dumb Waiter,* and *Landscape and Silence.*[37]

Considerable insight is thrown upon the nature of Pinter's and Vivien's early relationship from letters Pinter sent to Goldstein at the time and from Woolf's recollections. Writing on March 28, 1956 from the Palace Court Theatre Bournemouth, Pinter informed Goldstein that he was living with Vivien and that everything was fine. They lived without tension. In another letter written in the same month, he told Goldstein that he was living a more balanced life with Vivien than he has known before, lacking pretense and deceit. Following a brief autumn 1956 honeymoon at Mevagissey, a fishing port in Cornwall, he wrote Goldstein from the Pavilion Theatre Torquay that it was a shame Goldstein couldn't visit because their home was a haven.[38]

Similar sentiments are found in letters to Woolf. Pinter and Vivien married on September 14, 1956, the Day of Atonement or Yom Kippur, the most sacred day in the Jewish religious calendar. Pinter did not at once inform his parents of his marriage, much to their annoyance. Writing from Torquay in October 1956, Pinter described the registry office marriage ceremony, telling Woolf that he and Vivien are in their own quiet apartment/flat where they were very happy; they can feast in it, lie in bed, and wake in it. For Pinter, Torquay was splendid and Woolf was the first to know that he was married.[39]

A comment in a 1956 letter to Goldstein can be perceived as prefiguring what was to occur in the Pinter-Vivien relationship. Rather ambiguously, Pinter wrote that he is aware of the "lunacy and menace" in the world as he has never been before. His being married seems to be a contributing factor. Pinter may well have been reacting to the Suez Crisis; it is unclear, however, whether his being married contributes to what he calls the "lunacy and menace" in the world.

Pinter certainly was aware of Vivien's acumen. He wrote to Goldstein late in 1957 from the Playhouse Theatre Oxford after completing *The*

Birthday Party that he was glad that Vivien liked it, as she has an acute critical sense.[40] Goldstein recalled Vivien's abilities many years later, in a letter to Pinter written in 2000 after seeing a production of *Old Times*. Goldstein remembered an evening in May 1971 during the rehearsals for the London opening of the play when Vivien won a bottle of champagne awarded by the director, Peter Hall. Vivien, in the role of Anna, was the first one in the cast to get all their lines right.[41]

By August 1975, Pinter and Antonia Fraser began to live together at a house in Launcester Place, South Kensington, with Daniel. In a letter written from that address dated "Christmas Day. 1975," Pinter told Goldstein that the year has been total upheaval. His marriage was over, and he and Vivien would have to find another "shape" to their lives. [42]

Woolf's memoir *Barcelona is in Trouble* consists of short chapters. The twenty-ninth concerns "Vivien." Not all the memories are negative. Woolf remembers the time when his friend Pinter "couldn't stop writing about" Vivien and that it was unwise "to question anything Harold said about Vivien. She was Holy Ground. On the mantelpiece, in the drawing room of their grand house in Regent's Park, stood a pair of very high-heeled shoes, a tribute to her beautiful legs." Her legs were exploited by Pinter in his early plays, especially those on TV such as *The Lover* and when she played Ruth in *The Homecoming*. Vivien displayed considerable kindness toward Woolf and his wife, yet "Vivien was the most elusive person [Woolf] ever met. 'Now you see me, now you don't,' should have been her mantra." He remembers "her making beautiful shirts for [Pinter], in their early days, when they lived in a basement flat in Notting Hill Gate and he stoked the boiler as part of their rent. Then over the years, she drifted away, more and more, whenever it came over her to do so." For Woolf, Pinter's falling in love with Antonia came as "an awful shock to Vivien" and she "started to drink very heavily; she was determined to kill herself, I suppose. Not just to punish Harold, but to escape from an unbearable life." A small person physically, "she was one of the most frightening drunks [Woolf] ever encountered," and she needed looking after, a task undertaken at times by Woolf and his wife and Pinter's friend from drama school, Johnny Rees. Woolf believed that Vivien wanted to die as "she couldn't live without Harold." Her posthumous wish was to be left in peace (*Barcelona*: 209–13).

EDNA O'BRIEN

Born in Tuamgraney, County Clare, in 1930, Edna O'Brien's thinly disguised, largely autobiographical novel *The Country Girls* (1960) describes the attempt of a highly intelligent girl to free herself from her narrow Catholic family environment and to find herself. Married from 1954 to 1964 to the author Ernest Gébler, of Czech Jewish origins but born in

Dublin, O'Brien had two children whom she brought up. London-based, her prolific output includes novels, collections of short stories, poems, plays, and biographies. She gained many awards, including the *Los Angeles Times* Book Prize for Fiction (1990), the European Prize for Literature (1995), the Irish PEN Award (2001), the Lifetime Achievement Award in Irish Literature (2009), and the Frank O'Connor International Short Story Award (2009). A powerful second memoir, *Country Girl*, was published in 2012. Philip Roth described Edna O'Brien as "the most gifted woman now writing in English."[43]

Pinter noted their initial meeting took place at a party she gave on the evening of April 18, 1970. Their last recorded meeting occurred after Pinter was awarded the Nobel Prize, at 6:30 p.m. on December 31, 2005 and lasted probably an hour; he records that at 7:30 p.m. Betsy Reisz and Haya Clayton appeared to join him and Antonia for bridge (*Chronology*: 28, 289; see also *Must*: 299). In the years in between, Pinter and O'Brien met over one hundred times. Many of their meetings were either for lunch or dinner at a miscellany of restaurants including Le Caprice, where they met for dinner on five occasions during the 1996 to 2003 period. Other restaurants they went to include four times for dinner at Orsino's between 1999 and 2003, and on three occasions at the Ivy between 1995 and 1998. Other restaurants ranged from Thompson's in 1983 to Odin's for a lunch on November 8, 1972 with Pinter, Vivien, and their son Daniel.[44]

The "Appointment Diaries" record an December 11, 1977 evening meeting with O'Brien and Daniel. On January 29, 1978, the occasion of Daniel's twentieth birthday, there was an evening party at O'Brien's. Just over five years earlier, Pinter on November 13, 1972 went to see a performance of O'Brien's play *A Pagan Place* at the Royal Court. Following a rehearsal of his *The Hothouse*, on January 29, 1981, he saw her *Virginia* at the Haymarket Theatre (*Chronology*: 78, 79, 49, 104). On December 15, 1982, Pinter and presumably Antonia and O'Brien were joined by Laurence Olivier and his wife, Joan Plowright, and by Antonia's Czech-born "close friend" (*Chronology*: 120; *Must*: 30) Diana Phipps for dinner at Odin's. O'Brien, Phipps, and others also joined Pinter and probably Antonia on Christmas Day 1982. After a meeting that probably concerned theatrical designs with Eileen Diss at 6 p.m., the Pinters were joined at 8 p.m. on January 4, 1986 for dinner by Edna, Jeremy Irons and his wife, the actress Sinéad Cusak, and Robert Bolt, the dramatist and screenwriter. Other meetings of note with O'Brien included dining with Angus Wilson's partner, Tony Garrett, and Simon Gray and his wife on April 29, 1991. They dined with Carlos Fuentes, the Mexican novelist and essayist, at the Grill St. Quentin on August 4, 1992. On another occasion, Pinter and O'Brien met with Sir V. S. Naipaul, in 2001 the Nobel Prize–winning writer, and his wife, Nadira, just before Pinter's admission to the Princess Grace Hospital on the final day of August 2005. On October 2, 1996,

Pinter went with O'Brien to see the evening performance of his *Ashes to Ashes*. On April 14, 2001, O'Brien accompanied Pinter to a performance of Ibsen's *Ghosts* at the Comedy Theatre (*Chronology*: 120, 147, 188, 198, 297, 231, 265). In August of 2003, O'Brien stayed with Harold and Antonia at Kingston Russell in Dorset during the period Pinter was working on the film script of *Sleuth* (see *Must*: 271 and photographs 264–65).

The nature of O'Brien's relationship with Pinter and Antonia is found in Antonia's dedication to *Poems By Harold Pinter: Chosen by Antonia Fraser*, published by Greville Press Pamphlets in association with the Delos Press in 2002: "For Edna O'Brien our friend" (BR: I10). In *Barcelona* in his discussion about Pinter's fascination with women, Woolf asks, "And what about the enchanting Edna O'Brien, the writer (relationship with Harold Pinter undefined), who could have had the Guard's Brigade for breakfast if she felt like it?" (113). Clearly, Antonia's dedication to her choice of her husband's poems refutes Pinter's old friend's innuendo. In his diary entry for Tuesday September 7, 1976, Peter Hall provides insight into Edna's appeal. At London Weekend Television he "watched Russell Harty's *Aquarius* film on Edna O'Brien," describing it as "magnificent: as irritating and lovable as Edna herself, her vein of sentimentality is offset by that sharp eye and those acid little phrases" (*Diaries*: 255). A reconciliation between Hall and Pinter following their going separate ways in 1983 was assisted by O'Brien, who arranged for them to meet at a party she threw in the late 1980s following which Pinter wrote to Hall: "Life's too short—let's make it up" (cited Billington: 324, and see *Chronology*: 182, 194).

In the very early days of the Antonia-Pinter relationship, on February 25, 1975, Antonia, at O'Brien's request, met O'Brien for a drink. Antonia describes her as looking "like a beautiful fortune-teller in her shawl by the fire" with Antonia as "her client. 'He's much enraptured,' she said. Then: 'I'm glad this is happening to him. Last summer when he was writing [*No Man's Land*] . . . I almost thought, 'well,' she hesitated. 'He says he was waiting for death,' Antonia replied" (*Must*: 11–12). O'Brien's observations on Pinter, and especially his relationship with his first wife, are replete with insight. For O'Brien, Vivien Merchant's physical demeanor "illuminated" Pinter and his depiction of women in his drama. O'Brien told Michael Billington that she said "illuminated, because it would be impossible not to interconnect Vivien the person—as wife, lover, mistress—with the stage presence who had flesh, blood and very good legs." Such a comment applies especially to Pinter's *The Collection*, *The Lover*, and *The Tea Party*. According to O'Brien, Pinter was "snared, for better or worse, by the image of a woman who happened to be his and who happened to act—sublimely—in his plays." Vivien was his "muse," his inspirational flame; when their relationship deteriorated, gender relationships in, for instance, a play such as *No Man's Land*, "exist only in the form of competitive memory games." O'Brien's critical acumen is further revealed when she observes that Pinter's female characters appear "slippery" and "diffuse," qualities that allow women power over men (Billington: 134, 278, 136).

FRANCES PINTER (NÉE MOSKOWITZ) (1904–1992)

A succinct description of Pinter's mother is given by Antonia Fraser following her initial visit to Pinter's parents on January 3, 1978, almost three years after her fateful meeting with Pinter on January 8, 1975. She and Pinter visited them at their Hove flat/apartment, which "is extremely cosy, full of well-tended plants." Antonia describes Frances Pinter as tall, slender, with long legs and beautiful, thick, gray hair. She looks young for being in her mid-seventies.[45] She confirmed to Antonia that she and her husband didn't have another child "because Harold was so difficult." Pinter's father tells Antonia that they didn't go out when their son was young because "by the time the wife and I reached the street, there was a reproachful little figure standing at the window, holding back the curtains." On September 8, 1979, Antonia notes that Frances is enjoying reading Antonia's new historical best-selling biography, *Charles II and the Restoration*. She recounts receiving a charming letter from Frances Pinter saying how happy Antonia has made her son. His parents, Antonia adds, might justifiably "shrink" from a Catholic, divorced mother of six; in fact, they displayed great warmth. She contrasts this attitude with that of her husband, Hugh Fraser's mother, Lady Lovat, who didn't want Antonia to marry her son and wore black at their wedding (*Must*: 88–89, 108). In writing this, perhaps Antonia had in the back of her mind the fact that Frances Pinter was very concerned about her son's earlier relationship with the Irish Catholic–born Pauline Flanagan. Pinter's great friend Morris (Moishe) Wernick, had married "out"—a non-Jew—and following his 1956 marriage, Wernick left with his wife for Canada, returning home with her eight years later to introduce her and their children to his parents; this has been taken to be Pinter's stimulus for *The Homecoming*.[46]

Pinter's mother's family were real London/Jewish and tough. An uncle on the mother's side ran a Tottenham pub and was a Cockney. Pinter's mother's father, Harry Moskowitz, was born in Ukrainian Odessa, with its large Jewish population subject to cyclical waves of anti-Semitism. He got to London via Paris, around the beginning of the twentieth century. In common with many of the illiterate characters in his grandson's dramas, he survived by using his intelligence or wits. Family tradition, supported by photographs taken at the June 9, 1926 wedding of his daughter Frances to Jack Pinter, attest to his being stocky and well built—a physical characteristic Harold Pinter retained even in old age and sickness. Quick-witted and possessing considerable entrepreneurial skills, he remade trousers he saw in the windows of pawn shops, founded a clothing business under the name of "Richard Mann," and at one time had at least six commercial travelers working for the business. Following the death of his first wife, whom he'd met on a South African visit, he married the Polish-born Rose Franklin, who was from a family of three sisters with five children. All were part of the family circle when Harold Pinter was growing up. Rose and Harry had four children; Pinter's mother Frances (Fanny), the only girl, was the eldest, born in 1904. She taught her father how to write, and she maintained the accounts in his business. Her brother Ben's wife, Fay, died from cancer, and a distraught Ben subsequently took his own life and the life of his little daughter. As a young boy, Harold Pinter loved the baby, remembered her, and was very disturbed by what occurred. Judah, the third son, born in 1907, had a large physique, boxed using the name "Joe Mann," and was something of a black sheep who disappeared during the Blitz. He was last seen "hanging off the back of . . . [a] dustbin-van": (Pinter cited Billington: 4). The youngest son, Lou, was born in 1918.

Given that Harold was an only child and difficult when young, the forever protective Frances went with her son to Reading in 1941 when they were evacuated from London during the Blitz. In spite of disagreements—for instance, concerning Pauline Flanagan, failing to tell his parents that he had married and on the Day of Atonement too, and concerning Israel with his father—Pinter protected his parents. He initially set them up in a flat/apartment off the Hove seafront on the Sussex coast and traveled to see them regularly, celebrating their birthdays and anniversaries, taking them to see his plays. Pinter's powerful late play *Moonlight* has its origins in the period of his mother's death, and Antonia believes it came from his mother's dying in a Hove nursing home at age eighty-eight in October 1992. The play is the story of a dying person, a man nursed by his wife, whose sons refuse to come home to say goodbye to him. At the time of his mother's final illness, Pinter was rehearsing to play the role of Hirst at the Almeida revival of *No Man's Land.* He spent a good deal of the summer of 1992 interrupting rehearsals with three other actors to go to Hove and subsequently to see his father, who was alone and ninety. On the train, he began to scribble an outline of a dramatic scenario consisting of "a mother, a father, two brothers" and perhaps a daughter: the genesis of *Moonlight* (*Must*: 209–10). The play is dedicated "To Antonia with my love" (BR: A51).

BARBARA (CONDOS) STANTON

During the time Pinter was having an on-off relationship with Joan Bakewell, he had "a more intimate relationship . . . with the woman he called Cleopatra. Harold indifferent to the whole thing: 'It's all a long time ago'" (*Must*: 223). This refers to the New York socialite Barbara Stanton (then

Barbara Condos), whom Pinter first met in the autumn of 1968 when he was involved with the stage versions of *The Basement* and *The Tea Party*, which opened as a double bill at the Eastside Playhouse, New York, on October 10, 1968. According to Stanton, her affair with Pinter began in New York when he was directing the play that her then-boyfriend David Balding was producing, Robert Shaw's *The Man in the Glass Booth*, which opened on Broadway in September 1968.

Pinter described Stanton as being very beautiful; they became lovers "for many years," for instance staying together in expensive upmarket hotels such the Plaza Hotel New York in early March 1969. Aged seventy-seven in 2010, she told the *Daily Telegraph* about her "long, involved" relationship with Pinter: "Harold was not only a wonderful writer, he was a wonderful human being." According to Stanton, Pinter made her pregnant, but her doctor told her the embryo was dead or dying. Abortion was illegal in the United States, so Pinter made arrangements for her to terminate the pregnancy in Britain. Afraid of recognition, Pinter did not visit her in hospital. She also claimed that "during the 1960s she and Pinter took recreational drugs on holiday with friends at a villa in Mexico. They all spent the week 'stoned' and 'tripped' on hallucinogenic drugs."

Woolf says that she and Pinter remained in contact throughout his life, although there seems to be no mention of her in Pinter's "Appointment Diaries." Woolf is quoted in the *Daily Telegraph* as saying, "If she came to England, she and Harold would meet up, and the last time I saw her was in New York just before the attack on the twin towers."

Before meeting Pinter, whom she shared for a time in a triangular relationship with David Balding, Barbara ("Babsie") Stanton was married to the Broadway dancer Nick Condos, the former husband of the Oscar-winning comedy actress Martha Raye, as she relates in her memoir appropriately titled *Hard Candy: A True Story of Riches, Fame and Heartbreak* (1988). At least one head of state is said to have been among her other lovers. Her memoir reveals that her father, Hyme Caplan, was a fight promoter who ended up in jail. By the time he was released, his wife, "Babsie's" mother, had died. Her father then died, leaving three children to be bought up by uncaring relatives. Nick Condos was a drunk. Stanton had a child and then took to drugs. Her novel *Beautifully Kept* (1976) focuses on being rich men's mistresses. Stanton subsequently married Lari Stanton, who was eighty-six in 2014 and the former head of one of America's largest glove manufacturers, the Aris Glove Company. She and her husband had houses in New York and Florida.[47]

CONCLUSION

This chapter focusses upon the lives of twelve of the most important women in Pinter's life, including his mother, two wives, his literary agent, actresses who participated in his work, lovers, and close friends. All are highly intelligent and, with the exception of Pinter's mother, connected with the theatre in some form or other or with literary creative endeavors. Many were in positions of power and authority. Pinter's representation of women in his work has been a subject of considerable critical debate. There are critics who see in his drama "fetishistic exploitation of female sexuality." Some critics have seen in Pinter's work cryptofeminism, a celebration of female "strength and resilience." There is of course validity in both of these positions. As this chapter demonstrates, there is no doubt that Pinter "certainly adored women," and as his relationship with Vivien deteriorated, he reverted to a pattern of behavior prior to his marriage—a sequence of affairs. However, his plays "also constantly pit male weakness and insecurity against female strength and survival. No one can ever pin a decisive meaning on," for instance, "*The Homecoming*. But it seems clear that Ruth, in abandoning her husband to live with her in-laws and apparently work as a high-class prostitute, is making her own choice and feels personally empowered rather than enslaved."[48]

NOTES

1. BLADDMSS: 88880/4/17.
2. Shergold with whom Pinter appeared in repertory and from 1955 was married to his friend the actor Barry Foster (1927–2002).
3. Woolf writing in 2012.
4. 1928–2002. The actress.
5. Henry Woolf, *Barcelona is in Trouble*. Privately produced reminiscences in ring binder from 2013: 93–95, and subsequently published by the Greville Press, 2017. Woolf's observations are found on pp. 111–13; all references are to the Greville Press publication.
6. http://www.oxforddnb.com/view/article/39440, accessed November 23, 2016.
7. Email from Lady Antonia Fraser to the present writer April 27, 2017; for Billington, see n.6 above.
8. Owing to her hosting of a late-night TV arts program, *Late Night Line-Up*, that ran 1965–1972 and revived in 2008.
9. For Michael Bakewell's recollections of working with Pinter, see Billington: 266–67.
10. http://www.dailymail.co.uk/news/article-3434502/Why-thinking-man-s-crumpet-proud-husband-stealer-Joan-Bakewell-uses-Harold-Pinter-affair-plug-new-book-women-flaunt-betrayals-tear-families-apart.html%20Accessed%2026%20October%202016.
11. https://www.theguardian.com/stage/2017/apr/22/joan-bakewell-pinter-betrayal-affair-keeping-in-touch-radio-4, accessed April 25, 2017.
12. See Jones "Staging Pauses and Silences" in *Viva Pinter: Harold's Pinter's Spirit of Resistance*, Brigitte Gauthier, ed., Oxford, Bern et al., 2009: 58–59.

13. O'Connor "This much I know" interview with Joan Bakewell, *Guardian* (October 8, 2016), https://www.theguardian.com/lifeandstyle/2016/oct/08/joan-bakewell-this-much-i-know-thinking-mans-crumpet-not-insulting, accessed October 8, 2016.

14. See *The Letters of Samuel Beckett:. Volume III, 1957–1965*, D. Gunn et al., eds., Cambridge: Cambridge University Press, 2014: 694.

15. http://www.oxforddnb.com/view/article/102546, accessed 28 Oct 2016.

16. Pinter's letters to the critic Irving Wardle, drama critic for *The Times* (1963–1989) and the *Independent on Sunday* (1989–1995), among other journals, beginning with Pinter's letter of June 29, 1958 concerning Wardle's "most penetrating" observations on *The Birthday Party* published under a pseudonym in the *Bolton Evening News* through February 2002, now at BLADDMSS 88961/4, are instructive regarding Pinter's reactions to reviews of his work.

17. Personal knowledge.

18. Michael Codron and Alan Strachan, *Putting It On: The West End Theatre of Michael Codron*, London: Duckworth: Overlook, 2010: 217.

19. https://www.thestage.co.uk/features/interviews/2015/eileen-diss-50-years-set-design/, accessed November 31, 2016.

20. Eileen Diss Interview Ewan Jeffrey, http://sounds.bl.uk/related-content/TRAN SCRIPTS/024T-1CDR0032289X-0100A0.pdfhttp://sounds.bl.uk, Theatre Archive Project, accessed November 1–2, 2016.

21. BLADDMSS: 89094/1.

22. Letter written c/o Mrs McGinn, Dundalk, Co. Louth, Wed. July 29 [1953—year supplied by Goldstein]; Pinter to Goldstein, autograph letter (4 bifolia, [1]–16), with Goldstein's transcription. See more at http://searcharchives.bl.uk/primo_library/libweb/action/display.do?tabs=detailsTab&ct=display&doc=IAMS040-002765456&dis playMode=full&vid=IAMS_VU2#sthash.EAdBrV4H.dpuf letter (BLADDMSS: 89094/2).

23. BLADDMSS: 89094/2.

24. BLADDMSS: 89083/1/1/1 and cf. http://searcharchives.bl.uk/primo_library/libweb/action/display.do?tabs=detailsTab&ct=display&doc=IAMS040-002765456&dis playMode=full&vid=IAMS_VU2#sthash.EAdBrV4H.dpuf.

25. BLADDMSS: 89094/3; see also chapter 1.

26. BLADDMSS: 89094/2.

27. See https://en.wikipedia.org/wiki/Pauline_Flanagan, accessed November 3, 2016.

28. BLADDMSS: 88920/5/2.

29. BLADDMSS: 89094/5. Antonia's *The Weaker Vessel: Woman's Lot in Seventeenth-Century England* was published in 1984 by Weidenfeld & Nicolson.

30. See chapter 6.

31. https://www.theguardian.com/culture/2016/sep/17/antonia-fraser-harold-pint-er-israel-travel-diary, accessed November 3, 2016; Sam Carter at Oneworld acquired the English-language rights to publish it in book format-*The Bookseller*, October 19, 2016, subsequently published in 2017.

32. BLADDMSS: 89094/2.

33. BLADDMSS: 89083/1/1.

34. BLADDMSS: 89094/4.

35. Peter Gutteridge, http://www.independent.co.uk/life-style/those-choice-words-that- say-i-hate-you-1325795.html, *The Independent*, January 26, 1996.

36. See https://en.wikipedia.org/wiki/Vivien_Merchant, accessed November 4, 2016; cf. Billington: 276, 255, 278.

37. See BR: A1c, A2, A4, A10, A12, A22, A28.

38. BLADDMSS: 88920/5/2.

39. BLADDMSS: 89094/3.

40. BLADDMSS: 88920/5/2.

41. BLADDMSS: 89083/1/1.

42. BLADDMSS: 89083/1/1.

43. https://en.wikipedia.org/wiki/Edna_O%27Brien, accessed November 5, 2016.

44. See *Chronology*: 226, 229, 256, 269, 279, 253, 255, 263, 282, 262, 220, 240, 244, 124, 126, 126, 49.

45. For a photograph of Antonia and Harold with their respective parents taken at Bernhurst, East Sussex (on April 6?) 1980, see *Must*: 120–121 and 115.

46. See for instance Barry Supple, "Pinter's Homecoming," *Jewish Chronicle*, June 25, 1965: 7, 31.

47. http://www.telegraph.co.uk/culture/culturenews/6956929/Harold-Pinter-love-triangle-David-Balding-tells-of-anger-over-girlfriends-affair.html accessed November 7, 2016: *Daily Telegraph*, January 9, 2010: 3; cf. *Chronology*: 29–30.

48. Billington: Obituary of Pinter: https://www.theguardian.com/culture/2008/dec/25/pinter-theatre%20Accessed%2027%20April%202017; cf. Ann C. Hall, "Revisiting Pinter's Women: *One for the Road* (1984), *Mountain Language* (1988) and *Party Time* (1991)" in Mark Taylor-Batty, *The Theatre of Harold Pinter* (London: Bloomsbury, 2014): 232–48; and Drew Milne, "Pinter's Sexual Politics" in *The Cambridge Companion to Harold Pinter*, Peter Raby, ed., Cambridge: Cambridge University Press., 2001: 195–211.

FIVE

Politics and Religion

In "The Queen of all the Fairies," Pinter mentions the *43 Group*, a group of Jewish ex-servicemen formed in March 1946 to fight against the reemergence of Mosley's Fascist supporters and gangs in the East End of London. He was asked to join the *43 Group*; he simply laughed, considering it "such dross."[1] Pinter's overtly political *One For the Road* was first printed in 1984; its revised incarnation was published on October 3, 1985 (BR: A45, *a* and *b*). In May 1985, Pinter was interviewed by Nick Hern. In the interview, Pinter confessed that over the years following his 1948 political act of becoming a conscientious objector, he came to view politicians and political structures with detached contempt. Engaging in politics, he added, seemed futile to him (12).

In the immediate post-war years, Pinter had been engaged in direct physical resistance and combat with Fascists. Pinter told the present writer that he had "nasty encounters" with supporters of the British Fascist leader Oswald Mosley in 1946 and 1947 in the Ridley Road area of Dalston in North East London near Hackney.[2] The fact that Pinter sometimes wore glasses made him more vulnerable. At the time, he and his friends, possibly as a reaction to their hostile environment, retreated into their own fantasies.

In his "The Queen of all the Fairies," Pinter recalled the surroundings in which he lived. Many Jews lived in the district. There were mostly taxi drivers and pressers, machinists and cutters. The richer, upper-class Jews lived up the hill. They would strut around wearing mink coats and American suits and ties. They were bookmakers, jewelers, or farriers with gold shops in Great Portland Street, Central London.[3] There wasn't, however, a total retreat into his own imaginative universe, and Pinter didn't became a pacifist. Many years later, his second wife, Antonia Fraser, recalled that Pinter was asked what he'd have done if the Nazis had come to Britain. Pinter responded that he'd have retreated to the Welsh hills with a machine gun, resisted, and killed as many of them as he could. Indeed, his return to political engagement may be seen as partly due to Antonia, who was, with her father, deeply committed to radical causes.

To return to 1948 and his brave decision to declare himself a conscientious objector, Pinter and his friends were very disturbed by the Cold War, by the Russian suppression in Eastern Europe, and by McCarthyism in the United States. He strongly felt then, as he did when talking to Hern twenty-three years later, that people have obligations to subject their own actions and attitudes to an "equivalent critical and moral scrutiny" (9).

It was extremely difficult for Pinter to be a conscientious objector. It meant that such a tag would be on his record. According to a letter to Henry Woolf, his mother told him that being a conscientious objector would ruin his career[4] and prove costly in financial and emotional terms for his family. He could have been imprisoned for three months and fined. He told Hern that he had two tribunals and two trials and was prepared to go to prison. Indeed, he had his toothbrush with him, ready to go (10). At the time, two of his closest friends had been called up: Woolf in September 1948 was serving in the Royal Air Force on their Bridgnorth, Shropshire base, and Morris Wernick was serving in the Royal Artillery. Pinter went to stay at this time near Biggin Hill—a major RAF air base against the Luftwaffe in World War II—with a friend from school days. He wrote lengthy handwritten letters to Woolf in the autumn of 1948 from Biggin Hill, telling him that he had definitely decided to be a conscientious objector. He had several reasons, including the fear of dying in the army and principle. The horror of learning to kill appalled Pinter.

Such elements are powerfully rendered in his political plays such as *One for the Road* (1984) and *Mountain Language* (1988) as well as in confrontations between characters in his drama. In his early letters, Pinter told Woolf that he is, at heart, an artist who must save himself first. His poems helped him when he created a particularly beautiful phrase or image. He reported to Woolf that he had been writing more; he was alone with his poems and "clasping" them "for salvation."

Following his eighteenth birthday on October 10, 1948, Pinter received his call-up papers and returned them to the authorities. He spent a night in a prison cell. He was then called before a tribunal, where he said that he disapproved of the Cold War and wasn't going to assist it. His objection was rejected, but he was allowed to appeal and to bring a character reference to testify to his integrity. Pinter chose his contemporary Morris Wernick. The appeal tribunal was before senior army officers in Cumberland Place in Central London. His appeal was dismissed, and before the expected prison sentence, Pinter and Wernick went hitchhiking for a week around Cornwall during the summer of 1949. Back in London, Pinter's call-up papers came again, and he was summoned to attend a medical examination. Asked by an officer to undergo an examination, Pinter refused and was consequently arrested and faced a civilian magistrate, who gave him a choice of accepting his judgment or going before a jury. Pinter chose the former, and the magistrate fined him. Pinter's father, in an act for which Pinter remained deeply grateful, paid the relatively hefty fine of £50. The whole process was repeated a second time before the same magistrate, who this time fined Pinter £75, again paid by his father. This cycle might have continued, but the Board of Conscientious Objectors had gained a court victory that curtailed the pointless cycle of trial, imprisonment, release, medical attendance request, and imprisonment again and so on (Billington: 24). It should not be forgotten that at this time Pinter was experiencing considerable disillusionment with RADA (the Royal Academy of Dramatic Art), which he was attending from time to time. He told Woolf in a letter dated Tuesday January 4, 1949 that, as far as RADA was concerned, he refused to take any action at the moment. In the same letter, Pinter wrote of purchasing the works of Webster, attending art exhibitions, and watching the French Ballet perform *Swan Lake* on television.[5]

Pinter's correspondence with close friends such as Woolf, Mick Goldstein, and Wernick is largely devoid of overt political reference after around 1949–1950, the period in which Woolf and Wernick left compulsory conscription and Pinter was past his own call-up scare. Letters occasionally mentioned political situations, but Pinter didn't thump an ideological bandwagon. For instance, in a letter to Woolf from Torquay, dated November 8, 1956, he reacted to what became known as the Suez Crisis. Egypt's President Nasser nationalized the Suez Canal, Israel invaded, and on November 5, Britain and France sent troops into the Canal Zone. Pinter worried whether this would be a harbinger of war. He opined that the great powers, especially the Russians, were overreacting to the situation. For Pinter, "someone dropped a very big clangor a very long time ago, when apples were green." He added that he has long since ceased to pontificate on political issues.[6]

Pinter's focus was on personal concerns, work, his life as a repertory actor, marriage, and so on. But it would be incorrect to say that his political engagement lay dormant until his relationship with Antonia and the public engagement in the last decades of the twentieth century and beyond. Pinter's political concern was expressed earlier in different forms and in a different manner. In an interview in Ian Smith's *Pinter in the Theatre*, Pinter stated that his plays are preoccupied with "terrorizing" through verbal power and facility (83). This is evident in Pinter's initial performed drama, *The Birthday Party*. Its victim, Stanley, is subject to verbal and physical abuse from Goldberg and McCann, his visitors and interrogators. They shine a torch directly in Stanley's face and subject him to indignities. He loses the power of speech after resorting in desperation to attempt to put his spectacles lenses into his eyes—he has become an incoherent animal. In a 1958 letter to Peter Wood, the director of the initial 1958 production, Pinter wrote that Stanley is neither a hero nor a revolutionary. He asked whether we don't all find ourselves in Stanley's position at any given moment (*Various Voices*: 15). Writing on Pinter in the *New York Review of Books* (October 1999), Fintan O'Toole quoted Pinter as saying that he has always been surprised by the fact that people seem to have forgotten that it wasn't too long ago when the German Gestapo was knocking on people's doors. Further, that "knocking on people's doors" has been going on for centuries. Rather than expressing something un- usual, *The Birthday Party* actually expresses something quite common, Pinter said. He added that he was always aware that *The Birthday Party*, *The Dumb Waiter*, and *The Homecoming* were all political plays. He was aware of this at the time; he may have denied this on occasion because he believed that the plays spoke for themselves (38).

As Charles Grimes indicates in his *Harold Pinter's Politics: A Silence Beyond Echo* (2005), a key to a perception of Pinter's political politics is the Holocaust and the repetition of oppression and brutality and silencing throughout history, reoccurring from generation to generation. *The Birth- day Party* is a "political" play in its exploration of a "historically specific oppression that we in the present have apparently been fated to experi- ence, mutatis mutandis, again and again" (39). Sam Mendes's production of *The Birthday Party* at the National Theatre in 1994 was an overtly politi- cal one. In his *New Statesman* review, Aleks Sierks writes that the produc- tion sees "Stanley's situation as universal. He is Joseph K." Contempo- rary parallels are introduced: "Also anyone arrested under the Preven- tion of Terrorism Act. He is a victim of the Moonies, but also Salman Rushdie." Sierks adds that it is "more plausible now than ever, the dan- ger of arbitrary terror stalks a million homes" (March 11, 1994: 34–35).

Combining personal concerns with political ones, the one-act *The Dumb Waiter* was written just after *The Birthday Party* during the summer of 1958. Its first performance was on February 28, 1959 in Frankfurt am Main in the then–West Germany, with the first British production at the Hampstead Theatre Club on January 21, 1960 (BR: W7). Billington reads the play as an exploration "of the dynamics of power and the nature of partnership" and draws attention to a letter to Pinter from B. J. (Jimmy) Law, Pinter's friend from Hackney Downs school days, saying that both *The Birthday Party* and *The Dumb Waiter* are political plays concerning "power and victimization." Pinter responded to Jimmy Law in the affir- mative (90). In the play, characters Gus and Ben are hired killers waiting in a Birmingham basement for their victim to appear. Both are petrified of an unnamed boss. The two believe that they are being perpetually watched and under constant surveillance. There is, as the title of the play suggests, an antiquated serving mechanism that sends down increasingly strange food orders for them to fulfill, accompanied by an unseen person barking orders through a tube. Universal reverberations are developed from a seemingly ordinary instruction. In response to an order, Gus asks Ben, "What happens when we're not here? What do they do then?"—whoever "they" may be—"All those menus coming down, and nothing going up. It might have been going on for years."[7] Pinter's point is that it *has* "been going on for years": oppression, dominance, power play. The play may be seen as absurdist, with two gangsters passing their time in the world without any meaning or purpose—except, in their case, to kill.

In the drama, an envelope appears under the basement door. When opened, it contains twelve matches. This use of a stage prop—an envelope and matches—has led to speculation that the play presents humans as playthings, as the sport of a capricious Divine Power. Throughout the play, its two participants have continually bickered and played power games with each other. At the end, Ben is pointing a gun at Gus and slaps him. Ben seems obsessed with what he refers to as "this organization" (141). Their relationship is breaking down. The speaking tube continues to bark orders, which Gus questions and Ben obeys. Gus the questioner is destroyed by the system; the obedient Ben is not. Billington believes that the play features both an autobiographical element as well as a political one. Pinter rejected formalized Jewish religious practices and refused to be conscripted even at the risk of imprisonment, but he wrote "a strongly political play about the way a hierarchical society, in pitting the rebel against the conformist, places both at its mercy." Billington adds that *The Dumb Waiter* "was a deeply personal play about the destructiveness of betrayal"—something that obsessed Pinter (92).

A more obvious political play is *The Hothouse*. In common with other Pinter plays such as *The Birthday Party* and *The Dumb Waiter*, it focuses on oppression of the individual. *The Hothouse* was the immediate consequence of the temporary financial security that Roger Stevens had provided by taking out an option on Pinter's next three plays following his underwriting of *The Birthday Party*. Although written during the winter of 1958, it was put aside and not produced until 1980, with only a few omissions made during rehearsal (BR: W10). *The Hothouse* began as an hour-long BBC Radio play that Pinter submitted to the BBC Radio drama department in November 1958. Drawing upon Pinter's personal experience, the play is set in a psychological research center that has experiments and interrogation. In 1954, when not employed in repertory theatre, Pinter worked at the Maudsley psychiatric hospital, London, as a paid guinea pig to earn desperately needed money. Although Pinter was not subject to interrogation as experienced by the characters in the drama, the experience left a deep impression on him. The main character is Colonel Roote, who is in charge of the sinister government-directed psychiatric hospital. The play anticipates by almost three decades Pinter's dramatic rendition of the abuses of the state in his *Mountain Language* (1988). Charles Spencer, in his review of the 2007 National Theatre revival, refers to *The Hothouse* as "the missing link among Harold Pinter's plays." Spen-

cer writes that "what makes the piece so fascinating is that it seems to
unite Pinter's early plays of largely unspecified enigmatic menace," such
as for instance *A Slight Ache* (1958), "with the later . . . political playsa, in
which he specifically depicts the cruelty of the state against the individual."[8]

Pinter left *The Hothouse* unproduced until 1980 because he felt that it
was highly unlikely that it would be produced in the theatrical climate of
the time, especially after the failure of *The Birthday Party*. Pinter believed
"that in the late '50s London was still dominated by a safe commercial
theatre" (Billington: 102). Another factor may be that Pinter at the time
didn't wish to be perceived as a political dramatist.[9] He told Lawrence
Bensky in a 1966 interview that the world is a violent place, but he had
aesthetic issues with *The Hothouse* as it was heavily satirical. He never
liked any of the characters so he discarded the play.[10] Decades later,
successful and free of financial pressures, Pinter said in an interview with
John Tusa broadcast on BBC Television on September 28, 1985 that *The
Hothouse*, in common with *The Birthday Party* and *The Dumb Waiter*, dealt
with a totalitarian society and each with the individual at the mercy of an
authoritarian system (BR: K26). Three years later, he affirmed that the
play critically examined "authoritarian postures, such as state power,
family power, religious power, and power used to undermine, if not
destroy the individual, or the questioning voice."[11] Interestingly, in the
2007 production of *The Hothouse*, some elements of the play's origins as a
radio drama were restored: The audience could hear patients' sighs,
screams, and so on. The original scenes of dialogue that appear between
the patients, or "volunteers," and the staff remained omitted. The physical absence of the patients increases the audience's imaginative facilities
relating to the horrors that they may well be experiencing and "emphasizes the secrecy and sinister qualities of the institution" as well as under-
scoring "the fact that detainees are denied the right to speak out."[12]

Each of Pinter's plays from the 1960s and the following decade may be
viewed as containing some or more of these elements. For instance, *The
Caretaker* (1960) depicts a struggle for power or dominance over an individual who has been institutionalized and the overwhelming sense of
individual hopelessness and class deprivation. *The Homecoming* (1965)
may be perceived as a struggle for power and dominance within a family.
Old Times (1971) is preoccupied with a struggle for dominance, possession, and territory fought with the weapons of innuendo, ambiguity, and
latent threat. To take one more instance, *No Man's Land* (1975) exploits
memory and the past and its impact upon the present. It, too, focuses
upon sexual conflict, class dominance, and power play.

The perception that Pinter was apolitical before the 1980s, and before
his relationship with Antonia Fraser, should be taken into consideration
in the light of other evidence. It can well be argued, as Pinter suggests in
his 1988 interview with Anna Ford (BR: G63), that his work was political

but not in an overt form. In his compilation *File on Pinter* (1993), Malcolm Page writes that Pinter had a "reputation for reticence." As an exception, Page refers to remarks published in *Encounter* (December 1962), in which Pinter was asked his view on the European Common Market. He responds that he has no interest in the subject and doesn't care what happens (59). In Cecil Woolf and John Bagguley's *Authors Take Sides on Vietnam* (1967), Pinter succinctly observes that the Americans shouldn't have gone in, but they did so; they should "now get out, but they won't" (40; BR: H3A). Page writes that "in the eighties [Pinter] was prepared to discuss the political issues which increasingly concerned him" (101).

Somewhat curiously, Page's account omits Pinter's explicit condemnation and opposition to apartheid in South Africa in his early film work, especially *The Quiller Memorandum* (1965–1966), and in his 1967 direction of his friend Robert Shaw's *The Man in the Glass Booth*. In June 1963, Pinter was one of the signatories to a declaration opposing performances of plays in South African theatres that observed the color bar; other signatories included Samuel Beckett, Arthur Miller, Iris Murdoch, John Osborne, Muriel Spark, Arnold Wesker, and Angus Wilson.[13] On May 7, 1965, in an interview with Mercy Appet broadcast on the BBC Overseas Service for the program "Focus on Africa" (*Chronology*: 18; BR: J25), Pinter spoke out against apartheid. In his interview with Lawrence Bensky, Pinter recognized that politics are responsible for a good deal of suffering. Pinter added that he distrusted ideological statements of any kind. Pinter described watching politicians on television talk about Vietnam. He wanted to "burst through the screen with the flame-thrower and burn their eyes out and their balls off and then inquire from them how they would assess this action from a political point of view." In the same interview, Pinter discussed his adaptation of Robin Maugham's 1948 novel *The Servant*, Pinter's first movie script, which he worked on in 1962 and 1963, directed by Joseph Losey. It is preoccupied with male domination. Pinter told Bensky that he was attracted to the screenplay because of the battle for positions depicted in it.[14]

Joan Bakewell, intimately involved with Pinter from 1962 to 1969, recalled that she "dared to ask him why he didn't write about politics. He'd say 'hold on a minute. I write what I write. I write about what I know. I can't just write about politics to order.'" She added that in the 1960s, the dramatists David Mercer, Arnold Wesker, and others "were hammering at the system and Harold simply said, 'That's not what I do.'" For Bakewell, "although his work of course has changed in recent years, he was writing then about the psychic politics of people. Harold didn't write about world politics. He wrote about personal violence" (cited Billington: 204). There is also some truth in the view that Pinter was disconnected "from most forms of organized politics in the '50s through the late '70s" and that his "emergence as a political playwright in the early 1980s might be seen as somewhat surprising." Additionally, Pinter's "politics of detachment and disdain emphasize the playwright's distance from the traditional postwar political theater in Britain," a theater that looked "to socialism for its political vision" (Grimes: 22).

Political concerns and realities, and a preoccupation with what happened within his lifetime, are at the heart of Pinter's early film scripts and other creative activity. *The Quiller Memoradum* and *The Man in the Glass Booth* are both concerned with the Nazis. The former is Pinter's screenplay based on Adam Hall's (Elleston Trevor) espionage novel, *The Berlin Memorandum* (1965). It focuses on an intelligence operative who has been sent to post-war Berlin to uncover a neo-Nazi movement. In common with *The Quiller Memoradum*, Pinter's script reveals his preoccupation with the resistance to authority, suspense, power play, the strength that women possess, and moral ambiguity. The concern with revenge, guilt, and the past anticipate Pinter's 1987–1988 adaptation of Fred Uhlman's 1971 novel *Reunion*. Certainly, Pinter stresses domination, the Holocaust, interrogation, and fear in the script.

Pinter and friends Robert Shaw and Donald Pleasence formed Glasshouse Productions to stage Shaw's *The Man in the Glass Booth*. Pleasence, who also performed in *The Caretaker* in the mid-1960s, was a neighbor of Pinter who drove Pinter home after the initial rehearsals of the play, and they formed a close friendship. Indeed, Pinter moved in with Pleasence and his family and their Chiswick home when he left Vivien Merchant. Coinciding with the increasingly fraught nature of his relationship with Vivien, Pinter in the mid-1960s engaged in a multitude of activities, of which Shaw's play was one. May to July 1967 saw Pinter engaged with rehearsals and direction of *The Man in the Glass Booth*, which opened in Nottingham on July 11, 1967 prior to its opening in London at the St. Martin's Theatre. Shaw's play and Pinter's direction are both political. Shaw's play is a response to the Adolph Eichmann trial in Jerusalem. Eichmann, one of the leading architects of the gas chambers, was captured by Israeli agents and clandestinely flown back to Israel to face trial and execution. Billington observes that "Shaw's play was a tough moral thriller which raised the question, through the trial of a New York tycoon who poses as a concentration camp guard, as to whether the Germans should be absolved for the killing of the Jews. The play raised big issues" (193–94)—among them guilt, collective guilt, and forgiveness. The involvement with Shaw's play was not only an act of friendship but an illustration of Pinter's preoccupation with the Holocaust, which saw its culmination in what many discerning critics regard as Pinter's finest drama, *Ashes to Ashes* (1996).

Before turning to Pinter's very public political engagement from the 1980s and beyond, mention should be made of three film scripts that have political dimensions: *The Go-Between* (1970–1971), *The Last Tycoon* (1974–1975), and *The French Lieutenant's Woman* (1979–1980). The first and the third clearly explore the theme and politics of class within the British social system during different periods. In the case of *The Go-Between*, the focus is on the last years of the nineteenth century and the early years of the twentieth century, with the central historic event being the Boer War and the subsequent First World War. Class conflict, jealousy, rivalry, and sexual ambiguities are superbly exhibited at a cricket match. There is a deeply moving visual depiction of the character Leo, who in old age returns to the scenes of his youth. He goes past a memorial to the dead of the Boer War and of World War I, in which many of the cricketers and other spectators were slaughtered. Of course, this has a political resonance, especially from the perspective of a modern audience who would be aware of the subsequent World War II and other conflicts.

Pinter worked on his adaptation of L. P. Hartley's novel between 1969 and 1970; he worked on his adaptation of John Fowles's *The French Lieutenant's Woman* between 1978 and May 1980. Set at a slightly earlier historical period than Hartley's novel and juxtaposed with a contemporary one, Fowles's narrative explores class and gender conflict, mobility, and change. For instance, Sam, the servant of the central male figure Charles Smithson, asserts his independence by threatening to expose his master unless he gives him capital so that he can open a shop; Sam moves from the servant class upwards. Different historical periods are also juxtaposed in this film. Building upon suggestion of the film's director, Karel Reisz, Fowles's omniscient narrator is replaced with a twentieth-century storyline and the development of "a film-within-film structure" (*Sharp Cut*: 242). The film creates different realities, bringing past and present close together while being simultaneously distinct. Such a technique allows Pinter to reveal differences in attitudes. Sarah, the heroine, asserts her independence in both historical periods. Performed by Meryl Streep, in the 1970s she is a proto-feminist; in her mid-Victorian setting she is haunted by a relationship with a Frenchman who has deserted her. In this manner, sexual politics figure prominently in the film.

Much of 1974 was taken up with Pinter's adaptation of *The Last Tycoon* from the uncompleted F. Scott Fitzgerald 1941 novel. Although the director was Elia Kazan, a good deal of Pinter's work was done with its producer, Sam Spiegel, the eminent independent American film producer. Ironically, Kazan had been implicated in the anti–left wing witch hunts of Hollywood producers and others from the late 1940s and 1950s, some of whom, such as Joseph Losey and Spiegel, were close to Pinter personally.

Spiegel was important for Pinter. Charismatic, born in Galicia (now in Poland), educated at the University of Vienna, he left Europe in 1938 for Mexico and subsequently the United States. Committed to Zionism, his legacy includes large financial contributions to the Israeli film industry. He gained three Academy Awards for Best Picture, and his first contact with Pinter included negotiations with Joseph Losey for obtaining the rights for *Accident* during the early 1960s. It was Spiegel who commissioned Pinter for the screenplay of *The Last Tycoon*, and he also produced the film of *Betrayal* in 1982. An initial encounter between Pinter and Antonia Fraser was at an art benefit that Spiegel hosted in 1970, and Spiegel made his Grosvenor House flat available to Pinter at the time he left Vivien Merchant in April 1975. At the time, Pinter was working on adapting Fitzgerald's text. The script and the text reveal the fledgling film industry: the anti-union dogmatism of the central figure, the politics of the industry, and the use and abuse of power on the sexual and professional level. Pinter cut from his adaptation the confrontation between management and writers that figures in Fitzgerald's script. Pinter's focus was on the love element, the personal tragedy of the downfall of a dominant power player. His script reveals "the shallow incompleteness and insubstantiality of the Hollywood film world, as well as the hollowness of" its central figure, Monroe Stahr (*Sharp Cut*: 230, 232).

Feeling more socially and creatively secure, a public figure strongly supported by Antonia, Pinter turned to more political theatre from the early 1980s on. This turn is overtly represented in *One For the Road* (1984) and *Mountain Language* (1988), as well as through the majority of left-wing causes Pinter publicly identified with by writing letters to newspapers, jointly signing petitions, and other forms of expression such as participating in demonstrations. In a 1988 newspaper interview, Pinter explicitly expressed a catalyst that transformed his political attitudes from one of detachment and contempt. He believed the United States was responsible for the military coup in 1973 in Chile that overthrew the democratically elected government. It was done, he observed, in the name of Christianity, democracy, and freedom. In response, Pinter said, he could not sit back and not take responsibility for his own actions and thoughts, and instead act upon them, which he has been doing ever since. He added that he is making a nuisance of himself, especially as far as the United States is concerned.[15]

In early October 1981, Pinter directed a distinguished group of actors that included Jeremy Irons, Alec McCowen, Timothy West, Judi Dench, and others in "The Night and Day of the Imprisoned Writer." The project featured a reading of extracts that Christopher Hampton and Pinter's tennis and squash partner Ronald Harwood compiled from politically committed writers as diverse as Fugard, Solzhenitsyn, Havel, Neruda, and others. Pinter and Antonia were very active in PEN, regularly attending its meetings and advocating its causes on behalf of the freedom of writers and expression. At noon on Saturday February 27, 1982, Pinter, Antonia, the novelist Angus Wilson, and others protested outside the Polish Embassy in London on behalf of Solidarity, a protest that received nationwide media coverage. At this demonstration, the Pinters met Salman Rushdie. They would later give refuge to him when he fled from the fatwah imposed upon him for his *Midnight's Children* published in 1981. On Thursday March 11, 1982, Pinter attended a lunch on behalf of imprisoned writers (*Chronology*: 114).

In spite of Pinter's increasingly hostile anti-American and antiwar stance, as Antonia wrote in *Must*, the military "invasion of the Falkland Islands brings political unity to the family lunch table." On Saturday April 3, 1981, they listened "to the House of Commons debate with approval, Harold's patriotic feelings to the fore. Hateful Fascist Argentina is imposing its evil rule on the poor little Falkland Islanders: 'we should fight'" (135). Indeed, a pro-British Nationalist stand underpins Pinter's political approach and attitudes. For instance, one reason that he gave toward the end of his life for resisting pressure from the University of Texas at Austin to sell his papers to them was his patriotic belief that the papers should remain in the United Kingdom. Of course, by placing these on a loan basis to the British Library, he and Antonia were eventually able to sell them to the British Library at a considerable sum. In other words, Pinter's patriotism worked to his advantage.

Retrospectively, the 1980s may be viewed as a creative and active period for Pinter: He was involved in at least eight film adaptations, five of these being his own dramas, in addition to directing on the London stage. A further illustration of his political preoccupation during this period is reflected in his still unproduced but published screenplay adaptation of Joseph Conrad's novel *Victory*, which he began to draft on June 11, 1982 and completed by November 24, 1982 (BR: W46). For Gale, "the earlier versions" of Pinter's screenplays and *Victory* "are fuller, more information-packed; the final version is lean, keeping only the essentials required to express [Pinter's and Conrad's] meaning" (*Sharp Cut*: 288). From another perspective, Pinter's "reawakened interest in" the character of Axel Heyst in Conrad's novel "in the early 1980s might be read in autobiographical terms." His "work as writer and activist embraces the necessity of confronting and entering into the world as it is—with its aspects of contingency and compromise" (Grimes: 162).

On Thursday October 14, shortly after Vivien Merchant's death on Sunday October 3, 1982, Pinter attended press night at the Cottesloe Theatre on the South Bank of his triple bill *Other Places*. It consisted of his play *A Kind of Alaska*, written earlier at the turn of the year, *Victoria Station*, another product from the same year, and *Family Voices*, initially a radio play from 1980. *A Kind of Alaska* was inspired by his November 1981 reading of Oliver Sacks's *Awakenings*, the 1973 account of patients awakening from many decades or so of deep sleep and lost memories. Sacks's account and Pinter's drama may be perceived as having a political subtext. In his introduction to *A Kind of Alaska*, Pinter draws attention to the period of the 1916–1917 winter, a period when most of Europe was at war. An epidemic illness was spreading. It presented itself in innumerable forms: delirium, mania, sleep, insomnia, restlessness, and so on. A decade following that winter, the disease claimed millions of victims; more than a third died. Of the survivors, some escaped almost unscathed, but the majority moved into states of deepening illness that took the form of sinking into states of "sleep-consciousness, in which they were aware of their surroundings but motionless, speechless, and without hope. They were confined to asylums or other institutions" (BR: A41a[v]). Sacks's book is a medical account of twenty patients who were revived following the development of the L-DOPA drug fifty years later. *A Kind of Alaska* concentrates on a patient awakening, in which the past is the patient's present; in the play between worlds of time and memory, the past and what has happened subsequently become powerfully intertwined.

Pinter confessed in a letter to Woolf written on September 17, 1983 that he was feeling gloomy, worried that the world was on its "last legs" and would die by its own hand. He singled out a line from a speech given by then-U.S. President Ronald Reagan on August 13, 1983: "We're all Americans" and "We all pray to the same God." Pinter asked himself, "Which God would that be?"[16] *Precisely* (BR: A44) and *One For the Road* (BR: A45), Pinter's next plays, are both overtly political. The former was written for the actress and political activist Susannah York's efforts for the Peace Movement and plan for "Life: A Theatrical Show for Nuclear Disarmament" that she approached Pinter about on March 11 and 17, 1983 (BR: W47). It was performed as a sketch within the anti-nuclear-weaponry show *The Big One* at the Apollo Victoria Theatre on December 19, 1983. In the sketch, two men named "A" and "B," representing differing power elites, argue over the potential casualties involved in a nuclear disaster. "A" forces "B" into silence, and "A" may be regarded as the voice of a government forcing its populace into silence.

One For the Road continued Pinter's dramatic enactment of "a confrontation between power and powerlessness, between voice and voicelessness. It culminates in a silence that announces the brute fact of power as domination" (Grimes: 81). Antonia recorded that she and Pinter were dining at Le Caprice on May 19, 1983. They started "to talk about a play about imprisonment and torture," and Pinter remarked that the characters would be aware of their condition; further the play would not be explicit. There would be no blood or torture scenes. Pinter then cited the conclusion of Jacobo Timerman's memoir about being a political prisoner in the Argentine (*Must*: 142).

Timerman was born in the Soviet Union and went to Argentina with his family at the age of five. A journalist, he opposed the military dictatorship in Argentina and ran a left-leaning daily paper. A Zionist, he opposed and exposed increasing anti-Semitism in Argentina and was arrested and tortured by a section of the military, who subjected Timerman to electric shocks and beatings in solitary confinement. After being released in 1979, he spent some time in Israel, where he wrote and published *Prisoner Without a Name, Cell Without a Number* (1981), his memoir concerning his experiences in Argentina, to which he returned in 1984.[17] According to Antonia, Pinter told her that, in his work, Timerman "describes a woman taken down from her cell for the morning session. The guard is heard saying: 'Hurry up, you stupid bitch.' She's never seen again." Antonia added that "this was the first sighting of the play that became [*One For the Road*] but the image vanished until the following January" (*Must*: 142) when on January 7, 1984 Pinter read to her what became the drama. Its initial performance was on March 13, 1984 at the Lyric Theatre Studio, Hammersmith, in a double bill with *Victoria Station* and directed by Pinter (BR: W48).

Nuclear disarmament and the horrors of a nuclear war are not the concerns of *One For the Road*; abuses of human rights, power, and powerlessness are. Pinter told Mel Gussow that the play's world had been on his mind for years, and he had expressed it in one way or another in earlier plays. (*Conversations*: 86). The text does not describe a specific setting or country, except that the characters use and abuse the English language. The play has a cast of four: Nicolas, in his mid-forties (performed in the first production by Alan Bates), does most of the talking. The three others are presumably from the same family. There is a father, Victor, aged thirty; his wife, Gila, also aged thirty, and their seven-year-old son, Nicky. Nicolas interrogates them, although Victor mostly refuses to respond to his interrogator's taunts and chooses to remain silent. The dramatic text supplies scant information of the families' crime or opposition to what Nicholas represents—evidently, a religiously based totalitarian regime. A harrowing theatrical moment is when Gila loses control under interrogation. She loses the power to utter words, and all she can do is scream. The object is not to elicit information but to destroy.

There have been diverse critical observations on the play. For instance, for Basil Chiasson in his "Pinter's Political Dramas: Staging Neoliberal Discourse and Authoritarianism," Nicholas in *One For the Road* "strives to access the souls of his victims as a means to re-educate them, to bring them in line with the State, which means respecting it as an institution and therefore not turning against it." Chiasson adds that "the values perpetuated by the State which are to be respected and adopted are never mentioned in the play, just as the locale remains more or less blank." He observes that "ultimately *One For the Road* is not about informing spectators what these values are so much as dramatizing palpably the production of obedience through both discourse and marketing the body."[18]

One For the Road initially appeared in print in "Methuen's New Theatrescripts." A "revised and reset edition with illustrations and introduction" was published on October 3, 1985 (BR: A45, b; [iv]). The text of this later edition is prefaced by "a conversation between Harold Pinter and Nicholas Hern," dated "February 1985," in which Pinter tells Hern that he doesn't see the play as a metaphor. Rather, the play describes a state of affairs where people are victims of torture. The play features the torturer and the victims; two of the victims have been physically tortured (8). In a "Postscript" to his introductory conversation, dated "May 1985," Pinter relates that between March 17 and 22, 1985, he and Arthur Miller, as representatives of International PEN, visited Istanbul, where they met more than one hundred writers, academics, and trade unionists. Most of these people had spent some time in military prison, and the majority had been tortured. Pinter explains that all power, effectively, in Turkey remains with the military. The United States supports this in its fight to keep the world clean for democracy (24). Pinter neglects to mention that he and Miller were thrown out by the American ambassador from an embassy reception for their remarks on torture (*Chronology*: 140).

Shortly after leaving Turkey, Pinter began to draft his next play, *Mountain Language*, which had its genesis in his reactions to the oppression of the Kurds. Pinter had learned about the censorship of the Kurdish language, even among Kurds themselves. Pinter saw in this a bleak symbol of oppression, which was always so tightly connected in his mind to language (*Must*: 151). The play was put on the back burner until 1986 as Pinter became involved with myriad other activities, including completing the script of *Turtle Diary*, released in 1985, which is in itself a political film. Based upon Russell Hoban's 1975 novel of the same name, in spite of its romantic elements, it has an underlying political message relating to the release of animals from captivity—in this case, turtles from London Zoo.

In addition to PEN and allied activities, the early summer of 1985 saw Pinter directing Tennessee Williams's *Sweet Bird of Youth*, which opened at the Haymarket, London in June with the lead role performed by Lauren Bacall, who became close to Pinter (see *Chronology*: 336). It is sometimes forgotten that Williams was a political writer, and his play "was a symbol of [his] hatred of the Fascist instinct in American life." His career can be perceived "as an attack on a society that elevates crude energy and muscular materialism above delicacy of feeling" (Billington: 302).

Pinter performed Deeley in an American tour of *Old Times* from October 16 to November 27, 1985. Back in London, on February 17, 1986, Pinter participated in a roll call of Russian dissidents and two days later a demonstration at the Turkish Embassy. These may have provided the impetus for his resurrection on April 3, 1986 of *Mountain Language*, which he rewrote (*Must*: 150). Dedicated to Antonia and directed by Pinter, it was first performed at the Lyttleton, National Theatre on October 20, 1988 as an early evening platform performance. Pinter told Anna Ford that *Mountain Language* reflects a great deal what's happening in Britain. Pinter acknowledged to her that *One For the Road* and *Mountain Language* are both political in intent, associated with his visit to Turkey in 1985 and his concern for the plight of the Kurds; they also reflect his worries relating to what he considers to be Thatcherite authoritarianism at home.[19]

Pinter's mother recommended Fred Uhlman's little-known novella *Reunion* (1971) to her son. The initial script draft is dated "September 2, 1987." The final draft is dated "February 22, 1988" (BR: W50). On one level, Uhlman's novel is about the social and political forces that end the friendship and childhood of Hans Schwarz, a Jewish doctor's son in Germany before World War II, and Count Konradin von Hohenfels, an aristocratic schoolmate with whom Hans has become infatuated. "The short, poetic narrative chronicles their intense, innocent friendship and concludes with a revelation that counters superficial judgments about human character."[20] It also deals with political events that had profound and tragic consequences: the rise of Hitler, the Nazis, anti-Semitism, exile, and memory. There is a double-time frame: a wealthy Manhattan lawyer reflecting on the past, and that past itself, set in Stuttgart 1933, is just prior to Hitler coming to power. Through this device, Pinter brilliantly conveys the personal, social, and political dilemma of Hans and his family. His father declares himself to be both proudly Jewish and proudly German; for him, the country that produced Goethe, Schiller, and Beethoven will not succumb to Hitler. Still, he persuades his son to leave for America. In words reverberating with meaning, he tells Hans, "The Jewish problem is bound to be resolved, sooner or later." Konradin, Hans's German friend, adds that "he thinks it will resolve itself."

Following his own parents' suicides and the Holocaust, Henry, as he is now known, returns to confront the past and to visit a school that no longer exists. For half a century he hasn't spoken German, but does so to the headmaster in a new school. He sees a wall plaque at the former gymnasium/school commemorating the boys who died during World War II. The headmaster's silence, broken only by his use of "Umm," forces the normally reserved Henry to tell the headmaster that he has "had no contact with Germany at all, in fact, until now. I haven't read a German book or the German newspaper. I haven't spoken a word of the German language . . . in all that time."[21] Hans's attempt to find out what has happened to his friend leads to a deeply surprising conclusion to the film. He re-meets Konradin's cousin, Gräfin, whom Henry desired in his youth. Now aged, the once-blonde Wagnerian archetype with dangling pigtails, who adored the Hitler Youth Movement, pretends to be ignorant of her cousin and his fate. Uhlman's novella concludes with Henry discovering that his friend had been hanged for taking part in a singular act of bravery and ultimate political courage and defiance, the abortive 1944 plot to assassinate Hitler.

Director Jerry Schatzberg suggested to Pinter that he adapt Uhlman's work for the cinema. The film concludes with the headmaster's voice-over an "execution room" containing dangling butcher's hooks. The headmaster observes, "You don't know? He was implicated in the plot against Hitler. Executed." The stark fact is supplemented by the scriptwriter's addition of the butcher's hooks, seen in the light from the window (98–99). The film *Reunion* opened with a group of men being hanged from the butcher's blocks. All the executed men, the viewing audience subsequently finds out, participated in the plot to assassinate Hitler. Of course, if the 1944 plot had succeeded, then history would be different. This is to speculate; the film is interested in political realities and missed opportunities viewed from the hindsight of the present. This is particularly powerful when Henry overhears his father, a proud German who has been decorated for service to his country during World War I, behaving with contempt toward a Zionist who comes to warn him of the dangers they face. Henry's father tells the Zionist that Hitler and Fascism are "a temporary illness—like measles. Once the economic situation improves, Hitler will go out of fashion. He won't be necessary. Can't you see that? I know the German people." The unnamed Zionist leaves, saying, "You're mad," and Henry's father tells his mother that "they're such dangerous fools, these people!" (69). Shortly after, both husband and wife commit suicide.

Another Pinter cinematic adaptation with World War II as its backdrop is Elizabeth Bowen's novel *The Heat of the Day* (1949). In this case, it's a commissioned screenplay for television. The third draft of the adaptation is dated April 26, 1988 (BR: W51). Rehearsals were scheduled by Granada Television for October 4 to 14 of that year and the filming from October 17 to December 6, 1988. Directed by Christopher Morahan, it was initially broadcast on December 30, 1989 and starred Michael Gambon, Patricia Hodge, and Michael York, with roles also for Peggy Ashcroft and Anna Carteret, the director's second wife. Bowen's novel focuses on personal, sexual, and political treachery set in wartime London, mainly in 1942; in other words, "the masks we wear in our private lives and the threat of Fascism." According to Morahan, his "main discussions with [Pinter] were about how to make [the novel] visually exciting and how to get the texture of *film noir*. It mostly takes place at night in the middle of war and I found myself having to be an expert on the blackout: how people moved about, what they ate, how the traffic lights were partially blacked out and so forth" (Billington: 314).

The plot revolves around a divorcee, Stella Rodney (Patricia Hodge), who finds out through Harrison (Michael Gambon), who works in intelligence, that Robert (Michael York) an employee in a classified position in the War Office, is betraying the country by passing secrets to the Germans. Harrison is attempting to blackmail Stella in order to sleep with her, and Stella tries to suppress her awareness that Robert is committing treason. The main difference between Pinter's adaptation and the novel is Pinter's emphasis upon Harrison's sexual obsession with Stella. At the end of the novel, fifteen months after Robert's death, Harrison revisits Stella and after an air raid he asks her, "Would you rather I stayed till the All Clear?" (363). In Pinter's adaptation, Harrison doesn't ask her, he tells her, "I'll stay till the All Clear," and Pinter's directions that follow are: "They sit in silence. After a time, the All Clear Sounds. They do not move" (103). Both are connected by the events of the past; treachery has brought them together more than Robert's ironic belief in the Nazi cause. Politics and personal gain intertwine.

Mention too should be made of Pinter's adaptation of Ian McEwan's 1981 novel set in Venice, *The Comfort of Strangers*. Pinter worked on the script in 1988 and 1989 with the bound typescript dated "April 24, 1989" (BR: W54). Directed by Paul Schrader, the film was released in 1990 and focuses upon a British couple who holiday in Venice and become trapped by a dangerous maniac. The center of the story is possession and power on a personal level as opposed to a national or international level on the macrocosmic political stage. Pinter's adaptation is very political. Pinter sent his script to Simon Gray, who in a detailed typed letter to Pinter dated "May 7 [1989]," makes many astute observations. Pinter's script, not in the negative sense, is the most totally "hateful" script that Gray has ever read. When he finished reading it, Gray reacted physically "with shock and repulsion." In his script, Pinter explores "sexual fascism," lucidly depicts it as political, and even more, explores "the politics of lascivious destruction." Gray believes that this begins "in childhood," and explains in the film the character of Robert, whom Gray regards as a "monster." Gray asks why, however, "Colin the victim is so lacking in self-awareness, passive and ready to accept without self-questioning" the sexual evaluations others put on him? The answer may well be that Colin also needs a childhood rather than "drifting hollowly towards his fate" and consequently revealing "the kind of childhood he had." Colin is "a creature of a world in which the will has always come from other sources, not least the fashionable ones." He is a product of his 1960s upbringing and "his behavior after the blow to the stomach" in the film "so surely foretells his death that it was," for Gray, akin to "the death itself."

Somewhat ironically, Gray consequently finds himself loathing Colin more than he loathed his killer. This distressed Gray the most, as he finds "it's harder to forgive the victims than the violators. Their attraction to the brute current is almost as feeble as their resistance to it." Colin is neutered; "he really does belong to others, to do what they like with him." Gray asks, "Why shouldn't Robert have his final, filthy moment with him?" Colin is the partner of the divorcee Mary, who, with her two children, visits Venice with him. She "in the spite of her last minute fluttering, is deeply implicated, in spirit, in the sacrificial act" of Colin's abuse and murder. For Gray, "in its subtle and elegant fashion [Pinter's] script seems . . . to be an almost rabid savaging of the unfocussed, dilettante English male sexuality, Groucho-type chappies, who actually prefer to be objects of display, late-arousers, without much history and pretty pointless futures." In a postscript to his observations, Gray tells Pinter that "one of the cleverest strokes in the structure of the script is the way you draw us into the intricacies—*seduce* us into the intricacies—between Mary and Colin." This is the reason why in the film "the betrayal [is] so ghastly—it's a betrayal of our hopes for them, and our assumption of what they are."[22]

Following the February 14, 1989 memorial service for the travel writer Bruce Chatwin, Pinter and Antonia learned of the fatwa against Rushdie. Subsequently, Pinter garnered signatures of support for Rushdie, and he appeared frequently on TV and elsewhere, making the public aware of what had occurred. Protection of Rushdie placed them in personal danger. For instance, on March 12–13, 1989, Rushdie used the Pinters' house so that he could see his son and family; they were all surrounded by heavy security (*Must*: 159 and *Chronology*: 171). On March 1, 1989, meetings began to be held to discuss political issues; these became known as the "June 20th Group" meetings. In Rushdie's words, these meetings, at Pinter's home and elsewhere, were places "in which we might be able to thrash out ideas about what was happening in the country." He added that "it was never meant to be a pressure group or intellectual support system for the Labour Party" (cited Billington: 307–8 and see *Must*: 153–55).

From June 8 until June 12, 1989, the Pinters visited what was then Czechoslovakia. There were several reasons to do so. Antonia was then the president of English PEN. Louis Marks, the BBC director, producer, and scriptwriter, had suggested to Pinter that he consider working with him on a cinematic version of Kafka's *The Trial* (*Sharp Cut*: 339; BR: B8). Until then, Pinter had never ventured into Europe east of Germany. Pinter was also interested in meeting the Czech dissident and dramatist Václav Havel, who subsequently became the last president of Czechoslovakia (1989–1992) and then, from 1993 to 2003, the first president of the Czech Republic. Pinter and Antonia were also interested in the plight of dissident writers. The Pinter-Havel correspondence now in the Pinter Archive at the British Library dates back to April 1977. Pinter and Havel were represented in Germany by the same agent, Klaus Juncker, so they had a contact point. In a letter from Havel to Pinter, written in Prague and dated June 14 1988, Havel thanked Pinter for his assistance "and solidarity in the time of my stay in prison." Havel also mentioned Pinter's participation in BBC Radio productions of Havel's *Audience* and *Private View* in 1977. Havel wrote to Pinter on September 7, 1983, saying that Pinter's support for him when he was in prison "had a great importance not only for me, but also for my friends and . . . for ideals, which caused our suffering."

Antonia gives a vivid, detailed account of their five-day June 1989 visit, including their visits with former political prisoners, intellectuals, translators, and dissident writers, and their drinking "a lot of beer." They stayed with Havel and his wife, Olga, at their house at Hradecek in the countryside. "Havel himself was only just out of prison and the dreadful news of the deaths of the young at Tiananmen Square were filtering through to us: altogether it seemed a perilous time for civil-liberties worldwide." Among other activities, Pinter read *Mountain Language* to Havel and his compatriots (*Must*: 163–64, 66). On learning of the death of Olga, Pinter wrote to Havel on January 31, 1996 of his and Antonia's sorrow on hearing the news. He fondly recalled their visits, including the "unforgettable" visit to their house in the country in 1989.[23]

Their next visit was from February 7 to 11, 1990, when Havel was president. They visited Wenceslas Square, spent the evening of their second day at the theatre with Havel, and the next evening at a state dinner. On Saturday February 10, they went to Prague Cathedral, and Pinter viewed locations for the projected screenplay of Kafka's *The Trial*. On Sunday they visited East Berlin for the film festival and viewed Margaret Atwood's *The Handmaid's Tale*, for which Harold wrote the screenplay between October 1986 and February 1989 (BR: W53). During his visit, Pinter purchased for around £6 a portion of the Berlin Wall then being torn apart (*Chronology*: 178).[24]

The final decade of the twentieth century can be viewed as one of overt political commitment on Pinter's part. An example may be seen from 1990, the year in which Pinter turned sixty. January sees him meeting the radical authors Carlos Fuentes and Arthur Miller and their wives for dinner. Fuentes allied himself with the Socialist cause and, in company with Pinter, supported the Sandinistas. Five days later, on January 30, Pinter is assisting with a defense fund for Salmon Rushdie. On February 1, Pinter joined a breakfast to make people aware of the situation in Nicaragua. On February 6, he read Rushdie's "Herbert Read Memorial Lecture" on Rushdie's behalf. In February 1990, Simon Gray wrote to Pinter observing that Pinter's "reading of the Rushdie lecture was not only powerful but very *brave*." Gray was proud of Pinter even as he writes to him from his own "comfort and safety." He told Pinter that he "couldn't have done it." Revealingly, Gray comments on the information that Pinter has told him, which is that he has received an insulting, vitriolic letter replete with obscenities from his *bet-noire*, Ron Percival. Gray warned Pinter: "Do be careful—the anti-Semitism is also very personal . . . yet again—watch your back."[25]

Interestingly, in a contribution to the special issue of *Critical Quarterly* (52, no. 1, April 2010) devoted to Simon Gray, a friend with whom he grew up in Halifax, Nova Scotia, Louis Greenspan wrote that his parents, both of whom were Holocaust survivors, "were very fond of Simon, and his parents were so warm towards me that I was shocked to learn from the diaries Simon published many years later that they were anti-Semitic" (11). On February 5, 1990, Pinter sent his old school friend Henry Woolf a three-page diatribe from Ron Percival, their Hackney Downs School contemporary. The diatribe was against Salman Rushdie and Moslems and included anti-Jewish remarks, with Percival warning Pinter that he was "perceived as Rushdie's friend and collaborator" and consequently is in personal danger. Underneath Percival's letter, Woolf wrote in pencil, "A close friend once to us all. A primal member of our gang! Beautiful and brilliant and in some respects insane." Woolf's comment is followed by his initials and the date "24/x/12."[26]

On February 14, 1990, Pinter began auditioning for casting Jane Stanton Hitchcock's *Vanilla*, which he would direct at the Lyric Theatre, Shaftesbury Avenue, London. It opened on May 10, 1990 and closed on July 7. The choice of the play reflects Pinter's political stance. It is "a clumsy satire on the American super-rich and their groveling sycophancy towards foreign dictatorships, in this case that of Imelda Marcos and the Philippines." Billington observes that "one can only assume that Pinter's subscription to the play's attack on authoritarian cruelty blinded him to its technical gaucheness" (322). He took time from rehearsals on May 9 to record "Opinion" for Channel 4, broadcast on May 31, 1990 and published in *Various Voices* (190–200) under the title "Oh, Superman" (BR: I9a). This is a highly charged assault on American foreign policy, especially in South America, and a defense of the Sandinistas. Pinter asserted that U.S. foreign policy could be described as "kiss my ass or I'll kick your head in." He repeated his increasing concern regarding the distinctions between language and reality, where "language becomes a permanent masquerade, a tapestry of lies" (*Various Voices* 198–99).

The summer months of 1990 were also taken up with explorations as to whether "a Catholic marriage is possible" for Antonia and Harold, who celebrated their marriage on August 27, 1990 (*Must*: 190–91, 94). Pinter's sixtieth birthday party was celebrated on October 10 with sixty guests at Cibo's Restaurant and a four-hour program devoted to Pinter and his work broadcast on BBC Radio 3 (*Chronology*: 183). It was presented by Michael Billington and contains "reflections on Pinter's involvement with politics, film and cricket" (Billington: 323). Overt political activity worthy of note during the last two months of 1990 included a meeting on Sunday November 25 with the Chilean American writer and human rights activist Ariel Dorfman and on Sunday December 9 a visit from the Israeli activist Mordecai Vanunu, who had revealed in the British press details of his country's nuclear weapons activities and was lured back to Israel from Italy and subsequently imprisoned. Pinter continued to campaign on behalf of Vanunu—for instance, in front of the Israeli Embassy in London and on behalf of Amnesty International.

Pinter and Antonia visited Israel in May 1978. The highly successful visit is partly recorded in *Must* (see 93–96) and more fully in Antonia's *Our Israeli Diary, 1978: Of That Time, Of That Place*.[27] Pinter's father "was always a convinced Zionist." He and his son disagreed, sometimes violently, when Pinter criticized Israel (see Billington: 345). Indeed, an accusation that could be leveled against Pinter would be that, in his success and acceptance by the upper levels of British society, he didn't always remember the personal confrontations he himself experienced in the years after 1945 with Fascists; on the other hand, his father and mother never forgot the anti-Semitism they experienced in the pre- and post-World War II period. In her Israel travel diary, Antonia notes the scenes, shopping, discussions, and culture shock they experienced. Their base was Mishkenot Sha'ananim, the artists' colony near Jerusalem. On May 16, they had supper at the Rockefeller Museum in East Jerusalem, which, prior to 1967, was part of the Kingdom of Jordan. Pinter tells Antonia that he now knows that he is definitely Jewish—but he is also English, and this is an Arab town. Antonia replies that she "could live here in every way except one, and that's not being Jewish." In her diary, she observed that "for the first time, H[arold] says, he really does feel Jewish."[28]

Pinter was not above engaging in public and private controversy with his fellow dramatists. Early in 1979, during his time at the National Theatre, he objected strongly to the script of Howard Brenton's *The Romans in Britain* (see Hall's *Diaries*: 412), with its extreme indictment of imperialism and its rape scenes. It was in fact produced at the National, opening on October 16, 1980. Brenton's fellow radical dramatist Edward Bond, in his "The Roman's and the Establishment's Fig Leaf" published in the *Guardian*, November 3, 1980, defended Brenton's play and made a side-swipe at Samuel Beckett that roused Pinter's wrath. Two days later the same newspaper published a letter from Pinter, who wrote that Beckett remained "as human" in his concerns as Bond and, although Beckett may or may not be a socialistic dramatist, he knows as much about the "monster in man" as Bond does. Pinter added that Beckett does more than simply write essays about it; Bond does, which is his prerogative. Pinter's defense of Beckett continued; he observed that Beckett is never "self-righteous or woolly."

This latter remark elicited a personal letter from Bond to Pinter dated November 12, 1980, accusing Pinter of being "woolly" and defending himself against the charge of being "self-righteous." Bond told Pinter that "writers should concern themselves with describing and understanding the political and human horrors of our time. That concern seems so urgent and overwhelming that I don't have time, energy, or even the right to worry about the smallness of my own motives." Pinter replied forcibly on December 2, 1980. In his response, he told Bond that he regarded Bond's views as expressed in his letter to him, in his letter to the *Guardian*, and also in Bond's introduction to his play *Bingo* (1973) as complacent and arrogant. Pinter didn't mince his words, telling Bond not to lecture him about Fascism; Pinter is, after all, a Jew who grew up during World War II. After the war, Pinter added, he fought against English Fascists in London, and he can smell Fascism—including Bond's own brand. A decade later, Pinter seemed not to have borne a grudge against Bond, who on February 12, 1990 requested a contribution to the Soho Poly yearly choice of a new play by a new dramatist; Pinter financially contributed.[29]

The strength and direction of Pinter's political persuasion during the last two decades of his life are clearly reflected in his poetry, speeches, and other public pronouncements. Before turning to these, mention should be made of three of his theatrical works written during the period: *Party Time* (1992), *Moonlight* (1992–1993) and *Ashes to Ashes* (1996).

Pinter worked on *Party Time*, originally called *Normal Service*, from February 9 to 13, 1991. From April 19 to 21, 1991, a reading version was presented at the Pinter symposium at Ohio State University in Columbus, Ohio, celebrating Pinter's sixtieth birthday. As a stage play, it was first presented on October 31, 1991 at the Almeida Theatre in a double bill with *Mountain Language*, both directed by Pinter. The stage play was published on November 4, 1991, with a television version published April 10, 1994. Directed by Pinter, a television film of the play was broadcast on BBC Radio 4, November 17, 1992. (BR: W58). A short play, running for only forty minutes, it received an enthusiastic response at the Pinter Ohio symposium. A central figure in the drama, Jimmy, "speaks, paradoxically, only to tell us he has no words and no existence, as Pinter comes as close as possible to creating a voice for the disappearance of voice" (Grimes: 125). Billington wrote that *Party Time* "offers a powerful, developing image of an hermetic, heedless society so preoccupied with its own conspicuous consumption and health Fascism that it is blithely indifferent to the erosion of civil liberties" (333). Chiasson in his "Pinter's Political Dramas" goes even further, arguing that the play is "arguably the most overt attack on the realities at the heart of the implementation of neoliberalism across the globe, namely the re-signification of liberal and utilitarian concepts" (263).

Moonlight is less blatantly political and revisits many of Pinter's past themes and obsessions. Antonia Fraser writes that "in view of Harold's general preoccupation with politics and the oppressed in many, many countries, it should be recorded that the first play he wrote in the nineties could not possibly be argued to be political even by the most willy interpreter of his art." Initial notes for the play were made on December 11, 1992. The play's genesis "derived fundamentally from another very different human experience, his mother's death, peacefully in a nursing home in early October,[30] at the age of eighty-eight" (*Must*: 209). During the summer of 1992, Pinter had frequently been seeing his mother in her Hove nursing home while he was playing the role of Hirst in *No Man's Land* at the Almeida Theatre and comforting his father. The basic plot of *Moonlight* is a tale of a dying man, nursed by his wife, whose sons refuse to return home to comfort him and to say farewell to him on his final journey. As Pinter demonstrated in *The Homecoming*, family dynamics are a cauldron for politics, in the past and afterward.

Moonlight was initially performed at the Almeida Theatre, London, September 7, 1993, and then transferred to the Comedy Theatre in November 1993. Benedict Nightingale, in "Pinter Stages a Refreshing Return to the Family Business" in the *London Times*, was relieved that the play was not political and returned to old family Pinter territory of the battleground of the family (September 8, 1993), privileging the personal over the political. Francis Gillen's extensive, perceptive assessment of *Moonlight* captures the essence of the play. Gillen observed that "it is a play about the strangeness of death and of life viewed from that perspective as the characters who peopled one man's life appear as mirror images, the presences and absences of his life" (31). Furthermore, in the play "we fully encounter one of the most important paradoxes of Pinter's work. The struggle for identity which he portrays is necessary, but such struggle, carried on over a period of years, threatens to leave the individual finally separate and alone, locked in the 'I.'" [31]

Pinter spent a good deal of 1995 directing his friend Ronald Harwood's *Taking Sides*, a play that focused on the artist's position in a dictatorship, in this instance a Fascist one, and the question of whether art can transcend politics. Harwood's play centers upon the great conductor Wilhelm Furtwängler, who remained in Germany throughout the Nazi period. In the play, he is interrogated by an American officer after the war as a suspected Nazi. Pinter's direction and Harwood's script allowed the chief participants to speak for themselves, and the script supplies no clear-cut answers or simple solutions to a real dilemma. "In one fundamental respect the play reflects on Pinter's preoccupation with evasion of communication: not so much between persons . . . but between cultures as they shape persons. Furtwängler's anguished situation appears to derive from the impossibility of his recognizing the real tragedy—the *relationship between* the cultured Germany of Beethoven and the terrors of Kristallnacht. Against this, the possibility of his interrogator ever understanding him palls into insignificance." [32]

During a visit to Barbados from January 7 to 21, 1996, Pinter read Gitta Sereny's biography of Albert Speer, Hitler's favorite architect and, from 1942, his minister for Armaments and Munitions. The biography provided the inspiration for *Ashes to Ashes.* On January 19, 1996, Pinter told Antonia that he just realized that he would have been dead, at age ten, had the Nazis invaded. She records in her diary for January 24, 1996: "Harold started to scribble. He came over for supper" from his study, "having written a scene of great power which he read to me. A man and his wife. He then wrote on until after one. Rather erotic. Rather horrible. So far." Four days later, she records that "Harold wrote madly on Thursday" and that now she has "heard the whole thing, it may come from *Speer*." Two days later "the play has grown. Scenes came to Harold in the middle of the night. I found notes scribbled in the bathroom. He even wrote during breakfast." Nearly a month later Pinter read *Ashes to Ashes* to Salman Rushdie and others. Antonia observes that "this is taking place now, not in Nazi Germany." She records that "Harold said an interesting thing about the character of Rebecca in *Ashes to Ashes*: 'She is the artist

who cannot avoid the world's pain,' and he equated himself with her."
She adds that "this was the time of the savage war in Lebanon, for which
Harold, at a time of great physical weakness, was being asked on every
side to speak; sign petitions, etc. Devlin stands for the rest of the world
who ends up by being brutal towards her" and the play "ends on a note
of savage despair. Harold's own *weltschmerz* was very marked at times"
(*Must*: 214–16).

The play was finished on February 6, 1996. The initial rehearsal reading for *Ashes to Ashes* took place at the Ambassadors Theatre on Wednesday April 10. The initial private performance of *Ashes to Ashes* was on
May 28, 1996, following an afternoon dress rehearsal at Northwood
Town Hall the previous afternoon (*Chronology*: 227). Directed by Pinter,
the play opened on September 19, 1996 at the Royal Court Theatre. The
play "reveals the Holocaust to be at the root of Pinter's contemplations of
politics and power." The reality of the Holocaust is presented through
indirection with Pinter utilizing "allusion and . . . the traces of unreliable
personal memory rather than through direct reference or representation."
In *Ashes to Ashes*, "past and present, there and here, self and other emerge
inextricably, as political violence is located within the space of private
life."[33] In an interview with the Catalan academic Mireia Aragay, which
took place in Barcelona on Friday December 6, 1996, Pinter revealed that
his play is about the images of Nazi Germany; he doesn't think anyone
can ever get that out of their mind. He confessed to being haunted by
these images since he was young; he is sure that he is not alone in being
haunted by them.[34]

The play was performed again, with *Mountain Language*, at the Royal
Court in June 2001. In one of the most perceptive comments on Pinter's
late plays, Alastair Macaulay, then the chief theatre critic of the *Financial
Times*, conveyed the strength and importance of *Ashes to Ashes* in a detailed review of the June 2001 Royal Court revival: "Whether or not Rebecca's memories are false, they are true to some of the most appalling
events of the twentieth century." His comments were made at the time
when British television screens were full of horrifying images of the conflict that erupted following the breakup of Yugoslavia, immediately followed by images from Iraq and horrific pictures from various massacres
on the African continent. The other character in the play, Devlin, has a
"baffled inability to follow her message of involvement with scenes of
horror." For Macaulay, "the winged, elusive, uncapturable [sic] dark
poetry of Rebecca's confessed soul [is] probably Pinter's most extraordinary single achievement as a dramatist."[35]

Such a great play may be seen on many levels. Its title, *Ashes to Ashes*,
has multiple reverberations of meaning. It is a clear reference to the Holocaust, to the gas chambers, and to the Anglican funeral service, with its
use of the *Book of Common Prayer* and intermingling of passages in the
biblical books of *Genesis* (3.19, 18.28), *Job* (30.19) and *Ecclesiastes* (3.20). It

also may refer to Ash Wednesday. One of Pinter's favorite poets was T. S. Eliot. Antonia would have been aware of the significance of "Ash Wednesday," the title of Eliot's complex poem published in 1930, which takes place on the opening day of Lent, "the 40 days of fast and abstinence preceding Easter." On this day, Catholics "receive ashes in the sign of the cross on the forehead as a reminder of the repentance and penitence that will be required of them as they prepare to celebrate the spiritual fullness of Christ's coming resurrection from the grave and his triumph over death."[36] A fourth association is with cricket, to the seeming life and death conflict between England and Australia for an urn containing ashes.

Pinter turned seventy on October 10, 2000. His final play, *Celebration*, premiered at the Almeida March 20, 2000 in a double bill with his initial play, *The Room*. This coupling was Antonia's suggestion. According to Pinter, *Celebration* tapped accumulated memories and experiences. As discussed in chapter 3, Pinter was a frequent restaurant-goer, and the setting for the play is an upscale West End restaurant. Pinter began to write the play while on holiday in Dorset with his family. He read what he had written aloud to them and they collapsed with laughter; subsequently, the waiter began to emerge as a central character (Billington: 403–4).

There are two separate restaurant tables. Russell, a shady banker involved in investments, and his former secretary, Suki, sit at the small table. At a much bigger table is a group of former East Enders, now nouveau riche, celebrating loudly a wedding anniversary. They enjoy insulting one another, using foul language, and drinking heavily. The more they imbibe, the more extensive are the revelations and the more outrageous the insults. This leads the restaurant manager, a waiter, and a female assistant to intercede. The waiter eventually takes over the play in a series of monologues and reminiscences concerning famous people with whom his grandfather was apparently more than acquainted, including Mafia members, the Archduke Ferdinand who was assassinated in 1914, and Benito Mussolini. The waiter's penultimate ramblings to the diners, whose tables have joined together, overtly connects them to political brutality; his grandfather claimed to know great creative artists such as W. B. Yeats, T. S. Eliot, Picasso, and others "where they were isolated, where they were alone, where they fought against pitiless and savage odds, where they suffered vast wounds to their bodies, their bellies, their legs, their trunks, their eyes, their throats, their breasts, their balls" (66).

An examination of the drafts for the play shows that Pinter deliberately cut down specific political references such as those to Central America, and they do not appear in the printed text or when it was performed.[37] For Robert Gordon, *Celebration* in "its darkly comic representation of the duplicity, violence, and banal sexualization . . . revealed Pinter at the age of seventy to be as finely attuned to the changing landscape and values of

English society as always." Gordon also observes that *Celebration* "exposes the way postmodern culture not only fragments but flattens hierarchy of value so the difference between one pleasure or another is merely a matter of price." [38]

Violence, torture, brutality, betrayal, and political machinations are very Shakespearean themes and clearly evident in his great tragedy *King Lear*, a play that fascinated Pinter. One of his first theatrical experiences was going to see Sir Donald Wolfit as King Lear. He returned to the performance on no fewer than five occasions and subsequently performed the part of one of Lear's knights in a production of the play with Wolfit. It is not surprising that Pinter should be attracted by a cinematic adaptation of the play. He "completed" the script of his adaptation on the last day of March 2000, after working on it for about two years. In an interview published in the *Independent on Sunday* on February 6, 2000, Roth said, "What Harold Pinter will do is to rearrange, cut and then turn it from a stage piece into cinema" (10). Pinter eliminated the subplot, rather than altering Shakespeare's words or introducing his own language. Pinter's script omitted none of the suffering experienced by Lear and Gloucester or the evil enacted by Goneril and Regan in their political machinations. Pinter's adaptation reveals much about Pinter at work and his thematic preoccupations; it is unfortunate that it remains on the drawing board. [39]

The very late sketch *Press Conference* was performed at the Lyttelton Theatre, National Theatre, as part of two segments of Pinter sketches on February 8, 2002 (BR: W63). In spite of his serious medical condition and undergoing chemo on January 4, 2002, Pinter performed on the stage. An overtly political sketch, it "invokes torture and the fragile, circumscribed existence of dissent" (Grimes: 135). Pinter gave "a chilling performance of the totalitarian iron hand by none other than a Minister of Culture, who has assumed this role after tenure as the head of the Secret Police," playing the role "with chilling joviality." As the sketch develops, "the zealous abusers of freedom of expression seem to gain increasing control," so much so that "even the broken and the traumatized have disappeared under the swell of state controls. Even the gasps, sighs and screams, as well as the coded voice-overs, have vanished." [40]

Most of these illustrations of Pinter's political engagement have been drawn from his dramatic output and cinematic adaptations. During the last decades of his life, Pinter's political engagement is reflected in his non-fictional prose, letters, late poetry, and speeches as well as dramatic work. On July 11, 1996, after receiving an honorary degree from the University of Hull, where his friend the late Philip Larkin had worked, [41] Pinter focused his acceptance speech on the political. He told his audience that people are living with a distinct and palpable discrepancy: We are glad to be alive today and look forward to being alive tomorrow, while, at the same time, humanity draws closer and closer to destruction of the natural world and the end of civilization. Pinter considered it to be truly remarkable that people live in the shadow of utter catastrophe and manage not to think about it. For instance, he observed that some people consider nuclear war unimaginable and assume it won't happen. Pinter, however, believed that would happen *only* if we have the courage to find the language to describe it. In the speech, Pinter emphasized that we cannot allow others to do our thinking for us; if we submit to political rhetoric and political obstructions, we are doomed (BR: E39).

In a letter of January 4, 1997, Pinter told Mick Goldstein that political matters dominated his life and thoughts. He observed that Goldstein wouldn't believe the laws that were at the time being passed in the country. He said he would not shut up—which would make some people happy and others unhappy. His response is "bullocks!"[42] Four days after his letter to Goldstein, Pinter's letter titled "Scenario for the Bugging of a Home" was published in the *London Times* (BR: F32). The letter concerns police bills legalizing the bugging of private property. Anybody who found police installing bugs in their home and objected to it could be charged with obstructing the police in the course of their duties. Pinter asked Michael Howard, the home secretary at the time, to either confirm or deny such a scenario. In his response the next day, Howard wrote that given security issues, intrusive surveillance was justified. This caused a flurry of letters, with many amplifying the issue raised by Pinter's letter.

Another illustration of Pinter's persistent political engagement at this time may be found in his "First Person: Picking a Fight with Uncle Sam," in the *Guardian*, December 4, 1996. This was on a subject that increasingly preoccupied Pinter around the turn of the century: American foreign policy. His *Guardian* contribution concerned the incompatibility between American public rhetoric and the cruel impact of the United States upon other countries. Pinter outlined a catalog of crimes extending from the killing of "Communists" in Indonesia in 1965 to military coups in South America. He wrote that the crimes of the United States throughout the world have been systematic, constant, clinical, remorseless, and fully documented, but nobody talks about them (BR: E40).

Pinter's attacks on American foreign policy would not have fallen on unsympathetic ears among elements in the British establishment and intelligence services wishing to distance themselves from a perception of the United Kingdom's undue dependence upon the United States in the post-1945 world. Other factors came into play, too: disagreements with Prime Minister Tony Blair's perceived closeness to President George W. Bush's foreign policy, especially regarding the first Iraq war; personal antagonisms between intelligence services depicted, for instance, in the novels of "John le Carré" and life of their creator, David Cornwell; and a desire to reaffirm "freedom" of speech and dissent.[43] It should not be forgotten that for all Antonia and Pinter's anti-American stances, members of her family and good friends were in or had been in positions of considerable influence in the British ambassador service. For instance, Antonia's friend Sir Fred Warner was a senior British diplomat. William Waldegrave, with whom Pinter regularly played tennis and with Antonia bridge, served as a member of the Conservative government's cabinet between 1990 and 1997.[44]

Pinter's poem "The 'Special Relationship,'" dated "August 2004," was published in the *Guardian* (September 9, 2004) and in *Various Voices* (261; BR: C49). The poem, a savage indictment of the so-called Special Relationship between the United States and the United Kingdom, ends on the suggestion of sexual depravity: "A man bows down before another man I And sucks his lust." Other instances of a vitriolic anti-Americanism are reflected in Pinter's political poems from this period, such as "American Football I A reflection upon the Gulf War," dated "August 1991"; "God Bless America," dated "January 2003"; "The Bombs," dated "February 2003"; and "Democracy," dated "March 2003." They are included in the collection of largely political poems called *War* published by Faber in 2003 (BR: I12). The poems are also included in *Various Voices*. They contain a choice of words far from subtle, deliberately anti-poetic, with the word "fuck" repeatedly used. "Democracy," a four-line, single-verse poem with each line end-stopped, attempts to replicate the language of the aggressor. There is "no escape," "the big pricks are out," and "they'll fuck everything in sight." The last line of the poem contains a warning, an admonishment: "watch your back." The incidence of monosyllabic words, the movement from "The" at the start of the third line to the possessive adjectival "your"—the second word of the three-word final fourth line and sentence—serve to emphasize both the "violent, obscene, sexual and celebratory military triumphalism that followed the [first] Gulf War" and Pinter's "satirising" of such attitudes (Billington: 329; cf. Lin and Baker: 169).

"American Football I A reflection upon the Gulf War" was written as a response to the first Gulf War and the American invasion of Kuwait. With appropriate irony, given its satirical use of one of America's favorite sporting pastimes, the poem initially appeared in *BOMB*, a West Village New York radical magazine (issue 38 [Winter 1992]: 82; BR: C29a). This issue appeared in the first week of December 1991. Before this appearance, the poem had been rejected by the *London Review of Books*, the *Guardian*, the *Observer*, the *Independent*, and the *New York Review of Books*. Pinter was especially incensed by the decision of the *London Review of Books*,[45] as its rejection had been accompanied by "the assurance that the poem had 'considerable force' and that it shared the author's views on the United States" (Billington: 329). Following its appearance in *BOMB*, the poem was published in *The Pinter Review V: Annual Essays for 1991* (1991) and dated "August 1991" (41) and in a fortnightly paper called the *Socialist* (January 15–28, 1992). Founded in London in 1989 by the political activist Hilary Wainwright and others, it was subsequently closed down to reappear as the monthly *Red Pepper*, for which Pinter contributed and gave other significant support (BR: C29b and c). Pinter considers his involvement with *Red Pepper* part of the resistance and an independent and positive voice of critical dissent.[46]

The poem has nine brief verses of which the first and third have three lines, the second, fourth, fifth, and seventh two lines. Verses six, eight, and nine are each a single sentence. The last verse consists of the longest line and the penultimate verse the shortest: "We did it." There is considerable repetition with the biblical evocative "Hallelujah!" repeated twice, although in the second instance without the exclamation mark. Another repetition is the assertive "It works," repeated twice. "We blew" occurs five times, and in each instance with a varying continuance. In the first: "We blew the shit out of them," followed by, "We blew the shit right back up their own ass." Surprisingly, Pinter refrains from the possibly more evocative "arse," especially as the next instance of usage continues the metaphor: "We blew the shit out of them," as does "We blew them into fucking shit." The final instance is: "We blew their balls into shards of dust." Billington writes that the poem, "by its exaggerated tone of jingoistic, anally obsessed bravado, reminds us of the weasel-words used to describe the war on television and of the fact that the clean, pure conflict which the majority of the American people backed at the time was one that existed only in their imagination." The poem's final line and verse is startling with its movement in tense to the present, use of monosyllabic words, and ironic sense of submission to the aggressor combined with powerful pronoun usage characteristic of Pinter's finest poetry: "Now I want you to come over here and kiss me on the mouth." (*Various Voices*: 260).

In his "Foreword" to Peter Kennard's *Domesday Book: Photopoem (Critical Image)* (1999; BR: H50), Pinter writes that he believed that Kennard's work forced his readers to inhabit a grotesque and oppressive, unescapable prison—the human spirit—chained, shackled, wasted, reduced, and throttled. For Pinter, the vision is bleak one. As a consequence, people have two obligations: to recognize the existing structures of power for what they are and to resist them. Kennard's image of doomsday relates to military might and its relationship to market forces. Pinter addresses the then-U.S. President Bill Clinton's language: "We Americans have given freedom to the world." For Pinter, similar language would be used during the year 2000 and beyond. There would, he prophesized, be more moral outrage and humanitarian intervention and more language that Pinter referred to as lies, bombs, distraction. There would be more killing. Many of his poems from this period express disgust at American military intervention in Iraq and elsewhere. One example is his eight-poem collection *War* (2003).

At a degree speech at the University of Florence on September 10, 2001 when he received an honorary doctorate, Pinter drew attention to what he regarded as NATO's misuse of language in the way in which it justified the bombing of Serbia. Pinter drew special attention to the cruel facts of the innocent civilian casualties caused by the misdirected bombing of the town of Nis and its marketplace on May 7, 1999. He decried what he called America's brutal and malignant wild machine and said it must be resisted (*Various Voices*: 240). Such observations were followed by a brief statement to the Italian press made on September 13, 2001, in which Pinter condemned the terrorist attacks on New York and Washington. They were, he said, horrific, and no responsible person could see them in any other light. [47]

Pinter's prose and poetry during this period became more and more abusive toward the United States, its presidents, and foreign policy. In his poems, he uses plain idiomatic and obscene language with rather crude parody of American attitudes. His speeches are not that different, charged with venom and generalization. For instance, at the University of Florence, he told his audience that the United States has, since the end of World War II, pursued a brilliant strategy of exercising a sustained, systematic, remorseless, and clinical manipulation of power worldwide, while masquerading as a force for universal good. The country's foreign policy, in Pinter's view, is arrogant, indifferent, and contemptuous of international law. The country dismisses and at the same time manipulates the United Nations. Furthermore, the United States is the most dangerous power the world has ever known; it's a rogue state of substantial military and economic might. Pinter also verbally assaulted the actions of the British government, calling Europe, and especially the United Kingdom, compliant and complicit. Pinter then referred to Shakespeare's great political tragedy *Julius Caesar* and to Cassius's words in the second scene of the first act: We "peep about to find ourselves dishonourable graves." [48] As part of the resistance to American domination, Pinter instanced the Zapatistas, who define themselves rather than be defined by others and who refuse to accept American terms; the only way they could be eliminated is if America destroyed them, and they cannot be destroyed because they are free. [49] Pinter's specific attack was directed on a personal level at President Bush and Prime Minister Tony Blair. In a letter to the *Spectator*, Pinter referred to both as "terrorists" for whom he developed a particular contempt, although Blair had offered him a knighthood, which Pinter turned down with considerable disdain (October 30, 2004, BR: F54).

Pinter's address given when he received an honorary doctorate at the University of Turin on November 27, 2002 appeared, somewhat ironically, in the British Conservative daily newspaper the *Daily Telegraph* under the byline, "The American administration is a bloodthirsty wild animal" (December 11, 2002: 24; see BR: E54). Most of Pinter's speech consisted of a fierce attack on American hysteria, ignorance, arrogance, stupidity, and belligerence (*Various Voices*: 241) in relation to the prospect of the Bush regime's planned war against Iraq.[50]

Pinter received the Nobel Prize for Literature at a ceremony he was unable to attend in person due to illness. On September 14, 2005, he returned home after receiving treatment for pemphigus at the Princess Grace Hospital. On September 26, he was feeling unwell again, using a stick to move about. Due to the steroids, his feet started swelling and his voice was exceedingly croaky. Still, on October 6, he visited the Dublin Pinter Festival, traveling by private plane and in the evening attending a performance of *Old Times* at the Gate Theatre. The next evening, he saw *Family Voices*, the following day *The Caretaker*. He read to an audience his love poem "Paris." On Sunday October 9, in the afternoon, Pinter participated in readings from his poetry and prose and in the evening attended his seventy-fifth birthday party. The following afternoon, he had a bad fall at the VIP lounge at Dublin Airport and had to have stitches. He returned to London on Wednesday October 12, 2005 "scarcely able to walk, heavily dependent on a stick, with a white patch over one eye and a sailor's cap" (*Chronology*: 297–98; *Must*: 291). The following morning, he learned that he had been awarded the Nobel Prize for Literature and "now learned that the Nobel Prize transforms your life forever: in his opinion entirely for the better. His plays entered the stratosphere of productions. Equally dear to his heart was the fact that he would now have a political forum in his Nobel speech" (*Must*: 293).

On October 28, Pinter completed the first draft of the speech. In and out of hospital in November and early December, he realized that it would be impossible for him to go to Stockholm to accept the prize in person, so the speech was delivered via a recording made on December 4 in studios in London and transmitted through a satellite link on the day of the awards, December 7, 2005. The thirty-eight-minute speech called "Art, Truth and Politics" can be divided into various segments. It begins with an examination of his method of writing drama and then moves into reflections on the significance of art itself and the subject of linguistic precision. At this point, Pinter goes into a discussion of politics and the retention of power and the ways in which power is maintained by those in authority through the use of lies and dishonesty. For Pinter, the United States supported and in many cases engendered every right-wing military dictatorship in the world after the end of World War II. While praising the United States for its subtle manipulation of power while simultaneously pretending to be acting as a force for liberation and freedom of expression, Pinter sarcastically and humorously volunteers as the American president's speechwriter. The Nobel lecture most movingly concludes with a reading of his poem "Death" as a reminder of human mortality.[51] As Robert Gordon observes, "Speaking from a wheel-chair and appearing very weak, [Pinter] demonstrated his lifelong aversion to authority by using this media opportunity to deliver a powerful attack on the United States and Britain for initiating the Iraq war, and to demand that Tony Blair and George W. Bush be prosecuted for war crimes" (194).

It would be inappropriate to conclude this chapter on Pinter and politics without some consideration of his attitude to religion, which had political ramifications; he greatly admired the Sandinistas, who regarded religion and politics as one. At the Edinburgh International Festival Book Festival in an interview with the Australian journalist Ramona Koval on August 28, 2002, Pinter was asked about his Jewish upbringing. Pinter replied that he had a bar mitzvah when he was thirteen and never entered the synagogue again, other than attending a few marriages. Asked if he remembered the part of the Torah that he had to read, he responded that he did not. (BR: G117).[52] Given Pinter's negative attitude to Judaism as a religion, it is perhaps surprising that copies of the Talmud in Hebrew and English and J. H. Hertz's edition of *The Pentateuch and Haftorahs Hebrew Text English Translation and Commentary* were in his library when he died.[53]

When responding to Ramona Koval concerning entering a synagogue, Pinter forgot that he organized the memorial service for his good friend the film director Sam Spiegel and eulogized Spiegel at the West London Synagogue on Wednesday February 26, 1986 (*Chronology*: 148). Pinter's speech doesn't mention Spiegel's early years, his commitment to Zionism, or his deep Jewish commitment but focuses instead on their friendship. They worked together on two screenplays, *The Last Tycoon* and *Betrayal*, and Pinter remembered that in the worst crisis of his life—when he left his first wife, Vivian—he turned to Spiegel, who gave him shelter. For Pinter, Spiegel in spite of everything remained an optimist. He believed that the human spirit would prevail over the destructive forces within it. Pinter quoted the penultimate verse from Philip Larkin's poem "Bridge for the Living," which he believed would have meant a great deal to Spiegel. Following the lines from Larkin, Pinter concludes his Spiegel eulogy by saying that Spiegel would be remembered for many things but most of all the twinkle in his eye.[54]

In a discussion with Peter Stanford,[55] Pinter illuminated his attitudes to religion, Judaism, and Catholicism. The discussion with Stanford appeared under the title "Mystery at the Heart of Life and Death" in *The Tablet*, the leading Catholic intellectual weekly paper in the United Kingdom, following Pinter's death in the early evening of Christmas Eve 2008 and his burial on December 31, 2008. His funeral was private in West London's Kensal Green Cemetery and "a resolutely secular affair" with Pinter laying "down precise instructions for his Catholic wife, Lady Antonia Fraser, and selected readings on memory, mortality, politics and cricket, but nothing on religion." Stanford adds that this "makes perfect sense since Pinter never made any pretense to a religious faith." However, Pinter's attitude to religion and faith was complicated and Stanford draws upon a recorded interview with Pinter that they made in the autumn of 1992, broadcast on Thursday December 10, 1992 (*Chronology*: 201). The recording was intended as the pilot for a BBC Radio 4 series concerning those on the outer fringes of faith; however, the series as a whole never quite made it to the broadcasting state. Pinter told Stanford that he was aware that there is a mystery at the heart of life and death and admitted to having "religious inclinations," although they get him nowhere because he cannot believe in any formal God and can't, in fact, understand that idea. Those "religious inclinations" emerge in particular situations; for instance, he "derives an aesthetic pleasure from certain ceremonies and a great deal of religious music and even the physical presence of being in churches." Pinter would on occasion accompany his wife to Mass at their local Carmelite church in West London. Pinter told Stanford that he had great respect for his wife's faith but couldn't share the faith any further than that.

Pinter remembered that his parents were dutiful in their faith and never questioned the formal religious structure of their life. So he went through the paces until age thirteen and then left it entirely. His parents were deeply upset when he married Vivien Merchant on the most sacred day of the Jewish calendar, Yom Kippur. As a young man, Pinter had no belief whatsoever, although Judaism certainly influenced his thinking. He had close friends when an adolescent; a close-knit group, they used to discuss religion and the existence of God. Although he was not a believer, his friends were, and energetic conversations would go on for years. Such exchanges are at the heart of *The Dwarfs*, in which Pinter "refers to that period and the term 'God' dominates the book to a great extent."[56]

Terence Rattigan admired Pinter, and Pinter acknowledges a debt to Rattigan's work (cf. Billington: 55). An illustration of the elder dramatist's admiration for the younger one is found in a letter dated May 16, 1975, in which Rattigan wrote, "Dear Harold, You're a splendid poet and a very fine dramatist, and when it comes to sheer 'theatre'—there's no one else who can beat you—not even me, in the days when I still knew a trick or two. . . . Bless you."[57] Also, Rattigan commented to Pinter that *The Caretaker* was "about the God of the Old Testament, the God of the New, and all humanity." Pinter responded that it wasn't; rather, he said, it was about two brothers and a caretaker. He said he doesn't write allegories.[58]

During his visit to Nicaragua in the 1980s, Pinter met three priests: Father Miguel d'Escoto, the Sandinista foreign minister; the Jesuit Father Fernando Cardenal, minister of education; and his brother, the poet-priest Father Ernesto Cardenal, minister of culture. The encounters had a deep impact upon Pinter. He told Stanford that, over the years, he inherited a language in which the words "God," "Christianity," and "Christian values" have been totally abused. To Pinter, those words were used in damaging and hypocritical ways to justify actions that were, in themselves, evil. Pinter observed to Stanford that the idea of the vengeful, right, and just God has been used for many years to justify actions he believed are criminal. "But what [Pinter] observed the Sandinistas doing in Nicaragua was engendering an attitude to life that it seemed to [him], was actually informed by actual Christian values, if [he] understood actual Christian values to mean caring about other people, acknowledging the existence of other people, and objecting to strongholds of power which oppress the rest of society." Pinter added that the Sandinistas were on their way to embody an aspiration that was a synthesis of art, politics, and religion. Stanford asked Pinter how what he said had manifested itself. Pinter responded, perhaps rather naïvely, that there was no hierarchy and that everyone seemed to be part of the same thing. At least, that was the understanding. Pinter had rarely come across such stimulation, discovery, and excitement about a society that was possible to create. Pope John Paul humiliated Father Ernesto Cardenal in a very public rebuke at the Managua airport runway on a 1983 visit. Pinter's reaction to this was to view the Pope as representing a different facet of Catholicism than Ernesto Cardenal, who perceived politics and religion as one with no distinction between the fate of people on this Earth and their fate in a universal context.

Stanford questioned Pinter whether what he had witnessed in Nicaragua changed his views of Christianity and whether there had been subsequently a knock-on effect. Pinter responded that it made him aware of the antithetical state of affairs existing in Britain and in many European countries where no such synthesis between politics and religion existed. In Britain, people are separated from one another without a sense that individuals share the same world. The only thing that is shared is total misery by millions of people, being rejected by the status quo, or taking their place in the status quo as rejects. In Nicaragua, on the other hand, the respect for life is perhaps best expressed in the best minds of the Catholic priesthood. His Nicaraguan visit opened his heart to Catholicism. As an adolescent, he was opposed to Catholicism as he was very much influenced by the Spanish Civil War, when the Catholic Church institutionally was on the Fascist side. Consequently, Pinter became violently anti-Catholic, seeing Catholicism embodied in those sorts of terms and its relationship with Fascism. It took Pinter quite a while to move away from that. Pinter added that his experience of the Sandinista synthesis was a "profound" one. Stanford observed that it was "not profound enough, in the end, to carry [Pinter] forward to embrace any formal religious belief." Still, Stanford argued that the experience was "significant in reaching an evaluation of this extraordinary writer and inspiring human being" (*The Tablet*, January 10, 2009: 6–7).

As has been observed elsewhere in this book,[59] Simon Gray is a perspicacious judge of his close friend Pinter and his work. In a lengthy typed undated letter written on a Sunday night probably in early January [1990], Gray thanked Pinter for sending him a copy of the Anglo-Argentine Sister Pamela Hussey's *Free from Fear: Women in El Salvador's Church.*

It is a report dated "April 2, 1988" on behalf of the Catholic Institute for International Relations and published on January 1, 1990. In his lengthy comments on Sister Hussey's report, Gray revealed much about his possible beliefs and his perception of Pinter's attitude or non-attitude toward religious faith. Gray "struggled continuously" with particularly "bureaucratic prose" and commented that "she has almost no sense of God, or even interest in him." Gray referred to a hurried discussion that he and Pinter had over lunch concerning the differences in their "views of the use of religious metaphor," Gray's opinion being "that metaphor was only powerful if it attempted to *embody* a truth." For Gray, it seemed that Pinter held the opposite view of metaphor; in other words, "that metaphor was a helpful and persuasive and untruth—i.e. *if* [Gray] . . . [believed] in the virgin birth, it would be as an expression of God's intervention in the history of the human race." For Gray, Pinter doesn't "believe in God's intervention in the history of the human race" and regards "the virgin birth as a sort of fable about the need for the human race to believe that it can make itself better." In Gray's opinion, "*if* I believed it, the intervention would be a fact," whereas in Pinter's "view, the human race progresses . . . through a series of increasingly distancing interpretations of an archaic fable." Gray then confessed that as he doesn't "believe in anything very much except my *longing* to believe, [he] can't really quarrel with [Pinter]."

Gray reiterated that his objection to Hussey's work was due to its "prose that has no time or room (or gift) for metaphor, about a way of life that purposefully and no doubt sensibly doesn't care about the nature of metaphors." Gray wondered, "What does it mean to her to be a nun? Why bother to enlist the idea of God, when God seems not really even to be an idea?" Gray admitted that Pinter "might (rightly) reply—what does it matter, as long as there are people like her, and people like the people she met, to do what needs to be done?" Gray confessed to having no answer to this except to refer to "questions raised by stronger voices than mine—Eliot in *Four Quartets*, for instance." T. S. Eliot was a favorite poet of both. Gray concluded his letter: "But then again, in El Salvador, what is articulated doubt (and spasms of certainty) about God—or human purpose—but the luxury of the reasonably fed and the untortured?"[60] No response from Pinter is found in his archive.

Such perspectives are a considerable reversal to Pinter's excessive hostility to Catholicism expressed, for instance, in a letter to Henry Woolf written early in the period 1951 to 1953 when he was touring Ireland. Pinter told Woolf that, with Pauline Flanagan, he visited the hills surrounding Tipperary. He described poetically the autumn landscape covered in browns and dark green, with the evening sunlight slanting and hanging. The only blight on the landscape was a huge hillside statue of Jesus Christ. After several expletives and crudities and negative remarks about people crossing themselves everywhere, Pinter told Woolf that he certainly admires Jesus but it's just too much to have him shoved down his throat every day. He called religion an enormous mass cancer. In a letter also written to Woolf from Cashel, County Tipperary that dates from probably September 1953, when Pinter was close to turning twenty-three, he said that he knew all about the sterility and putrefaction of the inflicted systems of order, including religion.[61]

An insight on Pinter's dramatic characterization and attitudes is revealed in a June 20, 1964 letter to him from his former schoolmaster Joseph Brearley. Brearley and Woolf shared a taxi on the way back from the Aldwych Theatre, where they attended the opening night and party for the revival of *The Birthday Party* at the Royal Shakespeare Company on June 18, 1964.[62] Brearley recalled that Woolf remarked to him in the taxi that "this play is one of the most anti-Semitic ever." Brearley wondered if he noted in Pinter "a trace of fear?" and he asked Pinter if his mother was still afraid of anti-Semitism. However, another perspective opened in Brearley's mind. He thought that "Henry has forgotten" the character of McCann in *The Birthday Party*. Brearley told Pinter: "You see, you being a Jew and seeing things from inside, your portrait of Goldberg is complete—merciless and devastating." On the other hand, "McCann is different. More of a hint, a rough sketch. That's why the play is, for me (Christian that I am!) just a bit lop-sided." For Brearley, "nothing . . . is inconsequential."[63]

Essentially, Pinter's attitude to the divine, to religious belief, remained little changed from that reflected in a lengthy letter to Woolf written on a Sunday in the mid-1950s. He told his friend that both matter and mind exist and that God is only in the mind. He argued that God exists solely as a unifying factor; consequently, the dead are in the mind. When the dead appear to crop up following death, this can only be in the living mind, and they don't crop up at all. It is us, the living, who "crop 'em up." As far as Pinter is concerned, the mind and matter are not in opposition but complement each other and have connections. Pinter's commitment is to the outside world. For Pinter, there is no ultimate truth and there is no God. He further asserted that scientific humanism has dug its own grave, and, as was typical in his representative correspondence with Woolf, he referred to cricket. In this instance, he speculated that "if England make 400 [runs] tomorrow and the next day win the match." In other words Pinter was not a prophet and didn't have prophetic powers.[64]

Pinter and Antonia chose the readings for Pinter's memorial service. Michael Gambon read from *No Man's Land* and from Pinter's poem "Death"; Stella Powell-Jones (Flora Fraser's daughter) read a Pinter love poem to Antonia; Matthew Burton, close to Pinter in his later years, read Francis Thompson's "At Lords"; Penelope Wilton read from Eliot's "Little Gidding"; Antonia read Horatio's tribute to Hamlet: "Now cracks a noble heart/Goodnight, sweet prince, and flights of angels sing thee to thy rest!"[65] The traditional Hebrew prayer for the dead was not recited, and there is no evidence that Pinter himself recited it at his own father's burial at Hove Jewish cemetery following his death on September 10, 1997. Perhaps Antonia summed it up best when she wrote that "Harold had a deep sense of the spiritual, hence his love of such poets as Eliot, and when we were abroad liked to sit in dark churches while I tried to brighten them up by lighting candles to St. Anthony." She didn't add that her husband's admiration for a Sandinista leader such as Ernesto Cardenal was based upon what he perceived to be Cardenal's practical fusion of Catholicism with politics, yet another instance of Pinter's "deep sense of the spiritual" (*Must*: 189).

NOTES

1. BLADDMSS: 88880/4/17.
2. Personal letter August 12, 1971.
3. BLADDMSS: 88880/4/17.
4. BLADDMSS: 89094/1.
5. BLADDMSS: 89094/1.
6. BLADDMSS: 89094/3.
7. 145; the reference is to *The Birthday Party and Other Plays*. London: Methuen, 1960.
8. July 19, 2007, http://www.dailytelegraph.com, accessed November 30, 2016.
9. See Fintan O'Toole, "Our Own Jacobean," *New York Review of Books* (October 1999): 30.
10. *Paris Review* (Fall 1966): 30–31.
11. Cited Ronald Knowles, "Harold Pinter, Citizen," *Pinter Review* (1989): 25.
12. Mary Luckhurst, "Speaking Out: Harold Pinter and Freedom of Expression" in Peter Raby, ed., *The Cambridge Companion to Harold Pinter*, second edition, 2009: 110.
13. "48 Playwrights in Apartheid Protest," *London Times*, June 26, 1963: 12.
14. *Paris Review*: 30–31.
15. "Growth of an Angry Playwright," *The Observer*, October 16, 1988: 13.
16. BLADDMSS: 89094/5.
17. www.wikipedia.org, accessed September 3, 2016.
18. Basil Chiasson, "Pinter's Political Dramas: Staging Neoliberal Discourse and Authoritarianism" in Mark Taylor-Batty, *The Theatre of Harold Pinter*: 259. Chiasson's *The Late Harold Pinter* (2017) considers Pinter's "political" engagement in his work with an emphasis upon Pinter's late post-mid-1980s output with an emphasis upon applying critical theory to the work.
19. *Listener*, October 27, 1988: 5–6.
20. https://en.m.wikipedia.org/wiki/Fred_Uhlman, accessed September 5, 2016.
21. *The Comfort of Strangers and Other Plays*, London, Boston: Faber, 1990: 85, 98.
22. BLADDMSS: 88880/7/6: ff.20–21.
23. BLADDMSS 88880/7/5.
24. For a color photograph taken by Pinter of Antonia chipping away at the Berlin Wall, see *Must*: 264, facing.
25. BLADDMSS: 88880/7/6: f.37.
26. BLADDMSS: 89094/5.
27. Available on Amazon Kindle Singles from September 25, 2016 and published by Oneworld Publications, spring 2017.

28. https://www.theguardian.com/culture/2016/sep/17/antonia-fraser-harold-pinter- israel-travel-diary, accessed September 18, 2016; and cf. *Our Israeli Diary, 1978: Of That Time, Of That Place*: 83.

29. BLADDMSS: 88880/7/2.

30. In fact on Monday October 5, 1992.

31. Francis Gillen, "'Whatever Light is Left in the Dark?' Harold Pinter's *Moonlight*," *The Pinter Review* (1992–1993): 36–37.

32. Ronald Knowles, "From London: Harold Pinter 1994–95 and 1995–96," *Pinter Review 1995–1996*: 166.

33. C. Grimes, *Harold Pinter's Politics*: 195.

34. Mireia Aragay, "Writing, Politics and *Ashes to Ashes*: An Interview with Harold Pinter," *The Pinter Review Annual Essays 1995 and 1996*: 10.

35. Cited http://www.haroldpinter.org, accessed September 10, 2016.

36. R. E. Murphy, *T.S. Eliot A Literary Reference to His Life and Work*, New York: Facts on File, 2007: 58.

37. See BLADDMSS: 88880/1/16–17.

38. Robert Gordon, *Harold Pinter: The Theatre of Power*, Ann Arbor: The University of Michigan Press, 2012: 190–91.

39. See chapter 6 and *Sharp Cut*: 370–72.

40. Mary Luckhurst, "Speaking out: Harold Pinter and Freedom of Expression," in *The Cambridge Companion to Harold Pinter*, second edition (2009): 116–17.

41. See chapter 6.

42. BLADDMSS: 88920/5/2.

43. For an idea of the complex nature of the post-1945 Anglo-American relationship, see N.A.M. Rodger, "Grieve Not, but Try Again," a review of P. Hennessy and J. Jinks's *The Silent Deep: The Royal Navy Submarine Service Since 1945*, London: Allen Lane, 2016, *London Review of Books* 38 (18) September 22, 2016: 21–22; Geoffrey Wheatcroft, "Tony Blair's Eternal Shame: The Report," a review of the Chilcot Report into the Iraq War, *New York Review of Books* 63 (5) October 13, 2016: 42–44. For le Carré/David Cornwall, see Neal Acherson, "Which le Carré Do You Want?" a review of his biography and autobiography, ibid., 20–22.

44. See also chapter 3.

45. Inigo Thomas, then at the *London Review of Books*, recalls having to inform Pinter of the rejection. Pinter faxed an "explosive" reply. However, when the cricket season began months later, Pinter invited Thomas to play in the first match. Thomas describes the match. He accidentally bowled a ball that struck the chrome radiator of Pinter's beloved black Mercedes coupe called "Myrtle." "He exploded, but then gave me a wink: he was having me on. We never talked about 'American Football.'" http://www.lrb.co.uk/blog/2017/01/20/inigo-thomas/pinters-american-football/.

46. BLADDMSS: 88920/8.

47. See BR: E50; BLADDMSS: 88920/8.

48. ll.137–38: Riverside edition, eds. C. Blakemore Evans et al., *The Riverside Shakespeare*, Boston: Houghton Mifflin, 1974; *Julius Caesar*: 1108.

49. See BR: E50; BLADDMSS: 88920/8.

50. The full text is found in *Various Voices*: 241–43.

51. For analysis and citation from Pinter's Nobel Prize speech, see Baker, 2008: 13–32; Billington: 422–23; and Basil Chiasson, "Pinter's Political Dramas": 262–63; see also his *The Late Harold Pinter*. Pinter's text is found in *The Pinter Review: Nobel Prize/Europa Theatre Prize Volume: 2005–2008*, Tampa, FL: The University of Tampa Press, 2008: 6–17.

52. A transcript of the Koval interview available on http://www.abc.net.au/radionational/programs/booksandwriting/harold-pinter/3630860, accessed December 5, 2016; see also BLADDMSS: 89083/3/3 and *Guardian*, August 28, 2002.

53. See Baker, "Harold Pinter's Library," *Remembering/Celebrating Harold Pinter: The Pinter Review: Memorial Volume*, Tampa, FL: University of Tampa Press, 2011: 155.

54. Cited Andrew Sinclair, *Spiegel: The Man Behind the Pictures*, London: Weidenfeld and Nicolson, 1987: 140–41.

55. The biographer of Lady Antonia Fraser's father, Lord Longford (1904–2001), first published in 1994 and as *The Outcasts Outcast: A Biography of Lord Longford*, Stroud, Gloucestershire: Sutton Publishing, 2003, following Longford's death; the biography drew upon Longford's papers.

56. Peter Stanford, "Mystery at the Heart of Life and Death," *The Tablet*, January 10, 2009: 6–7; see also BLADDMSS: 89083/3/3.

57. BLADDMSS: 88880/7/14.

58. Cited in Stanford Interview; see BLADDMSS: 89083/3/3.

59. See chapter 3.

60. BLADDMSS: 88880/7/6: ff.62–64.

61. BLADDMSS: 89094/2.

62. See chapter 1.

63. BLADDMSS: 88880/7/2.

64. BLADDMSS: 89094/3.

65. *Hamlet* V, ii: 559–60; Riverside edition: 1185.

SIX

Literary Influences and Favorites

This final chapter, "Literary Influences and Favorites," follows the pattern of using hitherto untapped primary sources. Organized more or less chronologically, the chapter moves from Pinter's early reading and its impact upon him to subsequent literary influences and friendships. Pinter's correspondence is drawn upon to provide insight into literary authors and their work and their impact upon his creative imagination. The chapter provides information on Pinter's reading and his observations on his reading. The authors treated don't necessarily reflect a hierarchy of literary importance for Pinter. However, recently available materials make it possible to examine Pinter's personal and creative engagement with them. The writers discussed range from Shakespeare and some of his contemporaries to the Jacobean dramatist John Webster, then discussion moves forward chronologically to a great Romantic poet such as Wordsworth and then to W. B. Yeats, James Joyce, and Joyce Cary. Authors writing in languages other than English are examined, including Proust, Rimbaud, Tolstoy, Turgenev, and Goncharov, as well as the impact of Aldous Huxley and Henry Miller. Attention shifts to Pinter's relationship with three contemporaries: Samuel Beckett, W. S. Graham, and Philip Larkin. Each impressed Pinter in one way or another.

A comprehensive account of the literary influences on Pinter, whether conscious or not, would require at least one book. This chapter selectively focuses on a handful of his literary influences and his favorites. It draws upon hitherto unused letters to provide information on Pinter's reading and reaction to his reading. Unfortunately, space doesn't allow for more than an all-too-brief discussion of Pinter's interest in a visual medium such as painting—artists and their work.

A sense of the emotional impact upon Pinter of various aesthetic experiences is found in the letters he wrote to Henry Woolf during a particularly trying period in both his and his friend's lives. Woolf experienced a brutal mindless time during his RAF National Service in the autumn of 1948. In a letter postmarked September 16, 1948, Pinter referred to the awfulness of his friend's existence. Pinter also informed Woolf that he had made the difficult decision to be a conscientious objector—one reason being that he was a writer and intended to devote his time to his writing. Pinter was also experiencing moods of discontent with RADA (the Royal Academy of Dramatic Art), which he was attending from time to time in the autumn of 1948. He went to some of the performances and was touched, for instance, by Turgenev's *A Month in the Country*, a play that he saw at least twice more and one that his friend Simon Gray cinematically adapted (see *Chronology*: 359).

ARTISTS AND ART EXHIBITIONS

Plays and novels were not the only art form attracting the young Pinter. On January 4, 1949, he told Woolf that, the day before, he went to a modern art exhibition that "bewildered" him—an expression of his state at the time. One painting he considered to be superb was that by Yves Tanquy, the French surrealist. He compared it with the work of the French poet Arthur Rimbaud, whose work prefigured surrealism. Pinter told Woolf that Rimbaud's wish was to be a voyarite, meaning a mystic or seer. He then launched into a descriptive account of Tanquy's painting: Its foreground consists of delicately colored bones, probably human, that are propped up in harmony. The bones are large, tinted, and recede in size. These bones merge into an image of a stag shaded in quiet levels of integrating color. To Pinter, the effect was weird and wonderful, seeming to imply the horizon after the decay of the flesh.[1]

After becoming successful, Pinter visited art exhibitions, especially modern ones, and previews for prospective buyers of modern art. He participated in joint publishing ventures with painters, most notably the limited edition of *The Homecoming*, designed by the artist Harold Cohen, containing his lithographs accompanying Pinter's text (BR: A20e). He also collaborated with Guy Vaesen, a painter, theatrical manager, BBC radio producer, and close friend of Pinter and Pinter's first wife, Vivien Merchant. The published version of *Family Voices* was originally written for radio, and in its printed version interweaves Pinter's text with Vaesen's illustrations. There are a series of silkscreen prints designed and signed by both the artist and Pinter in a limited edition of forty. They also appeared in the year of the published version of *Family Voices*, 1981 (BR: A40a), but were never commercially distributed. In 2002, Enitharmon Editions produced *The Disappeared and Other Poems* in a signed limited edition. This contains twenty-nine poems from 1950 to 1998; "presented in reverse chronological order, the poems span the spare, impersonal tone of Pinter's mature years to the hurly-burly exuberance of his youth, when his poetry was influenced by Dylan Thomas and John Webster." In addition, the text is accompanied by twelve full-color plates reproducing the paintings of Tony Bevan; each signed and numbered copy contains an original Bevan etching.[2]

SHAKESPEARE

Pinter had a lifelong veneration of Shakespeare. His early letters to Woolf are replete with Shakespearian references. For instance, Pinter began a letter to his friend on a Tuesday evening, probably December 21, 1949, with: "'My fate cries out!' Hamlet's fate, our fate, the world's fate, old perhaps the same." Pinter then moved into a Wordsworthian allusion: "[T]he world rushes, hurries, for action, but yet the mind, groping . . . shows that it is indeed the still, sad music of humanity." In 1949, Pinter erratically attended the Royal Academy of Dramatic Art (RADA) for two terms before dropping out. He wrote to Woolf that, at RADA, he was involved in *Hamlet* and wanted to study it properly. However, shortly afterward, he complained to Woolf that RADA is diseased—echoing images from the play—and, in fact, so is the entire city. At Christmas, Pinter listened to a performance on the BBC Radio's Third Programme of *Hamlet* with John Gielgud in the title role. Pinter also heard Gielgud saying Prospero's speech "Our revels now are ended" from *The Tempest* and was moved to tears. The performance of *The Tempest* was masterly— fragile and at the same time strong and true, Pinter thought.

Pinter's ambition was to play a bloodied, soul-torn Macbeth or Othello. References from Shakespeare are not confined to letters from the 1940s. Pinter ended a July 1954 letter to Woolf referencing *King Lear*, observing that if Lear had more luck, "we'd all be better off."[3] During his tour of Ireland with Anew McMaster's company in 1951–1952 and again in late 1953, Pinter performed in various Shakespearian roles: Charles the Wrestler in *As You Like It*; Horatio in *Hamlet*; Edgar/Edmund in *King Lear*; Macduff in *Macbeth*; Cassio/Iago in *Othello*; Bassanio in *The Merchant of Venice*; and Hortensio in *The Taming of the Shrew*. In a letter to Wernick written either on Saturday September 22, 1951 or 1952, he called McMaster's Othello awesome. McMaster, he says, is an impressive actor and a simple, kind person. Pinter asks his friend if he recalls the fit that Othello falls into, then cites Othello's "Noses, ears, and lips" (IV, i. 42) and observes that McMaster is great in the role.[4] He must be great, Pinter says, because his Hamlet is so bad that he makes Hamlet a saint. In another letter to Wernick, this time from Tipperary, written on a Tuesday in the summer of 1952, Pinter reports that he is playing Bassanio, which he enjoys. He also says that one of his great successes was playing Hortensio in *The Taming of the Shrew*. It seems, Pinter observes, that he has a flair for comedy.

Gloucester's line in the opening scene from the fourth act of *King Lear*—"As flies to wanton boys are we to th' gods" (l.36)—are particularly meaningful to Pinter during this period. He cites them more than once in letters to Woolf. Indeed, Pinter wrote to Woolf from Carlow County on November 8, [1953] that he finds performing Edgar in *King Lear* a rare and interesting experience. In another letter to Woolf written from Galway in September [1953], slightly earlier toward the end of his second stint with McMaster's company, Pinter told Woolf that during the previous week, he played Iago in Galway and his performance was well received. In two weeks, he would play at the Opera House Cork. His Iago, he says, becomes more and more interesting. In a letter from Castlebar County Mayo written in November 1953 just before his final performances with McMaster's company, Pinter tells Woolf that he has finished the battlement scenes in *Hamlet*. He calls the wonderful work exhilarating, with another packed house; he had a great week.[5]

In Donald Wolfit's company at the King's Theatre, Hammersmith, from February until April 1953, Pinter played Jacques de Boys in *As You Like It*; a Knight in *King Lear*; the second Murderer in *Macbeth*; Salanio in *The Merchant of Venice*; Nicholas in *The Taming of the Shew*; and an officer in *Twelfth Night*.[6]

As mentioned in the first chapter of this book, Joe Brearley cast the youthful Pinter in the lead roles in the Hackney Grammar School productions of *Macbeth* and *Romeo and Juliet*, so it is hardly surprising that Pinter's semi-autobiographical novel *The Dwarfs* should be peppered with Shakespearian references. These may be found especially in its twenty-third chapter, in which Pete and Mark engage in a ferocious pub debate with each other on Shakespeare and morality. For Pete, Shakespeare was "only a jobbing playwright. A butcher's boy with a randy eye." He is "not a moral poet" who canvasses "for one kind of plug as opposed to another." Pete asserts that "Othello, Macbeth and Lear are men whose great virtues are converted by their very superfluity into faults" and "we're sympathizing with what they are when unhampered by the responsibility of action. The necessity of action smothers their virtue. They cease to be morally thinking creatures." The three tragic characters "are all forced in one way or another to account for what they do and they all failed to do it. Lear and Macbeth don't even attempt to." For Pete, "the point about Shakespeare . . . is that he didn't measure the man up against the idea and give you hot tips on the outcome." (*The Dwarfs*: 131–34). According to Francis Gillen's reading of Pinter's novel, for both Mark and Pete, "it is Shakespeare who finds the proper distance in a dramatic work. Beginning neither from a preconceived abstract moral principle nor a personal bias, he allows his characters to be themselves." Further, Shakespeare "takes them far enough that they reveal themselves and we have, instead of abstract or conventional morality, 'the simple fact of man as his own involuntary judge, because as a matter of choice he's finally obliged to accept responsibility for his actions.'"[7]

It should be self-evident that Pinter's knowledge of Shakespeare was extensive as was his ability to remember and quote lines from Shakespeare's work. For instance, Pinter told Mel Gussow when they were discussing *Old Times* that in it "so much is imagined and that imagining is as true as real." Then, he quoted from the opening of the final scene of *A Midsummer's Night's Dream* Theseus's lines to Hippolyta: "'imagination bodies forth | the form of things unknown.'"[8] In his personal library, Pinter owned various texts of Shakespeare. Pride of place went to the *Collected Shakespeare*, which his parents gave him when he turned fourteen. He also possessed thirty-five volumes of the forty-volume *New Temple Shakespeare*, published between 1949 and 1958. However, the set lacks *Twelfth Night*, the *Sonnets*, *Cymbeline*, *Macbeth*, and *Troilus and Cressida*. Texts that are well marked with linings and other evidence of being devoured include *Othello*, *Measure for Measure*, *Hamlet*, *King Lear*, and *Julius Caesar*.[9]

Shakespeare's pervasive influence is reflected in various Pinter texts. Two examples, one from his early career and one from late on, illustrate this: "A Note on Shakespeare" dated "1950" and the still-unmade film script of *King Lear* from 2000. The neglected "A Note on Shakespeare" first appeared in *Granta* in the autumn of 1993, is reprinted in *Various Voices*, and was written in 1951 during his tour in Ireland with Anew McMaster when Pinter took on various Shakespearian roles (BR: E32). It is a fourteen-paragraph prose piece extolling the bard. The first six paragraphs are short ones consisting of one or two sentences, followed by a lengthy one, then four briefer ones, a lengthier paragraph of a single sentence, followed by another lengthy one of eight short sentences, followed by a lengthy sentence held together by the repetitive "he," and then a final three-brief-sentence paragraph. Repetition is the key note as are inconsistences. There is an increasingly extended catalog of Shakespearian characteristics and cumulative pronouns, very similar to lists frequently found in Pinter's subsequent plays. Shakespeare "reports, he meanders, he loses his track, he overshoots his mark and he drops his glasses." The references to "glasses" might well refer to spectacles or to receptacles for beer and other beverages. The essay concludes with a single short paragraph replete with antithesis. There are three short staccato sentences: "The fabric never breaks. The wound is open. The wound is peopled" (*Various Voices*: 5–7).

Pinter's language in his essay on Shakespeare had an impact on an early important and influential study of his work by Martin Esslin, who worked with Pinter early in Pinter's career at the BBC.[10] In his *The Peopled Wound: The Work of Harold Pinter* (1970), Esslin emphasizes what he perceives to be the fundamental ambiguity of Pinter's dramatic universe. In the fourth paragraph of "A Note on Shakespeare," the young Pinter comments: "Shakespeare writes of the open wound and, through him, we know it open and know it closed." Ambiguity is also at the heart of Shakespeare. In his fifth paragraph, Pinter writes: "In attempting to approach Shakespeare's work in its entirety, you are called upon to grapple with the perspective in which the horizon alternately collapses and reforms behind you." Pinter's short essay is replete with dense, swirling metaphors, grounded in everyday existence yet forcing readers to create fresh connections between what they know, understood vocabulary, and unusual, disturbing ideas. Shakespeare "aborts, he meanders, he loses his track, he overshoots his mark and he drops his glasses." There is even a bullying, nagging, threatening perspective implicit in the repetitions found in Pinter's best writing, such as his "A Note on Shakespeare." The repetitions are juxtaposed with Pinter's emphasis on the gradual exposure of character and motivation found in Shakespeare; this effect is achieved by the use of seemingly meaningless repetition, by silences, by the use of the inconsistent, which suggest the baseline of the characters' action. Essentially, Pinter transforms Shakespeare's iambic rhythms into his own Pinteresque forms and rhythms: dense verbal texture, punctuated by the language of silence. Pinter writes that Shakespeare "is also a beggar; a road-sweeper; a tinker; a hashish-drinker; a leper; a chicken-fancier; the paper-seller; a male nurse; a son-worshiper and gibbering idiot" (*Various Voices*: 5–7).

Completed on March 31, 2000, "*The Tragedy of King Lear*" (BR: W67) is Pinter's cinematic adaptation of Shakespeare's great tragedy. It was planned to be directed by Tim Roth, with Dixie Lindner as producer. Pinter told the *Independent on Sunday* in February 2000 that it was a hefty piece; he wasn't interested in a bunch of people standing around a castle talking.[11] According to Steven H. Gale, it consists of an "eighty-eight page script (sixty scenes plus thirteen numbered subscenes)" that are "designed to make King Lear work on the screen."[12] Pinter does not change Shakespeare's words or introduce his own; he remains true to Shakespeare's language and to the structure of his tragedy, yet he removes the subplot. For instance, in the third scene of the second act, Edgar's speech beginning "I hear myself proclaimed" and concluding "That's something yet. Edgar I nothing am" (1–21) in which he decides to become Poor Tom, is omitted. In place of this, Edgar stares into a stagnant pond, then dirties himself and says, "Edgar, I nothing am." Pinter also includes scenes without dialogue. Lear rides out into the storm, deserting his knights who remain outside the castle, freezing. Dialogue cuts shorten the play, and its cinematic adaptation allows for visual action and scenery. The script starts with the depiction of Lear at the head of his troops after a battle that takes place in the year 1100. This is followed by a scene without dialogue that occurs a decade later. There are shots of the inside and outside of a Norman castle, of Lear, and of each of his daughters. At this point, Shakespeare's drama begins. Above all, Pinter's script demonstrates his consummate artistry as a cinematic adapter.[13]

JOHN WEBSTER

In Pinter's *monologue*, its speaker echoes Henry Woolf's reminiscences of his and Pinter's Hackney youth: "You introduced me to Webster and Tourneur." Woolf remembers that Joe Brearley took them to see John Webster's revenge tragedy *The White Devil* starring Robert Helpmann in the role of Flamineo and Margaret Rawlings as Vitoria Corombona at the Duchess Theatre in 1947. Looking back in his "Sixty years in Harold's gang," Woolf wrote that "we had never seen anything like it. We rushed about declaiming: 'There's a plumber laying pipes in my guts'; 'Oh, I have caught an everlasting cold'; 'My soul is like to a ship in a black storm driven I know not whither.'" Woolf adds that "sixty years later, Harold is still likely to come out with 'the time is ripe for the bloody audit and the fatal gripe' or 'I'll go hunt the badger by owl light,' [lines from] from *The Duchess of Malfi*.[14] In a letter written on Tuesday January 4, 1949, Pinter tells Woolf that on the previous day he bought a copy of Webster and is in awe of Webster's magnificence.

It is no wonder the 1947 Duchess Theatre performance had such a powerful impact. In his obituary of Margaret Rawlings in *The Independent*, Adam Benedick observes of Rawlings's performance: "In the great trial scene she cut a striking figure on the small stage of the Duchess Theatre—her ivory skin and flowing black hair like ivory starred with jet. The young Kenneth Tynan decided it was the most tragic acting he had seen in a woman—though he had seen Peggy Ashcroft's *Duchess of Malfi* a few seasons earlier." Benedick quotes Kenneth Tynan: "She is loud, demonstratively plangent and convincingly voluptuous: a plump, pallid nymphomaniac. And such control! In the great trial scene she eschewed pathos and gave us in its stead anger, mettlesome and impetuous. A stalwart piece of rhetoric and beautifully spoken."[15]

Many decades after Rawlings's performance, in March 1995, Goldstein thanked Pinter for sending him his short four-paragraph sketch "Girls," dated "1995" (in *Various Voices*: 106–107; BR: D10a), and referred to Pinter's directing of David Mamet's *Oleanna* in June 1993 at the Royal Court. Goldstein regarded "Girls" favorably and agreed with Pinter's point of view regarding *Oleanna* that "professors often" incorrectly "abuse their positions of power in seducing their students . . . absolutely without blush or blemish." Goldstein is reminded of lines in Act Four Scene Two from Webster's *Duchess of Malfi*: "Thou art a box of worm-seed, at best but a salvatory of green mummy. What's this flesh? A little crudded milk, fantastical puff-paste." This is "fantastic language." Goldstein adds that his friend Pinter "could never be the same after reading Webster." [16]

Pinter's poem "Chandeliers and Shadows," dated 1950, contains a Webster motto at its head: "I'll goe hunt the badger by owle-light: 'tis a deed of darknesse" [*Various Voices*: 123]. The sense of decadence, sexual depravity, images of rot and decay, and of the world being controlled by an oblivious "God" lessens after Pinter's marriage to Antonia Fraser but still reoccurs especially in his political poetry, which is replete with the anger and helplessness such as that experienced by the victims in Webster's dramatic universe. Apart from Webster, Pinter extols in a letter to Woolf (January 4, 1949) contemporaries of Webster such as Ben Jonson and Christopher Marlowe. He tells Woolf that Marlowe "rolls indefatigably on but Jonson is quite as glorious," although Marlowe's *Tamburlaine* and Jonson's *Bartholomew Fair* are very different from each other; however, Shakespeare was the master of both worlds. [17]

WORDSWORTH

As a young man, Pinter was also moved by a Romantic poet such as Wordsworth. In his December 21, 1949 letter to Henry Woolf, Pinter also referred to listening to John Gielgud's reading from Wordsworth's "Intimations of Immortality" and cites: "To me the meanest flower that blows can give | Thoughts that do often lie too deep for tears." These lines moved Pinter tremendously, and he called the poem one of the most wonderful in the language. Other lines from the poem that appealed to Pinter are "Behold the Child among his new-born blisses" and "Mighty prophet! Seer blest! | On whom those truths do rest | Which we are toiling all our lives to find."

W. B. YEATS

Pinter was not only influenced from an early age by classic English writers but great Irish ones, too, such as William Butler Yeats, James Joyce, and others. A detailed letter to Woolf, probably written during the summer of 1948, reveals Pinter's mood, poetic preferences, and creative preoccupations at the time. Pinter begins his letter by telling Woolf that all is a gradual development and maturity and awareness, helped by the most seemingly insignificant things. He is absorbed in the work of W. B. Yeats, whom he finds profound, and Henry Miller. There are various reasons why Pinter regarded Yeats as greater than T. S. Eliot and others. Poets such as Gerard Manley Hopkins, Keats, and D. H. Lawrence appealed to Pinter depending upon his mood. For Pinter, in the instance of Hopkins and Keats, there is a lack of image precision. Hopkins creates his images with a sensuous and immediate reaction to experience, and Keats's exactitude is wild and passionate. Only Keats's great genius manages to bring with it the necessary technique, some of which is often missing. Pinter tells Woolf that a whisper in his ear suggests that D. H. Lawrence is the greatest poet of them all, but Lawrence doesn't reach the objectivity found in Wordsworth or Yeats at their best. Pinter then writes out two nonconsecutive lines from Yeats's "The Second Coming": "Things fall apart; the centre cannot hold" followed by "the worst I Are full of passionate intensity." These are followed by other Yeats lines under Pinter's heading "insights of." He quotes, for instance, lines from the final stanza of Yeats's late poem "The Tower":

> Does the imagination dwell the most
> Upon a woman won or a woman lost?
> If on the lost, admit you turned aside
> From a great labyrinth out of pride [,]
> Cowardice, some silly over-subtle thought
> Or anything called conscience once

Such lines would apply to Pinter's bitterness concerning Dilys Hamlett's subsequent rejection of him two years later, in 1950. Pinter proceeds to quote a line from Yeats's "Byzantium" poem: "A starlit or a moonlit dome disdains." He omits the two lines that follow and most of the third one: "All that man is, I All mere complexities, I The fury and the mire of," writing down the two final words, "human veins." He also cites from the final verse of Yeats's "A Dialogue of Self and Soul" the line "So great a sweetness flows into the breast." He omits the next two lines, "We must laugh and we must sing, I We are blest by everything," and cites in his letter to Woolf the final line: "Everything we look upon is blest."

A reason Pinter finds Yeats greater than Eliot is because Yeats has conquered easy disillusion. He hasn't drifted into navel watching, Pinter says. He stresses that he is talking of Yeats's duty as a poet; Pinter thinks that Yeats surpasses Eliot in technique, diction, and style mainly owing to Yeats's greater insight and humanity. Pinter continues in his letter that everyone is dissecting Eliot. He doesn't completely agree with Yeats's point of view. He does respect and sympathize with his desire for order. Pinter then cites from Yeats's "A Prayer for My Daughter" the line: "Where all's accustomed, ceremonious." He follows this by saying that he wants a *natural* order and that it is unnecessary, for example, to believe in the circle of hell to grant Dante's greatness. Still, Pinter reports, he agrees with much of what Yeats says. Pinter reminds Woolf that Yeats also had sympathy with D. H. Lawrence.[18]

Pinter's passion for Yeats's poetry finds its reflection in his reactions to his September 1951 to autumn 1952 tour of Ireland. He made lifetime friendships, for instance, with the actor Barry Foster, whom he met at the Central School of Speech and Drama[19] and fell in love with a beautiful Irish actress named Pauline Flanagan. Four years after McMaster's death,

Pinter penned a moving tribute to him, "Mac," and used words from
Yeats's late poem "Lapis Lazuli" (1936), written in tetrameter lines, to
convey the essence of McMaster's acting and personality: "They know
that Hamlet and Lear are gay | Gaiety transfiguring all that dread." Fur-
thermore, Pinter's powerful description of "Mac" performing Lear—"At
the centre of his performance was a terrible loss, desolation, silence"—
penetrates to the depths of Pinter's own art and vision as well as Yeats's.
Indeed, more than half a century later, Flanagan reflected on her time
with Pinter during their period in McMaster's company by recalling: "He
was mad about Yeats . . . Yeats was highly influential. Harold introduced
me to Yeats's more difficult late poems, the poems I wasn't familiar with
like the one about the tin-can tied to a dog's tail." She recalled the opening of "The Tower" ([1925?])

> What shall I do with this absurdity—
> O heart, O troubled heart—this caricature,
> Decrepit age that has been tied to me
> As to a dog's tail?

Remembering such lines from an intense long-ago love affair is not without irony, as the poem reveals a youthful passion and sense of personal
mortality. Written in nineteen quatrains with the frequent use of monosyllables at the conclusion of the line—see, for instance, the last two lines
from the first verse—the poem uses a technique frequently found in Pinter's own poetry. Flanagan adds that Pinter "read Eliot and read *The Waste
Land* aloud" (cited Billington: 39–40).

Clearly, there are other influences at work on Pinter, and especially on
his poetry, including Dylan Thomas and T. S. Eliot. However, the impact
of Yeats during Pinter's formative years is seen in the poems written
during his time in Ireland. For instance, these include "The Islands of
Aran Seen from the Moher Cliffs," "Others of You," "Episode,"
"Poem,"—"I walked one morning with my only wife"—and "The Irish
Shape." "The Islands of Aran" exploits a five-verse quatrain—also used
by Yeats—to celebrate the overwhelming grandeur, beauty, and sheer
majestic power of the coastal scenery and the mythology of the west coast
of Ireland. Pinter's use of alliterative repetition of "d" in the opening two
lines of the final verse—"distended in distance . . . the stone of Connemara's head" (*Various Voices* 129)—as well as the topographical associations
are essentially Yeatsian features.[20]

Pinter's "Poem," dated "1953" (*Various Voices* 143), consists of five
stanzas of six lines each. Again, Pinter exploits Celtic mythology to convey his own emotions. Billington astutely observes that in this poem, "we
seem to be in the world Yeats and Synge—a world of peasants, shawls
and summer fairs—and there is even a faint echo of [Yeats's] 'The Lake
Isle of Innisfree' in the way the final stanza echoes the first." Billington
adds that "the poem, which deals with the loss of true love through the

cycle of the seasons, also has an aura of personal sadness as if Pinter is grafting his own feelings about the transience of passion onto a standard Irish form" (42). To oversimplify, a movement may be seen in Yeats's poetry "from the decorative, Pre-Raphaelite style of the early years towards an austere lyricism" (41). A similar movement may be traced in Pinter's poetry, a movement from syntactical irregularity, elaboration with inversions and enjambment, and the ornate earlier poetry, to a more usual word order later. Pinter's imagery moves from the lush to the pared down, the verse forms move from the lengthy to the brief, with the techniques and themes reflecting his own personal voyage of self-discovery.

JAMES JOYCE

James Joyce is among the earliest pervasive literary influences upon Pinter, whose first published essay was on the subject of "James Joyce." The essay appeared in the *Hackney Downs School Magazine* for Christmas 1946 (E1). Pinter describes *A Portrait of the Artist* as typical of Joyce: honest, true, and a work of great lyrical beauty. *Ulysses*, an enormous work, depicts a day in the life of the Dubliner, and it stands supreme among twentieth-century literature. Pinter calls it "outstanding as a feat of narration," using streams of consciousness to depict the thoughts of the subconscious mind. "Joyce omits nothing"—he describes every thought and word of this man. For the young Pinter, *Ulysses* was "one of the most complete works of art ever written." Its author "had great feeling for words," so much so that "no modern writer has used them to such effect" (32).

More than half a century later, Pinter was involved with a reading organized by PEN at a "Personal Wonderlands" event, a charitable evening of readings of fiction read by authors and actors, on Tuesday November 25, 2003 at the Bloomberg Auditorium, Finsbury Square. Pinter read an excerpt from *Ulysses*, choosing one of his favorite passages as a child and one that remained so. It is part of the exchange at Kiernan's pub between Dingham and Paddy with the lines: "You a strict TT says Joe?"; "Don't you know he is dead says Joe"; and "old digger smelling him all the time." In his introduction to the passage, Pinter recalled when he was thirteen years old and, in the Jewish tradition, had a bar mitzvah that represented a boy on the cusp of becoming a man. With his bar mitzvah money, Pinter walked the five miles or so from Hackney into London to the Charing Cross Road to purchase a copy of *Ulysses*, which he still possessed in 2003. However, the book was not in his library when he died.[21]

Letters written to Woolf during the period Pinter was touring in repertory theatre reveal a creative, playful Joycean-Joyce Cary sense of humor and playing with language. The letters are risqué and replete with puns. They play with names, many of them having Jewish associations, and feature innuendo mixed with crudity. A notable example is found in a typed letter to Woolf written during a midsummer weekend from Colchester in 1955. Titles are invented, such as "Freewheeling through the Talmud," which is known in Munich as "Up your dusty." Part of the comic effect has a foundation in the use of the very English idiomatic expression and the almost surrealistic title authored by someone named "Klaus," with its Germanic associations. Furthermore, Pinter tells Woolf that its author "approaches the whole problem with some delicacy." Given the German associations, this reads somewhat ironically.

Pinter then draws his friend's attention to a work conjured up in his imagination. It was published, Pinter speculates, in "Lower Lithuania" around 1906 and was titled "Birds, Bones and Detumescence," the final word having a sexual association with swelling and erection. The author is the invented "Boobafarski." Pinter refers to a subsequent commentary on this made-up title and author by "Rov" (playing on the shortened term for "rabbi") "Abrahamoff," who Pinter describes as a "Hindustani gentleman." It's all somewhat akin to the BBC *Goon Show* then being broadcast. Broadcast between 1951 and 1960, the *Goon Show*'s scripts "mixed ludicrous plots with surreal humor, puns, catchphrases and an array of bizarre sound effects" in addition to satirizing contemporary life in Britain. It was not without engaging in what today would be regarded as inappropriate ethnic stereotyping.[22] Pinter's letter then plays with names such as "Plotz," "Zitnick," "Mendel," and "Gruntz" and their sexual activities. He signs off his letter by asking Woolf, whom he calls "Sackstein," whether or not he is "[s]till pissing in an eyeglass."[23] There is the Joycean element evident in the word play in this letter. For instance, he uses Joyce's naming devices such as onomatopoeia, phononaesthesia (sound-symbolism), ironic juxtaposition, parody, puns, and polyphony among others.[24]

Joyce's lasting impact upon Pinter's work is seen, for instance, in his direction of Joyce's *Exiles* during the autumn of 1970 (from September 30 to December 12). The critic Mark Taylor-Batty writes perceptively that "we might speculate about the inspiration Pinter found in *Exiles* during a period of creative difficulty, before the purgation of any 'writers' block' with [*Old Times*] in 1971." This "was written immediately after the rehearsal period for *Exiles* and during the run of the first performances of the play." Taylor-Batty notes that "even the play's title can be found, perhaps quite coincidentally, within that play's dialogue when Robert invites Richard to his home: 'You must come some night. It will be old times again.'"[25] Michael Billington reaffirms the impact that *Exiles* had on Pinter's subsequent work, commenting that "although Pinter himself strenuously denies any direct cause and effect, the experience of working on *Exiles* also seems to have permeated his artistic imagination. He sat down to write [*Old Times*] in the winter of 1970 while saturated in Joyce's play; and while the two works are obviously very different, both deal with the contest between two figures for the soul and body of a third, and with the ultimate unpossessability of the triumphant heroine." Billington observes that "*Exiles* . . . planted seeds which were to germinate many years later in [*Betrayal*], in that it is the 'lover' Robert Hand who feels that it is he who has been deceived by the complicity between husband and wife about his advances" (210–11).

JOYCE CARY

There is a passing early reference in Pinter's correspondence to the Anglo-Irish novelist Joyce Cary and his *The Horse's Mouth* (1944), with its comic hero/anti-hero who uses his family and friends to earn a few quid. The young Henry Woolf discovered the novel and "made everyone read it" (Billington: 12). In a letter to Woolf on Monday September 6, 1948, Pinter praises the novel, although he notes that it has some faults: It's a little stylized, and he objects to the Penguin edition's introduction and biographical details concerning Cary on its back cover. Pinter writes that he doesn't want to know all the particulars about Cary; he just wants to read his art.[26] Toward the conclusion of his second tour in Ireland with Anew McMaster's company, on a Saturday in October [1953] written from Galway, Pinter observes to Woolf that Cary's novel is the "Bible."[27] Echoes of Cary's novel appear in Pinter's later work, including his film script of Anthony Shaffer's *Sleuth* (2003) and *Moonlight*. Both draw upon the quip "It's like farting Annie Laurie down a keyhole" — a line found in *The Horse's Mouth*.[28] In common with Cary, Pinter's work features rambunctious language, iconoclasm, punning, and onomastics.[29]

MARCEL PROUST

Another great author to have a significant lasting impact upon Pinter is the French author Marcel Proust, whose work is in common with Pinter's, similarly obsessed with time and memory. In a letter to Woolf written from Portstewart, County Londonderry, Northern Ireland, dated July 18, [1955], Pinter tells Woolf that he has, in addition to the sun in Jill's Johnson's eyes, the feeling of Proust's long cup of tea, his melancholy of passing, of distance, of image living though dead, the weight, the face, of gone occasion.[30]

A great deal of Pinter's time during the 1970s was taken up with his adaptation of Proust's *À la Recherche du Temps Perdu* (1871–1922) as a screenplay. Pinter reimmersed himself in C. K. Scott-Moncrieff's translation. Aware of the difficulties involved in such a task from early on, he consulted with Joseph Losey and also with the bilingual Barbara Bray, who possessed a detailed knowledge of Proust's work. Bray recalled that "the basic structural idea" for the adaptation originated with Beckett. She was "talking to [Beckett] about it, and he said that you really ought to start at the end with *Le Temps retrouvé* and so that's what we did." Bray continued: "Proust wrote the first part—*Du Côté de chez Swann*—and then the last part—*Le Temps retrouvé*—and then what he called the bit between. So we worked out a structure that starts with the party at the Prince de Guermantes' house in 1921, from the very end of the novel, and then goes back to Marcel as a boy of eight at Combray in 1888, which is the beginning of the book" (cited Billington: 223–24). Pinter, Losey, and Bray's script remained un-filmed but finally was published as *The Proust Screenplay* in 1977 (BR: B3). Pinter became obsessed with the Proustian project, telling Goldstein in a letter from 7 Hanover Terrace dated July 5, 1972 that he was trying to write a screenplay of *À la Recherche du Temps Perdu*. It was, he said, quite a task but deeply enjoyable. He added that Goldstein must read Proust, as Pinter himself loved reading him.[31]

Ronald Harwood wasn't alone in an enthusiastic approbation of Pinter's adaption of Proust.[32] Richard Round, the initial director of the New York Film Festival who had interviewed Pinter, Joseph Losey, and L. P. Hartley in the *Guardian* (March 16, 1971; BR: G35) regarding the film industry and issues of who contributes what to the final product, wrote a letter dated February 23, 1973 to Pinter. In it, he commented highly on the script. For Round, it is preferable not to interfere with the great works of fiction but in this instance, "there is such a meeting of minds, of temperaments, and of techniques, that the result can only be extraordinary; not Proust plus Pinter plus Losey, but Proust multiplied by Pinter multiplied by Losey. Fantastic."

Another interesting detailed reaction came from Gabriel Josipovici, the literary critic, novelist, dramatist, and short story writer. He and Pinter met on several occasions (for instance on December 5, 1970 and on December 12, 1984, *Chronology*: 34, 128). Pinter sent him pre-publication copies of his work, and Josipovici sent Pinter his work. In a letter dated February 24, 1973, Josipovici tells Pinter that he initially read Proust's *À la Recherche du Temps Perdu* at age seventeen, and that his critical study *The World and the Book* (1971) "was an attempt to come to terms with Proust." Josipovici is aware that Pinter had to rethink the novel "in cinematic terms." For Josipovici, Pinter has "succeeded almost beyond belief."[33]

Peter Hall on February 29, 1973 responded to the script adaptation without reservation. He approved of the "small cast and the sense of life. Time makes it epic." Furthermore, "the concentration on a few people is human and irresistible. It is why we all love long novels or become hooked on television [versions]. It is new ground for the cinema and must be recognized as such." The eminent New York–based Stanley Kauffmann, who for half a century was the film critic of the *New Republic*, observed that Pinter contacted him concerning a volume Kauffmann edited with Bruce Henstell: *American Film Criticism: From the Beginnings to "Citizen Kane"; Reviews of Significant Films at the Time They First Appeared* (1972). Pinter was "particularly struck" by an essay by Paul Goodman titled "The Proustian Camera Eye." Pinter told Kauffmann: "So the screenwriter may have felt a kinship with the novelist (and there was a link to Beckett, who had written about Proust)." [34]

Kauffmann wrote Pinter a lengthy letter dated "March 3, 1974." He told Pinter that, in his script, he has given "shape" to the Swann-Odette story, to the "color and development of their characters, the harmonic relation of their story to the whole work." This is "all interwoven with a quite subtle rhythm and structure of your own, developed here for" cinematic purposes. For Kaufmann, Pinter "has carefully dismantled" Proust's original "into its elements and reassembled them to produce the same effects in a different medium," as opposed to attempting to get "the effects of the book with the books methods, on film." There is a concern whether the film would be meaningful to a viewer who didn't know Proust's original. Pinter's script has succeeded and this isn't a worry. Kaufmann finds Pinter's time leaps "daring" and believes that Pinter would rely on Joseph Losey, the director, "to make sure that the viewer sees that, once the distinction is made." He also praises Pinter's "visual motifs [his] version of *idée fixe*"; these "tease us, rightly when we first see them, and there's a nice retrospective pleasure back along the lines when they are fulfilled." There is a problem with the character of Marcel, who is, in Proust's novel, "a passionate character, an observer, a camera eye." In the novel, this works as Marcel "*is* the camera and everything we see and hear comes to us through Marcel's sensibility." In the film, Marcel "is not the camera, he's in front of it." He becomes a non-active protagonist and "not the most interesting character in the script." Kauffmann adds that "this is irrelevant in the novel, substantially worrisome here."

Not everyone was as impressed by Proust and his characters as was Pinter. Sir Laurence Olivier wrote to Pinter on November 22, 1973, saying that he didn't want to play the part of Charles Swann because Olivier could not "see anything to him beyond his characteristic values and a plain dilettante decadent or plainer still a filthy old snob and nothing else." Olivier added that this "somehow doesn't feel interesting," and he gave Pinter a "word of warning about kaleidoscope insert-cum-flash techniques carried too far . . . when you meet a new person in an age jump." [35]

In spite of two years of haggling, film funding couldn't be found. It is no wonder, then, that the screenplay was never filmed. Pinter, Losey, and Barbara Bray looked for suitable locations during 1972. They discussed ideal casting, and Pinter "produced a first-draft screenplay—one eventually reduced from 468 shots to 455." Pinter subsequently continually tinkered with the Proust project. It was adapted for a two-hour radio play by Michael Bakewell, broadcast on BBC Radio 3 on the last day of 1995.

Pinter was the linking narration and John Wood was Charlus (Billington: 231). In November 2000 (*Chronology*: 224, 262), a stage-play version, *Remembrance of Things Past*, adapted by Pinter and Di Trevis, was performed at the Cottesloe Theatre (BR: A54). Marcel is present throughout until the conclusion, at which point the time that seemed to disappear reappears to gain permanence. John Peter astutely observes in the *Sunday Times*: "You are in a no-man's-land of reminiscence and recall, in-flight from the past but with a gnawing need to reconstruct it. Time as a sequence keeps stopping, suspended in interchange between past and present, just as it does in Pinter's *The Homecoming, Old Times* and *No Man's Land*" (December 3, 2000, Reviews Section:19). As Nicholas de Jongh observes in his extensive *Evening Standard* review of Pinter and Di Trevis: "'Ravishing' is the word for it. Marcel Proust's vast novel, his reminiscence of childhood, love and desire in high French society, has been triumphantly compressed, distilled and transmuted for performance on stage."[36]

ARTHUR RIMBAUD AND TOLSTOY'S *ANNA KARENINA*

In a letter from the summer of 1948, Pinter told Woolf that he was reading a fascinating study of poet Arthur Rimbaud and of Tolstoy's *Anna Karenina*: Pinter found reading Tolstoy's novel almost too much.[37] Arthur Rimbaud was one of the poets Pinter read in his adolescence when he obtained Rimbaud's work from Hackney Public Library. It may not be going too far to suggest that Rimbaud, whose work prefigured surrealism and influenced André Breton and Henry Miller—two writers mentioned in Pinter's *monologue*—remained a conscious or unconscious influence upon Pinter's work and technique. This can be seen especially in Pinter's use of synesthesia in his early poems such as "The Islands of Aran Seen from the Moher Cliffs" dated 1951, in which the terrain becomes a surrogate for the poet's state of mind (*Various Voices*: 129). Indeed, the importance of Rimbaud for the young Pinter is reflected in his intense affair in 1950 with the actress Dilys Hamlett, to whom he gave a copy of Rimbaud's *Une Saison en enfer*. The affair was short lived, ending when she dumped Pinter. Even two decades later, echoes of his bitterness emerged in *Old Times* (Billington: 35–36). However, *Anna Karenina* seems not to have left an impression on Pinter—assuming that he completed reading it. There is no evidence either that he ever toyed with a film adaptation of the novel, unlike his younger contemporary and friend Tom Stoppard, whose adaptation was distributed in 2012.

Other non-English writers that affected Pinter include Ivan Goncharov. In a 1957 letter to Goldstein, Pinter informs Goldstein that he has bought Goncharov's *Oblomov*[38] in a Penguin Books edition. There is no more discussion of the Russian novel published in 1859, translated by David Magarshack, and first published in Penguin in 1954. Still, its themes and concerns echo many of Pinter's. Its central figure is Ilya Ilyich Oblomov, one of Russia's decaying, indolent aristocrats. Relinquishing his civil service sinecure, he has put down his books, alienated his friends, and sunk into debt. Lethargic, he lives in a dilapidated apartment with his lazy former servant Zakhar. Oblomov stays in bed and dreams. He is depicted "as the ultimate incarnation of the superfluous man incapable of making important decisions or undertaking any significant actions. Throughout the novel he rarely leaves his room or bed. In the first 50 pages, he manages only to move from his bed to a chair."[39] Many of the characters in Pinter's early plays are worn down by the world; they are not aristocrats, but, on the lowest rungs of society, they have retreated into their own fantasy world surrounded by four walls in rundown circumstances.

Before turning to three writers whom Pinter knew, brief mention should be made of two who influenced him: Aldous Huxley and Henry Miller. Huxley's impact was primarily cinematic. In a letter dating probably from 1948, Pinter told Woolf that he and Jimmy Law saw *A Woman's Vengeance*, the stage adaptation of "Giaconda Smile," a short story in Aldous Huxley's collection of five short stories called *Mortal Coils*, written in 1921. Cinematic and stage versions highlighted the social satire, ambiguous triangular relations, and sexual components mixed in with a murder story, inherent in Huxley's work. A feature of the work was its use of allusions and citations from Shakespeare to Marvell, Shelley, and Modigliani to Cézanne—a feature present in Pinter's own work and especially in his short *monologue*. Pinter wrote to Woolf that Huxley is stimulating; he considered him a major artist, more than a witty satirist. Pinter called the play very good, the first scene brilliant.[40]

Another early influence was the contemporary American author Henry Miller. In *Barcelona is in Trouble*, Woolf recalls an early encounter with Pinter. In the lower sixth form, in 1946, at Hackney Downs Grammar School, Pinter thrust a copy of Henry Miller's second published novel, the semi-autobiographical *Black Spring*, initially published in 1936, into Woolf's hand. Pinter asked Woolf for his opinion. Woolf "was amazed by [Miller's] raucous delight in life and sexuality in particular." Woolf told Pinter that "there's no shortage of anal and genital activity." Pinter pressed Woolf to say whether he liked it or not. Woolf told Pinter that he "absolutely hated it . . . for waking me up, for being so full of life when I wasn't. It was a shot in the arm and kick up the arse." Woolf added that "this must have been the right answer because Pinter opened the door and let me in. We were friends for the next sixty years. Until death came to call that is" (48).

In a [1948] letter to Woolf, Pinter says that he adores Miller's glorious arrogance and manhood. Pinter quotes from *Black Spring* a passage that especially appeals to him: "Now I am never alone. At the very worst I am with God!"[41] For Pinter, these are words of wisdom. He enjoyed other lines from Miller, such as "He swims joyously ad lib in the amniotic fluid" and "In ordinary waking life the author suffers from normal vision."[42] Pinter probably truncated or misremembered Miller's "I believe that the whole world—not the earth alone and the beings which compose it, nor the universe whose elements we have charted, including the island universes beyond our sight and instruments—but the whole world, known and unknown, is out of kilter, [*sic*] screaming in pain and madness." Pinter quotes in his letter to Woolf, Miller's "I believe the whole of civilization is out of balance and has been from the beginning."[43]

In "The Queen of all the Fairies," Pinter writes that, in the words of Miller (whom he calls his "patron saint"), there is nothing like the pleasurable look of a man urinating.[44] Pinter tells Goldstein in a 1955 letter that in Miller's writing, there is always cancer and syphilis.[45] Earlier, on October 18, 1949, Pinter had written to Miller without, apparently, receiving a response.[46] At the age of nineteen, Pinter's interest in Miller is remarkable. Miller's work was banned in the United Kingdom until the 1960s, although his work was widely available in Paris and under the counter in London and the provinces. Miller had his advocates, such as George Orwell. In his "Inside the Whale" (1940), Orwell wrote of the appeal of Miller's "negative, unconstructive, amoral approach." Miller's was "the voice from the crowd, from the third class carriage, from the ordinary, non-political, non-moral, passive man." In the words of James Campbell in his "Miller's Fate," Miller was lacking in "cant and pretentiousness," the champion of the freedom of expression. Campbell cites Gore Vidal's praise of Miller, sentiments that the young Pinter would have agreed with and tried to imitate in some of his early prose writing, such as the "Queen of all the Fairies" and "A Note on Shakespeare." In Miller's *Tropic of Capricorn* (1939) "sentences swell and billow, engulfing syntax. Arcane words are put to use often accurately."[47]

SAMUEL BECKETT, W. S. GRAHAM, AND PHILIP LARKIN

Samuel Beckett

The first of the three writers, more or less Pinter's contemporaries, we shall discuss is Samuel Beckett, a writer with whom Pinter eventually became friendly. Pinter praised Beckett on numerous occasions and publicly acknowledged his debt to him. In 1954, Pinter wrote that Beckett was the most courageous, remorseless writer and that he was grateful to him. Beckett doesn't sell anything, but Pinter would buy his goods because Beckett leaves no stone unturned. His work, Pinter writes, is beautiful (*Various Voices*: 58; BR: E11). Beckett died on December 22, 1989. On the final day of January 1990, Pinter presented "A Wake for Sam" for BBC2, a televised tribute that was broadcast on February 8, 1990 (BR:

K31). Pinter recalled his initial meeting with Beckett in early January 1961. Pinter was visiting Paris for Roger Blin, the eminent French theatre producer and director who was producing *The Caretaker*. Pinter inscribed a copy for Beckett. In the TV reminiscence, Pinter recalled that Beckett had a sharp stride and quick handshake. An extremely fast driver who drove a small Citroën from bar to bar throughout the whole evening, they ended up around 4 a.m. in the morning having onion soup. By this time, Pinter was drunk and exhausted, and in a haze, went to sleep. When he woke up, he thought that Beckett had deserted him or that he was in a dream. Approximately three quarters of an hour later, Beckett appeared and told Pinter that he had been searching throughout the city for a tin of bicarbonate of soda, which worked wonders (*Various Voices*: 58–59).

On January 28, 1990, responding to a letter from Goldstein concerning the death of Beckett, Pinter replied that he remembered everything concerning his experiences with Beckett. Pinter tells Goldstein that he and Beckett spoke approximately three weeks before he died, and Pinter was pleased that he made Beckett laugh. He tells Goldstein how he sent Beckett his adaptation of Kafka's *The Trial*: The script was found in Beckett's room, but Pinter would never know what Beckett thought of it.

With his letter to Goldstein, Pinter enclosed a love poem called "It is Here" with "(for A)," Antonia, below the title. It was published in the *TLS* (February 2–8, 1990; BR: C27a; *Various Voices*: 169). It is a nine-line, five-verse poem, with its third verse having five lines, three of which end in questions; the other four verses are single end-stopped lines. The first line of the first verse is a question: "What sound was that?" Five of its lines begin with the pronoun "What," culminating in a question. Perhaps Pinter deliberately used "What" to evoke memories of Beckett's fictional *Watt* (1953), which sounds the same but is spelled differently. Pinter's poem is characterized by the transition from the past tense to the present: "Listen. It is here." The move from past to present, to affirmation, evokes the feeling of continuing with existence. In Antonia Fraser's words: "No one is ever dead in the Beckettian world, particularly not Beckett and particularly not the dead" (*Must*: 190). For Goldstein, "this poem is quite an inspired piece and must be one of [Pinter's] best" (February 13, 1990).[48]

Beckett's impact upon Pinter's drama has been noted by many, including those who worked for the Lord Chamberlain's Office, the official British government office to which all theatre scripts were submitted between 1824 and 1968. On the script of *The Birthday Party*, dated April 18, 1958, Charles David Heriot's "Readers' Report" begins: "An insane, pointless play. Mr. Pinter has jumbled all the tricks of Beckett and Ionesco with a dash from all the recently produced plays at the Royal Court theatre, plus the fashionable flavouring of blasphemy. The result is still silly. The Emperor is wearing no clothes." Apart from cutting a few lines that Heriot regarded as "the pointless pieces of blasphemy," the play was recommended for performance. St. Vincent Trourbridge, who also worked for the Lord Chamberlain's Office, opened his report on *The Care-taker* dated May 18, 1960: "This is a piece of incoherence in the manner of Samuel Beckett, though it has not that author's vein of nihilistic pessi-mism, and each individual sentence is comprehensible if irrelevant." Trourbridge added that the play was "received with enthusiasm by the high-brow critics." Apart from cutting words such as "piss off," "bugger it," "up your arse," and so on, he recommended it for license. Trour-bridge also enclosed with his report what must have been an advance copy of Harold Hobson's highly favorable review published in the *Sun-day Times*, June 5, 1960. Hobson concludes that he has "seen [*The Caretak-er*] twice, and I shall see it again at the first opportunity; and after that [will] see it a fourth time, and a fifth." Trourbridge had been in charge of the report that granted a license for the British production of *Waiting for Godot* in 1955 provided that twelve cuts were made; Beckett agreed to ten. In the opening paragraph of his report, Trourbridge noted the influence of Joyce on Beckett's play. Heriot's December 15, 1971 report on *Landscape* evoked the name of Beckett: "[T]he nearer to Beckett, the more porten-tous Pinter gets. . . . Since there is very little shape, the thing just stops— rather like a contemporary serial musical composition. And, of course, there have to be the ornamental indecencies." If seven small cuts were made, a license for *Landscape* was recommended.[49]

In a letter to Goldstein written from Portstewart, July 5, [1955], Pinter asked Goldstein to get him a ticket for *Godot*, which opened at the Arts Theatre on August 3, 1955. After seeing *Waiting for Godot*, Pinter wrote Goldstein a detailed letter about the experience and the play. He informs Goldstein several times that Godot does not appear and muses whether that is the crux of the matter. The play states two things: absence and attendance. If the question were explicitly answered, it would cease to exist. There would be no impulse, no work, and no play. Pinter adds that Beckett treats his material and manipulates it. Interestingly, in the revised 2005 edition of *Various Voices*, the second piece—not in the 1998 initial edition—is "On *Waiting for Godot*" (8–10).

Pinter then turns to Beckett's prose fiction *Malone meurt* (1951), which Pinter has read in French. He calls it more connected than *Watt* and grimmer than Beckett's novel *Murphy* (1938). If anything, he observes, it has points of contact with (the story) "The End" (1955): magnificent and terrible at the same time. In a July 5, [1955] letter, in addition to recount-ing the plot, Pinter provides Goldstein with an illustration of the clarity and beauty of the writing. As a postscript, Pinter says that he doesn't know whether the death of the character of Malone takes place in one moment or over a thirty-year period.[50]

Pinter wrote a letter to Woolf on November 6, 1955, observing that the intellectual climate had been "typhooned" by Beckett with *Waiting for*

Godot opening in London. Pinter added that he knew all about Beckett and had for a long time. In fact, Pinter wrote, it was Beckett who brought him to light. He suggested that Woolf read Beckett.[51] In a letter that was probably written in April 1957 from the Palace Theatre Leicester, Pinter asked Woolf to get him a copy of *Murphy*; at Zwemmers Bookshop in London, Pinter was told it was being reprinted. The Grove Press published it on March 15, 1957.[52]

On November 30, 1955, in a letter written to Goldstein, Pinter uses boxing and cricket metaphors to describe his encounter with Beckett's writings and their tremendous impact on him. He tells Goldstein that *Molloy* and *Malone* have "knocked me from here to yesterday." With *Murphy* and *Watt* to come, "it's an innings victory, whichever way you look at it." In a letter from the Palace Court Theatre Bournemouth postmarked February 14, 1956, Pinter tells Goldstein that he has been reading *Molloy*. He praises the "terrible silence" and calls the work great poetry.[53]

So eager was Pinter to read Beckett that it prompted him to his only criminal act. Unable to find a copy elsewhere, in 1951 he took out *Murphy* from Battersea Pubic Reserve Library. The copy, published by Routledge, had last been borrowed in 1938, the year of its publication. He kept the book, and it remained in Pinter's library. According to Joe McCann, who cataloged Pinter's library when it went to Maggs Brothers, the eminent London book dealers after Pinter's death, the copy "shows every sign of having been read nearly to death—it is a rebound in the library binding, the stitching is relaxed, a couple of pages have been reattached with librarians adhesive tape, and there is minor staining in a few places." McCann added that "Pinter himself appears to have been a notably careful reader, and even texts which he continually read show signs of abuse." Somewhat curiously, there are only two copies present in his library, from the sixty-two Becketts found there, that have been inscribed by Beckett to Pinter. "The first edition of *Mercier et Camier* has on the title page: 'For Harold, with love from Sam, Paris, Nov. 1970,' the year of its publication." Additionally, Beckett's *Breath* (1972) "is inscribed on its title page: 'To Harold and Vivien, with love from Sam, Paris, March 72.'"[54] Billington quotes Pinter as commenting that *Murphy* was "very funny." What impressed Pinter was the "quick" of the world. It was Beckett's own world, but it had so many references to the world we actually share (43). Pinter described Beckett, in a letter to Goldstein, as the most important writer of the 1950s and beyond.[55]

An illustration of the way in which Beckett pervades Pinter's thinking at this period may be found in the middle of a spring 1957 letter to Goldstein in which Pinter describes his own play *The Room*. Pinter moves from his own writing into discussing Beckett's work: "Not forgetting, of course, the mystery the fixity, of Mr. Knott's house where Watt was" in Beckett's *Watt* and he draws Goldstein's attention to "What *Watt* was not." In an undated letter to Goldstein from Bournemouth [1956?], Pinter describes a play that he had mentioned to Goldstein in London, *The End-game*. Patrick Magee,[56] with whom Pinter acted in rep, called the piece imitation Beckett, an observation Pinter disagreed with. When Pinter returned to London, he would send Goldstein a copy. In another letter, Pinter tells Goldstein that he has received *Malone Dies* from Zwemmers. After finishing its first chapter, Pinter comments that many readers will find it impossible as a novel. Pinter adds that once Beckett gets going, he can tie the whole lot of them in knots.[57]

Early in 1957, toward the end of his period in repertory at Torquay, Pinter wrote to Woolf asking him whether he liked *Murphy*. For his part, Pinter considered it a great comic work. He tells Woolf that, with Goldstein and others, he listened to Beckett's *All That Fall* broadcast by the BBC on Sunday evening January 13, 1957 and afterward had an argument concerning its meaning. He tells Woolf that he must also read *Molloy*, *Godot*, *Malone*, and other Beckett works.[58] In an interview with Harry Thompson in the *New Theatre Magazine* appearing in January 1961 (BR: G6), Pinter describes Beckett as a writer he has admired for years. If Beckett's influence shows in Pinter's work, he's fine with that. He observes that writers don't write in a vacuum; they are bound to absorb and digest other writing. He admires Beckett's work so much that something of its texture might appear in his own.

Pinter sent his work to Beckett, who at times suggested changes. For instance, Beckett recommended that Pinter should look again at a speech in *Silence*. Subsequently in rehearsal, Pinter decided that it didn't sound right, and he realized that Beckett was right. Pinter also pointed out that if he suddenly thought, "This is like Beckett," it might stop him dead in his tracks.[59] Beckett referred to "one speech (p. 19 beginning 'A long way')," which he suggested Pinter "reconsider."[60] Peter Hall thought that Pinter's famous "pause" has its origins in Beckett: "I have always supposed that Pinter gained confidence in this technique because of Beckett's use of pauses. Certainly Beckett is the first dramatist to use silence as a written form of communication." Hall adds that "Shakespeare's: 'Holds her by the hand silent' in *Coriolanus* [5.3.183] is the only other moment of complex drama" known to Hall "where words are deemed inadequate."[61]

It would be an oversimplification to suggest that Pinter was a disciple of Beckett. In an interview with Ramona Koval on September 15, 2002, Pinter reflected upon the influence of Beckett on him and Beckett's inspiration as a friend or as a writer. Pinter recalled reading Beckett's novels around 1949–1950, and he regarded them as extraordinary; he referred specifically to *Molloy*, *Malone Dies*, and *The Unnamable*. Pinter described Beckett as a charming man and recalled sending him a copy of *Old Times*. In response, Beckett sent Pinter one of his famous postcards, saying that he liked it very much. Beckett advised Pinter to look at speech five on page six. Pinter then remembered how the play went into rehearsal with

Peter Hall directing. They were having a problem with a speech; Pinter said to cut it. Beckett, as always, was right, and the speech was eliminated. Beckett had an unerring light on such things.[62]

The third volume of *The Letters of Samuel Beckett*, covering the years 1957 to 1965, contains their letters, the first being on August 18, 1960 in which Beckett thanks Pinter for a copy of *The Caretaker* (355). The other two are dated January 30, 1961 and January 27, 1965 following Pinter and Beckett's initial meeting in Paris on January 11, 1961 (see Beckett *Letters* III: 395–96). These particular letters largely concerned French responses to the January 1961 Paris performance of *Le Guardien* (*The Caretaker*) and Beckett's cordial thanks for *The Birthday Party* and *The Room* (January 30, 1961). Subsequently, Beckett writes that he is impressed by *The Homecoming*, telling Pinter, "It seems to me the best you have done since *The Caretaker* and perhaps the best of all." He adds that "the part of the father is tremendous and should play like a bomb" (January 27, 1965, *Letters*, III: 649–50).

The fourth and final volume of *The Letters of Samuel Beckett* covers the years 1966 to 1989 and contains fifteen letters revealing the strength of their friendship based on mutual admiration, friends in common such as Pat Magee and Barbara Bray, and a love of cricket.[63] Most of Beckett's letters respond to Pinter's work or contain information relating to performances. At the end of November or the beginning of December 1972, he tells Pinter that he is "very impressed by your *Proust* script so finely devised" (315). On May 14, 1977, Beckett thanks Pinter for sending him a copy of his poem "Message," which for Beckett is a "bang in the eye" (459; BR: C18). A mock-humorous, mock-satirical poem of seven lines in the first verse, eight in the second, and three final single-line verses, it uses colloquial expressions such as "Don't let the fuckers get you down," "find another tart" and "Kick the first blind man in the balls" with a final ironic line: "Your loving mother" (*Various Voices*: 161).

To sum up the relationship between Beckett and Pinter and Pinter's debt to Beckett: The editors of *The Letters of Samuel Beckett* write that, in the third volume covering the years 1957 to 1965, Pinter appears "as an eager, hopeful, and ambitious young actor and dramatist for whom discovering [Beckett] was a crucial experience." In light of Pinter's subsequent development, "Pinter saw himself as a kindred spirit of [Beckett], although with the years his increasing concern with political issues moved him farther and farther from Beckett's world." Consequently, "it is in the earlier work that we come closer to that world: work such as *The Dumb Waiter*, in which dialogue, represented in the language of the street, reveals above all the distance which separates people." Moreover, "Pinter retained a deep respect for [Beckett] and was an eager contributor to celebratory presentations of his work. As late as 2006, when he was already seriously ill, he performed *Krapp's Last Tape* at the Royal Court Theatre" (III: 701–2). Somewhat understating the case, on March 13, 2001,

Pinter replied to a schoolgirl who wrote to him concerning Beckett. Pinter said that he wouldn't call himself "influenced" by Beckett but always knew him to be a great writer.[64]

W. S. Graham

Pinter championed W. S. Graham; he helped publish his work, encouraged him, and financially supported him. In January 2001, Pinter wrote that Graham was a neglected master. He praised Graham's command of form, his range of operation. Graham could, Pinter observed, perform at any distance—a 100-metre funeral march to a 5,000-metre dash—and he did either and those in between with ease and dexterity. He worked intensely at his craft, Pinter said. He worked all the midnights all his life. In the course of doing so, Graham stumbled across moments of inspiration few other poets found. Pinter points to Graham's lines "the face | Turned to the heartbroke wall" from his poem "The White Threshold." For Pinter, the sinew of Graham's language is unique. Pinter observes that Graham opened his eyes wide many years ago, and they're still wide open to his one and only song, "I Leave This at Your Ear." For Pinter, this is one of the greatest love poems in the English language. [65]

The correspondence between Pinter and Graham extended for more than a decade. It reveals that Pinter continued to support Graham and his wife, Nessie, directly and indirectly for many years. Graham and his wife received aid from the Royal Literary Fund, which made it possible for them to survive materially. Following Graham's death, Pinter successfully wrote to the Fund to request financial assistance for Graham's widow, who was in straightened circumstances. He assisted Nessie with making sure that she received an adequate government pension to which she was entitled, and Pinter pestered publishers such as to ensure that Graham's work wasn't remaindered.[66] Pinter didn't need much persuasion for the Greville Press, then jointly run by Tony Astbury and Geoffrey Godbert, to publish pamphlets containing Graham's poems. Both Astbury and Godbert were Graham enthusiasts. Pinter was financing the press and suggesting ideas concerning distribution and presentation of its Graham and other publications. On October 29, 1986, he arranged a launching party at Methuen's, where Antonia's editor Christopher Falkus worked, to celebrate the publication of the Greville Press's and Methuen's *100 Poems by 100 Poets*. Poems were selected by Pinter, Godbert, and Astbury (BR: H8). The party was attended by Nessie, George Barker, and others (*Chronology*: 153). The anthology contained selections from Graham and others' work. It was dedicated "For George, Elspeth, Nessie | and in memory of W.S. Graham" ([v]). In his "Introduction," Pinter recounts that he, Godbert, and Astbury devised the book during a train journey to visit Nessie, and they had decided each poem should represent its author's finest work (xiii).

On Friday December 2, 1977, Pinter attended a Graham poetry reading at the Poetry Society. The following noon, Geoffrey Godbert met Graham and Nessie (*Chronology*: 77), who came to Pinter's home at 52 Campden Hill Square. After Graham returned home to 4 Mountview Cottages, Madron, Penzance, Cornwall, Graham wrote to Pinter, confessing apologetically that he infrequently visited London, that at their meeting he was "too greedy for attention and the drink," and acted, in short, as "an over-manic man." Graham described himself as "only a fool Gael from the West" who wasn't at his best when he visited Pinter at his home. Pinter's work shocked Graham as it made him realize that he hadn't, apart from in the cinema on television, actually witnessed a contemporary play performed in the theatre. He was especially gratified that Pinter liked Graham's late poem, "To My Wife at Midnight." In his reply dated December 20, 1977, Pinter told Graham that he has a lot on his plate personally and professionally. He doesn't reveal to the poet that he has moved into Antonia's home, is writing what became *Betrayal*, and needs to tell Joan Bakewell about it, which he did in the Ladbroke Arms on February 1, 1978 (*Must*: 90). Also among other professional activities, he was early in 1978 directing Simon Gray's *The Rear Column* and then would be involved with revising *The Homecoming*. Consequently, Pinter would not really be available to meet until the summer. At 3 p.m. on Monday June 19, 1978, he rehearsed for a Graham reading. The next day at 2:45 p.m. and at 5:30 p.m., the reading took place at the Olivier Theatre, the National Theatre on the South Bank (*Chronology*: 82). In his reply to Pinter, dated December 22, 1977, Graham, in addition to understanding Pinter's situation, confessed that he also got something from Pinter's work technically that he could use himself in his own verse.

Graham was most impressed with Pinter's reading of his poems, writing to Pinter on April 22, 1978, after viewing a Pinter reading on TV, that Pinter moved his "facial athletics very well." In a letter dated July 24, 1979, Graham observed that "every reading is unique" and that Pinter should hear Graham reading Gerard Manley Hopkins' "The Wreck of the Deutschland." In a letter dated September 7, 1979, Pinter expressed delight that Graham with others would be participating in the Greville Press launch at the Purcell Room on the South Bank. Pinter chaired the evening and introduced poetry readings by himself and others on Saturday September 29, 1979. Besides Pinter and Graham, other poets included George Barker, Lawrence Durrell, William Empson, David Gascoyne, Robert Graves, John Heath-Stubbs, Stephen Spender, and John Wain. Graham read his "Letter VI," "Hilton Abstract," "The Thermal Stair," and "To My Wife at Midnight." Pinter read his own six-line poem "I Know the Place." The selections are recorded in the Greville Press's *Poets*, selected by Anthony Astbury and G. H. Godbert (BR: I5), a publication underwritten, as so many other Greville Press publications, by Pinter.

George Barker is another poet who was accorded the honor of reading more than one of his poems at the Purcell Room on September 29, 1979. He read "Summer Song 1," "Battersea Park," and "In Memory of Robert MacBryde." A week or so before the Purcell Room event, Graham wrote to Pinter that his old friend George Barker was staying with him and Nessie and spoke of a recent meeting with Pinter (probably on Monday April 23, 1979 at the Olivier Theatre[67]) "with the greatest enthusiasm." Barker referred to Pinter as a "truly noble man." Graham on November 11, 1979 asked Pinter if he could participate in a December 1979 poetry reading. Pinter's personal assistant, replying on his behalf on November 13, 1979, explained that Pinter could not do so as he would be involved with the New York rehearsals for the upcoming American production of *Betrayal* opening on January 5, 1980.

On April 8, 1980, Pinter was made aware of the perilous state of Graham and Nessie's finances; they were living in poverty, from hand to mouth. In spite of his hectic schedule including his involvement with Simon Gray's *The Rear Column*, rehearsals of *The Hothouse* that opened at the Hampstead Theatre on April 24, 1980, and preliminary work for the filming of *The French Lieutenant's Woman*—shooting began on May 27, 1980 (*Chronology*: 97–98)—Pinter took the time to contact Victor Bonham-Carter, then secretary and chief administrator of the Royal Literary Fund that dispenses financial aid to indigent authors. On May 15, 1980, Pinter told Bonham-Carter that he was most concerned about Graham's health and financial state and asked whether the Royal Literary Fund would continue to award Graham a grant or would it take into account inflation and award him more. For Pinter, Graham ranked as one of the most important poets in England. Moreover, Graham was very proud but existing well below the poverty line. On the same day as contacting Bonham-Carter, Pinter received from Graham an inscribed copy of his *Collected Poems 1942–1977*, published by Faber & Faber. For Pinter, these poems were a wonderful achievement. Pinter told Graham that he was aware of his difficult financial straits. Not mincing words, Pinter disclosed that he wrote to the Royal Literary Fund to find out what was going on and wished that Graham and his wife would accept a £1000 gift. Enclosed with his letter is a money order for £250. Pinter suggested that Graham keep quiet about this and create a separate post office account. Pinter told the poet that his work has meant a great deal to him for a long time. Six days later, Graham reported to his benefactor that the gesture "is going to make a difference to" his and Nessie's lives. He also thanked Pinter for a copy of *The Hothouse*, published by Eyre Methuen on April 24, 1980 (BR: A39a).

Pinter's letter to Bonham-Carter and the Royal Literary Fund worked. Graham told Pinter in a brief letter dated June 12, 1980 that the Fund has awarded him £1000 for three years, which is a "great release from the wee worries." In spite of other commitments, Pinter responded to Graham on November 11, 1980 that he would be delighted to introduce a reading of Graham's poetry to be held at Pentameters Theatre in Hampstead Village North London on December 15, 1980. Three days after the reading, Pinter wrote to Graham that it was wonderful to see him and Nessie. For Pinter, the reading, following a slightly rocky start, gained and grew in power, life, and authority and was an inspiration. Pinter would like to receive copies of Graham's new poems that he read at the Hampstead Village reading. He also probably sent a copy of his *Family Voices* to be broadcast on BBC Radio's Third Programme on Thursday January 22, 1981 and published by Next Editions Ltd the following day (*Chronology*: 104; BR: A40). In a longish letter dated January 14, 1981 to Pinter, Graham offered his opinion on *Family Voices*. He regarded the radio play as "a strange object of some power," responding to it not as a drama "but a chamber trio of words," although Graham did not know what exactly Pinter's play is saying except for its title. For Graham, "the words" in *Family Voices* "are everything." On March 30, 1982, Pinter received a letter from Nessie thanking him for a copy of his *Victoria Station*, first presented October 14, 1982 (BR: W44). Nessie added that her husband "has not been well for some time now, having abdominal pain[s]" and other ailments.

Two years later, in the midst of National Theatre activities, directing Giraudoux's *The Trojan War*, and two days after Jimmy Wax's funeral, Pinter acted on Graham's behalf once again. He informed Victor Bonham-Carter on April 27, 1983 that W. S. Graham was ill and destitute and inquired as to whether the Royal Literary Fund award would continue. Two days later, in spite of lighting meetings and dress rehearsals for *The Trojan War* production (*Chronology*: 123), Pinter instructed his personal assistant to send a £500 check to Graham's account at Lloyd's Bank in Penzance. Nessie responded on May 3, 1983, expressing their "tremendous relief . . . and such an uplifting of" their "morale." In addition to news the next day from the Royal Literary Fund that Victor Bonham-Carter had retired and that they would increase their award, Pinter learned from Nessie in a letter dated June 13, 1983 that the Royal Literary Fund awarded them £500 more per year over a two-year period. Pinter suggested to Nessie that when her husband reached age sixty-five (he was born in 1918), he should apply for a retirement pension.

In the early summer of 1984, Pinter was involved with the production of Simon Gray's *The Common Pursuit*, which closed its London run at the Lyric on August 11 following negative reactions that infuriated Pinter. Other activities included the filming of *A Kind of Alaska* as a television script on Wednesday and Thursday, July 18/19 (see BR: W45f). On August 15, 1984, Nessie informed Pinter that her husband would have a bowel operation on August 22. She added that they received money from the Royal Literary Fund. On the last day of August, she wrote to Pinter that the operation was successful. On the last day of October, she told

Pinter that they are having problems with their landlord, the owner of their cottage, and thanked Pinter for a dollar check from "enthusiastic fans wherever they are." Still, her husband's recovery from his operation was slower than expected.

From September 24 to October 8, 1984, Pinter and Antonia visited New York and the northeast regions of the United States. Following their return, Pinter was briefly hospitalized at the Cromwell Hospital London from November 15–16 (*Chronology*: 135–36). On November 13, Pinter corresponded with Ruth Rosen, the South African–born actress and poet known for her poetry and prose readings and performances,[68] and Geoffrey Godbert concerning a reading of Graham's work. Pinter would read Graham's "The Nightfishing" and Graham's collection of poems of that name on the afternoon of December 7, 1984. Graham wrote to Pinter on November 20 that he should read the poems that require Pinter's "good voice and tuning." Pinter should not be afraid to give his readings from the stand-alone poem sequence "Johann Joachim Quantz's Five Lessons," which Graham described as a "big theatrical shoosh." Pinter should "make a play of it." He should where necessary read slowly and seriously and make "the sentimental bits tear ducters." No doubt Pinter agreed with Graham's sentiments, writing in a December 6 letter that listening to poetry being put into sound, especially words in an unexpected sequence, is not necessarily an unhappy thing.[69]

Antonia and Pinter were in St. Louis, Missouri, and then went to Los Angeles, Hollywood, and San Francisco from October 16 to November 28, 1985. On their return, a letter from Nessie dated November 5 awaited Pinter. It informed him that her husband had a second operation and that "sometimes he's very bright, and witty—at others, a bit drowsy." In spite of other engagements, two days prior to Christmas 1985, Pinter instructed his personal assistant to book a double room at the Abbey Hotel, Penzance, for the weekend of January 10, 1986 (*Chronology*: 146–47). On Thursday January 9, 1986, Graham died. Pinter, with Tony Astbury and Geoffrey Godbert, visited Nessie on what turned out to be a chilly day. On January 21, Nessie sent Pinter an account of the crematorium service at Truro, which she described as "beautiful, simple and dignified." The funeral address was given by Michael Snow, the literary administrator of the Graham estate and editor who, with his wife, Margaret, "with Nessie . . . surveyed all the W. S. Graham poems in Nessie's possession" following his death (*The Nighfisherman*: 394). Movingly, Nessie told Pinter that "it is difficult to think someone so vivid, so charged with life and imagination . . . can simply cease to be"—words that appropriately may be said of Harold Pinter.[70]

Pinter publicized Graham's work whenever he was able, most notably at the Ilkley Literary Festival from June 17–18, 1994, where he read Graham's poems. A year earlier, he encouraged the production of a projected "Selected Letters," which was eventually published on the final Thursday of November 1999 by Michael Schmidt's Carcanet Press in Manchester, following its rejection by Faber and other publishers apparently for economic reasons. In a letter dated September 8, 1995, Nessie thanked Pinter for a "marvelous speech" in praise of her husband and added, "[L]ong may you remain enigmatic, taciturn, tense, prickly, explosive, and forbidding!"[71] In a brief blurb on the back cover, Pinter wrote, "I said about W.S. Graham's poetry 'his song is unique and his work is an inspiration.' The same applies to this brilliant collection of letters. The subject is poetry. W.S. Graham drank and ate poetry every day of his life. These letters show an intelligence and sensibility ravished by language and conundrum of language. An explorer whose journey never ends." In a back cover endorsement of Ralph Pite's and Hester Jones's edited *W. S. Graham: Speaking Toward's You* (Liverpool University Press, 2004), Pinter recalled, "I first read a W. S. Graham poem in 1949. It sent a shiver down my spine. Forty-five years later nothing has changed. His song is unique and his work and inspiration."

Graham was also the subject of the most extraordinary coincidences ever experienced by Pinter. In a letter to the literary scholar Professor Geoffrey Moore dated September 25, 1995, Pinter related that before a performance of his *The Hothouse* in Bath on Saturday evening September 23, 1995, he was looking out of his dressing room window and the word "gentle" came into his mind. The word reminded him of the opening lines of Graham's "O Gentle Queen of the Afternoon." Pinter then proceeded to perform to an unresponsive audience apart from two people sitting in the front of the stalls. At the end of the performance, Pinter returned to his dressing room to find a letter from Moore, on the back of which were written the opening four lines from Graham's poem "O Gentle Queen of the Afternoon." After seeing the lines, Pinter was overcome and found it difficult to make sense of the coincidence. It sent a shiver down his spine.[72]

The impact of Graham's verse remained with Pinter. Antonia Fraser recalls that on April 16, 2002, shortly after her husband's cancer diagnosis at the Royal Marsden Hospital and prior to his operation, they went for a rest to Torquay. During their lunch "in a country pub"—"Harold's favourite thing"—they disagreed about a line in Graham's poem "I Leave This at Your Ear": "Was it the 'shining sea' as I thought, or the 'silent' sea as in Harold's version?" She adds that "Harold is always right about these things which doesn't stop me gamely arguing. So when at dinner he pronounced, 'It's actually the *speaking* sea,' it was a touching demonstration of his weakness, that he had forgotten one of his favorite lines" (*Must*: 256).

Philip Larkin

Pinter met, corresponded with, and admired Philip Larkin "from an early stage." Moreover, Anthony Thwaite, the editor of *The Selected Letters of Philip Larkin 1940–1985*, writes that "they also shared a great interest in and enthusiasm for cricket"—so much so that Pinter, with Larkin's friend Ansell Egerton, proposed Larkin for membership in the highly prestigious MCC (xxxii, xv). Larkin included W. S. Graham's "Letter V" in his selection *The Oxford Book of Twentieth Century English Verse* (500–2).

On February 11, 1967, Larkin replied to a letter from Pinter. For Larkin, it was "a great honour [*sic*] . . . to have such kind words from someone of [Pinter's] reputation." However, Larkin adds that "to be perfectly honest [he] shouldn't have thought" that his "grammar school Betjeman world would have" appealed to Pinter. Larkin apologizes to Pinter, as his "knowledge of modern English drama stops" at Noël Coward's 1924 play *Hay Fever*. Incidentally, Coward admired Pinter's work, and Pinter admitted to gaining much from Coward's stage craft and social comic technique. He directed Coward's *Blithe Spirit* at the National in May 1976 (Billington: 128–29, 255) and performed minor roles during his repertory company days in Coward's *South Sea Bubble* at the end of January 1957 and *Hay Fever* in July 1957. Larkin gathers that Pinter's "work is provocative and experimental"; consequently the letter from Pinter will "cheer [Larkin] up and give [him] new hope." Larkin confesses to Pinter that he has "never felt able to go on from" the last lines of his poem "Dockery and Son," first published in *The Listener* (April 11, 1963), with its title from Dickens's *Dombey and Son* (1847–48). In this poem, Larkin contrasts his own position with Dickens's character: "For Dockery a son, for me nothing, | Nothing with all a son's harsh patronage"[73]—ironic words in view of Pinter's own troubled relationship with his son, Daniel.

In his diary for Monday June 19, 1972, Pinter notes that at lunchtime, he heard John Betjeman reading Larkin (*Chronology*: 47). Betjeman and others introduced and read their favorite Larkin poems in a "Larkin at Fifty" broadcast on BBC Radio 3 on August 9, 1972. Betjeman read "Toads Revisited" and "The Whitsun Weddings."[74] Hearing an earlier version of Betjeman's reading may have encouraged Pinter to write to Larkin inviting him for lunch. On June 25, 1972, Larkin apologized to Pinter for not being able to meet him at Lord's during the England-versus-Australia Test Match. One month later, Larkin thanked Pinter for sending him a copy of *Landscape* and, in return, he sent Pinter copies of some of the poems that Betjeman read, although Larkin was unable to "imagine some of [his] lines coming out of [Betjeman's] mouth, but no doubt he handled them with his usual charm and tact." He informed Pinter that he would be in London on August 17, 1972 and suggested that they meet for lunch then.

Larkin wrote to Monica Jones, his "dearest Bun," on August 13, 1972 that a proposed meeting with Hallam Tennyson, the BBC Radio producer and great-grandson of the poet, would not prevent Larkin from lunching with Pinter. Larkin asked Jones if she was aware that "the prick [Pinter] is only 42 and has the CBE?" Consequently, Larkin felt "very dubious about meeting" Pinter.[75] Pinter booked a table for 12:30 p.m. on August 17 at the Vendome, a French restaurant located in Piccadilly—not one of Pinter's favorites, as he seems to have dined there only once more (*Chronology*: 372). In a letter to Pinter written the same day as Pinter booked the restaurant, Larkin perhaps revealed his nervousness at the upcoming meeting. He tells Pinter that Thomas Hardy "said that a man of fifty was an old man in winter and a young man in summer, but I think they must have had better summers in those days." The day following their lunch, Larkin wrote to Pinter, saying how much he enjoyed their meeting and only wished that it could have gone on later than it did. He attached to his letter a prose piece, "Not the Place's Fault." He wrote concerning his feeling for cricket and his childhood collecting cigarette cards in Coventry gutters and especially the "Famous Cricketers Series."[76] That may account for "the slight scholarly stoop in [his] bearing today" as he had to bend down to find the cards.[77] Larkin concluded with words on friendship using a cricketing metaphor that must have reverberated with Pinter: "In childhood friends are necessary: you cannot bowl to yourself." He added that, unlike Pinter, "I had none I remember until we moved to" a different area of Coventry.[78]

Following their lunch, Larkin sent Pinter a copy of the now exceedingly rare and highly priced *XX Poems*, privately printed in Belfast for Larkin in an edition limited to one hundred copies at the then cost of £14.[79] Thanking the poet for such a rare pamphlet and the cricket extract, Pinter sent him in return on August 21, 1972 something of his own on cricket, possibly his "Memories of Cricket," initially published in the *Daily Telegraph Magazine* (May 16, 1969: 25–26)[80] and also a copy of *The Homecoming* (see BR: E15 and A20). Pinter tells Larkin that his enjoyment was mutual and would appreciate it if Larkin would let him know when he is visiting London again. Pinter expresses surprise that Larkin is not including his own "Dockery and Son" in his *The Oxford Book of Twentieth Century English Verse*, as Pinter regards the poem as "undoubtedly one of [Larkin's] finest." Pinter encourages Larkin to fulfill a long-held cherished wish to become an MCC member by sending him the candidate's form for which a seconder is needed. Pinter, an MCC member, would propose him. He concludes optimistically that it is highly likely that Larkin would find himself next season elected a member.

On October 16, 1973, Larkin thanked Pinter for sending him a copy of *monologue*, lines from which made him "shudder a bit." He tells Pinter, with his typical modesty, that what he refers to as "a meagre collection" of his poems, *High Windows*, which is "very short weight," will appear in the next six months. It was published by Faber on June 3, 1974 and the impression of 6,142 copies sold out within three weeks of publication—apparently something of a record.[81] On October 25, Larkin returned the MCC form to Pinter. On March 23 1974, Pinter told Larkin that he was waiting anxiously for the appearance of Larkin's new volume of poetry. He informed Larkin that he was directing John Hopkins's drama *Next of Kin*, which opened at the National Theatre, the Old Vic, on May 2, 1974, and that they wished to include two Larkin poems in the program: "Home is So Sad" and "Talking in Bed." Pinter hoped that Larkin had no objections to their doing so. Replying to Pinter three days later, Larkin wrote that he of course did not object and would send Pinter a copy of *High Windows*, which he privately referred to as *Last Poems*—a title that Pinter refused to accept. Larkin became a country member of the MCC and agreed with Pinter's suggestion that they should meet at a county match as this would give them more time to chat. Larkin agreed with Pinter's hostile criticism of Luchino Visconti's Teatre di Romo production of *Old Times*, forcefully expressed by Pinter on the BBC Kaleidoscope program broadcast on BBC Radio 4 on May 10, 1973 (BR: J35) and other venues (see Billington: 237–38).

Although the date June 5, 1974 at Lord's cricket ground is mentioned in a April 23, 1974 letter from Pinter to Larkin, there is no mention of such a meeting in Pinter's "Appointment Diaries." The next meeting between Pinter and Larkin appears to be on March 22, 1975, when they met at the Mermaid Theatre. On June 16, 1975 Pinter, his friend, poet and literary editor Ian Hamilton, and the then–arts administrator Charles Osborne read a selection of Larkin's poems at "An Evening Without Philip Larkin" at the Mermaid (*Chronology*: 59, 61). On the occasion of the publication of *High Windows*, Pinter sent Larkin a congratulatory telegram. Their next communication seems not to be until the publication of Larkin's poem "Aubade" in the *TLS* (December 23, 1977, Bloomfield: A15, 47). Pinter also sent the poet a telegram of congratulation. Pinter found the poem that Larkin finished following his mother's death on November 17, 1977 at the age of ninety-one[82] "superb." Pinter liked the poem so much that he read it to Tom Stoppard and Henry Woolf on the last day of January 1978 (*Chronology*: 79). Formally, technically, and in the language used, however, Larkin's poem seems to have had little if any impact upon Pinter's poem written just after the death of his own father on September 10, 1997, "Death (Births and Death's Registration Act 1953)."[83]

In October 1980, Larkin sent copies of the poem printed on "Fabriano, Richard de Bas, Japanese handmade" papers by Charles Seluzicki, a poetry bookseller in Oregon, to some "people who had been nice about" the poem. These included Pinter and Stoppard.[84] On October 15, 1980, Larkin thanked Pinter for sending him a copy of "the funny and sad" *Family Voices* and suggested that they meet again for lunch, although no such meeting is recorded. On October 30, Larkin again wrote to Pinter, this time concerning Pinter's television reading of his poem that very evening; Larkin couldn't view the performance, as he didn't have access to a television set. Larkin "always remember[s] [Pinter's] telegram coming on Christmas Eve" praising "Aubade," and he is getting into training to listening, as did Pinter, to the Test Matches from Australia at six in the morning. Pinter replied on November 10 suggesting that they meet for lunch in December, but again there is no corroborating evidence to suggest that such a meeting took place.[85]

In 1982, Larkin turned sixty. Andrew Motion, who became poet laureate from 1999 to 2009, was then editor of the *Poetry Review*. He wrote to Pinter on November 25, 1981. Knowing that Pinter admired Larkin's work and recalling his television reading of "Aubade" (which Pinter reread on a BBC television program called *Word for Word* on October 18, 1982), Motion asked if Pinter would write a brief birthday tribute to Larkin. In it, he would say what Larkin meant to him and what he considered his special attributes. Pinter responded affirmatively on December 10, assuring Motion that his contribution would be brief. He sent his piece to Motion on February 4, 1982. The tribute appeared in the *Poetry Review* LXXII, 2 (June 1982): 5.[86]

Pinter's contribution is a five-verse unrhymed prose poem titled "Philip Larkin." It compares Larkin's skills to the great batsmen of the past, concluding: "He's Hutton and Compton. He warrants his own | personal Wisden," or cricketer's "bible." In his penultimate four-line verse, Pinter continues his cricketing allusions, writing that Larkin has "topped the averages for the last" quarter century and, consequently, Larkin is "now so far out in front as to be uncatchable, head and shoulders above the | rest." The structure of the poem is interesting and differs from Pinter's other poems. Each verse begins with a capital letter; however, none of the other lines of the five verses begin with capitals. The first verse consists of seven lines and five sentences, the second of five lines and four sentences; the third verse has five sentences and four lines. The fourth verse consists of a single sentence and the final verse has two lines, with two sentences. In the opening verse, the pronoun "he" has a repetitive effect used five times; "his" is used once; and the poem begins with the name "Larkin," which is its sole occurrence in the poem. In the second verse, "his" occurs thrice, in each instance at the start of a sentence, and interchanges with "him" used twice and "He's" once. In the third verse, "he's" occurs twice, at the start of a sentence and once within a sentence. In this verse, "you" is used twice, and in the penultimate single-sentence verse, "he's" once. In the final verse, "He's" opens the verse and "He" begins the second sentence. Such a poetic form and usage is highly unusual for Pinter, and he doesn't seem to have reissued or reprinted the poem; like its subject Philip Larkin, the poem is unique. Larkin's greatness is akin to that of Pinter's cricketing heroes.

Pinter sent Larkin his tribute to *Arthur Wellard* (BR: E21A) on January 5, 1983, and Larkin responded: "I love you knowing about cricket." Larkin was searching unsuccessfully to find a cigarette card of Wellard to send Pinter in return. He related to Pinter an anecdote concerning Larkin's friend Kingsley Amis. Amis recalled being in a box at Lord's and, while inebriated, witnessed someone hit a four. Amis called out that it was a "good shot." Pinter turned around and responded "thick edge off a long hop, and you call that a good shot" or words to that effect. Larkin adds that Amis "didn't call good shot anymore."

Some of the Pinter-Larkin correspondence during 1983 (April 29, May 3, May 10) concerns a copy of the first edition of *High Windows*, published on June 3, 1974 (Bloomfield: A10), which Larkin had sent to Pinter inscribed: "For Harold remembering his kindness in enabling me to have net practice—With kind regards—Philip." On April 25, 1983, Anthony Thwaite drew Pinter's attention to the fact that this copy appeared in a bookseller's catalog. Pinter forgot that he possessed this inscribed copy but then remembered, telling Larkin in a letter dated May 10, 1983 that there was a reason for his amnesia. In 1975, Pinter had separated from his then-wife Vivien, and many of his books remained in their Hanover Terrace home. Pinter was unable to regain them for another four years, and the copy of *High Windows* was one of the volumes that got away. Pinter told Larkin on June 28, 1983 that he has "finally got to the bottom of" what happened to the inscribed copy. He told Larkin that Vivien died in October 1982 and that the books in her house were sold at an auction; the copy of *High Windows* was one of them. This was the reason it reached the bookseller and his catalog. The volume subsequently has been sold to a New York book dealer. Pinter added that his recent reading of Larkin's "Aubade" has been of even more significance to him. Pinter's confusion and honesty is a reflection that he remained sensitive to the events surrounding his separation from Vivien and her later death.

At the Le Caprice restaurant on Thursday May 19, 1983, Pinter mentioned a play about imprisonment and torture that became the foundation for his subsequent *One For the Road* (*Must*: 142). The previous day, Larkin sent Pinter a copy of the initial paperback issue of *High Windows* that Faber had published in October 1979 (Bloomfield: A10c) as "some sort of consolation." He added that, for him, "life began to go downhill at fifty"—in Larkin's case, in 1972. He added that he was writing to Pinter on the way to the hospital to get a replacement for his hearing aid and that if he hadn't already written his poem "The Building"—his reaction to having to visit his mother in hospital after she fell (*Complete Poems*: 458) and published in *High Windows*—he'd need to begin it after his hospital visit. In his response dated July 7, 1983, Pinter thanked Larkin for his kindness in sending the copy, which Pinter would "guard . . . with my life." He also focused upon a common link between them: their mutual obsession with cricket and, specifically, a catch—one brilliantly depicted in Pinter and Alan Wilkinson's privately printed limited-edition *The Catch*, which concerns a fine catch Pinter made while playing for the Gaieties (BR: H69).

Pinter described in detail to Larkin another match, the conclusion of his Gaieties team's match against Sonning-on-Thames on Sunday July 3, 1983. With an over left, the Gaieties needed three runs to win and they had four wickets in hand. The opening bat was 92 not out and was not facing the bowling at the start of the final over. The Sonning captain who was bowling tossed the ball up and yorked the Gaieties number 8 batsman, who was facing his first ball. The next batsman, number 10, missed his first ball; hit the second only to be caught at mid-wicket. So there were three balls to be bowled and two wickets left. The next batsman swung at the first ball delivered to him and missed; he did the same with the next ball and was bowled. Number 11 came out to bat. On his way to the wicket Pinter advised the oncoming batsman to be calm and counseled him that the best position to adopt under the circumstances "was to do absolutely nothing." The last batsman seemed to agree, and after taking guard, smashed the last ball of the over and the game with all his strength only "to be brilliantly caught at mid-on." Pinter concluded his letter pointing out that his side "lost the match by two runs" with the final ball bowled and that the opposition captain had taken four wickets at the cost of no runs in the final over. He added that he still couldn't believe it.[87]

The focus and attention to detail on Pinter's account is perhaps a reflection of his escape from the sadness of life that he and Larkin were feeling with encroaching age and, in Pinter's case, the heavy weight of his professional commitments and mixed personal emotions. These are reflected in his poem dated "1983," "Ghost," published in the *TLS* (November 4, 1983: 1204; BR: C22). The poem was written following Vivien's death in October 1982. The six-verses of two lines each opens with an image of strangulation. Its interplay of monosyllables and personal pronouns powerfully conveys the sense of the living "I" being unable to communicate with the other, the dead body. A similar sense of the poet's physical touch with a dead body is found in Pinter's subsequent poetic lament for his deceased father.[88] Antonia remembers from this period a conversation between Pinter and Beckett in which the former says to the latter, "I'm sorry, Sam, if I sound very gloomy." Beckett responds, "Oh, you couldn't be more gloomy than I am, Harold" (*Must*: 145). Indeed, Beckett's despair was felt by others close to Pinter. For instance, Simon Gray, in an undated postcard sent to Pinter probably from February 1990, responded to a Beckett reading given by Pinter that expressed "a passionately felt aridity." Gray asked, "Is that really life? I refuse to believe so—with decreasing confidence," adding that Beckett is "a strange, desolating isolated genius."[89]

Larkin's October 12, 1983 letter to Pinter dwells upon mortality. His letter is to be the last extant one in the Pinter Archive at the British Library written by Larkin to Pinter. The opening of the letter refers to the death of Ralph Richardson, who died two days earlier and who played the part of Spooner in *No Man's Land*. It also refers to the increasing frailty of Larkin's friend John Betjeman, who died on May 19, 1984. In spite of a dwelling upon mutability, the subject of cricket isn't far away, and Larkin wonders what Pinter, a Yorkshire supporter since his early days, thinks of the business with Geoffrey Boycott, the former Yorkshire and England batsman. Media reports circulated of friction within the Yorkshire side.

Philip Larkin died on December 2, 1985. On December 16, 1985, Pinter applied to the chapter dean of Westminster Abbey for tickets for him and Antonia to attend Larkin's memorial service to be held at noon on Friday February 14, 1986.[90] On January 6, 1986, Pinter's reading of "The Whitsun Weddings" was shown just before "Newsnight" on BBC-2 television around 10:50 p.m. On the evening of March 3, 1986, Pinter participated in readings from Larkin's poetry at the Riverside Studios on the Thames in Hammersmith. As a tribute to Larkin, the Greville Press published in 2002 *Philip Larkin Poems Selected by Harold Pinter* in a limited edition of three hundred copies with the initial fifty signed and numbered by Pinter. On the second page of what turned out to be this final tribute, Pinter noted that he wished to include four poems from Larkin's *The Less Deceived* collection, but copyright permission had been refused (BR: H65). On Monday April 19 at 6:30 p.m. at the British Library Auditorium, Pinter gave a public reading of his favorite Larkin poems (*Chronology*: 288).[91]

CONCLUSION

This chapter illustrates Pinter's love for literature, especially for poetry and poets. This is revealed in his friendships with contemporaries such as W. S. Graham, to whom he gave financial support and other kinds of assistance; Philip Larkin; and the great dramatist, novelist, and correspondent Samuel Beckett. Pinter's letters to Woolf and Goldstein reveal influences and illuminate his enthusiasm for writers of diverse genres, periods, and nationalities extending from W. B. Yeats, James Joyce, and Joyce Cary, to Turgenev, Rimbaud, and Marcel Proust, to the American Henry Miller, to English Romantics such as Wordsworth, to the great Jacobean John Webster, and to Shakespeare, who "suffers, commits and survives them all" ("A Note on Shakespeare," *Various Voices*: 7).

NOTES

1. BLADDMSS: 89094/1.

2. http://www.enitharmon.co.uk/pages/store/products/ec_view.asp?PID=182, accessed August 20, 2016. BR: I11. For a review of *The Disappeared and Other Poems* see Ann C. Hall, *The Harold Pinter Review* I (2017): 149–51.

3. BLADDMSS: 89094/1.

4. For a photograph of McMaster as Othello and Pinter as Iago, see www. harold-pinter.org, accessed October 1, 2016.

5. BLADDMSS: 89094/2.

6. David Thompson, *Pinter: The Player's Playwright*, London: Macmillan, 1985: 128–29.

7. Francis Gillen, "Between Fluidity and Fixity: Harold Pinter's Novel *The Dwarfs*," *The Pinter Review* (1990): 56, citing *The Dwarfs*: 134.

8. *Midsummer Night's Dream* V, i: 14–15; cited Billington: 216.

9. See the present writer's "Harold Pinter's Library," *Remembering/Celebrating Harold Pinter. The Pinter Review* (2011): 148–155.

10. See *Chronology*: 312.

11. http://www.haroldpinter.org/films/films_kinglear.shtml, accessed November 10, 2016.

12. *Sharp Cut*: 372.

13. Pinter's unpublished script is at the British Library Pinter Archive; see Gale for a detailed discussion: 370–72.

14. https://www.theguardian.com/stage/2007/jul/12/theatre.haroldpinter, accessed June 7, 2016; and cf. *Barcelona is in Trouble*: 49.

15. http://www.independent.co.uk/news/people/obituary-margaret-rawlings-1335400.html, accessed June 7, 2016.

16. BLADDMSS: 88920/5/2.

17. BLADDMSS: 88920/5/2.

18. BLADDMSS: 89094/1.

19. See *Chronology*: 313.

20. See Helen Vendler, *Our Secret Discipline: Yeats and Lyric Form*: 400, n.9.

21. British Library Pinter Archive: "Harold Pinter in Conversation," CDRom r0025491; see also Baker, "Harold Pinter's Library": 149.

22. See https://en.m.wikipedia.org, accessed August 25, 2016.

23. BLADDMSS: 89094/3.

24. For a detailed discussion of such Joycean language usage, see K. Wales, *The Language of James Joyce*, 1992.

25. Taylor-Batty [2014]: 96.

26. BLADDMSS: 89094/1.

27. BLADDMSS: 89094/2.

28. Cf. Billington: 419.

29. See Ramona Kelley Stamm, "Joyce Cary's Onomastic 'Orchestration,': Name, Symbol and Theme in *The Horse's Mouth*," *Literary Onomastics Studies* 15 (1988), http://digitalcommons.brockport.edu/cgi/viewcontent.cgi?article=1019&context=los, accessed April 28, 2017.

30. BLADDMSS: 89094/3.

31. BLADDMSS: 88920/5/2.

32. Cited chapter 3.

33. These reactions to Pinter's cinematic adaptations are found in BLADDMSS: 88880/6/26.

34. S. Gale, *Sharp Cut*: 221.

35. BLADDMSS: 88880/5/4.

36. November 24, 2000: cited http://www.haroldpinter.org/plays/plays_remembrance.shtml, accessed April 29, 2017.

37. BLADDMSS: 89094/1; which study of Rimbaud Pinter had found eludes the present writer as does the texts of Rimbaud and Tolstoy's *Anna Karenina* he saw.

38. BLADDMSS: 88920/5/2.

39. https://en.wikipedia.org/wiki/Oblomov#, English_translations, accessed June 3, 2016.

40. BLADDMSS: 89094/1.

41. Third edition: 205 (Epigraph to "Walking Up and Down in China"), James Decker email June 17, 2016 to the present author. Decker adds that his references are "from the second Obelisk edition (1938)" and he does not "have access to the first edition. Second edition was based on first, but page numbers may be off slightly. . . . The third Obelisk edition (1945) was based on second edition—with same pagination—and was the first printed after the war (likely Pinter's copy). Fourth Obelisk edition appeared after [1954]. One variant second edition (green leather boards; same pagination as standard paper second edition) and one Chinese piracy (1939; same pagination as Obelisk second edition) also existed prior to 1950."

42. Ibid., 256.

43. Ibid., 215–16.

44. BLADDMSS: 88880/4/17.

45. BLADDMSS: 88920/5/2.

46. I have been unable to locate a reply from Miller; cf. BLADDMSS (Inventory) Pinter Archive.

47. Gore Vidal cited James Campbell, *TLS* 3 (June 2016): 4.

48. BLADDMSS: 89094/4.

49. For the Lord Chamberlain's responses, see D. Shellard, S. Nicolson, M. Handley, *The Lord Chamberlain Regrets . . . A History of British Theatrical Censorship*: plates 13, and 19, and 149–50, 160–61, 171.

50. BLADDMSS: 89094/4.

51. BLADDMSS: 89094/3.

52. BLADDMSS: 89094/4: See also *The Letters of Samuel Beckett: Volume III, 1957–1965*: 757. For Zwemmers, see Nigel Vaux Halliday, *More than a Bookshop: Zwemmers and Art in the Twentieth Century*, London: Philip Wilson Publishers, 2001.

53. BLADDMSS: 89083/1/1.

54. Baker, "Harold Pinter's Library": 153–54.

55. BLADDMSS: 89083/1/1.

56. For Magee and Beckett, see "Profiles" in *The Letters of Samuel Beckett: Volume III, 1957-1965*: 700.

57. BLADDMSS: 89083/1/1.

58. BLADDMSS: 89094/4.

59. Gussow, *Conversations*, 28, 106.

60. See *The Letters of Samuel Beckett: Volume IV, 1966-1989*: 158–59. Pinter discusses the implication in his discussion of "two silences" in his "Writing for the Theatre"; see *VV*: 24–25 (BR: E10).

61. Peter Hall, "Directing the Plays of Harold Pinter" in *The Cambridge Companion to Harold Pinter*, second edition, Cambridge: Cambridge University Press, 2009: 163.

62. BR: G117.

63. See chapter 2.

64. BLADDMSS: 88880/6/21.

65. BLADDMSS: 88920/8.

66. See for instance BLADDMSS: 88880/7/5.

67. *Chronology*: 89.

68. See W. S. Graham, *The Nightfisherman: Selected Letters*, eds. Michael and Margaret Snow, Manchester: Carcanet, 1997: 392.

69. BLADDMSS: 88880/7/5.

70. BLADDMSS: 88880/7/5.

71. BLADDMSS: 88880/7/5.

72. BLADDMSS: 88880/7/5.

73. *The Complete Poems Philip Larkin*, Archie Burnett, ed., NY: Farrar, Strauss and Giroux: 2012: 66–67.

74. William S. Peterson, *John Betjeman: A Bibliography*, Oxford: Clarendon Press, 2006: J 286, 352.

75. Larkin, *Letters to Monica*, Anthony Thwaite, ed., Faber and Faber: Bodleian Library Oxford, 2010: 438.

76. *Umbrella* I, 3 [Spring 1959], [107]–12.

77. See James Booth, *Philip Larkin Life, Art and Love*, New York: Bloomsbury Press, 2014: 22; B. C. Bloomfield, *Philip Larkin: A Bibliography 1933-1994*, London: British Library and New Castle, DE, 2002, c104: 104.

78. BLADDMSS: 88880/7/6.

79. Bloomfield: A4.

80. Reprinted in *Cricket '72*, J. A. Bailey and R. J. Roe, eds., London: The Test and County Cricket Board, Lord's Ground, 1972: 26, 28, as "Hutton and the Past."

81. See Bloomfield, A10: 39–41.

82. *Complete Poems*: 494–95.

83. BR: C37.

84. *Selected Letters of Philip Larkin 1940–1985*, Anthony Thwaite, ed., London, Boston: Faber and Faber, 1992: 629 and n.4.

85. BLADDMSS: 88880/7/5.

86. In addition, there are three prose pieces: by Gavin Ewart (1916–1995), whose poetry Larkin admired, "Larkin About" (6–7); A. N. Wilson (1950–), "Larkin's England" (7–9); and Mick Imlah (1956–2009), "Twenty Ways of Saying Happy Birthday" (9–11). Imlah's is a review of Anthony Thwaite's edited volume *Larkin at Sixty*. Described as a "poem" by B. C. Bloomfield in his *Philip Larkin: A Bibliography 1933–1994* (see "Appendix" item 244: 190).

87. BLADDMSS: 88880/7/5.

88. Cf. Baker (2008): 134–135.

89. BLADDMSS: 88880/7/6: f.57.

90. BLADDMSS: 88880/7/6: ff.131–181.

91. Pinter's reading is available at the British Library Pinter Archive C927/10413D1: 1 CD R0014600). A coda both Pinter and Larkin reveled in the use of the word "fuck" in their work; there isn't a single instance of the word in their correspondence [cf. Ryan Hibbert, "Philip Larkin, British Culture and [the] Four Letter Word" *Critical Quarterly* 43 no. 2 (June 2014): 120–38].

Conclusion

Let me conclude on a personal note. In many ways *Pinter's World: Relationships, Obsessions, and Artistic Endeavors* is an attempt to finally get out of my system something that has obsessed me for over half a century: Harold Pinter and his work. By utilizing primary materials and other materials that have come to light during the last decade or so, the writing of this book has allowed me to rethink Pinter's life and achievements. The initial experience of his drama frightened a sensitive adolescent almost to death and gave him nightmares for weeks afterward. In the early summer of 1960, when fifteen, *The Caretaker* was performed at the Theatre Royal Brighton, Sussex. What left such an impression sitting up with the gods in the cheapest seats at the Theatre Royal was the character of Mick, performed by Alan Bates, when he violently smashed his brother's Buddha into smithereens. That was the moment this author, William Baker, was hooked on Pinter. Whenever the opportunity came, I listened to his plays on the radio, watched them on TV, and started to collect everything by him, including newspaper interviews and ephemera.

That collection formed the foundation of my *Harold Pinter: A Bibliographical History*, completed in collaboration with John Ross and published by the British Library in 2005. My much earlier *Harold Pinter*, written collaboratively with Stephen E. Tabachnick, appeared in the Oliver and Boyd Modern Writers' series in 1973. Over thirty-five years later, in 2008, I revisited the subject with *Harold Pinter*, which appeared in the Continuum Writers' Lives series. The book was translated into Chinese; the country has an increasing interest in Pinter and his work. Drawing upon Pinter's yearly "Appointment Diaries" now in the Pinter Archive at the Manuscript Division of the British Library, my *A Harold Pinter Chronology* published in 2013 provided wherever possible a daily account of its subject's life, activities, and work.

Pinter's World: Relationships, Obsessions, and Artistic Endeavors is my attempt, based on a thorough immersion in the Pinter Archive, to reassess from the perspective of age a writer's life and work. It represents a personal finale undertaken through examining facets of Pinter's life, work, and relationships. The first chapter looked at his earliest years: the influence of his schoolmaster Joseph Brearley and their subsequent friendship after Pinter had left school. The chapter draws upon the relatively neglected *Peter Hall's Diaries: The Story of a Dramatic Life* to look at the frequently fractious relationship between the two that occupied many years of their professional and personal lives. Other topics treated in this chapter include Pinter's film work and creative collaboration with his close friend Simon Gray, also considered elsewhere, and reactions from actors whom Pinter directed and acted.

Pinter loved the game of cricket, a love I share. Pinter played cricket, had followed it avidly since childhood, and incessantly spoke about it especially in letters to his close friends. For Pinter, it epitomized the quintessence of Englishness. His obsession with the game forms the first part of the narrative of the second chapter. I also examine other nonliterary or dramatic obsessions, including his passion later in life for the mental game of bridge and the far more physically active games of squash and tennis, which he played vigorously. Even at the age of seventy-two, Pinter played tennis as opposed to table tennis, which he spent a good deal of his adolescence playing but then dropped, although he uses the game to open his one-act play *monologue*. This second chapter concludes with the examination of another lifelong love—a cerebral one—music.

The third chapter explores Pinter's friendships through the prism of his love for restaurants and reveals the supreme importance of loyalty in his life. It also examines the restaurants he particularly enjoyed and throws light upon his personal relationships. The fourth chapter is concerned with his love for and relationships with the opposite sex. The penultimate chapter treats the subjects of politics and the closely related topic of religion in his life. The final chapter looks at Pinter's engagement with the literature and writers who influenced him the most. It closes with an examination of his personal relationship with three contemporary authors.

The six chapters in *Pinter's World: Relationships, Obsessions, and Artistic Endeavors* are an attempt to illuminate aspects of a complex genius. In the fifth paragraph of Pinter's "A Note on Shakespeare" dated 1950, he writes of Shakespeare: "[I]n attempting to approach Shakespeare's work in its entirety, you are called upon to grapple with the perspective in which the horizon alternately collapses and re-forms behind you, in which the mind is subject to an intense diversity of atmospheric" (*Various Voices*: 5). Pinter here may be viewed as writing about his own life and work, his own world and company.

Bibliography

A comprehensive account of Pinter's output is found in William Baker and John C. Ross, *Harold Pinter: A Bibliographical History*. London: The British Library and New Castle, DE: Oak Knoll Press, 2005 [reference numbers to this are given in some instances in square brackets below, see for instance under POETRY] Much of Pinter's work is available either in the Faber and Faber collected editions of Pinter or in the same publisher's *Various Voices: Prose, Poetry, Politics, 1948-2005*, London: Faber and Faber, 2005, or subsequent editions.

The Harold Pinter Archive at the British Library [ADDMSS 88880: ff] contains a plethora of Pinter materials. References to specific items in this collection may be found in the footnotes to the present book.

PLAYS AND SKETCHES FOR
THE STAGE, RADIO, AND TELEVISION

Apart From That (2006), unpublished sketch.
Ashes to Ashes. London: Faber and Faber, 1996.
The Basement. BBC2 TV. 1967 (British Library Pinter Archive) in *Tea Party and Other Plays*. London: Methuen, 1967.
Betrayal. London: Eyre Methuen, 1978.
The Birthday Party. London: Methuen, 1963 [first published by Encore Publishing Co Ltd, 1959].
The Black and White (as short story, 1955) in *Sketches from One to Another*. London: Samuel French, 1960. Includes "Trouble in the Works."
The Caretaker. London: Methuen, 1960 [first published Encore Publishing Co Ltd, 1960].
Celebration (1999) in *Celebration* and *The Room*. London: Faber and Faber, 2000.
The Dwarfs in *A Slight Ache and Other Plays*. London: Methuen, 1961.
The Dumb Waiter (1957) in *The Birthday Party and Other Plays*. London: Methuen, 1960.
The Examination (as story in *Prospect* [summer of 1959]: 21–25), also in *Ten of the Best British Short Plays*, ed. Ed Berman. London: Inter-Action, 1979.
Family Voices: A Play for Radio With Seven Paintings by Guy Vaesen. London: Faber and Faber, 1981.
Five Screenplays: The Servant, The Pumpkin Eater, The Quiller Memorandum, Accident, The Go-Between. London: Methuen, 1971.
The Homecoming. London: Methuen, 1965.
Limited edition of *The Homecoming*, designed by the artist Harold Cohen, containing his lithographs accompanying Pinter's text. London: Karnac, Curwen, 1968.
The Hothouse (1958). London: Eyre Methuen, 1980.
Landscape (1967) in *Landscape* and *Silence*. London: Methuen, 1969. Also as BBC Radio Play, April 1968.
The Lover (1962) in *The Collection* and *The Lover*. London: Methuen, 1963.

"Mixed Doubles": [W30 (2) (3)]

monologue. London: Covent Garden Press, 1973. Reprinted in *Plays 4*. London: Eyre Methuen, 1981.

Moonlight. London and Boston: Faber and Faber, 1993.

Mountain Language. London and Boston: Faber and Faber, 1988.

The New World Order (1991) in *Party Time and the New World Order*. New York: Grove Press, 1993.

Night (1969) in *Landscape* and *Silence*. London: Methuen, 1969.

A Night Out (1961) in *A Slight Ache and Other Plays*. London: Methuen, 1961.

Night School (1966) in *Tea Party and Other Plays*. London: Methuen, 1967.

No Man's Land. London: Eyre Methuen, 1975.

One for the Road. London: Methuen, 1984 [a Methuen New Theatrescript].

Other Places: Four Plays. New York: Dramatists Play Service, Inc., 1984.

Other Places: Three Plays. London: Methuen, 1982.

Old Times. London: Methuen, 1971.

Party Time and The New World Order: Two Plays. New York: Harold Pinter Grove Press, 1993.

Precisely (1983) in *The Big One: An Anthology of Original Sketches, Poems, Cartoons and Songs on the Theme of Peace*. Susannah York and Bruce Bachle, ed. London: Methuen, 1984.

Press Conference. London: Faber, 2002.

Remembrance of Things Past, 1972 (adapted by Harold Pinter). London: Faber and Faber, 2000. (with Di Treves).

The Room (1957) in *The Birthday Party and Other Plays*. London: Methuen, 1960.

Silence (1968) in *Landscape and Silence*. London: Methuen, 1969.

"Sketches (I and II)": [W63 (1)]

A Slight Ache (1958) in *A Slight Ache and Other Plays*. London: Methuen, 1961. [A12]

"Something in Common" [W8]

"Special Offer" in A. P. Hinchliffe, *Harold Pinter*. Boston: Twayne Publishers [G. K. Hall], 1967: 73–74 [A25]

Tea Party and Other Plays. London: Methuen, 1967.

"*Tess: A Short Story By Harold Pinter.*" *Tatler*, November 2000: 75–76. Short story performed as a dramatic sketch.

"That's Your Trouble" in *The Dwarfs and Eight Revue Sketches*. [New York] Dramatists Play Service, 1965.

"3 by Harold Pinter." *The Pinter Review*, 1997 and 1998 (Tulsa, FL: Tulsa University Press), 146–50.

Victoria Station (1982) in *Other Places: Three Plays*. London: Methuen, 1982.

[And James Clarke] "Voices." BBC Radio 3, 10 October 2005.

FILM ADAPTATIONS

Some of Pinter's screenplays may be found in the Faber edition of his *Collected Screenplays*, 3 vols. London: Faber and Faber, 2000.

The Caretaker [in US, *The Guest* (1964)] screenplay 1962–1963. Script at British Film Institute.

The Go-Between (1964, 1969) in *Five Screenplays*. London: Methuen, 1971. Also in *Collected Screenplays*, Vol. 2. London: Faber and Faber, 2000.

The Comfort of Strangers and Other Screenplays. London and Boston: Faber and Faber, 1990.

"The Dreaming Child" (1997) [screenplay published but not yet filmed] in *Collected Screenplays*, Vol. 3.

The Dwarfs. Initially screened on BBC 4 in October 2002, in April 2003 at the Tricycle Theatre, Kilburn, an adaptation of Pinter's biographical novel *The Dwarfs*, by Kerry Lee Crabbe. London: Faber and Faber, 2003.

Five Screenplays. London: Methuen, 1971.

The French Lieutenant's Woman (1981) in *The French Lieutenant's Woman and Other Screenplays.* London: Methuen, 1982. Also see *Collected Screenplays*, Vol. 3.

The Go-Between (1964, 1969) in *Five Screenplays.* London: Methuen, 1971. Also in *The Servant and Other Screenplays.* London and Boston: Faber and Faber, 1991.

Heat of the Day. London and Boston: Faber and Faber, 1989. Also in *Collected Screenplays*, Vol. 3.

Langrishe Go Down in *The French Lieutenant's Woman and Other Plays.* London: Methuen, 1982. Also in *Collected Screenplays*, Vol. 1.

The Last Tycoon (1975) in *The French Lieutenant's Woman and Other Plays.* London: Methuen, 1982. Also in *Collected Screenplays*, Vol. 1.

Lolita (1994) [screenplay not used] in the British Library Pinter Archive.

The Proust Screenplay: À la Recherché du Temps Perdu (screenplay not filmed, 1972, published as *The Proust Screenplay* [in collaboration with Joseph Losey and Barbara Bray]. London: Eyre Methuen, 1978).

The Pumpkin Eater (1963) in *Five Screenplays.* London: Methuen, 1971. Also in *Collected Screenplays*, Vol. 1.

The Quiller Memorandum (1966) in *Five Screenplays.* London: Methuen, 1971.

The Remains of the Day [screenplay, mainly not used, not published (1990)] British Library Pinter Archive.

Reunion (1987–1988) in *The Comfort of Strangers and Other Screenplays.* London: Faber and Faber, 1990. Also in *Collected Screenplays*, Vol. 2.

Servant in *Five Screenplays.* London: Methuen, 1971. Also in *Collected Screenplays*, Vol. 1.

Shakespeare's *The Tragedy of King Lear* [2000]. Film adaptation not made, British Library Pinter Archive.

Sleuth (2002–2005). British Library Pinter Archive.

The Trial (1989–1992). London and Boston: Faber and Faber, 1993.

Victory (1982) [unproduced screenplay] in *The Comfort of Strangers and Other Screenplays.* London: Faber and Faber, 1990.

POETRY

Various Voices: Prose, Poetry, Politics, 1948-2005. London: Faber and Faber, 2005. Contains some of Pinter's poetry, referred to below as *VV*.

"American Football (Reflection on the Gulf War)." *BOMB*, XXXVIII (Winter 1992): 82 and *The Pinter Review, V: Annual Essays for 1991.* (1991): 41. In *VV* and *War*.

"Body." *Saturday Guardian* (25 November 2006): 23.

"The Bombs." *Independent* (15 February 2003). In *VV* and *War*.

"Cancer Cells." *Guardian* (14 March 2002), G2: 5. In *VV*.

"Chandeliers and Shadows." *Poetry London* 5 (19 August 1950): 8–10. As Harold Pinta. In *VV*.

"Cricket at Night." *Guardian* (3 June 1995) Guardian Features: 29 [C33]

"Dawn." *Hackney Downs School Magazine* 161 (Spring 1947): 27.

"Death" (Births and Deaths Registration Act, 1953). *Times Literary Supplement* 4932 (10 October 1997): 11. In *VV* and *War*.

"Democracy." *Spectator* (15 April 2003): 13. In *VV* and *War*.

The Disappeared and Other Poems. Images by Tony Bevan. London: Enitharmon Press, 2002. [I11]

"Episode" (1951) in *Poems*, 1968.

"The Error of Alarm" in Kathleen Nott, C. Day Lewis, and Thomas Blackburn's *New Poems 1957.* London: Michael Joseph, 1957. In *VV* [C10].

"Ghost." *Times Literary Supplement* 4205 (4 November 1983): 1204. In *VV*.

"God Bless America." *Guardian* (22 January 2003), G2: 4. In *VV* and *War*.

I *Know the Place*. Warwick: The Greville Press, 1979.

"I Shall Tear off my Terrible Cap." *Poetry Quarterly* 13, 2 (Summer 1951): 59. As Harold Pinta.

"The Irish Shape" [I8].

"The Islands of Aran Seen from the Moher Cliffs" (1951). *Poems*, 1968. In *VV*.

"It is Here 'For A.'" *TLS* 4531 (2–8 February 1990): 113 [C27a].

"Joseph Brearley 1909–1977" in *Soho Square* II (1982): 182. In *VV*.

"Kullus" (1949) in *Poems*. London: Enitharmon Press, 1968.

"Message." *The New Review* 4: 39/40 (June/July 1977): 26 [C18].

"New Year in the Midlands." *Poetry London* 5 (19 August 1950): 8–10. As Harold Pinta. In *VV*.

"O Beloved Maiden." *Hackney Downs School Magazine* 162 (Summer 1947): 14.

"One a Story, Two a Death." *Poetry London* 6: 22 (Summer 1951): 22–23. As Harold Pinta.

"Others of You" [I8].

"Paris" (1975) in *Bananas* 9 (Winter 1977): 35. In *VV*.

"Philip Larkin" *Poetry Review*, LXXII, 2 (June 1982): 5 [prose poem: tribute to Larkin's sixtieth birthday]

"Poem" (1953) ["I walked one morning with my only wife"] [I3a1(i)] in *Poems*, 1968. In *VV*.

Poems. London. Enitharmon Press, 1968.

Poems [second edition with nine added poems]. London: Enitharmon Press, 1971.

Poems by Harold Pinter: Chosen by Antonia Fraser. Warwick: The Greville Press, 2002.

"Requiem for 1945" (1999). *Sunday Times* (13 May 1999, Book Section 4). In *VV*.

"Restaurant" [C26].

"School Life" (1948). In *VV*.

Six Poems for A. (2007). Warwick: The Greville Press, 2007.

"The Special Relationship" (August 2004). *Guardian* (9 September 2004), G2: 4. [C49] In *VV* and *War*.

Ten Early Poems. Warwick: The Greville Press, 1992.

"To My Wife" (June 2004). *Guardian* (22 July 2004), G2: 4. In *VV*.

"A View of the Party" (1958) in *Poems*, 1968.

War. London: Faber, 2003. [I12]

"Weather Forecast." *Guardian* (20 March 2003), G2: 2. In *VV* and *War*.

FICTION

"The Black and White. An Unpublished Text by Harold Pinter." *Flourish* 4 (Summer 1965): 4. "The Royal Shakespeare Club Newspaper." Also in *Transatlantic Review* 21 (Summer 1966): 51–52.

The Dwarfs: A Novel. London: Faber and Faber, 1990. Adapted from the novel as a play by Kerry Lee Crabbe. London: Faber and Faber, 2003.

"Girls." *Sunday Times*, Section 7 (1 October 1995): 8b.

"The Mirror." *Areté* 23 (Summer/Autumn 2007): 59. [prose piece].

ALL OTHER, INCLUDING INTERVIEWS AND EDITIONS OF COLLECTED OR SELECTED WORKS

Ian Smith, compiled and edited. *Pinter in the Theatre*. London: Nick Hern Books, 2005; and Mark Taylor-Batty. *About Pinter: The Playwright and the*

Work. London: Faber and Faber, 2005 contain previously published interviews with Pinter, as does Mel Gussow, *Conversations with Harold Pinter*, London: Nick Hern Books, 1994.

"The American administration is a bloodthirsty wild animal." *Daily Telegraph* (11 December 2002) 24. Speech [E54].

Address to Hull University Congregation, 11 July 1996, on the occasion of being awarded an honorary degree. Text on website: http://www.haroldpinter.org/politics/politics_freedom.shtml (E39).

Ando, Robert. "Ritratto di Harold Pinter." *RAI-SAT*. 1998. [Italian television interview].

"The Art of the Theatre" (interview with Lawrence Bensky). *Paris Review* 39 (Fall 1966): 13–37.

"*Art, Truth and Politics.*" *The Pinter Review: Nobel Prize/Europa Theatre Prize Volume: 2005-2008*. Tampa, FL: University of Tampa Press, 2008: 6–17, University of Turin, 27 November 2002.

Arthur Wellard. London: Villiers, 1981. In *VV*.

[Contribution to] *Authors Take Sides on Vietnam: Two Questions on the War in Vietnam Answered by the Authors of Several Nations*. Cecil Woolf and John Bagguley, eds. London: Owen, 1967: 40 [H3A].

Back cover endorsement, Ralph Pite, Hester Jones, ed. *W. S. Graham: Speaking Toward's You*. Liverpool: Liverpool University Press, 2004.

"Beckett" in *Beckett at Sixty: A Festschrift*, John Calder, ed. London: Calder and Boyars, 1967 [E11].

"Blood Sports." *Hackney Downs School Magazine* 163 (Autumn 1947): 23–24.

Letter "Bush and Blair 'terrorists.'" *Spectator* (30 October 2004): 38 [F54].

Cambridge University Magazine. Programme note to *The Room* and *The Dumb Waiter*, 1956. In Gussow, *Conversations*.

The Catch a Correspondence [introduction by Alan Wilkinson]. Charingworth: Alan Wilkinson, The Evergreen Press, 2003.

Ciment, Michel. "*Reunion*: Harold Pinter Visually Speaking." *Film Comment*, XXV, no. 3 (May–June 1989): 20–22.

Collected Poems and Prose. London: Methuen, 1986. And London and Boston: Faber and Faber, 1991.

[Contribution to "Jimmy"]. *Jimmy. Jonathan Wax*. London: Pendragon, 1984. In *VV*.

Desert Island Discs. 14 June 1965. http//www.bbc.co.uk/radio4/features/desert-island discs/find-a-castaway.

[Pinter and Alan Haydock]. Discussion within the "Options" program on BBC Radio 4, broadcast 15 November 1970. This was recorded at the Mermaid Theatre and relates to the production of Joyce's *Exiles* [J33].

"Filming *The Caretaker*: Harold Pinter and Clive Donner Interviewed by Kenneth Cavander." *Transatlantic Review* 13 (Summer 1963): 17–26.

Pinter, and Andy Bull [final interview]. *Guardian* (27 December 2008). https://www.theguardian.com/culture/2008/dec/26/harold-pinter-final-interview.

"First Draft, *The Homecoming*." *The Pinter Review Collected Essays 1997 and 1998*: [1]–30.

"First Person: Picking a Fight with Uncle Sam." *Guardian* (4 December 1996). Section 2.4 (E40).

"Foreword" to Peter Kennard's *Domesday Book: Photopoem (Critical Image)*. Manchester: Manchester University Press, 1999 [H50].

"Foreword," Simon Gray in *An Unnatural Pursuit*. London: Faber, 1985.

"48 Playwrights in Apartheid Protest." *London Times* (26 June 1963): 12 [Pinter signatory].

"Growth of an Angry Playwright." *The Observer* (16 October 1988): 13 [interview: G61].

Gussow, Mel. "A Conversation (Pause) with Harold Pinter." *New York Times Magazine* (5 December 1971): 115.

———. *Conversations with Harold Pinter*. London: Nick Hern Books, 1994.

[Harold Pinter] In Conversation at the Royal Court Theatre, 20 October 2005. British Library Sound Archives.

"Harold Pinter OM" interview in Brian Johnston, *A Further Slice of Johnners*, Barry Johnston, ed. London: Virgin Books, 2002: 298–307.

"Humanitarian Intervention." *Spokesman* 73 (2001): 47–49. Degree speech to the University of Florence, 10 September 2001 [E50].

"In view of its progress in the last decades, the Film is more promising in its future as an art form than the Theatre." *Hackney Downs School Magazine* 164 (Spring 1948): 12.

Interview on the hostile criticism of Luchino Visconti's production of *Old Times* for the Teatro di Roma in Italy, "Kaleidoscope" program, BBC Radio 4, broadcast 10 May 1973 [J35].

Interview with John Tusa. In "Saturday Review" program, BBC, 28 September 1985: 7.10–8pm [K26].

Interview with Kenneth Tynan, BBC, 19 August 1960. In Gussow, "A Conversation (Pause) with Harold Pinter" in the *New York Times Magazine* (5 December 1971), 53.

Interview with Mercy Appet. On the subject of apartheid in South Africa, within program "Focus on Africa," BBC Overseas Service, recorded 7 May 1965, broadcast 11 May 1965 [J25].

"Introduction" *"Fortune's Fool": The Man Who Taught Harold Pinter: A Life of Joe Brearley*, G. L. Watkins, ed. Aylesbury: Twig Books, 2008: 7–9.

"Introduction." Simon Gray, *Key Plays*. London: Faber, 2002.

"James Joyce." *Hackney Downs School Magazine* 160 (Christmas 1946): 32.

"Just a simple little love story?" *Radio Times*, 16–22 September 1978, 80–83, 85 (Harold Pinter with Judi Dench and David Jones talk to Jack Emery regarding *Langrishe Go Down*).

"Latest Reports from the Stock Exchange" [1953]. *VV*: 82–84.

Letter in response to Edward Bond's "The Roman's and the Establishment's Fig Leaf." *Guardian* (5 November 1980).

"Letter to Peter Wood, Directed of *The Birthday Party*," dated 30 March 1958. *Kenyan Review*, III, no. 3 (Summer 1981): 2–5.

Letter "Scenario for the Bugging of a Home." *Times* (8 January 1997) section 1:17 [F32].

Lyall, Sarah. "Still Pinteresque." *New York Times*, "Arts and Leisure" (October 7, 2007): [1], 16. Contains extracts from discussion with Pinter.

Mac [London]: Emanuel Wax for Pendragon Press, 1968. In *VV*.

"Memories of Cricket." *Daily Telegraph Magazine* (16 May 1969): 25–26. Reprinted in *Cricket '72*, J. A. Bailey and R. J. Roe, eds. London: The Test and County Cricket Board, Lord's Ground, 1972: 26, 28, as "Hutton and the Past."

"The Night and Day of the Imprisoned Writer" [readings]. 4 October 1981.

"A Note on Shakespeare" [prose essay dated 1950]. *Granta* 59 (Autumn 1993): 252–54. In *VV*.

"O Superman." Broadcast for *Opinion*, Channel 4, 31 May 1990. *VV*: 190–200.

[With Ramona Koval]. "On cancer, war and cricket.s . . ." *Guardian* (28 August 2002): Section G2: 2–4.

[On *King Lear*] [film]. *Independent on Sunday* (February 2000). http://www.haroldpinter. org/films/films_kinglear.shtmls.

100 Poems by 100 Poets, selected by Harold Pinter, Geoffrey Godbert, and Anthony Astbury. London: Methuen, Greville Press, 1986.

"Orange Screen Writers Season at the British Library." Harold Pinter interviewed by Peter Florence at the British Library, 9 February 2004. British Library Sound Archives.

"Personal Wonderlands." PEN Discussion (25 November 2003). British Library Sound Archives.

Philip Larkin Poems Selected by Harold Pinter. Warwick: Greville Press, 2002 [H65].

[Pinter on] *The Trial. The Pinter Review* [1992–1993]: 61–62.

"A Play and Its Politics' Conversation between Harold Pinter and Nicholas Hern." In *One for the Road*. London: Methuen, 1985: 7–23.

"Preface" *Pinter in the Theatre*, Ian Smith ed. London: Nick Hern Books, 2005.

Presenter of play: "A Wake for Sam" [i.e., Samuel Beckett], BBC2, broadcast 8 February 1990, 10-15-10.30pm [K 31].

The Proust Screenplay, radio adaptation of (1995). National Sound Archive London.

"The Queen of all the Fairies" [1952?], unpublished autobiographical prose work, British Library Pinter Archive.

"Radical Departures: Harold Talks to Anna Ford." *Listener* 120, no. 3086 (27 October 1988): 5–6. In Smith.

"Realism and Post-Realism in the French Cinema." *Hackney Downs School Magazine* 163 (Autumn 1947): 13.

"Reply to Open Letter By Leonard Russell." *Sunday Times* (14 August 1960): 21.

Silence (August 1970) as a radio drama. British Library BBC Sound Archives.

Speech, "Writing for the Theatre." First published as "Pinter: Between the Lines," *Sunday Times* (4 March 1962): 25. In *VV*.

A Speech of Thanks [David Cohen Award]. London: Faber, 1995.

With Harry Thompson. "Harold Pinter Replies." *New Theatre Magazine* II:2 (January 1961): 8–10.

With Richard Round. "Take Three on *The Go-Between*." *Guardian* (16 March 1971), *Arts Guardian*: 8 [G35].

"Trying to Pin Pinter Down: Interview with Marshall Pugh." *Daily Mail* (7 March 1964): 8.

"Two People in a Room: Playwriting." *The New Yorker* 43 (25 February 1967): 34–36.

University of Turin Speech, 27 November 2002. In *VV*.

Various Voices: Prose, Poetry, Politics, 1948-2005. London: Faber and Faber, 2005.

War. London: Faber and Faber, 2003. http://www.independent.co.uk/arts-entertainment/theatre-dance/features/when-harold-met-ronald-118150.html.

"Writing, Politics, and *Ashes to Ashes*: An Interview With Harold Pinter," with Mireia Aragay and Ramon Simó. *The Pinter Review Annual Essays 1995 and 1996* (1997): [4–15]. http://www.haroldpinter.org.

SECONDARY SOURCES

Writings About Pinter

This listing is restricted to those books and articles mentioned in this study. An excellent guide to the many studies of Pinter is found in Steven H. Gale, *Harold Pinter: An Annotated Bibliography*. Boston: G.K. Hall and Co., 1978. This needs supplementing with Steven H. Gale, *Critical Essays on Harold Pinter*, Boston: G.K. Hall and Co., 1990; Susan Hollis Merritt, *Pinter in Play: Critical Strategies and the Plays of Harold Pinter*, Durham, NC and London: Duke University Press, 1990; and Peter Raby, ed., *The Cambridge Companion to Harold Pinter*, Cambridge: Cambridge University Press, 2001, revised second edition 2009. Merritt provides an indispensable listing of primary and secondary Pinter materials in her "Annual Bibliography" found in *The Pinter Review*, Francis Gillen and Steven H. Gale, eds., Tampa, FL: University of Tampa Press, 1987–2011. There is also a selective listing of recent work about Pinter on the Pinter website at http://www.haroldpinter.org.

Books

Baker, William. *Harold Pinter*. London: Continuum, 2008.

———. *A Harold Pinter Chronology*. Houndmills, Basingstoke, Hants: 2013.

Baker, William and John C. Ross. *Harold Pinter: A Bibliographical History*. London: The British Library and New Castle, DE: Oak Knoll Press, 2005.

Baker, William, and Steven E. Tabachnick. *Harold Pinter*. Edinburgh: Oliver and Boyd, 1973.

Billington, Michael. *Harold Pinter*. New and updated edition. London: Faber and Faber, 2007.

Burkman, Catherine H. *The Dramatic World of Harold Pinter*. Columbus: Ohio State University Press, 1971.

Chiasson, Basil. *The Late Harold Pinter*. Houndmills, Basingstoke, Hants: Palgrave Macmillan, 2017.

Esslin, Martin. *The Peopled Wound: The Work of Harold Pinter*, 1970.

———. *Pinter: A Study of His Plays*. Third and expanded edition. London: Eyre Methuen, 1977.

Fraser, Antonia. *Must You Go? My Life with Harold Pinter*. London: Weidenfeld and Nicolson, 2010.

———. *Our Israeli Diary, 1978. Of That Time, of That Place*. London: Oneworld Publications, 2017.

Gale, Steven. *Butter's Going Up: A Critical Analysis of Harold Pinter's Work*. Durham, NC: Duke University Press, 1977.

———. *Critical Essays on Harold Pinter*. Boston: G.K. Hall and Co., 1990.

———, ed. *The Films of Harold Pinter*. Albany, New York: SUNY Press, 2001.

———. *Harold Pinter: An Annotated Bibliography*. Boston: G.K. Hall and Co., 1978.

———. *Sharp Cut: Harold Pinter's Screenplays and the Artistic Process*. Lexington, KY: University Press of Kentucky, 2003.

Gordon, Lois, ed. *Pinter at Seventy: A Casebook*. London and New York: Routledge, 2001.

Gordon, Robert. *Harold Pinter: The Theatre of Power*. Ann Arbor: University of Michigan Press, 2012.

Gouthier, Brigitte, ed. *Viva Pinter: Harold Pinter's Spirit of Resistance*. Bern: Peter Lang, 2009.

Grimes, Charles. *Harold Pinter's Politics: A Silence Beyond Echo*. Cranberry, NJ: Associated University Press (Fairleigh Dickinson University Press), 2005.

Hayman, Ronald. *Contemporary Playwrights: Harold Pinter*. London: Heinemann, 1976.

Merritt, Susan Hollis. *Pinter in Play: Critical Strategies and the Plays of Harold Pinter*. Durham, NC and London: Duke University Press, 1990.

Page, Malcolm. *File on Pinter*. London: Methuen Drama, 1993.

Raby, Peter, ed. *The Cambridge Companion to Harold Pinter*. Cambridge: Cambridge University Press, 2001. Revised second edition 2009.

Smith, Ian, compiled and edited. *Pinter in the Theatre*. London: Nick Hern Books, 2005.

Taylor-Batty, Mark. *About Pinter: The Playwright and the Work*. London: Faber and Faber, 2005.

Taylor, John Russell. *Anger and After: A Guide to the New British Drama*. London: Methuen, 1962. Harmondsworth, Middlesex: Penguin Books, revised edition 1963.

Thompson, David T. *Pinter The Player's Playwright*. Houndmills, Basingstoke, 1985.

Woolf, Henry. *Barcelona is in Trouble*. Warwick: Greville Press, 2017.

Articles and Reviews

Baker, William. "Harold Pinter's Library." *The Pinter Review Memorial Volume*. Tampa, FL: University of Tampa Press, 2011: 148–55.

Balding, David. *The Daily Telegraph* (9 January 2010): 3. http://www.telegraph.co.uk/culture/culturenews/6956929/Harold-Pinter-love-triangle-David-Balding-tells-of-anger-over-girlfriends-affair.

Ben-Zvi, Linda. "*Monologue*: The Play of Words" in *Pinter at Seventy: A Casebook*, Lois Gordon, ed. London: Routledge, 2001: 81–93.

Billington, Michael. "Familiar Spirits." *Guardian* 7 (July 1976): 8 [Noël Coward's impact on Pinter]. https://www.theguardian.com/stage/2012/feb/26/hay-fever-review; http://www.telegraph.co.uk/culture/theatre/theatre-reviews/9108057/Hay-Fever-Noel-Coward-Theatre-review.html). [comparisons with Pinter]

"Harold Pinter and the Hackney Gang." *Daily Telegraph Magazine* (29 November 2014). https://www.theguardian.com/stage/2014/nov/29/harold-pinter-and-the-hackney-gang.

Obituary of Pinter: https://www.theguardian.com/culture/2008/dec/25/pinter-theatre.

Birmingham Weekly Post, 6 September 1957. Review of production of Arthur Miller, *All My Sons* [HP in].

Bovell, Andrew. "Harold Pinter at the Ivy." *Daily Review* (27 November 2016). https://dailyreview.com.au/xenophobia-and/52522.

Brown, Craig. Review of Hytner [*Balancing Acts*]. *Daily Mail* (29 April 2017). http://www.dailymail.co.uk/home/event/article-4447988/Nicholas-Hytner-Balancing-Acts-review-gossipy-delight.html.

Bryden, Ronald. "Pinter's New Pacemaker." Review of *Old Times*. *The Observer* (6 June 1971): 27.

Review of *The Lover*. *The Observer* (29 November 1970).

Chiasson, Basil. "Pinter's Political Dramas: Staging Neoliberal Discourse and Authoritarianism" in Mark Taylor-Batty, *The Theatre of Harold Pinter*: 249–66.

Darges, Manohla. Review of *Sleuth*. *New York Times* (October 12, 2007): B14

De Jongh, Nicholas. Review of *Remembrance of Things Past*. *Evening Standard* (24 November 2000). Cited http://www.haroldpinter.org.

Derbyshire, Harry. "Pinter as Celebrity" in *The Cambridge Companion to Harold Pinter*, second edition, Peter Raby, ed. Cambridge: Cambridge University Press, 2009, 266–82;

Dickson, Wheeler Winston. "The Eternal Summer of Joseph Losey and Harold Pinter's *Accident*" in Gale, *Films*, 27–37.

Enfield Gazette and Observer (3 January 1958): 14; ibid., 34. Review of production of R. C. Sherriff's *The Telescope* [HP in].

Enfield Gazette and Observer (26 March 1958): 11. Review of production of John Osborne's *Look Back in Anger* [HP in].

Esslin, Martin. "Harold Pinter: From *Moonlight* to *Celebration*." *The Pinter Review 1999 and 2000*: [23]–30.

Joyce's *Exiles*, *Plays and Players*. January 1971 [HP directed].

Fowles, John. "Afterword: Harold Pinter and Cricket" in Peter Raby, ed., *The Cambridge Companion to Harold Pinter*, second edition (2009), 310–12.

Gascoigne, Bamber. Review of *The Birthday Party*, 21 June 1964. http://www.haroldpinter.org/directing/directing_bday.shtml.

Gillen, Francis. "From Chapter Ten of *The Dwarfs* to *Mountain Language*: The Continuity of Harold Pinter." *The Pinter Review* II: i (1988): 1–4.

———. "Between Fluidity and Fixity: Harold Pinter's Novel *The Dwarfs*." *The Pinter Review* (1990): 50–60.

"Isak Dinesen with a Contemporary Social Conscience: Harold Pinter's Film Adaptation of 'The Dreaming Child'" in Gale, *Films*, 147–58.

———. "Pinter at Work: An Introduction to the First Draft of *The Homecoming* and Its Relationship to the Completed Drama." *The Pinter Review Collected Essays 1997 and 1998*: [31]–47.

———. ". . . 'Whatever Light Is Left in the Dark,': Harold Pinter's *Moonlight*." *The Pinter Review Collected Essays, 1992-1993*: 31–37.

Gordon, Robert. "Experimental Drama and the Well-Made Play: Simon Gray and Harold Pinter as Collaborators" in Katherine Burkman, ed., *Simon Gray: A Casebook.* London: Garland, 1992: 3–24.

Hackney Downs School Magazine 162 (Summer 1947), 11. Review of HP in *Macbeth.*

———. 165 (Summer 1948), 16. Review of HP in *Romeo and Juliet.*

Hall Ann C. "*The Disappeared and Other Poems*" [review]. *The Harold Pinter Review* I (2017): 149–51.

———. "Revisiting Pinter's Women: *One For the* Road (1984), *Mountain Language* (1988) and *Party Time* (1991)" in Mark Taylor-Batty, *The Theatre of Harold Pinter* (London: Bloomsbury, 2014): 232–48.

Hall, Peter. "Directing Pinter." *Theatre Quarterly* IV, 16 (November 1974–January 1975): 4–17.

———. "Directing the Plays of Harold Pinter" in *The Cambridge Companion to Harold Pinter*, Peter Raby, ed., second edition. Cambridge: Cambridge University Press, 2009, 160–69.

Hobson, Harold. "Paradise Lost." Review of *Landscape* and *Silence. Sunday Times* (6 July 1969): 52.

———. "The Screw Turns Again." Review of *The Birthday Party. Sunday Times* (25 May 1958).

Hudgins, Christopher. "Harold Pinter's *The Comfort of Strangers*: Fathers and Sons and Other Victims," *Pinter Review: Annual Essays 1995-1996* (1997): 54–72.

———. "Harold Pinter's *Lolita*: 'My Sin, My Soul" in Gale, *Films*: 123–46.

Jones, Alice. "Voices." *The Independent* (7 October 2005). http://www.independent.co.uk/voices.

Jones, David. "Staging Pauses and Silences" in *Viva Pinter: Harold's Pinter's Spirit of Resistance*, ed., Brigitte Gauthier. Bern: Peter Lang, 2009: 43–65.

Knowles, Ronald. "Harold Pinter, Citizen." *The Pinter Review* (1989): 24–33.

"From London: Harold Pinter 1994-95 and 1995-96." *The Pinter Review: Annual Essays 1995 and 1996* 8 (1997): 152–67.

Lin, Qin, and William Baker. "Pinter's Poetry: A Diachronic Analysis." Style 50, no. 2 (2016) 158–71.

Losey, Joseph, on *The Go-Between. Time* (9 August 1971): 45.

Luckhurst, Mary. "Speaking Out: Harold Pinter and Freedom of Expression" in *The Cambridge Companion to Harold Pinter*, second edition, Peter Raby, ed. Cambridge: Cambridge University Press, 2009, 105–120.

Macaulay, Alastair. [*Ashes to Ashes*] *The Financial Times* (27 June 2001). Cited http://www.haroldpinter.org.

———. "Master of the Pause Had an Unmistakeable Sense of Rhythm." *New York Times* (January 9, 2009). http://www.nytimes.com/2009/01/10/arts/dance/10pint.html.

Marks, Louis. "Producing *The Trial: A Personal Memoir*" in Gale, *Films*, 109–121.

Miles, Tim. "Playing cricket shots in my mind: Cricket and the drama of Harold Pinter." *Studies in Theatre and Performance* 31, i (2011), 17–31.

Milne, Drew. "Pinter's Sexual Politics" in *The Cambridge Companion to Harold Pinter*, Peter Raby, ed. Cambridge: Cambridge University Press, 2001, 195–211.

Nightingale, Benedict. "Pinter Stages a Refreshing Return to the Family Business." *Times* (8 September 1993).

O'Toole, Fintan. "Our Own Jacobean." *New York Review of Books* (October 1999): 30, 38

Pennington, Michael. "Harold Pinter as Director" in *The Cambridge Companion to Harold Pinter*, second edition, Peter Raby, ed. Cambridge: Cambridge University Press, 2009, 146–59.

Peter, John, on *Proust. Sunday Times* (3 December 2000, "Reviews"): 19.

Powell, Dilys. Review of *Accident. Sunday Times*. Cited http://www.haroldpinter.org/films/films_accident.shtml.

"Profile: Playwright on his own." *The Observer* (15 September 1963): 13.

Roth, Tim, on *King Lear* adaptation. *Independent on Sunday* (6 February 2000): 10.

Rosselli, John. "Between Farce and Madness." Review of *The Caretaker*. *Manchester Guardian* (29 April 1960): 13.

Shuttleworth, Martin. Review of *The Collection*. *The Listener* (21 June 1962).

Sierks, Aleks. Review of *The Birthday Party*. *New Statesman* (11 March 1994): 34–35.

Silverstein, Marc. "'Talking about Some Kind of Atrocity': *Ashes to Ashes* in Barcelona." *Pinter Review* [1997 and 1998]: 74–85.

Spencer, Charles. "Pinter's Prescient Missing Link." Review of the National Theatre revival of *The Hothouse*. *The Daily Telegraph* (19 July 2007). http://www.telegraph.co. uk.

———. [Review of Simon Gray's *Life Support* directed by Pinter]. *Daily Telegraph* 7 (August 1977).

Supple, Barry. "Pinter's Homecoming." *Jewish Chronicle* (25 June 1965): 7, 31.

Taylor, John Russell. Review of *The Dwarfs* [as a drama] *Plays and Players*. November 1963.

Taylor, Paul. Review of Simon Gray's *Enter a Fox*. *The Independent* [directed by HP]. Cited http://www.simongray.org.uk.

Taylor-Batty, Mark. "Harold Pinter Directing." http://www.haroldpinter.org/direct ing/directing_lover.shtml.

Thomas, Inigo. http://www.lrb.co.uk/blog/2017/01/20/inigo-thomas/pinters-american-football/.

Thomson, Peter. "What's in a name? Cricket in *No Man's Land*." *Studies in Theatre and Performance* 31, i (2011) 5–15.

Tynan, Kenneth. Review of *The Birthday Party*. *The Observer* (25 May 1958): 15

———. "A Verbal Wizard in the Suburbs." Review of *The Caretaker*. *The Observer* (5 June 1960): 16.

Walker, Alexander. Review of *The Go-Between*. *Evening Standard*. Cited http://www. haroldpinter.org/films/films_gobetween.shtml.

Woolf, Henry. "My Sixty Years in Harold's Gang." *Guardian* (12 July 2007), G2: 23–25.

General Works

Abse, Dannie.*Goodbye, Twentieth Century: An Autobiography*. London: Hutchinson 2001

———. ed. *Poetry and Poverty*. London: [D.Abse] [1949–1954]

———. *Verse* . London: Deacon Press, 1947.

Acherson, Neal. "Which le Carré Do You Want?" A review of his biography and autobiography. *New York Review of Books* 63 (5) October 13, 2016: 20–22.

Archibald, William. *The Innocents*. New York: Coward-McCann, 1950.

Atwood, Margaret. *The Handmaid's Tale*. London: Cape, 1986.

Baker, William. 'Litvinoff, Emanuel (1915–2011).' *Oxford Dictionary of National Biography*, Oxford University Press, Jan 2015. http://www.oxforddnb.com/view/article/ 104147.

Bailey, Paul. 'Crisp, Quentin (1908–1999).' *Oxford Dictionary of National Biography*, Oxford University Press, 2004. http://www.oxforddnb.com/view/article/73162.

Bakewell, Joan. *The Centre of the Bed*. London: Hodder and Stoughton, 2003.

———. *Keeping in Touch* (drama). Premiere BBC Radio 4, April 22, 2017.

———. "One Women's Week." *Sunday Times* (15 June 1975): 28.

Barker, George. *Selected Poems*. Robert Fraser, ed. London: Faber, 1995.

Baron, Alexander. *With Hope, Farewell*. London: Jonathan Cape, 1952.

Beckett, Samuel. *All That Fall*. London: Faber, 1957.

———. *Endgame*. London: Faber, 1958.

———. *Krapp's Last and Embers*. London: Faber, 1959.

———. *The Letters of Samuel Beckett*. George Craig, Martha Dow Fehsenfeld, Dan Gunn and Lois More Overbeck, eds. 4 vols. Cambridge: Cambridge University Press: 2009–2016.

———. *Malone meurt*. Paris: Les Éditions de Minuit, 1951.

———. *Mercier et Camier*. Paris: Les Éditions de Minuit, 1970.

———. *Murphy*. London: Routledge, 1938.

———. *The Unnamable*. New York: Grove Press, 1958.

———. *Waiting for Godot*. London: Faber and Faber, 1956.

———. *Watt*. Extracts: *Envoy* (Dublin January 1950); Poetry Ireland, David Marcus, ed. (Dublin 1951). Paris: Olympia Press, 1953.

Benedick, Adam. Obituary "Margaret Rawlings." http://www.independent.co.uk/news/people/obituary-margaret-rawlings-1335400.html.

Billington, Michael. "Ashcroft, Dame Edith Margaret Emily [Peggy] (1907–1991)." *Oxford Dictionary of National Biography*, Oxford University Press, 2004; online edition, January 2010, http://www.oxforddnb.com/view/article/39440, accessed 10 July 2017.

Bloomfield, B. C. *Philip Larkin: A Bibliography 1933-1994*. London: British Library and New Castle, DE, 2002.

Bond, Edward. *Bingo: Scenes of Money and Death*. London: Eyre Methuen, 1974.

———. "The Roman's and the Establishment's Fig Leaf." *Guardian* (3 November 1980).

Booth, James. *Philip Larkin Life, Art and Love*. New York: Bloomsbury Press, 2014.

Bowen, Elizabeth. *The Heat of the Day*. London: Jonathan Cape, 1949.

Brecht, Bertolt. *The Mother* (1930–1931) *Die Mutter, Versuche*, Heft 7 (1933). London: Methuen, 1978.

Brenton, Howard. *The Romans in Britain*. London: Methuen, 1980.

Brookes, Christopher. *English Cricket: The Game and Its Players through the Ages*. Newton Abbott: Readers Union, 1978.

———. *His Own Man: The Life of Neville Cardus*. London: Methuen, 1985.

Brown, Georgia. Review of Simon Gray's *Enter a Fox*. *The Mail on Sunday*. Cited http://www.simongray.org.uk.

Campbell, James. "Miller's Fail." *TLS*, 3 June 2016:4. http://www.the-tls.co.uk/articles/public/millers-fail/.

Candos, Barbara. *Beautifully Kept*. New York: Warner Books, 1976.

———. *Hard Candy: A True Story of Riches, Fame and Heartbreak*. New York: Morrow, 1988.

Carroll, Lewis. *Alice's Adventures in Wonderland*. London: Macmillan, 1865.

Cary, Joyce. *The Horse's Mouth*. London: Michael Joseph, 1944.

Casey, John. *After Lives: A Guide to Heaven, Hell and Purgatory*. Oxford: Oxford University Press, 2010.

———. "Language, Sincerity and the Self." British Academy Chatterton Lecture, 19 May 1977.

———. *The Language of Criticism*. London: Methuen, 1966, reissued 2011.

———. *Morality and Moral Reasoning*. London: Methuen, 1971.

———. *Pagan Virtue: An Essay in Ethics*. Oxford: Clarendon, 1991.

Chalke, Stephen, with illustrations by Ken Taylor. *Runs in the Memory: County Cricket in the 1950s*. Bath: Fairfield Books, 1997.

Christie, Agatha. *Witness for the Prosecution and Other Stories*. London and New York: Dodd Mead, 1948.

Codron, Michael, and Alan Strachan. *Putting It On: The West End Theatre of Michael Codron*. London: Duckworth: Overlook, 2010.

Conrad, Joseph. *Victory*. New York: Doubleday and Co., 1915.

Coward, Noël. *Ace of Clubs*. London: Warner/Chappell, 1950.

———. *Blithe Spirit*. London: Heinemann, 1942.

———. *Hay Fever*. Ernest Benn, 1925.

———. *Sigh No More*. London: Novello, 1945.

———. *South Sea Bubble*. London: Heinemann, 1951.

Davis, Barbara. "Why Is the Thinking Man's Crumpet So Proud of Being A Husband Stealer? As Joan Bakewell Uses Her Harold Pinter Affair to Plug A New Book, How Women Flaunt The Betrayals Which Tear Families Apart." *Daily Mail* (October 26, 2016). http://www.dailymail.co.uk/news/article-3434502/Why-thinking-man-s-crumpet-proud-husband-stealer-Joan-Bakewell-uses-Harold-Pinter-affair-plug-new-

book-women-flaunt-betrayals-tear-families-apart.
html%20Accessed%2026%20October%202016.

Dickens, Charles. *Dombey and Son*. London: Bradbury and Evans, 1848.

Dimond, Guy [restaurant review: The Ivy]. *Time Out* (17 June 2015). http://www.
timeout.com/london/restaurants/the-ivy posted 17 June 2015.

Dinesen, Isak (Karen Blixen-Finecke). *The Dreaming Child*. New York: Random House,
1942.

Dudley-Smith, Trevor [Elleston Trevor]. *The Berlin Memorandum*. London: Collins,
1965.

East, Robert. *Incident at Tulse Hill*. Playscript 1981. BLMss MPS 1450

Fitzgerald, F. Scott. *The Last Tycoon*. New York: Charles Scribner's, 1941.

Fowles, John. *The French Lieutenant's Woman*. London: Jonathan Cape, 1969.

Fraser, Antonia. *Desert Island Discs* 2 June 1969, 27 July 2008. http//www.bbc.co.uk/
radio4/features/desert-island discs/find-a-castaway.

———. *Charles II and the Restoration: His Life and Times*. London: Weidenfeld and Nicolson, 1993.

———. *The Gunpowder Plot: Terror and Faith in 1605*. London: Weidenfeld and Nicolson
Jemima Shore series [BBC TV].

———. *King Charles II*. London: Weidenfeld and Nicolson, 1979.

———. *Mary Queen of Scots*. London: Weidenfeld and Nicolson, 969.

———. *My History: A Memoir of Growing Up*. London: Weidenfeld and Nicolson, 2015.

———. *Perilous Question: the Drama of the Great Reform Bill 1832*. London: Weidenfeld
and Nicolson, 2015.

———. *The Weaker Vessel: Woman's Lot in Seventeenth-Century England*. London: Weidenfeld and Nicolson, 1984.

Gaur, Albertine. "Remembering David Goldstein (1933–1987)." *British Library Journal*,
1989: 6–15. http://www.bl.uk/eblj/1989articles/pdf/article1.pdf%20accessed%2027%
20November%202016.

Goldstein, David, ed. Translated. *Hebrew Poems from Spain*. London: Routledge and
Kegan Paul, 1969.

———. *The Jewish Poets of Spain 900-1250*. Harmondworth: Penguin Books, 1971.

Goncharov, Ivan. *Oblomov*. Translated David Magarshack. Harmondsworth, Middlesex: Penguin Books, 1954.

Graham, W. S. *Collected Poems 1942-1977*. London: Faber, 1979.

———. *The Nightfisherman: Selected Letters*. Michael and Margaret Snow, eds. Manchester: Carcanet, 2012.

"Graveney, Tom" [obituary]. *The Daily Telegraph* (3 November 2015).

Gray, Simon. *An Unnatural Pursuit*. Forward H. Pinter. London: Faber, 1985.

———. *Butley*. London: Eyre Methuen, 1971.

———. *Cell Mates [Fate Chance]*. London: Faber, 1995.

———. *Enter a Fox: Further Adventures of a Paranoid*. London: Faber, 2001.

———. *The Holy Terror [Melon Revised]*. In Gray Four Plays. London: Faber, 2004.

———. *The Last Cigarette: Smoking Diaries Volume 3*. London: Granta Books, 2008.

———. *Life Support*. London: Faber, 1995.

———. *The Old Masters*. London: Faber, 2006.

———. *Otherwise Engaged*. London: Methuen, 1986.

———. *Quartermaine's Terms*. London: Eyre Methuen, 1981.

———. *The Rear Column*. London: Eyre Methuen, 1978.

———. *Simon Gray: Plays 3*. London: Faber, 2010.

———. *The Smoking Diaries*. London: Granta Books, 2004.

———. *The Year of the Jouncer*. London: Granta Books, 2006. http://www.simongray.
org.uk.

Greene, R. et al. *The Princeton Encyclopedia of Poetry and Poetics*, fourth edition. Princeton: Princeton University Press, 2012.

Greenspan, Louis. "The Early Simon [Gray]: the Canada Years." *Critical Quarterly* 52, I
(April 2010): 9–16.

Gunn, Dan. "Bray, Barbara (1924–2010)." *Oxford Dictionary of National Biography*, Oxford University Press, January 2014. http://www.oxforddnb.com/view/article/102546.

Gutteridge, Peter. *The Independent* (26 January 1996). http://www.independent.co.uk/life-style/those-choice-words-that-say-i-hate-you-1325795.html.

Hartley, L. P. *The Go-Between*. London: Hamish Hamilton, 1953; Harmondsworth, Middlesex: Penguin Books, 1965.

Hall, Adam. *The Berlin Memorandum*. London: Collins, 1965.

Hall, Peter. *Diaries*. John Goodwin, ed. London: Hamish Hamilton, 1983.

Halliday, Nigel Vaux. *More than a Bookshop: Zwemmers and Art in the Twentieth Century*. London: Philip Wilson Publishers, 2001.

Harwood, Ronald. *Sir Donald Wolfit: His Life and Work in the Unfashionable Theatre*. London: Amber Lane, 1983.

———. *Taking Sides*. London: Faber and Faber, 1995.

Hertz, J. H., ed., *The Pentateuch and Haftorahs Hebrew Text English Translation and Commentary*. London: Soncino Press, 1936 etc.

Hibbert, Ryan. "Philip Larkin, British Culture and [the] Four Letter Word." *Critical Quarterly* 43 no. 2 (June 2014): 120–38.

Higgins, Aidan. *Helsingør Station and Other Departures: Fictions and Autobiographies, 1956-1989*. London Secker and Warburg, 1989.

———. *Langrishe Go Down*. London: John Calder, 1966.

Hoban, Russell. *Turtle Diary*. London: Cape, 1975.

Hopkins, Gerard Manley. "The Wreck of the Deutschland." See *The Later Poetic Manuscripts of Gerard Manley Hopkins in Facsimile*. Norman H. MacKenzie, ed (New York and London: Garland Publishing), 1991.

Hotten, Jon. *The Meaning of Cricket*. London: Vintage: Penguin/Random House, 2016.

Hussey, [Sister] Pamela. *Free from Fear: Women in El Salvador's Church*. London: Catholic Institute for International Relations, 1990.

Hutton, Leonard. *Cricket is My Life*. London: Hutchinson, 1954.

Huxley, Aldous. *Mortal Coils*. London: Chatto and Windus, 1922.

Hytner, Sir Nicholas. *Balancing Acts: Behind the Scenes of the National Theatre*. London: Jonathan Cape, 2017.

Ishiguro, Kazuo. *The Remains of the Day*. London: Faber and Faber, 1989.

James, Henry. *The Turn of the Screw*. London: Heineman, 1898.

Jeffrey, Ewan. Eileen Diss Interview, http://sounds.bl.uk/related-content/TRANSCRIPTS/024T-1CDR0032289X-0100A0.pdfhttp://sounds.bl.uk Theatre Archive Project.

Jones, Inigo. "Beware Bouncers." *LRB* (blog), 27 November 2014.

Josipovici, Gabriel. *The World and the Book. A Study of Modern Fiction*. London: MacMillan; Stanford: Stanford University Press, 1971.

Joyce, James. *Exiles*. London: Grant Richards Ltd., 1918.

———. *Finnegan's Wake*. London: Faber and Faber, 1939.

———. *Portrait of an Artist as a Young Man*. London: The Egoist Ltd., 1917.

———. *Ulysses*. Paris: Shakespeare and Co., 1921.

Kafka, Franz. *The Trial*. [London: Secker and Warburg (1937?)].

Kauffmann, Stanley, and Bruce Henstell, eds. *American Film Criticism: From the Beginnings to "Citizen Kane"; Reviews of Significant Films at the Time They First Appeared*. New York: Liveright, 1972.

Larkin, Philip. *The Complete Poems Philip Larkin*. Archie Burnett, ed. New York: Farrar, Strauss and Giroux: 2012.

——— ed. *The Oxford Book of Twentieth Century English Verse*. Oxford: Clarendon Press, 1973.

———. *High Windows*. London: Faber, 1974.

———. *The Less Deceived*. Hull: The Marvell Press, 1955.

———. "Not the Place's Fault." [Prose] *Umbrella* I, 3 [Spring 1959], [107]–12.

Philip Larkin Letters to Monica. Anthony Thwaite, ed. Faber and Faber: Bodleian Library Oxford, 2010.

———. *The Selected Letters of Philip Larkin 1940-1985*. Anthony Thwaite, ed. London: Faber 1999.

———. *XX Poems*. Belfast: [Carswells]. Privately printed for the author, 1951.

———.*The Whitsun Weddings*. London: Faber, 1964.

Litvinoff, Emanuel. *Journey Through a Small Planet*. London: Michael Joseph, 1972. With an Introduction by Patrick Wright. London: Penguin Books [Penguin Modern Classics], 2008. [Contains "To T.S. Eliot": 194–95]

McEwen, Ian. *The Comfort of Strangers*. New York: Simon and Schuster, 1981.

Mamet, David. *Oleanna*. New York: Pantheon Books, 1992.

Maugham, Robin. *The Servant*. London: Falcon Press, 1948, republished London: Heineman, 1964.

Millar, Ronald. *Waiting for Gillian: A Play in Three Acts* from the novel *A Way Through the Woods* by Nigel Balchin. London: S. French, 1954.

Miller, Henry. *Black Spring*. Paris: Obelisk Press, 1936.

———. *Tropic of Capricorn*. Paris: Obelisk Press, 1939.

Mortimer, Penelope [interview]. *The Daily Telegraph* (3 September 1971): 11.

———. *The Pumpkin Eater*. London: Hutchinson, 1962.

Mosley, Nicholas. *Accident*. London: Hodder and Stoughton, 1965.

———. *Efforts at Truth*. London: Secker and Warburg, 1994.

Murphy, R. E., *T.S. Eliot: A Literary Reference to His Life and Work*. New York: Facts on File, 2007.

Nabokov, Vladimir. *Lolita*. Paris: Olympia Press, 1955.

Nadel, Ira. *Double Act: A Life of Tom Stoppard*. London: Methuen 2002.

Nairn, Ian. *Nairn's London*. Harmondsworth, Middlesex: Penguin Books, 1966.

O'Connor, Joanne. "This much I know," interview with Joan Bakewell. *Guardian* (8 October 2016). https://www.theguardian.com/lifeandstyle/2016/oct/08/joan-bakewell-this-much-i-know-thinking-mans-crumpet-not-insulting.

O'Brien, Edna. *Country Girl* . London: Faber, 2012.

———. *The Country Girls* . 1960.

———. *A Pagan Place* [drama]. London: Faber, 1973.

———. *Virginia* [drama]. London: Hogarth Press, 1981.

Orwell, George. *Inside the Whale and Other Essays*. London: Gollancz, 1940.

Peterson, William S. *John Betjeman: A Bibliography*. Oxford: Clarendon Press, 2006.

Proust, Marcel. *A la recherché des temps perdu* [1913]. Translated C. K. Scott Moncrieff and Andreas Mayor. 12 vols. London: Chatto and Windus, [1922–1931].

Rattigan, Terence. *Separate Tables*. London: Hamilton, 1955.

Rimbaud, Arthur. *Une Saison en enfer. Une saison en Enfer = A season in Hell; Les illuminations = The illuminations / Arthur Rimbaud; a new translation by Enid Rhodes Peschel*. New York and London: Oxford University Press, 1973.

Rodger, N.A.M. "Grieve Not, but Try Again." Review of P. Hennessy and J. Jinks's *The Silent Deep: The Royal Navy Submarine Service Since 1945*. London: Allen Lane, 2016. *London Review of Books* 38 (18) (22 September 2016): 21–22.

Rose, Reginald. *Twelve Angry Men*. Chicago: Dramatic Publishing Co., 1955.

Rushdie, Salman. *Midnight's Children*. London: Jonathan Cape, 1981.

———. *The Satanic Verses*. London: Penguin/Random House, 1988.

Sacks, Oliver. *Awakenings*. New York: Harper Perennial, 1973, 1990.

Salvador Dali and Luis Buñuel's 1924 silent film, *Un Chien Andalou*.

Schiller, Friedrich. *Mary Stuart*. Translated Jeremy Sams. London: Royal National Theatre and Nick Hern,1996.

Sereny, Gitta, *Biography of Albert Speer*. New York: Knopf, 1995.

Shaffer, Anthony. *Sleuth*. London: Calder and Boyars, 1971.

Shakespeare's *The Tragedy of King Lear* [c. 1605].

Shakespeare, William. *The New Temple Edition*. M. R. Ridley, ed., illustrations after Eric Gill. London: J. M. Dent, [1943]–[1958].

———. *The Riverside Shakespeare*. C. Blakemore Evans et al., eds. Boston: Houghton Mifflin, 1974.

Shaw, Robert. *The Man in the Glass Booth*. New York, Harcourt, Brace and World, 1967.

Shellard, Dominic, Steve Nicholson, and Miriam Handley. *The Lord Chamberlain Regrets . . . A History of British Theatre Censorship*. London: The British Library, 2004.

Sherriff, R. C. *Journey's End*. New York: Brentano's, 1930.

Shorter, Eric. :https://www.theguardian.com/stage/2011/oct/17/denis-cannan-obituary, accessed 17 June 2017.

Sinclair, Andrew. *Spiegel: The Man Behind the Pictures*. London: Weidenfeld and Nicolson, 1987

Sinyard, Neil. *Jack Clayton* . Manchester: Manchester University Press, 2000 .

Smurthwaite, Nick. [interview with Elieen Diss]. *The Stage* (21 May 2015). https://www.thestage.co.uk/features/interviews/2015/eileen-diss-50-years-set-design/.

Stamm, Ramona Kelley. "Joyce Cary's Onomastic 'Orchestration,': Name, Symbol and Theme in *The Horse's Mouth*." *Literary Onomastics Studies* 15 (1988). http://digitalcommons.brockport.edu/cgi/viewcontent.cgi?article=1019andcontext=los.

Stanford, Peter. "Mystery at the Heart of Life and Death." *The Tablet* (January 10, 2009): 6–7.

———. *The Outcasts Outcast: A Biography of Lord Longford*. Stroud, Gloucestershire: Sutton Publishing, 2003.

Stoppard, Tom. *The Coast of Utopia: Voyage, Shipwreck, Salvage*. London: Faber, 2008.

———. *Rock 'n' Roll*. London: Faber, 2006.

———. *Voyage The Coast of Utopia, Part I*. London: Faber, 2002.

Stothard, Peter. Review of A Fraser *My History*, TLS July 10, 2015: 21.

Timerman, Jacobo. *Prisoner Without a Name, Cell Without a Number*. Translated from the Spanish by Toby Talbot. New York: Alfred A. Knopf, 1981.

Uhlman, Fred. *Reunion*. New York: Farrar, Straus and Giroux, 1977.

Vendler, Helen. *Our Secret Discipline: Yeats and Lyric Form*. Harvard, MA: Harvard University Press: 2007.

Vosper, Frank and Agatha Christie, *Love From a Stranger* (based on "Philomel Cottage"). London: William Collins, 1936.

Wales, Katie. *The Language of James Joyce*. Houndmills, Basingstoke, Hants: Macmillan, 1992.

Wheatcroft, Geoffrey. "Tony Blair's Eternal Shame": The Report.," Review of the Chilcot Report into the Iraq War. *New York Review of Books* 63, no. 5 (October 13, 2016): 42–44).

White, Patrick. *Voss*. New York: Viking, 1957.

WEBSITES

Pasolini's *Teorema*. Wikipedia. https://en.wikipedia.org/wiki/Teorema_(film).

2 November 2011: http://www.telegraph.co.uk/news/obituaries/culture-obituaries/theatre-obituaries/8865604/Denis-Cannan.html.

https://en.wikipedia.org/wiki/Philip_King_(playwright); and Doolee.com, http://www.doollee.com/PlaywrightsK/king-philip.html.

"Pacifism." Wikipedia. https://en.wikipedia.org/wiki/Pacifism.

Index of Works by Pinter

AUDIO-VISUAL MATERIALS

"Oh Superman." Television Talk, for
 Opinions' Series, 164
Participant in: "Late Night Line-Up,"
 111; "A Wake for Sam" BBC2, 202

FICTION

"The Black and White," 131
The Dwarfs, xi, 4, 9, 13, 22, 69, 78–79, 80,
 82, 121, 132, 188
"The Examination," 11, 131
"Girls," 191
"Latest Reports from the Stock
 Exchange," 83

INTERVIEWS, PRINTED IN
NEWSPAPERS OR MAGAZINES

"The Art of the Theatre III: Harold
 Pinter: An Interview" (L. M.
 Bensky), 68, 150, 151
"A Conversation [Pause] with Harold
 Pinter" (with M. Gussow), 157
"Harold Pinter Replies" (H.
 Thompson), 206
"[Interview with Nick Hern]," 145, 146
"[Interview] in Ian Smith, ed.," Pinter
 in the Theatre, 147
"Mystery at the Heart of Life and
 Death" (P. Stanford), 176–177
"On Cancer, War and Cricket" (R.
 Koval), 59–60
"The Oval, 25 August 1990" (B.
 Johnston), 50
"Pinter on Pinter: The Lincoln Center
 Interviews" (M. Gussow), 189

"Radical Departures: Harold Talks to
 Anna Ford," 150, 158

MISCELLANEOUS: MINOR
PIECES, COLLABORATIVE
WRITINGS, EDITING, ETC.

Authors Take Sides on Vietnam
 (contribution), 150
The Catch (A. Wilkinson), 47, 54, 219
[Endorsement to R. Pite and H. Jones
 ed., W. S. Graham Speaking Toward
 You], 212
"Foreword by Harold Pinter" (P.
 Kennard, Doomsday Book), 173
"Foreword" An Unnatural Pursuit (S.
 Gray), 92
"Humanitarian Intervention," (degree
 speech University of Florence),
 173–174
100 Poems by 100 Poets, 208
"Philip Larkin" (prose poem), 217
"Remarks on Common Market"
 (Encounter), 150
Various Voices, 11, 56, 79, 83, 103, 147,
 172, 173, 174, 189, 191–192, 194, 200,
 202, 203, 204, 207
War, 172, 220

PLAYS AND SKETCHES FOR
THE STAGE, RADIO, AND
TELEVISION

Ashes to Ashes, 21, 56, 71, 89, 102, 115,
 120, 123, 137, 152, 166, 167–168
The Basement, 11, 18, 123, 124, 139
Betrayal, x, 19–20, 38–39, 65, 79, 87, 96,
 105, 111, 115–117, 120, 123, 125, 176,

197, 209, 210

The Birthday Party, xi, 4, 5, 10, 12, 14, 15, 16, 17, 18, 27, 28, 30, 36, 56, 61, 65, 67, 105, 109, 119, 134, 137, 147–148, 149–150, 180, 203, 207

The Birthday Party and Other Plays, 134

The Caretaker, xi, 5, 9, 17, 21, 36, 55, 88, 120, 125, 134, 150, 152, 175, 177, 202, 203, 207, 225

The Caretaker and The Dumb Waiter, 134

Celebration, xi, 77–78, 89–90, 102, 109, 120, 123, 124–125, 169–170

The Collection, 27, 33, 35, 88, 132, 137

Dialogue for Three, 19

The Dumb Waiter, 11, 15, 27, 78, 106, 148–150, 207

The Dwarfs, 18, 28, 115, 119, 177

The Examination, 115

Family Voices, 20, 113, 114, 155, 175, 186, 210, 216

The Homecoming, 2, 6, 9, 12, 17, 19, 21, 28, 31, 36, 77, 88, 132, 135, 141, 147, 150, 166, 186, 199, 207, 209, 215

The Hothouse, 17, 20, 27, 95, 99, 119, 136, 138, 149–150, 210, 213

A Kind of Alaska, 20, 62, 105, 155, 210

Landscape, 38, 62, 113, 114, 203, 214

Landscape and Silence, 134

The Lover, 18, 28, 132, 135, 137

monologue, 18–19, 21, 22, 57, 65, 66, 85, 191, 200, 201, 215, 226

Moonlight, 53, 87, 103, 139, 166, 197, 226

Mountain Language, 21, 101, 114, 146, 149, 154, 158, 162, 168

A Night Out, 119, 132

No Man's Land, 7, 8, 31, 36–37, 61, 83, 102, 104, 106, 128, 137, 139, 150, 166, 180, 199, 220

Old Times, 17, 34, 37, 91, 107–108, 119, 133, 135, 150, 158, 175, 189, 196–197, 200, 206, 216

One for the Road, 106, 114, 145, 146, 154, 156–157, 158, 218

Other Places: Three Plays, 20, 27, 82, 105, 155

Other Places: Four Plays, 82

Party Time, 21, 87, 166

Precisely, 156

Press Conference, 107, 170

Proust: Remembrance of Things Past (with Di Trevis), 35, 38, 98, 105, 132, 199

Review Sketches, 115

The Room, 13, 13–14, 15, 64, 66, 80, 102, 119, 124, 125, 132, 169, 205, 207

The Room and The Dumb Waiter, 134

Silence, 206

A Slight Ache, 19, 91, 105, 119, 132, 133, 150

A Slight Ache and Other Plays, 134

Tea Party, 5, 115, 123, 124, 125, 132, 137, 139

Victoria Station, 20, 155, 156, 210

POETRY

Collections

The Disappeared and Other Poems, 186

I Know the Place, 209

Poems (1968), 13, 82

Poems By Harold Pinter: Chosen by Antonia Fraser, 137

Poems, Second Edition, 82

Published Shorter Poems

"American Football—(A Reflection on the Gulf War)," 172–173

"The Bombs," 172

"Cancer Cells," 102

"Chandeliers and Shadows," 192

"Cricket at Night," 56

"Daylight," 13

"Death," 89, 175, 180, 216, 219

"Democracy," 172

"Episode," 194

"The Error of Alarm," 11

"Ghost," 219

"God Bless America," 172

"The Irish Shape," 194

"I Know the Place," 209

"The Islands of Aran Seen from the Moher Cliffs," 194, 200

"It Is Here," 129, 203

"Joseph Brearley 1909–1977," 3

"Kullus" (prose poem), 11

"Message," 207
"New Year in the Midlands," 79, 88
"Old Man at a Cricket Match," 48
"Others of You," 194
"Paris," 103, 175
"Poem" (Hutton), 50
"Poem: I walked one morning with my
only wife," 194
"Restaurant," 90
"School Life," 81
"The Special Relationship," 102, 172
"To My Wife," 102, 131

PROSE NONFICTION: ESSAYS,
ARTICLES, PUBLISHED
SPEECHES

Address to Hull University
congregation, 170
"The American administration is a
bloodthirsty wild animal"
(University of Turin), 174
"American Foreign Policy if it Never
Happened," (Opinion: Picking a
Fight with the Bulldog of the West)
(First Person: Picking a Fight with
Uncle Sam) (Commentary: Land of
the Free? It Never Happened), 171
"Art Truth & Politics," ix, 98, 175
"Arthur Wellard (1902–1980):
Somerset, England and Gaieties,"
58, 218
"Beckett," 202
Fortunes Fool, 2
"Introduction to Simon Gray's Plays,"
92
"In View of its progress . . . Film is
more promising . . . Theatre," 22
"James Joyce," 195
Jimmy [contribution], 17, 121
"The Knight has been Unruly —
Memories of Sir Donald Wolfit," 9
Larkin Poems, 220
"Mac," 193
"Memories of Cricket" ("Hutton and
the Past"), 48, 49, 52, 61, 215
"A Note on Shakespeare," 189, 202,
220, 226

"On *Waiting for Godot*," 204
"Preface" *Pinter in the Theatre*, ed. Ian
Smith, 26–27
"Realism and post-realism in the
French cinema," 22
"A Speech of Thanks" (Receipt of
David Cohen Award), 88

PUBLISHED LETTERS TO
NEWSPAPERS, MAGAZINES,
ETC.

"[Bond on Beckett]" (letter), 165
"[Brenton, *The Romans in Britain*]"
(letter), 165
"Bush and Blair 'terrorists'" (letter),
174
"Scenario for the Bugging of a Home,"
171

SCREENPLAYS AND
ADAPTATIONS

Accident, 23–24, 132, 153
Betrayal, 123, 153
The Caretaker (*The Guest*), 5, 18, 34
The Comfort of Strangers, 161
The Compartment, 18
Five Screenplays, 25
The French Lieutenant's Woman, 1, 20,
62, 63, 120, 152–153, 210
The Go-Between, 4, 24–25, 152–153
The Handmaid's Tale, 62, 163
The Heat of the Day, 160
King Lear, 170, 190
The Last Tycoon, 152, 153, 176
The Pumpkin Eater, 85
The Quiller Memorandum (*The Berlin
Memorandum*), 6, 61, 151, 152
The Proust Screenplay, 98, 105, 115,
119–120, 197–199, 207
Reunion, 123, 152, 158–159
The Servant, 5, 34, 61, 151
Sleuth, 67, 137, 197
The Trial, 21, 95, 162, 163, 203
Turtle Diary, 158
Victory, 155

SOUND ITEMS

Desert Island Discs, *Castaway*, 69
Interview: Luchino Visconti
    production of *Old Times*, 215
Interview with Andy Bull, 68
Interview with Brian Johnston, 50
Interview with Mercy Appet, 151
Interview with Ramona Koval, 59–60,
    176
"The Night of the Day of the
    Imprisoned Writer," 154
"Players," 105
"Take Three on *The Go-Between*" (with
    Richard Round: interview Pinter,
    Losey, L. P. Hartley), 198
Voices (with James Clarke), 71

UNPUBLISHED, PROJECTED
WRITINGS, AND ALTERNATIVE
TITLES

"Appointment Diaries," ix, x, xii, 16,
    23, 35, 46, 65, 66, 67, 69, 70, 72, 81,
    93, 95, 99, 100, 104, 112–113, 115,
    118, 119–120, 122, 125, 130, 132, 136,
    140, 216, 225
One Final Summer, 9
The Proust Screenplay, adapted for
    Radio by Michael Bakewell, 199
Queen of All the Fairies, 51, 80, 145, 202
The Shaft, 15
"[Radio Interview Peter Stanford],"
    174, 177–178
"Something in Common," 115
Torcello, 116
"[Tribute to Alan Schneider]," 27
"[Tribute to Jack Clayton]," 63
"[Tribute to Joseph Brearley-Memorial
    Service]," 3
"[Tribute to Karel Reisz—Funeral
    Oration]," 62–63
"[Tribute to Sam Spiegel—Funeral
    Oration]," 176
"Unsolicited Manuscript," 116

Index of People

Abse, Dannie: *Poetry and Poverty*, 85
Adams, John: *Nixon in China*, 72
Akhmatova, Anna, 33
Amis, Kingsley, 218
Anouih, Jean: *Point of Departure*, 10
Appleyard, Bob, 56
Aragay, Mireia, 168
Archer, Jeffrey, 106
Archibald, William: *The Innocents*, 70, 127
Armstrong, Anthony and Philip King: *Here We Come Gathering*, 9
Ashcroft, Dame Peggy, 35, 47, 105, 112–114, 160, 191
Astbury, Anthony, 95, 208–209, 212; *Letters*, x; *Memories*, x
Atkins, Eileen, 33
Atwood, Margaret: *The Handmaid's Tale*, 62
Aukin, David, 104, 125
Austen, Jane: *Mansfield Park*, 34

Bacall, Lauren, 158
Bach, Johanes, 1, 6, 68, 72, 78; *Brandenberg*, Nos 4 and 6, 69; *Cantatas*, 71; *Orchestral Suite* No.3, 69
Badcock, Jack, 59
Badel, Alan, 132
Bagguley, John, 151
Bailey, Paul, 80
Bailey, Trevor, 57–58
Baker, Stanley, 23
Baker, William, 172, 225; *Chronology*, ix, 31, 33, 36, 48, 49, 50, 56, 60, 63, 65, 67, 69, 70, 72, 81, 93, 95, 97, 100, 101, 102, 104–108, 113, 114, 118, 119–120, 122, 125, 127, 128, 130–131, 132, 136, 151, 154, 157, 158, 162, 163, 164, 168, 176, 185, 198, 208–209, 210–211, 212,

214–215, 216, 220, 225
Bakewell, Harriet, 115
Bakewell, Dame Joan (née Rowlands), 61, 105, 111–112, 114–118, 133, 139, 151, 209; *Centre of the Bed*, x, 114; *Keeping in Touch*, 114, 116; *Late Night Line-Up*, 111
Bakewell, Michael, 115, 116–117, 199
Balding, David, 139, 140
Bannnerman, A. C., 91
Barker, George, 208, 209–210; "Battersea Park," 210; "In Memory of Robert MacBryde," 210; "Summer Song," 210
Baron, David, 9, 12, 13, 16, 18
Barrett, Philip: New Malvern Company, 12
Bateman, Colin, 48
Bates, Alan, 32, 108, 122, 157, 225; *Butley*, 92; *Caretaker*, 7; *The Go-Between*, 24; *Life Support*, 92; *Melon*, 14; *Otherwise Engaged*, 92
Beckett, Samuel, xii, 8, 27, 51, 61, 65, 68, 83–84, 118, 119, 120, 151, 165, 185, 197, 198, 202–207, 219, 220; *All that Fall*, 206; *Breath*, 205; *The End*, 204; *Endgame*, 206; *Film*, 18; *Krapp's Last Tape*, 207; *Letters of*, 207; *Malone meart (Dies)*, 204, 205–206; *Mercier et Camier*, 205; *Molloy*, 205, 206; *More Pricks than Kicks*; *Murphy*, 204, 205, 206; *The Unnameable*, 206; *Waiting for Godot*, 4, 34, 51, 203–204, 206; *Watt*, 203, 205
Beethoven, Ludwig von, 68, 72, 158, 167; *Fidelio*; *Grosse Fugue*, 72; *String Quartet Op. 132*, 69; *Symphony No.9*, 69
Béjart, Maurice: *Ballet of the 20th Century*, 72

Bellini, Vincenzo, 72
Benedick, Adam, 191
Benney, Jack, 2
Bensky, Lawrence, 68, 150, 151
Berlioz, Hector, 72
Betjeman, Sir John, 214, 220
Bevan, Tony, 186
Billington, Kevin, 132
Billington, Michael, 3, 30, 39, 51, 90,
    116, 140, 164, 172; *Ashcroft, Dame
    Edith Margaret (Peggy)* [ODNB], 113,
    114; *Harold Pinter*, ix, 9–10, 11, 14,
    17, 20, 24, 29, 33, 40, 57, 67, 68, 79,
    82, 86, 93, 98, 99, 100, 101, 109, 116,
    118, 119, 127, 131, 133, 137, 146,
    148–149, 150, 151, 152, 158, 160, 162,
    164, 166, 169, 172, 177, 194, 196, 197,
    200, 205, 214, 215
Billington, Rachel (née Pakenham), 128
Birtwistle, Harrison, 70; *The Minotaur*,
    70, 72
Blair, Tony, 171, 174, 175
Bloom, Claire, 100
Bogarde, Dirk, 23
Bolt, Sir Robert, 136
Bond, Edward, 165; *Bingo*, 165
Bonham-Carter, Victor, 210–211
Boulez, Pierre, 68, 71; "Pli Selon Pli," 70
Boycott, Geoffrey, 54, 55, 220
Bradman, Sir Donald, 52–53
Bradshaw, Peter, 33
Brand, Daniel (HP's son), 3, 6, 14, 65,
    85–86, 115, 128, 133, 135, 136, 214
Bray, Barbara (née Jacobs), 61, 112,
    118–120, 207; *Á la Recherche du
    Temps Perdu (Proust Screenplay)*, 197,
    198, 199
Bray, Francesca, 118
Bray, John, 118
Bray, Juliet, 118
Brearley, Joseph, x, xi, 1–3, 4, 5–7, 22,
    40, 51, 86, 180, 188, 225; *Fortune's
    Fool*, 2
Brearley, Michael, 60
Brendel, Alfred, 72
Brenton, Howard, 165; *The Romans in
    Britain*, 165
Breton, André, 200

Britten, Benjamin: *Billy Budd*, 70; *Death
    in Venice*, 70; *Gloriana*, 70; *A
    Midsummer's Night's Dream*, 70;
    Owen Wingrave, 70; *Peter Grimes*, 70;
    The Turn of the Screw, 70; *War
    Requiem*, 70
Brookes, Christopher, x, 47–48
Brown, Craig, 108
Brown, Georgina, 30
Bryden, Ronald, 28, 35
Buchan, Rita, 17
Bull, Andy, 67
Bunker, Dr. Chris, 96
Buñuel, Luis: *Un Chien Andalou*, 22
Burton, Harry (Matthew), x
Burton, Matthew, 180
Burtt, Tom, 52
Bury, John, 35
Bush, George, 171, 174, 175

Caine, Michael, 67
Campbell, James, 202
Camus, Albert, 33
Cannan, Dennis: *You and Your Wife*, 10
Caplan, Hyme, 140
Carcanet Press, 213
Cardenal, Ernesto, 177, 180
Cardenal, Fernando, 177
Cardus, Neville, 52
Cargill, Patrick, Jack Beale: *Ring for
    Cathy (Carry on Nurse)*, 12
Carné, Marcel: *Les Enfants du Paradis*,
    22
Carroll, Lewis: *Alice in Wonderland*, 126
Carteret, Anna, 160
Cary, Joyce, 185, 195, 197, 220; *The
    Horse's Mouth*, 197
Casey, Dr. John, 77, 100–101
Casey, Rosemary: *Late Love*, 9, 56
Celine, Louis Ferdinand, 22
Cézanne, Paul, 201
Chalke, Stephen: *Runs in the Memory*,
    56
Chatwin, Bruce, 162
Chiasson, Basil, 157, 166
Chopin, Frédéric, 72
Christie, Agatha: *Love from a Stranger*,
    12; *Murder at the Vicarage*, 9; *Peril at
    End's House*, 12; *Ten Little Niggers*,

10, 56; *Witness for the Prosecution*, 11; *Spider's Web*, 3, 12, 15

Clarke, James, 71; *Voices*, 71

Clayton, Haya, 63, 136

Clayton, Jack, 63

Clinton, Bill, 173

Close, Brian, 54

Cocteau, Jean, 68

Codron, Michael, 17, 123

Cohen, David, 88

Cohen, Harold: *The Homecoming*, 186

Coleman, Uncle, 88

Colgan, Michael, 95

Compton, Denis, 49–50, 51, 58, 60, 217

Condos, Nick, 140

Conrad, Joseph: *Victory*, 155

Cookson, Cherry, 105

Cooper, Sir Robert, 64, 69. *See also* Uchida, Mitsuko

Cornwall, David ("John Le Carré"), 171

Coward, Noël, 3; *Ace of Clubs*, 132; *Blithe Spirit*, 38, 214; *Hay Fever*, 3, 15, 214; *Private Lives*, 102; *Sign no More*, 132; *South Sea Bubble*, 3, 214

Crisp, Quentin (Dennis Charles Pratt), 80

Cusack, Cyril, 19

Cusack, Sinéad, 136

Daish, Judy, 87, 95, 104, 107, 112, 118, 120–122

Dali, Salvador, 22

Dante, Alighieri, 193

Davies, Barbara, 115

Delderfield, R. F.: *A Worm's Eye View*, 16

Delos Press, 137

Dimond, Guy, 91

Diss, Eileen, 29, 92, 112, 123–125, 136

Dench, Judi, 20, 33, 154

Derbyshire, Harry, 71

Dickens, Charles: *Dombey and Son*, 214

Doggart, G. H. G., 52

Donner, Clive, 5, 18

Dostoevsky, Fyodor, 33; *The Brothers Karamazov*, 57

Druten, John Van: *Bell, Book and Candle*, 12

Du Garde, Peach, L., 9

Duras, Marguerite, 119

Durrell, Lawrence, 209

East, Robert, 125

Edrich, Bill, 49

Egerton, Ansell, 214

Eichmann, Adolf, 152

Eliot, T. S., 78, 84–85, 100, 168, 169, 192, 193; *Ash Wednesday*, 168; *Four Quartets*, 178; *Little Gidding*, 180; *Selected Poems*(1948), 85; *The Waste Land*, 84, 193

Engel, Susan, 14, 92

Empson, William, 209

Engels, Friedrich, 85

d'Escoto Miguel, 177

Esslin, Martin, 28, 85, 189

Everett, Dany, 125

Eyre Methuen, 210

Ezra, Rabbi Ben, 84

Faber and Faber, 210, 212, 215, 218

Falkus, Christopher, 63, 65, 208

Falkus, Gila, 63

Fay, Stephen, 39

Feast, Michael, 7

Ferdinand, Archduke, 169

Fingleton, Jack, 90

Firth, Colin, 21

Fitzgerald, Edward, 107

Fitzgerald, F. Scott, 152, 153

Flanagan, Pauline, 7, 82, 84, 126–127, 131, 138, 139, 179, 193–194

Flaubert, Gustave, 119

Florence, Peter, 22

Ford, Anna, 150

Foster, Barry, 79, 108, 132, 193

Foster, Judith, 111

Fowles, John, 20, 67, 153

Fox, Edward, 32, 95

Fraser, Lady Antonia (née Pakenham: HP's second wife), 19, 31, 36–37, 38, 39, 47, 50, 61, 64, 69–72, 85–87, 88, 91, 93, 96, 100, 101, 104, 106–107, 111–112, 113, 114, 121, 128–131, 133, 135, 137, 138, 139, 145, 147, 150, 153–154, 156, 158, 162, 168, 171, 176, 180, 192, 203, 208–209, 212, 219, 220; "Death v. Harold Pinter," 61;

"Desert Island Discs," 69; *Diaries*, ix;
"For My Partner," 63; *The
Gunpowder Plot*, 88, 129; Jemina
Shore Series, 130; *King Charles II*, 86,
138; *Mary Queen of Scots*, 130; *Must
You Go?*, 60, 61, 62, 63–65, 67, 70–71,
72, 83, 95, 96, 97, 101, 102–104, 106,
107, 111, 112, 116, 120, 122, 128–130,
136, 137, 138, 139, 155, 156, 158, 162,
164, 166, 167, 180, 203, 209, 213, 218,
219; *My History: A Memoir of
Growing Up*, 129, 131; *Our Israeli
Diary*, 131, 164; *Perilous Question*,
131; *The Weaker Vessel*, 128
Fraser, Benjie, 130
Fraser, Damian, 63, 130; with Paloma
    Fraser, 88, 106
Fraser, Flora, 105, 106–107, 130, 180
Fraser, Hugh, 130, 138
Fraser, Orlando, 63, 105, 107, 130
Fraser, Natasha, 130; with John-Pierre
    Cavassoni, 130
Fraser, Rebecca, 107, 130. *See also*
    Fitzgerald, Edward
Freed, Donald: *Circle and Bravo*, 95
Fuentes, Carlos, 107, 136, 163
Fugard, Athol, 33, 154
Furtwängler, Wilhelm, 98, 167

Gale, Steven H., xiii, 24, 25, 31, 92, 119,
    123, 153, 155, 162, 190
Gambon, Michael: *Heat of the Day*, 160,
    180
Garrett, Tony, 70, 136
Gascoigne, Bamber, 5
Gascoyne, David, 209
Gaur, Albertine, 89
Gébler, Ernest, 135
Genet, Jean, 119
Gielgud, Sir John, 7, 36, 37, 113; *Hamlet*,
    187; *The Tempest*, 35, 187
Giordano, Umberto, 72
Gilchrist, Roy, 54
Gillen, Francis, xiii, 79, 166, 189
Giraudoux, Jean: *The Trojan War Will
    Not Take Place*, 21, 32, 39–40, 70, 211
Gluck, Christoph Willibald, 72
Godbert, Geoffrey, 208–209, 212
Goethe, Johann Wolfgang von, 158

Godfrey, Derek, 124
Goldstein, David, 89
Goldstein, Helen, 85
Goldstein, Michael (Mick), xi, 3, 7, 11,
    12, 13, 14, 15, 18, 19–20, 21, 22, 33,
    51, 52, 53–56, 60, 61, 66, 68, 72, 77,
    81–84, 85–91, 97, 111, 118, 126, 128,
    132, 134–135, 147, 171, 191, 197, 200,
    202, 203, 204, 205, 220
Gonchorov, Ivan: *Oblomov*, xii, 185, 200
Gooding, Ossie, 45, 108
Goodman, Harold, 105
Goodman, Paul, 198
Goodwin, John: *Peter Hall's Diaries*,
    34–35, 40, 225–226
Gordon, Robert, 29, 169, 175
Gottwald, Klement, 83
Gounod, Charles, 72
Gower, David, 55
Graham, Nessie, 208–209, 210, 212
Graham, W. S., xii, 185, 208–213, 220;
    Collected Poems 1942–1977, 210;
    "Hilton Abstract," 209; "Johann
    Joachim Quartz," 212; "I Leave This
    at Your Ear," 208, 213; "Letter V,"
    214; "Letter VI," 209;
    "Nightfishing," 212; *The
    Nightfisherman*, 212; "O Gentle
    Queen of the Afternoon," 213;
    Selected Letters, 212; "The Thermal
    Stair," 209; "To My Wife at
    Midnight," 209; "The White
    Threshold," 208
Graveney, Tom, 54
Graves, Robert, 209
Gray, James (SG's father), 96
Gray, Simon, 1, 21, 25–26, 29–31, 40, 61,
    77, 92–96, 104, 108, 122, 125, 136,
    161, 163, 178–179, 185, 219, 225;
    Butley, 29, 92, 123; *Cell Mates*, 123;
    Close of Play, 29, 120; *Common
    Pursuit*, 92, 94, 211; *Coda*, ix; *Enter a
    Fox*, ix, 30; *The Holy Terror*, 121; *Last
    Cigarette*, ix; *The Late Middle Classes*,
    30, 92; *Life Support*, 92, 123; *The Old
    Masters*, 29, 120, 123, 125; *Otherwise
    Engaged*, 92, 123; *Quartermaine's
    Terms*, 123; *The Rear Column*, 29, 32,
    86, 102, 123, 209, 210; *Smoking*

Diaries, ix; *An Unnatural Pursuit*, ix, 93; *Year of the Jouncer*, ix, 29, 50, 64, 67, 120–121
Greenspan, Louis, 163
Gregory, Jack, 61
Greig, Geordie, 30
Greville Press, 209, 220; pamphlets, 137
Grimes, Charles, 148, 151, 155, 156, 166
Gross, Susanna, 63
Guard, Dominic, 24
Gunn, Dan, 118
Gussow, Mel: *Conversations*, ix, 38, 189

Hall, Adam. *See* Elleston, Trevor
Hall, Jacky, 37
Hall, John, 14
Hall, Sir Peter, 4, 19, 20, 26, 27, 34–40, 70, 72, 95–96, 106, 112–113, 114, 132, 134, 198; *Diaries*, ix, 1, 19, 27, 29, 39–40, 112–113, 128, 137, 165; *Directing Harold Pinter*, 206
Hamlett, Dilys, 10, 111, 193, 200
Hamilton, Hamish (Publishers), 39
Hamilton, Ian, 216
Hamilton, Patrick: *Rope*, 8
Hammerstein, James, 125
Hammond, Walter, 59
Hampton, Christopher, 154
Handel, George Frideric, 72
Hardstaff, Joe, 48
Hardy, Thomas, 215
Hartley, Leslie Poles, 153, 198; *The Go-Between*, 4, 24–25, 152–153
Harty, Russell: *Acquarius*, 137
Harvey, Neil, 53, 56
Harwood, Sir Ronald, 3, 8, 20, 64–65, 77, 98–99, 104, 108, 154, 198; *The Pianist*, 98; *Taking Sides*, 31, 32, 72, 98, 107–108, 123, 167
Hassett. Lindsay, 53, 57
Havel, Olga, 162–163
Havel, Václav, 125, 154, 162–163; *Audience*, 162; *Private View*, 162
Haydn, Franz Joseph, 68, 87
Heath-Stubbs, John, 209
Helfgott, Daniel: *Shine*, 89
Helpmann, Robert, 191
Henstell, Bruce, 199
Heriot, Charles D., 203

Hern, Nick, 157
Hitchcock, Alfred, 8; *Frenzy*, 132
Hitchcock, Jane Stanton: *Vanilla*, 164
Hoban, Russell *Turtle Diary*, 158
Hobson, Harold, 16, 17, 203
Hodge, Patricia, 160
Holm, Ian, 19
Hopkins, Gerald Manley, 192; "The Wreck of the Deutschland," 209
Hopkins, John *Next of Kin*, 215
Horwitz, Ronald. *See* Harwood, Sir Ronald
Howard, Michael, 171
Howitt, Peter, 21
Hudson, Anne, 97
Hussey, Sister Pamela: *Free from Fear*, 178–179
Hutchinson (Publishers), 50
Hutton, Sir Len, 48–52, 53, 54, 56, 58, 60, 217; *Cricket in my Life*, 50
Huxley, Aldous, xii, 185, 201; "Giaconda Smile," 201; "Mortal Coils," 201
Hytner, Sir Nicholas, 108–109

Ibsen, Henrik: *Ghosts*, 136; *John Gabriel Borkman*, 112
Ikin, Jack, 53
Inigo, Thomas, 45
Inshaw, David, 60, 104
Ionesco, Eugene, 203; *The Hard-Boiled Egg*, 18
Irons, Jeremy, 136, 154; *The French Lieutenant's Woman*, 26, 63
Ives, Kenneth: *The Birthday Party*, 30; *A Kind of Alaska*, 105

Jacobi, Derek, 34
James, Henry: *The Turn of the Screw*, 16
Jarrott, Charles, 6, 124
Jay, Peter, 63
Jeffrey, Ewan, 124
John Paul XXXIII, Pope, 177
Johnson, Brian, 50
Johnson, Jill, 10, 84, 90, 105, 107, 131–132, 197
Jones, Alice, 71
Jones, David, 83, 96, 117, 122, 125
Jones, Hester, 213

Jones, Monica, 215
Jongh, Nicholas de, 199
Jonson, Ben, 192
Josipovici, Gabriel, 198
Joyce, James, 51, 185, 192, 195–196, 220;
    Exiles, 28, 119, 123, 124, 125, 196; *A
    Portrait of the Artist*, 195; *Ulysses*, 195
Juncker, Klaus, 162

Kafka, Franz: *The Trial*, 95, 126, 162
Kant, Immanuel, 85
Kaufmann, Stanley, 198–199
Kazan, Elia: *The Last Tycoon*, 153
Keats, John, 192
Kelvern, Beryl Mary (SG's first wife),
    93, 96
Kemp-Welch, Joan, 132
Kendal, Felicity, 104
Kennard, Peter: *Doomsday Book*, 173
Kennedy, Jacqueline (Onassis), 6
Kenyon, Don, 58
King, Norman: *Shadow of a Doubt*, 12
King, Philip: *Serious Charge*, 10
Kingston, Jeremy, 31
Kitchen, Michael, 114
Koval, Ramona, 59, 176, 206
Kristeva, Julia, 119
Kubelik, Rafael, 72
Kustow, Michael, 65

Lane, Lupino, 46
Larkin, Philip, xii, 61, 170, 185, 202,
    214–220; "Aubade," 216–217, 218;
    "Bridge for the Living," 176; "The
    Building," 218; *Complete Poems*, 218;
    "Dockery and Son," 214, 215; *High
    Windows*, 215–216, 218; "Home is So
    Sad," 215; *Larkin: Poems*, 214; *Last
    Poems*, 216; *The Less Deceived*, 220;
    "Not the Place's Fault," 215; *Oxford
    Book of Twentieth Century English
    Verse*, 214, 215; *Philip Larkin Poems*,
    220; *Selected Letters of*, 214; "Talking
    in Bed," 215; "Toads Revisited,"
    214; "The Whitsun Weddings," 214,
    220; *XX Poems*, 215
Law, Jimmy, 4, 79, 82, 148, 201
Law, Jude, 67
Lawrence, D. H., 192, 193

Leavis, F. R., 1, 34, 96
Lechner, Geno, 107
Leichhardt, Luwig, 89
Lillie, Dennis, 54
Lin, Qin, 172
Lindner, Dixie, 190
Lindwall, Ray, 58
Lipstein, Isidor (HP's uncle), 68
Lipstein, Sophie (née Pinter; HP's
    aunt), 68
Litvinoff, Emanuel, 84–85; *Journey
    Through a Small Planet*, 84; "To T. S.
    Eliot," 85
Lloyd-Pack, Roger, 26
Longford, Elizabeth (née Harman),
    129. *See also* Pakenham, Frank
Losey, Joseph, 23, 87, 89, 151, 153,
    197–198, 199; *Á la recherche du temps
    perdu (Proust Screenplay)*, 119, 198,
    199; *Accident*, 23, 34; *The Go-Between*,
    24; *The Servant*, 34
Lovat, Lady, 138
Löytved, Mara, 2, 6
Lumet, Sidney: *The Offence*, 132
Lumley, Joanna, 32
Luther, Martin, 4

Macaulay, Alastair, xii, 33, 68, 168
McCann, Joe, 205
McCowen, Alec, 154
MacDonald. Edward A. (Ted), 61
McEwan, Ian: *The Comfort of Strangers*,
    161
McFerran, Douglas, x
McGilvray, Alan, 49
McKern, Leo, 124
McMaster, Anew, 4, 8, 15, 51, 105, 126,
    187–188, 189, 193, 197
McWhinnie, Donald, 19
MacLaren, Archie, 57
Magarshack, David, 200
Magee, Patrick, 8, 15, 205, 207
Mailer, Norman, 6
Main, Ian: *Subway in the Sky*, 16
Mamet, David: *Oleanna*, 123, 191
Marcos, Imelda, 164
Markham, Kiki, 124
Marks, Louis, 95, 106, 162
Marlowe, Christopher, 192

Marriott, R. B., 28
Marvell, Andrew, 93, 201
Massey, Anna, 32
Maugham, Robin, 151
Melville, Alan: *Simon and Laura*, 12
Mendes, Sam, 26, 148
Mercer, David, 151
Merchant, Vivien (née Thomson; HP's first wife), 3–4, 12, 14, 15, 17, 19, 20, 23, 35, 37, 84, 85–86, 87, 91, 93, 104, 111–113, 115, 116, 124, 128, 132–135, 136, 140, 152, 153, 155, 177, 186, 205, 218, 219
Merritt, Susan Hollis, x
Methuen, 208
Miles, Tim, 61
Miller, Arthur, 151, 157, 163; *All My Sons*, 3, 15; *Death of a Salesman*, 2
Miller, Henry, xii, 185, 192, 200, 201–202, 220; *Black Spring*, 126, 201; *Tropic of Capricorn*, 202
Miller, Keith, 52–54, 57
Miller, Max, 2
Modi (Indian cricketer), 55
Modigliani, Amedeo, 201
Moore, Geoffrey, 213
Morahan, Christopher, 65, 160
Morris, Arthur, 53, 56, 58
Mortimer, John, 19
Mortimer, Penelope: *The Pumpkin Eater*, 64, 85
Moscowitz, Ben (HP's uncle), 138
Moscowitz, Fay (HP's aunt), 138
Moskowitz, Harry (HP's maternal grandfather), 138
Moskowitz, Judah (HP's uncle), 138
Moskowitz, Lou (HP's uncle), 138
Moscowitz, Rose (née Franklin; HP's maternal grandmother), 138
Mosley, Nicholas,: *Accident*, 23–24
Mosley, Oswald, 145
Motion, Andrew, 217
Mozart, Wolfgang Amadeus, 38, 68–69, 72; Piano Concerto, No 23, 69; Piano Concerto, No 27, 64, 69
Muir, Frank, 114
Mulligan, Gerry, 69
Munk, Thelonius, 69
Murdoch, Iris, 151

Mussolini, Benito, 71, 169
Mussorgsky, Modest, 72

Nadel, Ira, 103
Naipaul, Nadira and Sir V. S., 136
Nairn, Ian: *Nairn's London*, 81
Nasser, Gamel Abdel, 147
Neruda, Pablo, 154
Nightingale, Benedict, 19, 29, 166
Normington, John, 19
Nugents, Valerie, 80
Nunn, Trevor, 33

O'Brien, Edna, 40, 108, 135–137; *Country Girl*, 135; *The Country Girls*, 135; *A Pagan Place*, 136; *Virginia*, 136
O'Conner, Francis, 33
Olivier, Sir Laurence, 5, 136, 199
Orwell, George: "Inside the Whale," 202
Osborn, Paul: *Mornings at Seven*, 13
Osborne, John, 151; *Look Back in Anger*, 16; *An Epitaph for George Dillon*, 16
Osborne, Charles, 216
O'Toole, Fintan, 147
O'Toole, Peter, 5
Owen, Wilfred, 70

Packer, Kerry, 56
Padgett, Doug, 51
Page, Malcolm, ix, 150–151
Pakenham family, 129
Pakenham, Frank (Lord Longford), 129
Pakenham, Sir Michael and Mimi, 107
Pakenham, Thomas, 129
Parker, Charlie, 69
Parks, Jim, 54
Pasolini, Pier Paolo: *Teorema*, 6
Pennington, Michael, 32
Percival, Ron, 2, 51, 78, 80, 87, 91, 111, 163
Peter, John, 31, 199
Petit, Roland, 68
Phipps, Diana, 136
Picasso, Pablo, 169
Pinta, Harold, 9
Pinter, Fanny (née Baron; HP's paternal grandmother), 68

Pinter, Frances (née Moskowitz; HP's mother), 4, 87, 127, 138–139, 158, 166, 180

Pinter, Hyman (Jack; HP's father), 87, 89, 138, 139, 164; and Frances, 87, 89, 138, 146, 180

Pinter, Nathan (HP's paternal grandfather), 68

Pite, Ralph, 212

Planchon, Roger, 120

Pleasence, Donald, 5, 31, 32, 152; *The Caretaker*, 5, 21

Plowright, Joan, 136

Pope, the, 84. *See also* John Paul XXIII

Popplewell, Jack: *The Vanity Case*, 16

Posner, Lindsay, 30

Powell, Dilys, 23

Powell-Jones, Stella, 180

Priestley, J. B.: *Mr. Kettle and Mrs. Moon*, 13

Proust, Marcel, xii, 84, 98, 119, 185, 197–199, 220; *À la Recherche du Temps Perdu*, 6, 35, 197–199

Puccini, Giacomo, 72

rabbi(s), 84

Ramadhin, Sonny, 52

Rattigan, Terence, 177; *Separate Tables*, 12

Rawlings, Margaret, 5, 191

Raye, Martha, 140

Read, Sir Herbert, 85

Redgrave, Corin, 103

Redgrave, Sir Michael, 5, 7

Rees, Jasper, 66

Rees, Johnny, 135

Regan, Ronald, 156

Reisz, Betsy, 63, 136

Reisz, Karel, 62–63; *The French Lieutenant's Woman*, 25–26, 63, 152–153; *Morgan: A Suitable Case for Treatment*, 62; *Saturday Night and Sunday Morning*, 62; *This Sporting Life*, 62

Reitman, Max, *Love on the Never-Never*, 12

Richards, I. A., 1

Richardson, Ralph: *No Man's Land*, 7, 36–37, 220

Richardson, Tony, 16

Riehle, Natasha, 98

Rigby, Terence, 19, 23, 106

Rimbaud, Arthur, xii, 185, 186, 200, 220

Robertson-Glasgow, R. C., 55

Rogers, Paul, 19

Rossini, Gioachino, 72

Rostropovitch, Mstislav, 72

Roth, Philip, 100, 135

Roth, Tim, 170, 190

Rothschild, Victoria (SG's second wife), 93, 96, 104, 120

Rosen, Ruth, 212

Ross, Alan, 49

Ross, G and C. Singer: *Any Other Business*, 17

Round, Richard, 198

Rozema, Patricia, 34

Rushdie, Sir Salman, 148, 162, 163, 167; "Herbert Read Memorial Lecture" (Pinter), 163; *Midnight's Children*, 154; *Satanic Verses*, 87

Sacks, Albie: *Jail Diary of*, 32

Sacks, Oliver: *Awakenings*, 155

Sams, Jeremy, 107

Saro-Wiwa, Ken, 107

Sartre, Jean-Paul: *Huis Clos*, 4

Saville, Philip, 4

Schatzberg, Jerry: *Reunion*, 159

Schiller, Friedrich, 158; *Mary Stuart*, 107

Schmidt, Michael, 212

Schnabel, Artur, 69

Schneider, Alan, 27

Schrader, Paul: *The Comfort of Strangers*, 161

Schulman, Milton, 29

Scofield, Sir Paul, 133

Scott-Moncrieff, C. K., 197; translation prize, 119

Scruton, Roger, 100

Seluzicki, Charles, 216

Sereny, Gitta, 167; *Albert Speer*, 56, 167

Shaffer, Anthony: *Sleuth*, 67, 197

Shakespeare, William, xii, 2, 3, 32, 68, 78, 79, 170, 174, 185, 187–190, 191, 192, 201; *As You Like It*, 187, 188; *Collected Shakespeare*, 189; *Coriolanus,*

206; *Cymbeline*, 189; *Hamlet*, 5, 79, 180, 187–188, 189, 193; *1 Henry IV–2 Henry IV*, 83; *Julius Caesar*, 174, 189; *King Lear*, 126, 170, 187–188, 189, 190; *Macbeth*, 2, 132, 187, 188–189; *Measure for Measure*, 83, 126, 189; *Merchant of Venice*, 7, 187, 188; *A Midsummer Night's Dream*, 189; *Othello*, 7, 33, 187–189; *Romeo and Juliet*, 2, 188; *Sonnets*, 189; *The Taming of the Shrew*, 187, 188; *The Tempest*, 35, 187; *Troilus and Cressida*, 189; *Twelfth Night*, 188

Shaw, Robert: *The Man in the Glass Booth*, 139, 151, 152

Shelley, Percy Bysshe, 50, 201

Sher, Anthony, 32

Sherriff, R.C.: *The Telescope*, 3, 15

Shuttleworth, Martin, 27

Sierks, Aleks, 148

Silverstein, Marc, 123

Simpson, N. F.: *The Form*, 19; *The Hole*, 16; *A Resounding Tinkle*, 16

Simpson, Reg, 48, 57

Sims, Jim, 48

Smith, Ian: *Pinter in the Theatre*, 26

Smurthwaite, Nick, 123

Snow, Margaret, 212

Snow, Michael, 212

Solzhenitsyn, Aleksandr, 154

Sophocles: *Oedipus*, 7, 9; *Oedipus at Colonus*, 8; *Oedipus Rex*, 8

Soros, Peter, 105, 106

Souza, Edward de, 105

Spark, Muriel, 151

Speer, Albert, 56, 167

Spencer, Charles, 3, 92, 149

Spender, Stephen, 85, 209

Spielberg, Stephen, 103

Spiegel, Sam, 176; *The Last Tycoon*, 153

Stafford, Winston, 46

Stalin, Joseph, 83

Stamp, Terence, 6

Stanford, Peter, 176, 177–178

Stanton, Barbara (Condos), 112, 116, 133, 139–140

Stanton, Larry, 140

Starker, Janos, 69

Steinbeck, John: *Of Mice and Men*, 10

Stephens, Robert, 5

Stevens, Roger, 17, 149

Stockhausen, Karlheinz, 72

Stoppard, Miriam, 101, 102, 104

Stoppard, Tom, 58, 77, 100, 101–104, 120, 200, 216; *The Coast of Utopia*, 104; *Rock 'n' Roll*, 101

Stoppi, Maurice, 106

Strachey, Lytton: *Elizabeth and Essex*, 70

Streep, Meryl, 26; *The French Lieutenant's Woman*, 63, 152–153

Strindberg, August: *Playing with Fire*, 27

Sussard, Jacqueline, 23

Synge, John Millington, 194

Taylor-Barry, Mark, 27, 196

Tanquy, Yves, 186

Taylor, John Russell, 28

Taylor, Ken, 56

Taylor, Paul, 30

Tchaikovsky, Pyotr Ilyich, 72, 146

Tennyson, Hallam, 215

Thomas, Dylan, 186, 194

Thompson, David J., 11, 16

Thompson, Francis: "At Lord's," 180

Thompson, Harry, 206

Thomson, Ada. *See* Merchant, Vivien

Thomson, Peter, 61

Thurston, Ernest Temple: *The Wandering Jew*, 8

Thwaite, Anthony, 214, 218

Timmerman, Jacobo, 156

Tippett, Michael: *The Knot Garden*, 72

Tolstoy, Leo, xii, 185; *Anna Karenina*, 200

Tourneur, Cyril, 3, 191

Trelford, Donald, 47

Trevis, Di: *À la Recherche du Temps Perdu*, 35, 38, 98, 105

Trevor, Elleston, 6, 152; *The Berlin Memorandum*, 152

Trourbridge, St. Vincent, 203

Trueman, Fred, 54

Trumper, Victor, 90

Turgenev, Ivan, xii, 185, 220; *A Month in the Country*, 185

Turing, Alan, 34

Tusa, John, 150

Tynan, Kenneth, 191

Uchida, Mitsuko, Dame, 64, 69, 72. *See also* Cooper, Robert
Uhlman, Fred: *Reunion*, 123, 152, 158–163

Vaesen, Guy, 17, 18, 28, 113, 126, 133, 186
Valentine, Alf, 52
Vanunu, Mordecai, 164
Verdi, Giuseppe, 72
Verneuil, Louis: *Affairs of State*, 10, 56
Vidal, Gore, 202
Visconti, Luchino, 215
Vogel, George, 127

Wagner, Richard, 1, 6, 71; *Die Meistersinger*, 72; *Die Walküre*, 72; *Götterdämerung*, 72; *Lohengrin*, 72; "Ring Cycle," 39; *Tristan and Isolde*, 72
Wain, John, 209
Walcott, Sir Clyde, 52
Waldegrave, William, 171; and Caroline, 63, 120
Walker, Alexander, 24
Wallace, Merv, 51
Wardle, Johnny, 57
Warner, Sir Fred, 171
Washbrook, Cyril, 51, 57
Watling, E. F., 8
Watson, Willie, 57–58
Wax, Emanuel (Jimmy), 14, 15, 17, 20, 24, 121, 122
Webern, Anton, 68
Webster, John, 2, 3, 146, 185, 186, 191–192, 220; *Duchess of Malfi*, 32, 191; *The White Devil*, 5, 32, 191
Weidenfeld, Lord George, 107, 130
Weidenfeld and Nicholson, 63, 86, 88, 130, 131
Wellard, Arthur, 58–59, 105, 218
Wernick, Moishe, xi, 6, 7, 66, 82, 85–86, 97, 111, 118, 138, 146–147, 187
Wesker, Arnold, 151
West, Timothy, 154
White, Patrick, *Voss*, 89
Whitemore, Hugh: *Breaking the Code*, 34

Whittington, R. S., 53
Wilde, Oscar: *An Ideal Husband*, 7; *Lady Windermere's Fan*, 7
Wilder, Thornton: *The Matchmaker*, 17
Willes, Peter, 65
Wilkinson, Alan: *The Catch*, 47, 54, 218
Williams, Tennessee: *Sweet Bird of Youth*, 158
Willis, Ted and R. Gordon: *Doctor in the House*, 14, 15
Wilson, Sir Angus, 70, 136, 151, 154
Wilton, Penelope, 32, 180
Wolfit, Sir Donald, 2–3, 8, 12, 98, 126, 170, 188
Wood, John, 102, 199
Wood, Peter, 15, 147; *The Birthday Party*, 5
Woolf, Cecil: *Authors Take Sides on Vietnam*, 150
Woolf, Henry, x, xi, 2, 4, 7–8, 9, 10, 11, 13, 14, 15, 16, 18–19, 20, 22, 33, 45, 50, 51, 52–53, 56–57, 60, 61, 66, 72, 79, 82, 85–86, 91, 96, 97, 111, 118, 126–127, 128, 131, 133, 134, 135, 179–180, 187, 188, 191, 192, 193, 195, 197, 200, 201, 204, 206, 216, 220; *Barcelona*, x, 78, 82, 111, 135, 137, 140, 146, 147, 156, 163, 201
Woolley, Frank, 55, 61
Wordsworth, William, 185, 187, 192, 220; "Intimations of Immortality," 192
Wright, David, 97

Yeats, William Butler, 169, 185, 192–194, 220; "Byzantium," 193; "A Dialogue of Self and Soul," 193; "The Lake Isle of Innisfree," 194; "Lapis Lazuli," 193; "A Prayer for My Daughter," 193; "The Second Coming," 192; "The Tower," 193, 194
York, Michael, 23, 160
York, Susannah: *The Big One*, 156; "Life: A Theatrical Show ...," 156

Index of Places and Miscellaneous

43 Group, 145

"Abrahamoff," 196
actor, Pinter as, 33–34
African, 168
alcoholism, 133, 135
Aldeburgh, 70
Alfie, 132
America/American, 91, 126, 145, 153, 156, 157, 172, 173, 174; American Embassy, Istanbul, 157–158; foreign policy, 164, 171, 174; anti- (Pinter), 50, 155, 171–172, 174
Amnesty International, 164
Anglican funeral, 168
anti-Semitism, 71, 83, 85, 138, 156, 158, 163, 164, 180
Arab, 164
Argentina, 155, 156
Aris Glove Company, 140
art exhibitions, 186
Ascot, St Mary's Convent, 129
associated rediffusion, 33, 132
Australia, 85, 89, 97, 118, 176; Adelaide, 56; Brisbane, 53; cricketers, 90; Cricket XI, 49, 56, 57, 59–60, 216; Melbourne, 54, 57; Sydney, 91; Test Match, 49; Victoria, 54; Waverley Cemetery, 90; Waverley Philharmonic Orchestra, 87
Austria/Austrian: Burgtheater, Vienna, 35; English Theatre, Vienna, 132; University of Vienna, 153

badminton (game), 67
ballet, 68
Barclays Theatre Awards, 30
baseball (game), 50
Batley Grammar School, 1

BBC, 11, 17; European service, 124; "Goon Show," 196; overseas service, 151; symphony orchestra, 72; third program, 118–119, 210; TV center, 119
BBC2, 124, 202, 220
BBC4, 91
BBC Radio, 105, 115, 123; Radio 3, 71, 105, 113, 164, 199, 214; Radio 4, 114, 132, 166, 176, 215; Radio Drama, 149
Belarus Free Theatre, 104; *Being Harold Pinter*, 104
Biggin Hill, 146
Birmingham, 21; Alexandra Theatre, 3, 15; *Birmingham Weekly Post*, 15
"Boobafarski," 196
Boer War, 152–153
BOMB, 172
Book of Common Prayer, 168
boxing, as metaphor, 205
Bradford, 21
bridge (game), xi, 45, 47, 62–64, 67, 226
Bridgnorth, Shropshire, 146
Bristol, 14, 70, 102; Old Vic, 14; St. Brendan's College, 100
British, 102; British Academy, 100; British Academy of Film and Television Arts (BAFTA), 123, 132; British Board of Jewish Deputes, 88; British Establishment, 171; British Film Academy, 25; British Intelligence, 100; British Library (auditorium), 220; British Library (Pinter archive), x, xii, 51, 104, 155, 162, 220, 225; *British Library Journal*, 89; British Nationalist (Pinter), 155; British Nazism, 145

Cambridge, 100, 117; Arts Theatre, 15, 16, 51, 91; Emmanuel College, 62;

Girton College, 118; Gonville & Caius College, 100; Newnham College, 114; St Catherine's College, 34; St John's College, 1; Trinity College, 96
Campaign for Nuclear Disarmament (CND), 113, 156
Canada, 97, 107, 138; Halifax, Nova Scotia, 96, 163; Dalhousie University, 96; Montreal, 6; Ontario, 47; Saskatchewan, Summer Festival, Saskatoon, 21
cancer, 96, 104
Cardiff, 6, 10
Carmelite, 176
Catalan, 168; Barcelona, 123, 168
Catholic/Catholicism, 127, 129, 130, 135, 138
conscientious objector/s, 45, 70, 145, 146, 185; Board of, 146
conservative, 171, 174
Cornwall, 111, 129, 146; Abbey Hotel, Penzance, 212; Lloyd's Bank, Penzance, 211; Mevagissey, 12, 134; Madron, Penzance, 209; Truro, 212
Coventry, 215
cricket, xi, 26, 29, 45–61, 64–65, 72, 91, 94, 96, 98, 100, 124, 126, 180, 214, 217–218, 220, 226; as metaphor (significance), 46, 48, 49, 50–51, 53, 54, 57, 59–61, 67, 68, 86, 87, 152, 205, 207, 215; The Ashes, 49, 53, 56, 57, 82, 168
Cricket World, 45
Critical Quarterly, 163
criminal act, 205
Critics, The (BBC Radio), 120
Cyprus, 118
Czechoslovakia/Czech Republic, 83, 135, 136, 162; Hradecek, 162; Prague, 162; Prague Cathedral, 163; Wenceslas Square, 163

Daily Mail, 100, 108, 115
Daily Telegraph, 54, 92, 100, 101, 140, 174
Daily Telegraph Magazine, 49, 215
directing, Pinter as, 26–33

Dorset, 90; Kingston Russell, 136; Westbrook House, 71

Ecclesiastes, Book of, 168
Egypt, 147; Alexandria, 118; Cairo, 118; Suez, 147
El Salvador, 178–179
England/English, 45, 59–60, 67, 85, 94, 100, 164, 180, 226
England v. Australia, 52–53, 54, 55, 56, 59, 61, 82, 95, 169, 214
England v. India, 50
England v. New Zealand, 51
England [MCC] v. South Africa, 54
England v. West Indies, 47, 52, 54
English fascism, 165
Enitharmon Editions, 186; Press, 13
Eton College, 63
Evening Standard, 24, 29, 83, 100, 132, 199
Exeter, 63

Falkland Islands, 12, 155
"Famous Crickets Series," 215
fascist/m, 82, 145, 155, 158, 159–160, 161, 164, 165, 167, 178
Fernleigh, 103
films (Pinter and), 22–26
Financial Times, The, 33, 168
food, 77–109. *See also* restaurants
football (soccer), 61, 65, 67
France/French, 22, 147; Cannes, Film Festival, 23, 24; Combray, 197; food, 93, 106, 119; Gallimard, Publishers, 120; Paris, 119, 120, 138; Théâtre Montparnasse, 119
friendship/s, 77–109, 176

Genesis, Book of, 168
Germany/German, 1, 3, 6, 111, 123, 152, 158–159, 160, 167; Bayreuth, 39; Berlin, 107, 152; Berlin Film Festival, 18; Berlin Wall, 163; East Berlin, 163; Frankfurt am Main, 148; Gestapo, 147; Munich, 195; Nazi/s, 123, 152, 158, 160, 167, 168; Nürnberg, 3; PEN, 107; Stuttgart, 123, 158
Gloucestershire: Cheltenham, 14, 18

God, 71, 177, 178–179, 180, 192, 201. *See also* religion
Granta, 189
Greece/Greek, 81; food, 120
greyhound (dog) racing, 67
Guardian, The, 10, 30, 33, 55, 59, 67, 165, 171, 172, 198; Cricket XI, 47, 54
Guatemala, 107
Guinness, 81, 84, 88, 92
Gulf War, 172

Hampshire: Barry O'Brien Company, The Palace Court Theatre, Bournemouth, 134; Bournemouth, 12, 14, 84, 91, 132, 205; Hayling Island, 96
Harold Pinter XI, 54
Hebrew prayers, 181
Holocaust, 148, 152, 159, 163, 168
Honeywell (computers), 87

ill health, 91, 93, 96, 97, 99, 102, 107, 131, 170, 175, 207, 212, 213
Indonesia, 171
Independent, The, 30, 99, 172
Independent on Sunday, 170, 190
Iraq, 91, 168, 171, 174, 175
Ireland/Irish, xi, 7, 11, 15, 51, 129, 131, 187, 193, 194; Carlow, County Carlow, 126, 188; Castlebar, County Mayo, 126, 188; Catholic, 127, 138; Connemara, 194; Cork, Opera House, 188; Dundalk, County Loath, 15, 57; Dublin, 10, 88, 135; Dublin Airport, 175; Dublin Pinter Festival, 62, 95, 175; Galway, 197; Gate Theatre, Dublin, 33, 88, 129, 175; Listowel, 126; PEN, 135; Portstewart, County Londonderry, 10, 197, 204; Protestant Ascendancy, 129; Seatown, Dundalk, 126; Sligo, 127; Tipperary, 83, 179–180, 187; Tuamgraney, County Clare, 135; Waterford, 126; Westport, County Mayo, 126
Israel, 139, 147, 152, 164; film industry, 153; Jerusalem, 152, 164; Mishkenot Sha ánanim, 164; Rockefeller Museum, 164

Italy/Italian, 164; food, 81, 93, 99, 118; Grand Hotel dis Castelli, nr.Genoa, 94; Neapolitan food, 81; Palermo Festival, 57, 64; Turin, Europa Theatre Prize, 122; University of Turin, 174; Venice, 161
Iver Grove, 102

Japanese handmade paper, 216
jazz, 68, 69
Jesuit, 177
Jewish/Jews, 80, 83, 84, 123, 138, 145, 149, 152, 158, 164, 180, 195
Job, Book of, 168
Jordan, Hashemite Kingdom, 164
Joycean devices, 196–187
Judaism, 176–177
"June 20th Group," 162

Kent, 55; Sissinghurst, 63
Kurds, 158
Kuwait, 172

Labour Party, 114, 162
Lancashire : County Cricket Club, 51, 53; Liverpool University Press, 212; Manchester, Old Trafford, 58, 94
Lebanon, 168
Leicester, 14; Palace Theatre, 14, 204; University of, 47
Leicestershire, 55
Lent, 168
library (Pinter's), 50, 55, 176, 189, 205
Listener, The, 214
literary influences, 185–220
London, 6, 9, 25, 27, 55, 63, 70, 81, 82, 87, 91, 109, 111, 119, 130, 131, 132, 135, 138–139, 146, 155, 160, 165, 175, 205, 209, 214, 215; Acton, 120; Athenaeum, 99; Barbican Centre, 36, 64, 70, 72; Battersea Public Reserve Library, 205; Beaufort Street, 80; Bethnal Green, 84; Blackheath, 133; Bloomberg Auditorium, Finsbury, 195; Brent, 118; Campden Hill Square, London W8 (No. 52), 38, 55, 77, 86, 88; Central School of Speech and Drama, 51, 132; Charing Cross Road, 195; Chiswick, 152; Chiswick

High Road, London W4 (No. 373), 17, 88; Clapton Pond, 3; Coliseum, 70, 72; Compton Street, 80; Conway Hall, Red Lion Square, 68; Covent Garden, 70, 72, 91, 106; Covent Garden Press, 18; Coventry Street, 81; Cromwell Hospital, 212; Cumberland Place, 146; Dalston, 82, 84, 145; Dean Street, 80; Ealing Studios, 124; East End, x, 9, 67, 77, 80, 84, 87, 90, 96, 109, 145; Finsbury Park, 3; Gaieties Cricket Club, x, 26, 45–46, 47, 49, 50, 55, 56, 58, 65, 67, 83, 95, 101, 108, 218–219; Garrick Club, 99, 101; Gower Street, 51; Great Portland Street, 145; Grosvenor House, 145; Gunnersbury Lane, 120; Gunnersbury Park, 54; Hackney, x, 5, 46, 49, 60, 79, 80, 84, 89, 126, 145, 195; Hackney Boys' Club, 66, 82; Hackney Downs Grammar School, 2, 7, 48, 52, 64, 82, 89, 148, 188, 201; *Hackney Downs School Magazine*, 2, 22; Hackney Film Society, 22; Hackney Public Library, 200; Hampstead, 39, 56; Hampstead Cricket Club, 83; Hampstead Theatre Club, 13, 15, 20, 104, 148, 210; Hanover Terrace, Regent's Park, London NW1 (No. 7), 86, 128, 133, 197, 218; Haymarket Theatre, 107, 136, 158; Holland Park, 81, 100, 104, 118, 133; House of Commons, 107, 155; Institute of Contemporary Arts, 85; Kensal Green Cemetery, 101, 176; Kentish Town, 115; King's Cross, 9; Launceston Place, South Kensington (No. 33), 85, 128; London Weekend Television, 137; London Zoo, 158; Lord Chamberlain's Office, 203; Lord's Cricket Ground, 46, 47, 48, 49, 50–53, 54, 57, 61, 67, 82, 101, 214, 216, 218; Lyric Studio, Hammersmith, 10, 15, 156; Madame Tussaud's, 119; Maggs, 205; Maida Vale, West London, 118; Manor Avenue, 3; Maudsley Hospital, 20,

99, 149; North London, 2, 3; Northwood Town Hall, 168; Notting Hill Gate, 17, 135; Old Compton Street, 80; Oval Cricket Ground, 50, 52; Palladium, 2; Piccadilly, 106, 215; Poetry Society, 209; Preston Manor Grammar School, 118; Princess Grace Hospital, 96, 136, 175; Queen Elizabeth Hall, 70; Queen Elizabeth Hall, Purcell Room, 209–210; Queen Mary College, 96; Raine's Foundation School, 82; Regent's Park, 119, 135; Ridley Road, 82, 145; Riverside Studios, 220; Royal Academy of Dramatic Art (RADA), 51, 146, 185, 187; Royal Albert Hall, 70; Royal Society of Arts Club, Waterloo, 47; Royal Festival Hall, 70; Royal Marsden Hospital, 93, 97, 121, 213; Royal Opera House, Covent Garden, 70, 72; Russell Gardens, 82; St George's Square, 111; St Martin's Central School of Arts and Crafts, 123; St Mary's Hospital, 61; Shaftesbury Avenue, 81; Shepherd's Bush, 64, 124; Society of West End Theatre Managers', 39, 111; Soho, 80; Soho Poly, 165; South Kensington, 81; Southgate, 6; Stamford Hill, 3; Stoke Newington, 5, 11; Thistlewaite Rd (No. 19), Hackney, 127, 131; Thurloe Place, 81; Tottenham, 124, 138; Vanderbilt Club, West London, 64; West End, 90; West London Synagogue, 176; Westminster Abbey, 114, 220; Whitechapel, 84; Wigmore Hall, 72; Wimbledon, 64; Zwemmers, 204, 205

London Embassies: Mexican Embassy, 107; Polish Embassy, 154; Turkish Embassy, 158

London Magazine, The, 49

London Review of Books, 172

London Theatres: Aldwych Theatre, 5, 18, 27, 28, 33, 35, 180; Almeida Theatre, 21, 87, 103, 123, 124, 139, 166; Ambassadors Theatre, 20, 125,

168; Ambiance Almost Free Theatre, 11; The American Film Theatre/Cinebill, 29; Apollo Theatre, 156; Arts Theatre, 4, 16, 34, 204; Arts Theatre Club, 18; Comedy Theatre, 21, 40, 87, 103, 136, 166; Cottesloe Theatre, South Bank, 20, 107, 132, 155, 199; Criterion Theatre, 19, 29, 92, 108; Donmar Warehouse, 33; Duchess Theatre, 19, 30, 191; Duke of York's Theatre, 32, 120; Fred Tripp Company, Intimate Theatre, Palmers Green, 16; Gaiety Theatre, Strand, 46; Hackney Empire, 2; King's Theatre, Hammersmith, 12, 126, 188; Hampstead Theatre, 125; Lyric Theatre, 211; Lyttelton Theatre, South Bank, 29, 37, 38, 88, 107, 158, 170; Mermaid Theatre, 28, 119, 123, 125, 216; National Theatre, 19, 20, 31, 34, 35, 37, 38, 39, 70, 108, 112, 114, 120, 148, 149, 214; New Arts Theatre, 28; Old Vic, 37; Olivier Theatre, 104, 209, 210; Pentameters Theatre, 210; Royal Court Theatre, 15, 16, 21, 136, 168, 191, 203, 207; Royalty Theatre, 37; St Martin's Theatre, 152; Theatre Royal, Haymarket, 108; Wyndham's Theatre, 37, 95, 108
Lord Chamberlain's Office, 21

Mail on Sunday, The, 30
MCC, 49, 50, 52, 54, 56–57, 89, 214, 215
McCarthyism, 146
Mexico, 130, 136, 140, 153; Mexico City, 83, 88; Oaxaca, 83; Puerto Vallarta, 83
Middlesex: County Cricket Club, 47, 48, 49; Teddington, 46
milk bars, 80
Miramax, 34
modern jazz quartet, 69
Moslem, 163
music, 45, 68–72, 226

national service, 51, 146, 185
NATO, 173
Next Editions, 211

New Republic, 198
New Statesman, 19, 29, 148
New Theatre Magazine, 206
New York, 6, 8, 39, 83, 86, 122, 127, 129, 132–133, 139–140, 172, 173, 210, 212, 218; Broadway, 62; Manhattan, 158; New York Grove Press, 18, 204; Plaza Hotel, 140
New York City Theaters: Booth Theater, 27; Eastside Playhouse, 139; Lincoln Center, 62; Manhattan Theatre Club, 27; Morosco Theatre, 92
New York Review of Books, 147, 172
New York Times, The, 68
New Yorker, The, 48
Newcastle upon Tyne, 45
Nicaragua/Nicaraguan, 163, 177–178; Managua Airport, 178
Nobel Prize, 67, 97, 136, 175
Northamptonshire, 34
Nottinghamshire: Cricket Club, 48; Nottingham, 152

Oare, Wiltshire
Observer, The, 28, 35, 47, 49, 172
Odessa, 138
Ogoni, Nigeria, 107
Old Testament, 177
Olympia typewriter, 88
Oxford, 89, 129; Christ Church College, 129; Dragon School, 129; Lady Margaret Hall, 130; Magdalen College, 86; New College, 121; Oxford Playhouse, 15, 29, 92, 134; University, 8
Oxfordshire Manor, 129

Pedragon Press, 121
PEN, 81, 98–99, 101, 104, 107, 128, 154, 157, 158, 162
PEN Translation Prize, 119
pemphigus, 97, 175
ping pong (game). *See* table tennis
Paris Review, 68
patriotism (Pinter), 50, 155
"Pauses," 206
"Pinter [cricket] XI," 47
Pinter Review, The, 123

Plays and Players, 28
Plymouth, Devon, 30
Poetry London, 88
Poetry Review, 217
Poland/Polish, 153; Galicia, 153; solidarity, 154
politics, 113, 120, 145–176, 226
Portugal: Algarve, 54
pre-Raphaelite, 194
Prevention of Terrorism Act, 148
pubs, 79, 81, 213. *See also* restaurants

Red Pepper, 172
Reading, Berkshire, 139; Leighton Park School, 62
restaurants, xi, 77, 78–108, 109, 226; La Barca, 114, 118; Belvedere, 104–105, 114, 118, 122, 132; Le Caprice, 48, 99, 118, 122, 136, 156, 218; Café Royal Grill, 118; Café Torino, 80; Chez Moi, 93, 100, 122; Cibo, 81, 99, 118, 132, 164; Clarke's, 118; Cock Tavern, Fleet Street, 81; Connaught Hotel, Mayfair, 106; Da Mario, 99; L'Epicure, 122, 125; Giovanni's, 99; Grill St Quentin (GST), 132, 136; Groucho, 93, 94–95; Hilaire, 99; Ivy, 91, 104, 106, 114, 136; Kingfisher, 99; Ladbroke Arms, 209; Little Acropolis, 118, 120; Odette's, 118; Odin's, 93, 95, 99, 104, 118, 119, 136; Orsino's, 81, 99, 118, 122, 132; Pegasus, 99; Ritz, 99; Ritz bar, 81; Running (Athletics), 64, 67; St. James, Piccadilly, 106; Sheekey's, 118; Thompson's, 99, 122, 136; Vendome, 215; Venezia's, 93; Waldorf, 98, 118; Ward's Irish House, 81; Whitbread Pub, 111; Wilton's, 114
religion, 94, 100, 176–180, 226
Routledge, 205
Royal Literary Fund, 98, 208, 210–211
Royal Shakespeare Company, 27, 28, 33, 34, 35, 113, 132, 180
Russia/Russian, 78, 146, 147; dissidents, 158; Moscow, 83

Salisbury, 130

Salisbury Review, The, 100
Sandinistas, 100, 163, 164, 176, 177–178, 181
Schlinder's List, 103
Scotland, 128; Edinburgh International Book Festival, 176
Shenley Cricket Centre, 49
sidcup, 55
Serbia/Serbian, 173; Nis, 173
"Silences," 206
silkscreen prints, 186
Soho Square, 3
smoking, 96, 108
Somerset, England, 58; Bath, 21, 213; Theatre Royal, Bath, 30
Sonning-on-Thames, 219
sociability, 77–109
Socialist, 172
South Africa/African, 98, 138, 151, 212; Cape Town, 98
South America, 164, 171
Soviet Union, 156
Spanish Civil War, 178
Spectator, The, 100
squash (game), 45, 64–65, 67, 98, 154, 226; sexual associations, 65
The Stage, 28, 123
Stockport, Cheshire, 114
Suez Crisis, 134
Suffolk, 70; Bury St Edmunds, 34
The Sunday Times, 16, 17, 23, 31, 61, 100, 199, 203
Surrey: Croydon, 113; Guildford, 21; Richmond, 17–18, 30; Richmond Theatre, 17–18; Woking, 30; Yvonne Arnaud Theatre, Guildford, 92, 107
Sussex : Ambrose Place, Worthing (No, 14), 17, 85; Brighton, Sussex, 30; Chichester, 108; Chichester, Minerva Theatre, 32; Eastbourne, 10, 59, 109; Glyndebourne Opera House, 70; Grand Hotel, Eastbourne, 39, 130; Horsham, Collyer's School, 1; Hove, 54, 138, 139, 166; Hove Jewish Cemetery, 180; Hove Town Hall, 89; Sussex v. Yorkshire, 54; Theatre Royal, Brighton, 225; Worthing, 2, 81; Worthing, Connaught Theatre, 17

Sutton Coldfield, West Midlands, 54
Sweden/Swedish: Academy, 97;
    Stockholm, 97, 175

table tennis (game), 66, 67, 82
Talmud, The, 176, 195
Tangier, 61
Teatre di Romo, 216
tennis (game), 45, 47, 61, 63, 64–65, 67,
    98, 154, 171, 226
Time Out, 91
Times, The, 31, 89, 166, 171
Times Literary Supplement (*TLS*), 129,
    203, 216, 219
totalitarianism, 71
Torquay, 11, 14, 147, 206, 213; Pavilion
    Theatre, 3, 12, 13, 57, 134
Turkey, 157–158; Istanbul, 157

Ukraine, 138
unions, 37
United Kingdom, 27, 39, 130, 155,
    171–172, 174, 176
United States, 100, 140, 146, 153–154,
    157, 171–172, 174, 175, 212;
    Academy of Motion Pictures, 123,
    153; Beverley Hills, Gregory Peck
    Collection, Margaret Herrick
    Library, 119; Hollywood, California,
    153; Los Angeles, California, 212;
    Los Angeles Times Book Prize, 135;
    Ohio State University, Columbus,
    166; Oregon, 216; St Louis, Missouri,
    212; San Francisco, California, 212;

University of Texas (Ransom
    Collection, 104, 155; Washington,
    D.C., 173

versification, 103
Vietnam, 151
visual medium, 185, 186

Wales, 7; Welsh Hills, 145; Welsh
    National Opera, 70
Wallingford, 128
Watford, Palace Theatre, 30
West Indies, 56; Barbados, 96, 120, 167;
    Coral Reef Club, 96
Whitebread Ale, 88
Wisden's, 55, 57, 217
women, HP relationship with, 84,
    111–141, 152
Worcestershire, 58
World Cricket Series, 56

Yiddish, 57, 84
Yom Kippur (Day of Atonement), 88,
    134, 139, 177
Yorkshire, 111; Huddersfield
    Repertory Company, 10, 56; Ilkley
    Literary Festival, 212; Leeds, 70;
    Stokesley, 47; Whitby Spa Repertory
    Company, 9, 127; Yorkshire Cricket
    Club, 56, 220
Yugoslavia, 168

Zapatista, 174
Zionism, 153, 156, 159, 164, 176

About the Author

William Baker is distinguished professor emeritus of English, Northern Illinois University, and visiting professor of English, Zhejiang University, PR China. The author/coauthor of more than thirty books, this is his fifth book on Pinter.